Personnel Selection

FIFTH EDITION

Personnel Selection

Adding Value Through People

FIFTH EDITION

Mark Cook

WILEY-BLACKWELL

A John Wiley & Sons, Ltd., Publication

This fifth edition first published 2009
© 2009 John Wiley & Sons Ltd.
Edition history: John Wiley & Sons Ltd. (1e, 1988; 2e, 1993; 3e, 1998 and 4e, 2004)

Wiley-Blackwell is an imprint of John Wiley & Sons, formed by the merger of Wiley's global
Scientific, Technical, and Medical business with Blackwell Publishing.

Registered Office
John Wiley & Sons Ltd, The Atrium, Southern Gate, Chichester, West Sussex, PO19 8SQ, UK

Editorial Offices
The Atrium, Southern Gate, Chichester, West Sussex, PO19 8SQ, UK
9600 Garsington Road, Oxford, OX4 2DQ, UK
350 Main Street, Malden, MA 02148-5020, USA

For details of our global editorial offices, for customer services, and for information about how
to apply for permission to reuse the copyright material in this book please see our website at
www.wiley.com/wiley-blackwell.

The right of the Mark Cook to be identified as the author of this work has been asserted in
accordance with the Copyright, Designs and Patents Act 1988.

Wiley also publishes its books in a variety of electronic formats. Some content that appears in
print may not be available in electronic books.

Designations used by companies to distinguish their products are often claimed as trademarks.
All brand names and product names used in this book are trade names, service marks,
trademarks or registered trademarks of their respective owners. The publisher is not associated
with any product or vendor mentioned in this book. This publication is designed to provide
accurate and authoritative information in regard to the subject matter covered. It is sold on
the understanding that the publisher is not engaged in rendering professional services. If
professional advice or other expert assistance is required, the services of a competent
professional should be sought.

Library of Congress Cataloging-in-Publication Data
Cook, Mark, 1942–
    Personnel selection : adding value through people / Mark Cook. – 5th ed.
      p. cm.
    Includes bibliographical references and index.
    ISBN 978-0-470-98645-5 (cloth) – ISBN 978-0-470-98646-2 (pbk.)   1. Employee selection.
I. Title.
    HF5549.5.S38C66 2009
    658.3'112–dc22

                                                                        2008049821

A catalogue record for this book is available from the British Library.

Set in Palatino 10/12 pt by SNP Best-set Typesetter Ltd., Hong Kong
Printed in Singapore by Markono Print Media Pte Ltd

1   2009

Contents

Preface to the first edition

When I first proposed writing this book, I thought it self-evident that personnel selection and productivity are closely linked. Surely an organization that employs poor staff will produce less, or achieve less, than one that finds, keeps and promotes the right people. So it was surprising when several people, including one anonymous reviewer of the original book proposal, challenged my assumption and argued that there was no demonstrated link between selection and productivity.

Critics are right, up to a point – there has never been an experimental demonstration of the link. The experiment could be performed, but might prove very expensive. First, create three identical companies. Second, allow company A to select its staff by using the best techniques available, require company B to fill its vacancies at random (so long as the staff possess the minimum necessary qualifications), and require company C to employ the people company A identified as least suitable. Third, wait a year and then see which company is doing best, or – if the results are very clear-cut – which companies are still in business. No such experiment has been performed, although fair employment laws in the USA have caused some organizations to adopt at times personnel policies that are not far removed from the strategy for company B.

Perhaps critics meant only to say that the outline overlooked other more important factors affecting productivity, such as training, management, labour relations, lighting and ventilation, or factors which the organization cannot control, such as the state of the economy, technical development, foreign competition, and political interference. Of course all of these affect productivity, but this does not prove that – other things being equal – an organization that selects, keeps and promotes good employees will not produce more, or produce better, than one that does not.

Within-organization factors that affect productivity are dealt with by other writings on industrial/organizational psychology. Factors outside the organization, such as the state of world trade, fall outside the scope of psychology.

Centre for Occupational Research Ltd
10 Woodlands Terrace, Swansea SA1 6BR, UK

Preface to the fifth edition

Every chapter of this fifth edition has been revised to incorporate new research and new ideas, so the amount of change in each chapter gives an indication of how much interesting new research has appeared in each area. The chapters on assessment centres, personality questionnaires and interviewing include a lot of new material. There have also been very important developments in methodology covered in Chapter 2. The issue of adverse impact continues to be exceedingly important in the USA. Chapter 11 reviews emotional intelligence, which has attracted a lot of attention, and some research. The areas of references and biographical methods have altered least. Chapter 1 includes new material analysing type of information, which is also used in later chapters, especially Chapter 8. Every chapter has been rewritten, even where there is not much new research to report.

The field seems to be entering a period of uncertainty. Previously accepted 'truths' are being questioned. Structured interviews may not be any better than traditional interviews. Tests may after all have lower validity for ethnic minorities. It may be necessary to review all existing validity data. The issue of whether people tell the truth about themselves when applying for jobs has been addressed, especially for personality questionnaires.

A new feature of this fifth edition is the inclusion of sections on Research Agenda, to make suggestions where the field should go next.

To keep the book to a reasonable length, references are not necessarily given for points that are not central to selection, e.g. heritability.

The key references for each chapter are selected to be accessible, meaning published, and written in English, which unfortunately excludes one or two important references.

Finally, I would like to thank the many people who have helped me prepare this fifth edition. First, I would like to thank the many researchers in the selection area who have generously sent me accounts of research in press or in progress. Second, I would like to thank Karen Howard for her help with the figures. Finally, I would like to thank John Wiley & Sons for their support and help over the five editions of *Personnel Selection*.

Centre for Occupational Research Ltd
10 Woodlands Terrace, Swansea SA1 6BR, UK

CHAPTER 1

Old and new selection methods

We've always done it this way

Why selection matters

Clark Hull is better known, to psychologists at least, as an animal learning theorist, but very early in his career he wrote a book on aptitude testing (Hull, 1928) and described ratios of output of best to worst performers in a variety of occupations. Hull was the first psychologist to ask how much workers differ in productivity, and he discovered the principle that should be written in letters of fire on every manager's office wall: *the best is twice as good as the worst*.

Human resource (HR) managers sometimes find that they have difficulty convincing colleagues that HR departments also make a major contribution to the organization's success. Because HR departments are neither making things, nor selling things, some colleagues think they are not adding any value to the organization. This represents a very narrow approach to how organizations work, which overlooks the fact that an organization's most important asset is its staff. Psychologists have devised techniques for showing how finding and keeping the right staff adds value to the organization. The *rational estimate* technique (described in detail in Chapter 14) estimates how much workers who are doing the same job vary with regard to the value of their contribution. For computer programmers, Schmidt, Gast-Rosenberg and Hunter (1980) estimated that a good programmer is worth over $10,000 a year more than an average programmer. This implies that HR can add a great deal of value to the organization by *finding* good managers in the first place (the subject of this book), *making* managers good through training and development, and *keeping* managers good by avoiding poor morale, high levels of stress, and so on. Differences in value of the order of £16–28,000 per employee mount up across an organization. Hunter and Hunter (1984) generated a couple of examples for the public sector in the USA:

- A small employer, the Philadelphia police force (5,000 employees), could save $18 million a year by using psychological tests to select the best.
- A large employer, the US Federal Government (4 million employees), could save $16 billion a year. Or, to reverse the perspective, the US Federal Government is losing $16 billion a year by not using tests.

Some critics see a flaw in Schmidt and Hunter's calculations. Every company in the country cannot employ the best computer programmers or budget analysts; someone has to employ the rest. Good selection cannot increase national productivity, only the productivity of employers that use good selection methods to grab more than their fair share of talent. At present, employers are free to do precisely that. The rest of this book explains *how*.

Recruitment

Traditional methods

Figure 1.1 summarizes the successive stages of recruiting and selecting an academic for a British university. The *advertisement* attracts applicants (As) who complete and return an *application form* (AF). Some As' *references* are taken up, while the rest are excluded from further consideration. Applicants with satisfactory references are shortlisted and invited for *interview*, after which the post is filled. The employer tries to attract as many As as possible, then passes them through a series of filters, until the number of surviving As equals the number of vacancies.

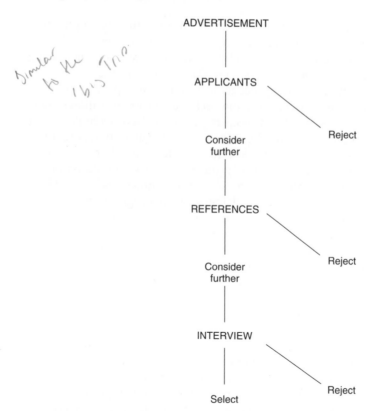

Figure 1.1 Successive stages in selecting academic staff in a British university.

Recruitment sources

There are many ways in which employers can try to attract As, for example through advertisements, agencies (public or private), word of mouth, 'walk-ins' (people who come in and ask if there are any vacancies) or job fairs. Employers should analyse recruiting sources carefully to determine which find good employees who stay with them. Employers also need to check whether their recruitment methods are finding a representative applicant pool in terms of gender, ethnicity and disability. Sometimes, employers or their agents seek out likely candidates for a vacancy and invite them to apply ('headhunting').

Realistic job previews (RJPs)

Many organizations paint a rosy picture of what is really a boring and unpleasant job because they fear no one would apply otherwise. In the USA, RJPs are widely used to tell As what being, for example, a call-centre worker is really like – fast-paced, closely supervised, routine to the point of being boring and solitary. The more carefully worded the advertisement and the job description, the fewer unsuitable As will apply. RJPs tend to reduce turnover, preventing people from leaving as soon as they find what the job is really like.

Informal recruitment

Applicants are sometimes recruited by word of mouth, usually through existing employees. Besides being cheaper, the grapevine finds employees who stay longer (low *turnover*), possibly because they have a clearer idea what the job really involves. Zottoli and Wanous (2000) report that informal recruits, on average, do slightly better work; the difference is small (d = 0.08) but is achieved very cheaply. However, fair employment agencies, for example the (British) Commission for Racial Equality (CRE), generally dislike informal recruitment. They argue that recruiting their white workers' friends is unfair because it tends to perpetuate an all-white workforce.

New technology and recruitment

Advertising, making applications, sifting applications and even assessment can now be carried out electronically, which can make the whole process far quicker. People talk of making 'same-day offers', whereas traditional approaches took weeks or even months to fill vacancies. On the downside, Internet recruitment can greatly increase the number of As, which is good for the employer if it broadens the field of high-calibre As, but it does also create work sorting through a mountain of applications.

- More and more jobs are advertised on the Internet through the employer's own website or through numerous recruitment sites.

- People seeking jobs can post their details on websites for potential employers to evaluate. This gives the job seeker an opportunity that did not exist before. People could make speculative applications to possible employers, but could not advertise themselves on a global scale.
- Many employers now use electronic application systems, eliminating the conventional paper AF.
- Interactive Voice Recognition (IVR) can be used by As to make their application, and by the employer to screen them. The A presses keys to indicate his/her responses, or – in more sophisticated systems – speech recognition software allows A to speak his/her answers.
- 'Headhunting' can be done electronically by systems that scan databases, newsletters and 'blogs' for any information about people who are outstanding in the field of, for example, chemical engineering.

Application sifting

The role of the AF, or its new technology equivalent, is to act as first filter, choosing a relatively small number of applications to process further, which is called *sifting*. Sifting can take up a lot of time in HR departments so any way of speeding it up will be very valuable, so long as it is fair and accurate. Research suggests that sifting is not always done very effectively. Machwirth, Schuler and Moser (1996) used policy-capturing analyses to reconstruct how HR sifted applications. Policy capturing works back from the decisions that HR makes about a set of applications, to infer how HR decides. Machwirth *et al.* showed what HR does, according to the policy-capturing analysis, often differ from what they say, when asked to describe how they sift. Managers say they sift on the basis of proven ability and previously achieved position, but in practice reject As because the application looks untidy or badly written. McKinney *et al.* (2003) analysed how US campus recruiters use grade point average (GPA; course marks) to select for interview. Some choose students with high marks, which is the logical use of the information, given that GPA does predict work performance to some extent, and that it is linked to mental ability, which also predicts work performance. A second large group ignore GPA altogether. A third group select for lower GPA, screening out any As with high grades. This does not seem a good way to sift, given the link between work performance and mental ability. The choice of strategy seems essentially idiosyncratic and cannot be linked to type of job or employer.

Accuracy and honesty

Numerous surveys report that alarming percentages of AFs, résumés and CVs contain information that is inaccurate, or even false. These surveys often seem to have a 'self-serving' element, being reported by organizations that offer to verify information supplied by As. Not much independent research regarding this has been reported. Goldstein (1971) found that many As for nursing vacancies exaggerated both their previous experience and salary. More seriously, a quarter gave a reason for leaving that their previous employer did not agree with, and 17% listed as their last employer someone who denied ever having employed them. McDaniel, Douglas and Snell (1997) surveyed marketing, accounting, management and computing professionals, and found that 25 to 33% admitted misrepresenting their experience or skills, inflating their salary, or suppressing damaging information, such as being sacked. Keenan (1997) asked British graduates which answers on their AFs they had 'made up ... to please the recruiter'. Hardly any admitted to giving false information about their degree, but most (73%) admitted they were not honest about their reasons for choosing that employer, and 40% felt no obligation to be honest about their hobbies and interests. Electronic media, such as the Internet, do not bypass these problems. It is just as easy to lie through a keyboard as it is on paper or in person, and just as easy to give the answer you think the employer wants to hear.

RESEARCH AGENDA

- The accuracy of CV and AF information
- What sort of information is wrongly reported
- What sort of people report false information
- Why do people report wrong information
- Whether the rate of incorrect information is increasing
- The role of careers advice, coaching, self-help books and websites.

Fairness and sifting

Equal opportunities (EO) agencies in the USA have produced long lists of questions that AFs should not ask for one reason or another. Some are obvious: ethnicity, gender and disability (because the law forbids discrimination in all three). Others are less obvious: for example, AFs should not ask about driving offences, arrests or military discharge, because some minorities have higher rates of these, so the question may create indirect discrimination. Questions about availability over holidays or weekends may discourage, for instance, some religious minorities. A succession of surveys (reviewed by Kethley & Terpstra, 2005) have consistently shown that most US employers seem unaware of, or unconcerned by, this guidance and continue to ask questions that the agencies say they should not. Kethley and Terpstra reviewed 312 US Federal cases involving AFs and found complaints centred on sex (28%), age (25%) and race (12%). Some questions listed as 'inadvisable' – military discharge, marital status, arrest – have never been the subject of a court case.

Internet recruitment and selection could raise another set of 'fairness' issues. Not everyone has access to the Internet. Any gender, ethnicity or age differences in access to the Internet might have possible legal implications.

Bias in sifting

Many studies have used the paper applicant method, which prepares sets of equally suitable As who differ in one key feature – for example gender, age or having a beard – then has HR staff rate their suitability. This is an easy type of research to do and one that usually 'gets results' by finding evidence of bias:

- Davison and Burke (2000) reviewed 49 studies of gender bias and found both male and female sifters biased against female As. The less information about the job was given, the greater the bias.
- In The Netherlands, As with Arabic-sounding names are four times as likely to be rejected at sifting (Derous, Nguyen & Ryan, 2008).
- Gordon and Arvey (2004) summarized 25 studies of age bias and found that older As rated less favourably, especially their 'potential for development'. However, bias was not large and seemed to be decreasing.
- Ding and Stillman (2005) report New Zealand data showing that over-weight female As tend to be sifted out.
- Correll, Benard and Paik (2007) found women with children tend to be sifted out, but men with children are not, and may even be favoured.

Paper applicant research has a flaw, however. The sifters know they are being scrutinized by psychologists, so may be on their best behaviour. Also, they are not really hiring As and will not have to work with the people they 'select'. Research on sifting in the USA had reached the reassuring conclusion that it seemed free of racial bias, but a recent study by Bertrand and Mullainathan (2004) suggested there may be a serious problem after all. They used a different technique. They sent their 'paper applicants' to real employers, applying for real jobs, and counted how many were shortlisted for interview. Choice of first name identified A as white or African American. (Americans will assume 'Brad' and 'Carrie' are white, while 'Aisha' and 'Leroy' are African American.) For every 10 'white' As called for interview, there were only 6.7 'African Americans'; African Americans were being sifted out, by ethnicity. Bertrand and Mullainathan could argue that their data show what is really happening in the real US job market, which justifies the slightly unethical practice of sending employers fake job applications. Some research, described in Chapter 4, takes this method a step further, by accepting invitations to interview. There is one partly similar study in Britain, where Hoque and Noon (1999) wrote to employers enquiring about possible vacancies, not applying for a specific job, calling themselves 'Evans' implying a white person, or 'Patel' implying a South Asian person. 'Evans' got, on average, slightly longer and more helpful replies..

Improving application sifting

Behavioural competences

Applicants are asked to describe things they have done which relate to key competences for the job. *Ability to influence others* is assessed by A describing an occasion when A had to persuade others to accept an unpopular course of action. This method might improve the AF as a selection assessment, but there is no research on whether it does.

Weighted application blanks (WABs) and biodata

AFs can be converted into WABs by analysing past and present employees for predictors of success (Chapter 9). One study found that American female bank clerks who did not stay long tended, for instance, to be under 25, single, to live at home or to have had several jobs (Robinson, 1972), so banks could reduce turnover by screening out As with these characteristics. (Robinson's list probably would not be legal today however because it specifies female bank clerks.) Most WABs are conventional paper format, but the technique would work equally well for electronic applications. Biodata also uses biographical items to select, but collects them through a separate questionnaire, not from the AF.

Training and experience (T&E) ratings

In the USA, application sifting has been assisted by T&E ratings, which seek to quantify As' T&E by various rating systems, instead of relying on arbitrary judgements. T&E ratings seem to have been overtaken in the USA by application coding systems such as Resumix. Note, however, that T&E ratings had extensive research (McDaniel, Schmidt & Hunter, 1988), showing they do actually predict work performance – information not provided for Resumix or any other system.

Minimum qualifications (MQs)

The advertisement says that As need a civil engineering qualification plus minimum five years' experience; the intended implication being that people who lack these will not be considered, so should not apply. MQs are generally based on education and experience. However, educational MQs may exclude some minorities, while length of experience may exclude women who tend to take more career breaks. Hence, in the USA, MQs may be challenged legally and so need careful justification. Buster, Roth and Bobko (2005) described elaborate systems of panels of experts, discussions and rating schedules for setting MQs. (As opposed to setting an arbitrary MQ, or using the 'one we've always used', or the 'one everyone uses'.) For example, the experts might be asked to 'bracket' the MQ; if it is suggested that three years' experience is needed, then ask the experts to consider two and four years as well, just to make sure three years really is the right amount. Buster *et al.* noted that MQs should define the 'barely acceptable' applicant, so as to weed out 'no hopers'. They suggest that MQs have tended to be set unnecessarily high, making recruitment difficult, and possibly excluding too many minority persons.

Background investigation aka positive vetting

AFs contain the information As choose to provide about themselves. Some employers make their own checks on As, covering criminal history, driving record, financial and credit history, education and employment history, possibly even reputation and lifestyle. Background checking is rapidly growing in popularity in the USA, from 51% employers in 1996 to 85% in 2007 (Isaacson *et al.* 2008), possibly driven by several high-profile cases where CEOs have been caught falsifying their CVs. In Britain, background investigations are recommended for childcare workers and used for government employees with access to confidential information (known as *positive vetting*). The Criminal Records Bureau was set up to supply information on criminal records of people applying for work which gives access to children. Presently, there is little or no research on whether background checks succeed in selecting 'good' employees and rejecting unsuitable ones. Isaacson *et al.* compared As who failed a background check with those who passed and found those who failed scored slightly higher on test of risk taking. The closest they could get to work performance was a realistic computer simulation of manufacturing work, where the failed group worked slightly faster, but slightly less well. Roberts *et al.* (2007) report a long-term follow-up of a New Zealand cohort of 930 26-year-olds, which found no link between criminal convictions before age 18, and self-reported counterproductive behaviour at work. (Counterproductive behaviour is discussed in detail in Chapters 7 and 12.)

Structured questioning

Internet application systems can be structured to include qualifying (or disqualifying) questions at the beginning. People who lack necessary expertise or experience, or who are not eligible to work in the USA, or who have criminal records, are speedily eliminated. This saves time for both applicant and employer. (Politer employers tell As they have little chance of success and ask if they wish to proceed.) These systems can also screen out As who, for instance, are unwilling to work shifts, wear uniform or smile all the time.

Internet tests

Some employers are replacing their conventional paper AFs with short tests completed over the Internet. Some assess job knowledge; it is useful to screen out people who know little or nothing about subjects (e.g. Microsoft Excel) they claim expertise in. Testing can improve the whole selection process by screening out, early on, As who lack the mental ability necessary for the job. (Chapter 6 will show that mental ability is generally a good predictor of work performance.) In conventional selection systems, tests are not normally used until the shortlist stage, by which time many able As may have been screened out. It is theoretically preferable to put the most accurate selection tests early in the selection process, but the cost of conventional paper-and-pencil testing tends to prevent this. Some Internet tests assess personality or fit. Formerly, HR inferred, for example, leadership potential from what As said they did at school or university. Some new systems assess it more directly by a set of standard questions. No research has been published on how well such systems work.

Application scanning software

Numerous software systems can scan applications and CVs to check whether they match the job's requirements. This is much quicker than conventional sifting of paper applications by HR. The Restrac system is said to be able to search 300,000 CVs in 10 seconds. One of the best-known systems is Resumix, subsequently called Hiring Gateway, which started operations as long ago as 1988 and boasts many major employers as customers, including the American armed services. Resumix does more than just scan and file applications; it is also a job analysis system (Chapter 3). Resumix has a list of 25,000 KSAs (Knowledge Skill Ability). Employers use this list to specify the essential and desirable skills for their particular vacancy, and Resumix searches applications for the best match. MacFarland (2000) listed some of the competences Resumix uses, including leadership, budget planning and forecasting, performance assessment, staff education, performance management, performance evaluation and others. Resumix may save employers time and money, but may not make life all that easy for job As, judging from the number of consultancies and websites in the USA offering help on how to make Resumix applications. Automated sifting systems can eliminate bias directly based on ethnicity, age, disability or gender because they are programmed to ignore these factors. They will not necessarily ignore factors linked to ethnicity, disability, age or gender, such as sports and pastimes. Sifting software will do the job consistently and thoroughly, whereas the human sifter may get tired or bored and not read every application carefully.

Sifting electronically is not necessarily any more accurate. Accuracy depends on the decision rules used in sifting, which in turn depend on the quality of the research the employer has done. Reports (Bartram, 2000) suggested that some scanning systems do nothing more sophisticated than search for keywords. Once As realize this, they will try to include as many as possible. Resumix say their software does not use simple word counting, nor is there a list of 'buzzwords' that As can include to improve their chances of being selected. The system is described as 'intelligent' and as able to recognize the contextual meaning of words. The software is copyrighted and no details are released. There is an urgent need to know what application-sifting programs actually do. Psychologists tend to be rather sceptical for one fairly simple reason. If these systems are doing something tremendously subtle and complex, where did the people who wrote them acquire this wisdom? There is no evidence that human application sifters are doing anything highly complex that software can model, nor is there any body of research on application sifting that has described any complex subtle relationships to put into software.

RESEARCH AGENDA

- The link between various application sifting systems and later work performance, for competence-based applications, background investigations, internet testing, application scanning and sorting software systems.
- Policy-capturing research on application scanning and sorting software systems.
- Investigation of how application sifting software operates, and what it can achieve

---

Overview of selection methods

The first column in Table 1.1 lists the main techniques used to select staff in North America, Europe and other industrialized countries. The list is divided into traditional and 'new', although most 'new' methods have been in use for some time. Table 1.1 also indicates which chapter contains the main coverage of each method.

What is assessed in personnel selection?

The short answer to this question is: ability to do the job. A much more detailed answer is provided by job analysis, which lists the main attributes successful employees need (*see* Chapter 3). Table 1.2 lists the main headings for assessing staff.

Mental ability

Mental ability divides into general mental ability (GMA or 'intelligence'), and more specific applied mental skills, for example problem solving, practical judgement, clerical ability or mechanical comprehension. Some jobs also need sensory abilities: keen hearing, good balance, or good eye–hand co-ordination.

Physical characteristics

Some jobs need specific physical abilities: strength, endurance, dexterity. Others have more implicit requirements for height or appearance.

Table 1.1   Traditional and new(er) selection assessment methods.

Traditional methods	Chapter	Alternative names
Application form / CV / résumé	1	
Traditional interview	4	
References	5	
New(er) methods		
Electronic application	1	
Structured interview	4	
Peer rating	5	
Mental ability test	6	Aptitude test
Job knowledge test	6	Achievement test, trade test
Personality questionnaire	7	Personality inventory
Honesty test	7	Integrity test
Projective test	8	
Graphology	8	Handwriting analysis
Biodata	9	Weighted Application Blank
Assessment centre	10	Extended interview
Group exercise	10	
Simulation	10	
Emotional intelligence	11	Situational judgement Social intelligence
Work sample test	11	Trainability test, in tray / basket
Physical ability test	11	
Drug use testing	11	

Table 1.2   Seven main aspects of applicants assessed in selection.

Mental ability
Personality
Physical characteristics
Interests and values
Knowledge
Work skills
Social skills

Personality

Psychologists list from 5 to 30 underlying dispositions, or personality traits, to think, feel and behave in particular ways. An extravert person, for instance, likes meeting people and feels at ease meeting strangers. The employer may find it easier to select someone who is very outgoing to sell insurance, rather than trying to train someone who is presently rather shy.

Interests, values and fit

Someone who wants to help others may find charity work more rewarding than selling doughnuts; someone who believes that people should obey all the rules all the time may enjoy being a traffic warden. People cannot always find work that matches their ideals and values, but work that does may prove more rewarding. 'Fit' means the A's outlook or behaviour matches the organization's requirements. These can be explicit: soldiers expect to obey orders instantly and without question. 'Fit' may be implicit: the applicant does not sound or look 'right for us', but there is not a written list of requirements, or even a list that selectors can explain to you.

Knowledge

Every job requires some knowledge: current employment law, statistical analysis, or something much simpler, such as how to use telephones or how to give change. Knowledge can be acquired by training, so it need not necessarily be a selection requirement. Mastery of higher-level knowledge may require higher levels of mental ability. Several types of knowledge are distinguished:

Declarative – knowing that: London is the capital of Britain.
Procedural – knowing how: to get from Heathrow to Piccadilly.
Tacit   – knowing how things really happen: when and where it is not safe to walk in London.

Work skills

The ability to do something quickly and efficiently: bricklaying, driving a bus, valuing a property, diagnosing an illness. Employers sometimes select for skills and sometimes train for them. Mastery of some skills may require levels of mental or physical ability not everyone has.

Social skills are important for many jobs and essential for some. They include, for instance, communication, persuasion, negotiation, influence and leadership and teamwork.

Nature of the information collected

Discussions of selection methods usually focus on the merits of personality questionnaires (PQs) or structured interviews, or work samples. They do not usually address the issue of what sort of information the method generates. Table 1.3 sorts selection methods by five qualitatively different types of information.

Table 1.3 Five categories of qualitatively different information obtained by selection tests.

Self	Information provided by the applicant. *Application form, including online application, T&E rating, biodata, personality questionnaire, honesty test, projective test, interest questionnaire, interview.*
Reported	Information provided by other people about the applicant. *References, peer rating.*
Demonstrated a) Test	The applicant performs a task or demonstrates a skill. *Work sample, mental ability test, job knowledge test, physical ability test.*
b) Behavioural	*Group exercise, behavioural test.*
Recorded	The applicant has obtained a qualification, or made a recorded achievement.
Involuntary	*Graphology, drug use testing, polygraph, psychophysiology, voice stress analysis.*

Self-report evidence

Self-report evidence is information that is provided by the applicant, in written or spoken form, on the AF, in the interview, and when answering PQs, attitude measures and biographical inventories. Some self-reports are free form or unstructured, for example, some interviews or AFs. Others are more structured, such as PQs, biodata or structured interviews. Some self-reports are fairly transparent, notably interviews and PQs. (Transparent in the sense that As will have little difficulty working out what inference will be drawn from what they say.) Other assessments may be less transparent, such as biodata or projective tests; As may find it less easy to decide what answer will be seen as 'good' or 'poor'.

Self-report data have some compelling advantages in selection. It is generally very cheap and very convenient; As are present, and eager to please, so collecting information is easy. Self-report can also be justified as showing respect and trust for As. However, self-report also has a fundamental disadvantage in selection; As provide the information and the employer generally has no way of verifying it. Self-report has two other limitations: coaching and lack of insight. There are many books on how to complete job applications; career counselling services advise students what to say at interviews. The second problem is lack of self-insight. Some As may genuinely think they are good leaders or popular or creative, and incorporate this view of themselves into their application, PQ or interview. However, by any other criterion – for example, test, others' opinion and achievement – they lack the quality in question. This issue has not been researched much, if at all, in the selection context. These problems make it important to confirm what As say about themselves by information from other sources.

Other report evidence

Information about the applicant is provided by other people, through references or ratings. Other reports vary in the degree of expertise involved. Some require no special expertise, such as peer ratings and the letter of reference. Others use experts, generally psychologists.

Demonstrated evidence

The applicant performs a task or demonstrates a skill. Tests include GMA / intelligence tests, as well as tests of aptitudes, and specific knowledge (trade or job knowledge or achievement tests). These are real tests, with right and wrong answers. Demonstrated evidence also includes work samples, group exercises, simulations and other behavioural exercises typically included in assessment centres. Demonstration evidence has fewer limitations than self-reports or other reports. Ability tests cannot generally be faked. On the downside, demonstrated evidence tends to be more difficult and expensive to collect.

Recorded evidence

Some information used in selection can be characterized as recorded fact. The applicant has a good degree in psychology from a good university. The information is recorded and is verifiable. (Although some employers make the mistake of relying on self-report data, and fail to check As' qualifications at source.) Work history can also provide a record of achievement, for example the applicant was CEO/MD of organization XYZ during a period when XYZ's profits increased. Published work, grants obtained, inventions patented, prizes and medals, for instance, also constitute recorded evidence.

Demonstrated and recorded information tends to have an asymmetric relationship with self- or other reported information. Evidence that someone cannot do something disproves the statement by the applicant or others that he/she can. However, the converse is not true: being told that someone cannot do something does not disprove demonstrated or recorded evidence that he/she can. To this extent, demonstrated and recorded evidence is superior to self and other reported evidence, which implies that selectors should prefer demonstrated and recorded evidence.

Involuntary evidence

Some evidence is provided by As, but not from what they tell the assessors, nor from things they do intentionally. The classic example is the polygraph, which is intended to assess A's truthfulness from respiration, heart rate and electrodermal activity, not from the answers that A gives. In fact, the polygraph is used to decide which of A's self-reports to believe, and which to classify as untrue. Two other involuntary assessments are graphology and drug-use testing. The former seeks to infer As' characteristics from the form of their handwriting, not from its content. Drug-use testing assumes that drug use can be more accurately detected by chemical analysis than by self-report.

Work performance

Selection research compares a *predictor*, meaning a selection test, with a *criterion*, meaning an index of the worker's work performance. The criterion side of selection research presents greater problems than the predictor side because it requires researchers to define good work performance. The criterion problem can be very simple when work generates something that can be counted: widgets manufactured per day or sales per week. The criterion problem can be made very simple if the organization has an appraisal system whose ratings can be used. The supervisor rating criterion is widely used because it is almost always available (in the USA), because it is unitary and because it is hard to argue with.

On the other hand, the criterion problem can soon get very complex, if one wants to dig a bit deeper into what constitutes effective performance. Questions about the real nature of work or the true purpose of organizations soon arise. Is success better measured objectively by counting units produced, or better measured subjectively by informed opinion? Is success at work unidimensional or multidimensional? Who decides whether work is successful? Different supervisors may not agree. Management and workers may not agree. The organization and its customers may not agree.

Objective criteria are many and various. Some are more objective than others; *training grades* often involve some subjective judgement in rating written work. *Personnel criteria* – advancement / promotion, length of service, turnover, punctuality, absence, disciplinary action, accidents, sickness – are easy to collect. Analyses of selection research (Lent, Aurbach & Levin, 1971) have shown that a subjective criterion – the global supervisor rating – was clearly the favourite, which was used in 60% of studies. Criteria of work performance are discussed in greater detail in Chapter 12.

Fair employment law

Most people know it is against the law to discriminate against certain classes of people when filling vacancies. These protected classes include women, ethnic minorities and disabled people. Most people think discrimination means deciding not to employ Mr Jones because he is black or Ms Smith because she is female. Direct discrimination is illegal, but is not the main concern in personnel selection. The key issue is indirect discrimination or *adverse impact*. Adverse impact means the selection system results in more majority persons getting through than minority persons. For example, some UK employers sift out As who have been unemployed for more than six months on the argument that they will have lost the habit of working. The

CRE argued that this creates adverse impact on some ethnic minorities because their unemployment rates are higher. Adverse impact assesses the effect of the selection method, not the intentions of the people who devised it. Adverse impact means an employer can be proved guilty of discrimination, by setting standards that make no reference to ethnicity or gender. Adverse impact is a very serious matter for employers. It creates a presumption of discrimination, which the employer must disprove, possibly in court. This will cost a lot of time and money, and may create damaging publicity. Selection methods that do not create adverse impact are therefore highly desirable, but unfortunately not always easy to find. Fair employment issues are discussed in detail in Chapter 13.

Current selection practice

Surveys of employers' selection methods appear quite frequently, but should be viewed with some caution. Return rates are often very low: Piotrowski and Armstrong (2006) say 20% is normal. There is also the grey (and black) side of selection. Some methods are not entirely legal or ethical, so employers are unlikely to admit to using them. Rumours suggest that some employers gain unauthorized access to criminal records by employing former police officers or use credit information to assess As. There are even rumours of secret databases of people to avoid employing because they are union activists or troublemakers. Many organizations forbid the use of telephone references, but Andler and Herbst (2002) suggest many managers nevertheless both ask for them and provide them.

Selection in Britain

Table 1.4 presents two recent UK surveys, by IRS (Murphy, 2006) and the Chartered Institute of Personnel and Development (CIPD, 2006), covering the service, manufacturing and production, and public sectors. Table 1.4 confirms earlier UK surveys, showing that most UK employers are still using interviews of various types, that most still use references, that most use tests at least some of the time, but less frequently online. Only half use assessment centres or group exercises, while biodata are very rarely used. Neither survey gives any information about return rate.

Graduate recruitment

Keenan (1995) reported a survey of UK graduate recruitment. At the screening stage, employers use AFs, interview and reference; for the final decision, all employers use the interview again, and nearly half use assessment centres. Clark (1992) surveyed British executive recruitment agencies, used by many employers to fill managerial positions. They all used interviews; most (81%) used references; nearly a half (45%) used psychological tests; they rarely used biodata or graphology.

PERSONNEL SELECTION

Table 1.4 Two surveys of ...
and IRS (2006). CIPD % are en...
method (rarely/occasionally/...
are employers who use that met...
unspecified).

Sample size	
AF	
CV	
Interview	
Face-to-face IV	98
Panel IV	28
Structured panel	88
Structured one to one	81
Competency-based	85
Telephone	56	32
References	
References	85
Employment ref (pre interview)	49
Academic ref (pre interview)	36
Tests	
Tests for specific skills	82
General ability tests	75
Literacy/numeracy	72
Personality/aptitude Qs	60
Psychometric tests (mostly PQs)	64
Online test	25
Biodata	4
Behavioural	
Assessment centre	48	35
Group exercise	48	

University staff

Foster, Wilkie and Moss (1996) confirmed that staff in British universities are still selected by AF, reference and interview, and that psychological tests and assessment centres are virtually never used. Nearly half of Foster *et al.*'s sample said they used biodata, but had probably confused it with the conventional AF. Most universities, however, do use a form of work sample test – they ask the applicant to make a presentation about their research.

Small business

Most surveys look at large employers, who have specialized HR departments who know something about selection. One-third of the British workforce

...rk for small employers, with fewer than 10 staff, where HR exper-... be lacking. Bartram *et al.* (1995) found that small employers rely on ...rview at which they try to assess As' honesty, integrity and interest in the job, rather than their ability. One in five use work samples or tests of literacy and numeracy; a surprising one in six use tests of ability or aptitude. Bartram characterized small employers' approach to selection as 'casual'.

Selection in the USA

Piotrowski and Armstrong (2006) report the most recent US survey of 151 companies in the Fortune 1000 (Table 1.5). US employers use AF, résumé and reference check virtually without exception. Half used 'skills testing' and a substantial minority used personality tests and biodata. A few employ drug-use testing. Pietrowski and Armstrong did not enquire about use of interviews.

Chapman and Webster (2003) reported a survey of present and intended use of new technologies in selection. Presently, employers sift paper applica-tion, use phone interviews (but not for low-level jobs), face-to-face interviews in the preliminary or sifting phase. In future, they expect to use keyword searching, computerized scoring of AFs, IVR, online mental ability tests and videoconferencing. But, when it comes to the final decision, most employers do not envisage much change, except more use of video conferencing.

Reasons for choice

One survey (Harris, Dworkin & Park, 1990) delved a little deeper and asked why personnel managers choose or do not choose different selection methods. Factors of middling importance were fakability, offensiveness to applicant

Table 1.5 Survey of selection methods used by 151 companies in the Fortune 1000 in the USA.

	% Yes
Résumé	98
Application form	97
Reference	97
Skills testing	50
Biodata	25
Personality	19
Honesty	29
Violence potential	22
Background	11
Online pre-employment check	9
Drug-use testing	5

Data from Piotrowski & Armstrong (2006).

and how many other companies use the method. Interviews, although very widely used, were recognized not to be very accurate, as well as easy to fake. Harris *et al.* suggest that personnel managers are aware of the interview's shortcomings, but continue using it because it serves other purposes besides assessment. Terpstra and Rozell (1997), by contrast, asked personnel managers why they did not use particular methods. Some they did not think useful: structured interviews and mental ability tests. Some they had not heard of: biodata. They did not use mental ability tests because of legal worries. Wilk and Cappelli (2003) tried to discover why employers put more or less effort into selection. They showed that employers use more selection tests when the job pays more, when it has longer training and when skill levels are rising. These data suggest that employers are behaving rationally; the more workers cost in pay and training, the more carefully they are selected, and the more skill levels are rising, the more carefully workers are selected. Muchinsky (2004) notes that the most common question managers ask about selection tests are 'How long will this take?' and 'How much will it cost?' not 'How accurate is it?'.

In Europe

European countries favour a social negotiation perspective on selection, which emphasizes employee rights, applicant privacy and expectation of fair and equitable treatment. Salgado and Anderson (2002) conclude that MA tests are now more widely used in Europe than in the USA. The most recent comprehensive survey of European practice remains the Price Waterhouse Cranfield survey from the early 1990s (Dany & Torchy, 1994), which covers 12 Western European countries and nine methods. Table 1.6 reveals a number of interesting national differences:

- The French favour graphology but no other country does.
- AFs are widely used everywhere except in The Netherlands.
- References are widely used everywhere but less popular in Spain, Portugal and The Netherlands.
- Psychometric testing is most popular in Spain and Portugal and least popular in West Germany and Turkey.
- Aptitude testing is most popular in Spain and The Netherlands and least popular in West Germany and Turkey.
- Assessment centres are not used much but are most popular in Spain and The Netherlands.
- Group selection methods are not used much but are most popular in Spain and Portugal.

Further afield

Less is known about selection in other parts of the world. Recent surveys of New Zealand (Taylor, Keelty & McDonnell, 2002) and Australia (Di Milia,

Table 1.6 The Price Waterhouse Cranfield survey of selection methods in 12 countries (Dany & Torchy, 1994). Percentage of employers using method.

	AF	IV	Psy	Gph	Ref	Apt	AC	Grp
UK	97	71	46	1	92	45	18	13
Ireland	91	87	28	1	91	41	7	8
France	95	92	22	57	73	28	9	10
Portugal	83	97	58	2	55	17	2	18
Spain	87	85	60	8	54	72	18	22
Germany	96	86	6	6	66	8	13	4
Netherlands	94	69	31	2	47	53	27	2
Denmark	48	99	38	2	79	17	4	8
Finland	82	99	74	2	63	42	16	8
Norway	59	78	11	0	92	19	5	1
Sweden	n.a.	69	24	0	96	14	5	3
Turkey	95	64	8	0	69	33	4	23

Methods: AF = application form; IV = interview panel; Psy = psychometric testing; Gph = graphology; Ref = reference; Apt = aptitude test; AC = assessment centre; Grp = group selection methods.

2004) find a very similar picture to Britain; interview, references and application are virtually universal, with personality tests, ability tests and assessment centres used by a minority, but gaining in popularity. Arthur *et al.* (1995) describe selection in Nigeria and Ghana; interviews were nearly universal (90%), references widely used (46%); paper-and-pencil tests are less frequently used, as were work samples (19%) and work simulations (11%). Ryan *et al.*'s (1999) survey covered no less than 20 countries, although some samples are rather small. Mental ability tests are used most in Belgium, The Netherlands and Spain, and least used in Italy and the USA. Personality tests are used most in Spain, and least used in Germany and the USA. Projective tests are used most in Portugal, Spain and South Africa, and least used in Germany, Greece, Hong Kong, Ireland, Italy and Singapore. Drug tests are used most in Portugal, Sweden and the USA, and least used in Italy, Singapore and Spain. Ryan suggested that the data confirmed a prediction from Hofstede's (2001) discussion of national differences in attitudes to work: countries high in uncertainty avoidance (Box 1.1) use more selection methods, use them more extensively and use more interviews. Huo, Huang and Napier (2002) surveyed 13 countries including Australia, Canada, China, Indonesia, Taiwan, Japan, South Korea, Mexico, the USA and Latin America. They found that interviews are very widely used, but less so in China and South Korea. Some countries including Mexico, Taiwan and China base selection partly on connections (school, family, friends, region or government). Selection in Japan emphasizes ability to get on with others, possibly because Japanese employers traditionally offered people lifelong employment.

Box 1.1   Uncertainty avoidance

Uncertainty avoidance means organizations do not like unpredictable situations, and maintain predictability by adhering to formal procedures and rules. Countries that tend to be high in uncertainty avoidance include Greece and Portugal, while countries low in uncertainty avoidance include Singapore.

Asking applicants

All the surveys discussed so far ask HR how they select. Billsberry (2007) presented 52 UK accounts of selection procedures by those on the receiving end. The accounts amply confirm the hypothesis that some of the 80% of the employers who do not reply to surveys have something to hide. Applicants describe rudeness, unprofessional behaviour, blatant lying, obvious bias and sexual harassment. The most generally favoured form of assessment seems to be the interview, often conducted very incompetently. Billsberry's data suggested that a large survey of job As is an urgent necessity to find how many employers are behaving badly towards As. Surveys of As might also offer a second set of data on the use of selection methods or at least those visible to As.

RESEARCH AGENDA

- Employers' reasons for choosing selection methods
- Information from applicants about use of selection methods

Key points

In Chapter 1 you have learned the following.

- Employees vary greatly in value, so selection matters.
- How employees are recruited may be linked to turnover.
- Deciding which application to proceed with and which to reject is called sifting and is often done inefficiently or unfairly.
- Sifting can be improved by T&E ratings and careful setting of MQs.
- Conventional paper application methods can be improved.
- The Internet may greatly change the application process.
- Sifting software is something of an unknown quantity.
- Selection uses a range of tests to assess a range of attributes.
- Information used in selection divides into five main types.
- Selection methods must conform with fair employment legislation.
- The problem with fair employment is not deliberate or direct discrimination, but adverse impact, meaning the method results in fewer women or

minority persons being successful. Adverse impact will create problems for the employer, so should be avoided if possible.
- Selection in developed countries follows broadly similar patterns with some local variations.

Key references

Bartram (2000) discusses the role of the Internet in recruitment and selection.

Bertrand and Mullainathan (2004) describe discrimination in selection in the USA.

Billsberry (2007) presents 52 accounts of how applicants experienced selection.

Buster *et al.* (2005) describe a system for setting minimum qualifications.

Chapman and Webster (2003) review the likely impact of 'new technology' on selection.

Dany and Torchy (1994) describe the Cranfield Price Waterhouse study, which describes selection methods in 12 European countries.

Davison and Burke (2000) review research on gender bias in application sifting.

Gordon and Arvey (2004) review research on age bias in sifting.

McKinney *et al.* (2003) describe how information on college grades is used in sifting.

Ryan *et al.* (1999) describe selection methods in 20 countries, including the USA and the UK.

Useful websites

checkpast.com. A (US) background checking agency.
factsfinder.com. Another (US) background checking agency.
hrzone.com. offers advice on range of HR issues in USA
incomesdata.co.uk. Income Data Services, UK company that reports interesting research on HR issues, including surveys of selection tests.
siop.org. (US) Society for Industrial and Organisational Psychology includes details of conferences and The Industrial/Organisational Psychologist.

CHAPTER 2

Validity of selection methods

How do you know it works?

Introduction

Assessment methods themselves need to be assessed against six main criteria. An assessment should be:

- *reliable*   giving a consistent account of applicants (As).
- *valid*   selecting good As and rejecting poor ones.
- *fair*   complying with equal opportunities legislation.
- *acceptable*   to As as well as the organization.
- *cost-effective*   saving the organization more than it costs to use.
- *easy to use*   fitting conveniently into the selection process.

Selection methods do not automatically possess all these qualities. Research is needed to show which possess what. Few assessment methods meet all six criteria, so choice of assessment is always a compromise. Chapter 15 will offer an overview.

Reliability

Reliability means consistency. Physical measurements, for example the dimensions of a chair, are usually so reliable that their consistency is taken for granted. Most selection assessments are less consistent. At their worst, they may be so inconsistent that they convey little or no information. Several different sorts of reliability are used in selection research.

1] *Retest reliability* compares two sets of scores obtained from the same people, on two occasions, typically a month or so apart. The scores may be interview ratings or ability test scores or personality questionnaire profiles. If the test assesses an enduring aspect of As, as selection tests are meant to, the two sets of information ought to be fairly similar. Reliability is usually given as a correlation (Box 2.1). Retest reliability is also calculated for work performance measures, such as monthly sales figures, or supervisor ratings. These too ought to be fairly consistent month by month.
2] *Inter-rater reliability* is calculated by comparing ratings given by two assessors for people they have both interviewed or both supervised at work. If

Box 2.1   Correlation

Height and weight are correlated; tall people usually weigh more than short people, and heavy people are usually taller than light people. Height and weight are not perfectly correlated; there are plenty of short fat and tall thin exceptions to the rule. (Figure 2.1).

The correlation coefficient summarizes how closely two measures like height and weight go together. A perfect one-to-one correlation gives a value of +1.00. If two measures are completely unrelated, the correlation is zero – 0.00. Sometimes two measures are inversely, or negatively, correlated: the older the people are, the less fleet of foot they (generally) are.

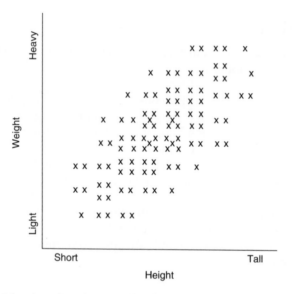

Figure 2.1   Height plotted against weight, showing a positive correlation of 0.75.

Box 2.2   Split-half reliability

The test is divided in two, each half scored separately and the two halves correlated, across a large sample. If the test is too short, the halves will not correlate well. The usual way of splitting the test is to separate odd numbered items from even numbered.

the assessors do not agree, one at least of them must be wrong, but which? Inter-rater reliability should be calculated from ratings that have not been discussed.

3] *Internal consistency reliability.* Psychological tests usually have a dozen or more component questions or 'items'. Internal consistency reliability checks whether all questions are measuring the same thing. Suppose a personality test asks 10 questions, each of which actually assesses a different trait. Calculating a score from the ten questions will generate a meaningless number. Internal consistency reliability for this 'test' will give a value near zero. The same will happen if a test consists largely of questions that do not assess anything at all. One reason why employers should avoid 'home-made' tests is the risk of finding they do not measure anything. Poor internal consistency reliability can also mean the test is too short. Earlier research used split half reliability (Box 2.2), but modern research uses the alpha coefficient (Box 2.3).

Box 2.3 Alpha coefficient

Based on examining the contribution of every item of the test to the total score. Mathematically equivalent to the average of every possible split half reliability. This procedure gives a coefficient that does not vary according to how the test is split.

Retest reliability requires the same people to do the test twice, whereas internal consistency reliability can be computed from a single set of data. Hence, internal consistency data are more popular with test publishers. However, the two types of reliability provide different sorts of information about the test, so are not really interchangeable.

Box 2.4 Standard deviation

The standard deviation does two things: 1) it describes how one person compares with another and 2) it summarizes the variability of the whole distribution. Standard deviation is usually abbreviated to SD.

A distribution is completely summarized by its mean and SD, so long as it is normal, that is bell-shaped and symmetrical. (Distributions of some natural scores, like height, are normal; distributions of constructed scores, like IQs, are made normal.)

The SD can be used to describe someone's height, without reference to any particular system of measurement. A man 6'2" high is 2 SDs above the mean. Anyone who understands statistics will know how tall that is, be the local units of height metres, feet and inches, or cubits.

Error of measurement

A simple formula based on reliability and standard deviation (Box 2.4) of scores gives the test's error of measurement, which estimates how much test scores might vary on retest (Box 2.5). An IQ test with a retest reliability of 0.90 has an error of measurement of five IQ points, meaning one in three retests will vary by five or more points, so clearly it would be a mistake for Smith who scores IQ 119 to regard himself as superior to Jones who scores 118. If they take the test again a month later, Smith might score 116 and Jones 121. One of many reasons psychologists avoid using IQs is they tend to create a false sense of precision. One reason untrained people should not use psychological tests is that they tend not to understand error of measurement.

Box 2.5   Standard error of measurement (s.e.m.)

s.e.m. is calculated by the simple formula $SD \times \sqrt{(1-r)}$, where SD is the standard deviation of test scores and r is the test's reliability.

Validity

A valid selection method is one that measures what it claims to measure, that predicts something useful, one that works. A valid test is backed by research and development. Anyone can string together 20 questions about accepting diversity. It takes patient research, studying large groups of people, collecting follow-up data, to turn the list of questions into a valid selection test. Up to 10 different types of validity can be distinguished (Table 2.1). They differ in convincingness, suitability for different sample sizes, legal acceptability and their centrality to selection.

Table 2.1   Core and marginal types of validity in selection research.

Core types of validity in selection	
Criterion	Test predicts work performance
Content	Test looks plausible to experts
Construct	Test measures something meaningful / important
Incremental	Test measures something not already measured
Convergent/divergent	Tests that 'should' correlate do correlate, while tests that 'should not' correlate do not.
Cross-validation	Test predicts work performance in two separate samples
Synthetic	Tests measure component traits and abilities that predict work performance (covered in Chapter 3)

Marginal types of validity in selection	
Faith	Person selling the test is very plausible
Face	Test looks plausible
Factorial	Test measures five separate things
Peripheral	Test measures something that might be relevant to work performance
Mythical	People think research has shown the test is valid

Criterion validity

The test predicts productivity. Ninety years ago, Link (1918) published the first selection validation study for American munitions workers, using a battery of nine tests. The most successful test, the Woodworth Wells Cancellation test, correlated very well – 0.63 – with a month's production figures for 52 munitions inspectors. Criterion validation looks for evidence that people who score highly on the test are more productive – no matter what the test is called, what the questions are, how they are selected or how plausible the test looks. What matters is predicting the criterion – work performance. Since 1918, thousands of similar studies have been reported. Early validation research was summarized by Dorcus and Jones (1950) and Super and Crites (1962).

Predictive vs. concurrent validity

Criterion validity has two main forms: predictive and concurrent.

Predictive validity

The test predicts who will produce more. This parallels real-life selection: HR select today, then find out later if their decisions are correct.

Concurrent validity

The test 'predicts' who is producing more. Test and work performance data are collected at the same time, that is concurrently. This is also referred to as present employee validity.

Concurrent validation is much quicker and easier than predictive validation because there is no need to wait for the outcome. Consequently, a lot of validation research is concurrent. Over 40 years ago, Guion (1965) said the 'present employee method is clearly a violation of scientific principles'. Morgeson *et al.* (2007) agreed: 'only studies that use a predictive model with actual job applicants should be used to support the use of personality in personnel selection'. Concurrent validation has three possible problems and one possible advantage.

1. *Missing persons.* In concurrent studies, people who left or who were dismissed are not available for study. Nor are people who proved so good they have been promoted or left for a better job somewhere else. In concurrent validation, both ends of the distribution of performance may be missing which may restrict range and reduce the validity correlation (see page 42).

2. *Unrepresentative samples.* Present employees may not be typical of applicants, actual or possible. The workforce may be all white and/or all male when As include, or ought to include, women and minorities.
3. *Direction of cause.* Present employees may have changed to meet the job's demands. They may have been trained to meet the job's demands. So it may be trivial to find that present successful managers are dominant, because managers learn to command influence and respect, whereas showing dominant As become good managers proves that dominance matters. This is a particular problem with personality, but could affect abilities as well.
4. *Faking good.* Present employees may be less likely to fake PQs and other self-reports than applicants, because they have already got the job and so have less need to describe themselves as better than they are. Faking is not normally a problem with ability tests.

The missing persons argument tends to imply that concurrent validity might be lower, through restriction of range, while the faking good argument tends to imply that predictive validity might be lower. Chapter 7 looks at predictive and concurrent validity for PQs.

Selective reporting and 'fishing expeditions'

Psychologists have traditionally relied on tests of statistical significance to evaluate research. A result that could arise by chance more often than one time in 20 is disregarded, whereas one that could only be found by chance one time in 100 is regarded as a real difference or a real correlation. However, this system can be misleading and can sometimes be used to mislead. Suppose research is using the 16PF personality questionnaire and 10 supervisor ratings of work performance. This will generate 160 correlations. Suppose eight correlations are 'significant' at the 5% level, that is larger than would arise by chance one time in 20. Researchers should conclude they have found no more 'significant' correlations that would be expected by chance, given so many have been calculated. But researchers have been known to generate plausible explanations of the link between, for example, 16PF dominance and supervisor rating of politeness, and add their results to the 16PF literature. This is called a 'fishing expedition'; it would not be published by a refereed journal, but might be cited by, for example a test publisher as evidence of validity. Unscrupulous researchers have also been known to omit tests or outcomes that did not 'get results', to make the research look more focused.

Box 2.6   Variance refers to the variability of data

Workers vary in how good their work is. The aim of selection is to predict as much of this variation as possible. Variance is computed as the square of the standard deviation.

Effect size

Wiesner & Cronshaw's (1988) review reported a correlation of 0.11 between traditional selection interview and work performance. What does a correlation of 0.11 mean? Correlations are interpreted by calculating how much variance they account for, by squaring and converting to a percentage: $0.11^2 = 0.01$, that is 1% of the variance (Box 2.6) in later work performance. The other 99% remains unaccounted for. This type of interview is not telling the employer much about how employees will turn out.

The 0.30 barrier?

Critics of psychological testing argue that tests rarely correlate with 'real world' outcomes, such as work performance, better than 0.30. The intended implication is that tests are not very useful. Critics seem to have chosen 0.30 because a 0.30 correlation accounts for just under 10% of the variance. Harpe (2008) notes that in the USA, the principal fair employment agency, the Equal Employment Opportunities Commission, tends to consider a correlation below 0.30 as failing to establish validity, which certainly makes 0.30 a barrier for American employers.

The largest correlations obtainable in practice in selection research (0.50 to 0.60) account for only a quarter to a third of the variance in performance. It may not be realistic to expect more than 0.50 or 0.60. Performance at work is influenced by many other factors – management, organizational climate, co-workers, economic climate, the working environment – besides the assessable characteristics of the individual worker.

The d statistic

The d statistic describes the size of a difference between groups of people. Chapter 1 (page 3) noted there is a small difference in work performance between employees recruited informally by word of mouth and those recruited formally through press advertisement. The d statistic computes how many SDs separate the means. For informal versus formal recruitment, d is 0.08, meaning less than a tenth of an SD separates the averages, so the difference is not very great. Very small effect sizes, such as a correlation of 0.11, or d statistic of 0.08, mean the selection or recruitment procedure is not making much difference. This tends to be a reason to look for something better. However, it can sometimes be worth using something that achieves only modest results. Informal recruiting only makes a small difference in subsequent output but this improvement is achieved very easily and cheaply, and can mount up across a lot of vacancies filled. (But recall also from Chapter 1 that fair employment agencies do not like informal recruiting.)

Content validity

The test looks plausible to experts. Experts analyse the job, choose relevant questions and put together the test. Content validation was borrowed from educational testing, where it makes sense to ask if a test covers the curriculum and to seek answers from *subject matter experts*. Content validation regards test items as *samples* of things employees need to know, not as *signs* of what employees are like. Devising a content valid test for fire fighters might have three stages:

1. An expert panel, of experienced firefighters, assisted by HR and psychologists, write an initial pool of test items – things firefighters need to know, for example *Which of these materials generate toxic gases when burning?* or be able to do, for example *Connect fire appliance to fire hydrant.*
2. Items are rated by a second expert panel for how often the problem arises or the task is performed and for how essential it is.
3. The final set of knowledge and skill items are rewritten in a five-point rating format, for example *Connect fire appliance to fire hydrant. 5 (high) quickly & accurately assembles all components … 1 (low) fails entirely to assemble components correctly.*

Content validation has several advantages: it is plausible to applicants, and easy to defend because it ensures that the selection test is clearly related to the job. It does not require a large sample of people presently doing the job, unlike criterion validity. Content validation also has limitations. It is only suitable for jobs with a limited number of fairly specific tasks. Because it requires people to possess particular skills or knowledge, it is more suitable for promotion than for selection. Content validity is subordinate to criterion validity. Content validation is a way of writing a test that ought to work. The organization should also carry out criterion validation to check that it really does.

Construct validity

The test measures something meaningful. When a new selection system is devised, people sometimes ask themselves: What is this assessing? What sort of person will get a good mark from it? One answer should always be 'People who will do the job well.' But it is worth going a bit deeper and trying to get some picture of what particular aspects of applicants the test is assessing: for example, abilities, personality, social background and specific skills. There are several reasons why it is important to explore construct validity:

- If a new test is mostly assessing personality and HR already use a personality test, HR may well find that the new test is not adding much. The new test may not be called a personality test. It may be labelled emotional intelligence or sales aptitude.

- If a two-day assessment centre measures the same thing as a 30-minute ability test, it would be much cheaper to use the 30-minute test.
- If As complain about selection methods and HR have to defend them in court, HR may want to be able to say exactly what the test assesses, and what it does not. They may be made to look very silly if they cannot!
- If the new test turns out to be mostly assessing mental ability (MA), HR will be alerted to the possibility of adverse impact on certain groups.

Construct validity is usually assessed by comparing one selection method, for example interview ratings, with other methods (e.g. psychological tests). Construct validity reveals what a method is actually assessing (which is not necessarily what it is intended to assess). For example, the traditional unstructured interview turns out to be assessing MA to a surprising extent (Chapter 4).

Convergent / divergent validity

Assessment centres (Chapter 9) seek to assess people on a number of dimensions, for example problem-solving ability, influence and empathy, through a series of exercises (e.g. group discussion and presentation). Figure 2.2 illustrates three types of correlations:

- Those at AAA are for the same dimension rated in different exercises which 'ought' to be high; this is *convergent validity*.
- Those at bbb are for different dimensions rated in the same exercise, which 'ought' to be lower; this is *discriminant validity*. (They need not be zero – the dimensions may be correlated).
- Those at ccc are for different attributes rated in different exercises, which 'ought' to be very low or zero.

	A - group discussion			B - presentation		
Dimensions	1	2	3	1	2	3
A - group discussion						
1 - influence						
2 - empathy	bbb					
3 - planning	bbb	bbb				
B - presentation						
1 - influence	AAA	ccc	ccc			
2 - empathy	ccc	AAA	ccc	bbb		
3 - planning	ccc	ccc	AAA	bbb	bbb	

Figure 2.2   Three types of correlation in an assessment centre with three dimensions (1 to 3) rated in each of two exercises (A and B).

In AC research in particular, and in selection research in general, it often turns out that both convergent and divergent validity are low. Low convergent validity means that different measures of the same dimension do not correlate: influence measured by PQ does not correlate with influence assessed by group discussion, which implies one or other measure is not working, or that something complex and unexpected is happening. Low divergent validity means that a test intended to measure several conceptually different dimensions is failing to differentiate them and that all the scores derived from, for example a group discussion, are highly correlated. This problem is also referred to as method variance: how data are collected often seems to explain correlations better than what the data are intended to assess.

Cross-validation

This means checking the validity of a test a second time, on a second sample. Cross-validation is always desirable, but becomes absolutely essential for methods likely to capitalize on chance, such as multi-score PQs, and empirically keyed biodata (Chapter 8). Locke (1961) gave a very striking demonstration of the hazards of not cross-validating a test. He found students with long surnames (7+ letters) were less charming, happy-go-lucky, and impulsive, liked vodka, but did not smoke, and had more fillings in their teeth. Locke's results sound quite plausible, in places, but all arose by chance, and all vanished on cross-validation.

Incremental validity

A selection test, for example a reference, may not be very accurate in itself, but it may improve the prediction made by other methods, perhaps by covering aspects of work performance that other selection methods fail to cover. On the other hand, a method with good validity, such a job knowledge test, may add little to selection by MA test, because job knowledge and MA tests are highly correlated, so cover the same ground.

Figure 2.3 illustrates incremental validity, showing two predictors and an outcome, work performance. Where the predictor circles overlap the outcome circle, the tests are achieving validity. In Figure 2.3a, the two predictors – MA test and reference – do not correlate much, so their circles do not overlap much, whereas in Figure 2.3b the two predictors – job knowledge and MA – are highly correlated, so their circles overlap a lot. Note the effect on the overlap between predictor and outcome circles. In Figure 2.3a, the predictors explain more of the outcome, where in Figure 2.3b, they explain less, because they both cover the same ground.

Incremental validity is very important when assembling a set of selection tests. It is too easy otherwise to find that the selection procedure is measuring the same thing over and over again. Incremental validity needs data on the intercorrelation of selection tests, which is very patchy in its coverage. Sometimes there is a lot (e.g. MA tests and interviews); sometimes there is hardly

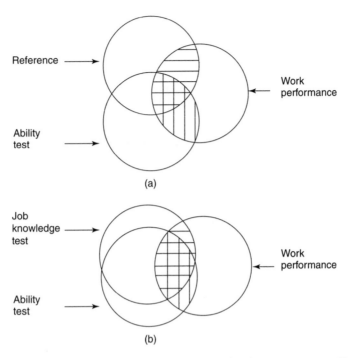

Figure 2.3   Schematic representation of the relationship between two predictors, e.g. mental ability test and reference, and work performance, where (a) the predictors are not highly correlated and (b) where they are highly correlated.

any (e.g. references). Schmidt and Hunter (1998) offered estimates of the correlation between MA and other tests, and of likely incremental validity, discussed in Chapter 14.

Marginal types of validity

Face-validity. The test looks plausible. Some people are persuaded a test measures dominance, if it is called 'Dominance Test', or if the questions all concern behaving dominantly. Face-validity does not show the test really is valid, but does help make the test more acceptable to employer and applicants.

Faith validity. The person who sold me the test was very plausible. Some people are easily impressed by expensively printed tests, smooth-talking salespersons and sub-psychodynamic nonsense. But plausibility does not guarantee validity, and money spent on glossy presentation and well-dressed sales staff is all too often money not spent on research and development.

Factorial validity. The test measures five things but gives them 16 different labels. Knowing how many factors (Box 2.7) a test measures does not reveal what the factors are, nor what they can predict.

Box 2.7   Factor analysis

Table 2.2 shows (fictitious) correlations between performance on six typical school subjects, in a large sample. The correlations between English, French and German are all fairly high. People who are good at one tend to be good at the others. Similarly, the correlations between Maths, Physics and Chemistry are fairly high. However, correlations between subjects in different sets – e.g. English Literature and Physics – are much lower. All of which suggests that people who are good at one language tend to be good at another, while people who are good at one science are good at another. There are six school subjects, but only two underlying abilities.

Table 2.2   (Fictitious) correlations between school subject marks.

	Maths	Physics	Chemistry	English	French
Maths					
Physics	0.67				
Chemistry	0.76	0.55			
English	0.33	0.23	0.25		
French	0.23	0.31	0.30	0.77	
German	0.11	0.21	0.22	0.80	0.67

Peripheral validity. Sometimes research in other areas of psychology suggests a measure might be useful in selection. For example, Graziano, Jensen-Campbell and Hair (1996) found that people low on the personality factor of agreeableness tend to have personal relationships characterized by conflict and discord. This suggested low A scorers may be a problem in some workplaces, but does not definitely prove it because the research was done on college students.

Mythical validity. Sometimes people assume that tests are valid because they are widely used, or heavily advertised, or have been around a long time. Sometimes people think validity data are better than they really are because research evidence is not very accessible, or is seldom or never read. Zeidner, Matthews and Roberts (2004) said that Goleman (1995) described a study at Bell Laboratory showing that top performers were higher on emotional intelligence (EI). Subsequently, this study has been widely quoted as showing the value of EI. However, 'careful reading of the original shows this is pure conjecture – Bell Laboratory engineers were never actually tested with any instrument designed to assess EI' – a classic example of mythical validity.

Meta analysis

For some selection methods, hundreds of validity studies had accumulated by the 1960s. This created problems in summarizing and interpreting research, especially when studies gave inconsistent results. It proved difficult, at first, to answer the apparently simple question: does it work?

Narrative reviews

Earlier reviews of selection research did not use any quantitative means of summarizing research. They often failed to enlighten readers because they first listed 10 studies that find that interviews do predict job performance, then listed 10 studies that find that they do not, and finished by listing 20 studies that are inconclusive. Readers typically react by exclaiming 'Do interviews work or not? The psychologists don't seem able to make up their minds!'. At their worst, narrative reviews can be exercises in preconception: reviewers read into the research whatever conclusions they want to find.

Ghiselli's Meta-analysis

Meta-analysis pools the results of many different researches and generates a single numerical estimate of link between selection test and work performance, usually average correlation, weighted by sample size (because research based on 1000 persons carries more weight than research based on 50 persons). Ghiselli (1966b, 1973) collated hundreds of validity coefficients for MA tests, classified by test type, job type and measure of work performance. Figure 2.4 presents his distributions of validities for four test × job combinations. These days, meta-analyses are usually presented as tables, as in Table 2.3, where k is the number of correlations and r is the average correlation. Current meta-analyses also give N, the total pooled sample size, but Ghiselli's first meta-analysis did not include this information.

Meta-analysis proved a very useful development in selection research. Large bodies of research could be summarized in a single overall validity. Meta-analysis sometimes found fairly encouraging results. Average validity for some selection methods turned out to be greater than zero, despite the many 'negative' results. Meta-analysis could generate 'league tables' of selection validity. One of the first, by Hunter and Hunter (1984), concluded that MA tests achieved good validity, whereas the conventional unstructured interview achieved very poor validity.

Moderator variables

Suppose a test had good validity for men, but poor validity for women (something which does not seem to happen very often in reality). Pooling data from men and women would obscure this important point. Meta-analysis can code

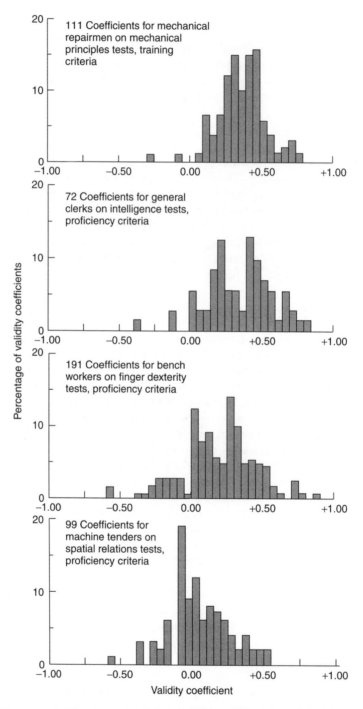

Figure 2.4   Four distributions of validity coefficients for four combinations of test and criterion (Ghiselli, 1966b). (Reprinted by permission of John Wiley & Sons, Inc.)

Table 2.3   Ghiselli's (1973) meta-analysis of ability test validity.

Job	Mechanical repair worker	Bench worker	Clerk	Machine tender
Test	Mechanical principles	Finger dexterity	General mental ability	Spatial relations
1) k – number of validities	114	191	72	99
2) N – total sample size	Not reported	Not reported	Not reported	Not reported
3) r – average validity	0.39	0.25	0.36	0.11

every correlation for any variable that might be relevant, and for which there are enough studies to allow a comparison. So if gender is important, moderator variable analysis could uncover this fact.

Problems with meta-analysis ✳

Meta-analysis first appeared, in as many as four places more or less simultaneously, in the 1970s. The idea of averaging across different researches had occurred to people before then, but had been dismissed on the 'chalk and cheese' argument: that pooling results from different tests, or different workforces, or different work performance measures was wrong. Critics still argue that combining different measures can be a mistake: Hogan and Holland (2003) argued that meta-analysis pools good personality measures with poor, which may obscure the former's contribution. Hogan also noted that different measures of conscientiousness are based on different concepts of conscientiousness, so it is misleading to pool them. Sackett (2003) argued that 'counterproductivity' is a 'catch-all term' covering absence, lateness, disciplinary problems, theft, accidents and so on, which have in common that all are contrary to the organization's interests, but which could 'have different underlying motives: greed, retaliation, laziness, inattention', so pooling them could be psychologically meaningless.

Disagreement

Table 2.4 summarizes four meta-analyses of the same relationship, between MA and interview ratings. The four analyses reach four different conclusions:

- The more structured the interview, the less it correlates with MA (Huffcutt, Roth & McDaniel, 1996).
- The more structured the interview, the more it correlates with MA (Cortina *et al.*, 2000).

Table 2.4 Summary of four meta-analyses of the correlation between interview and mental ability.

Interview structure

	Low		Medium		High	
Huffcutt	Low		Medium		High	
Salgado	Conventional				Behaviour	
Cortina	Level 1		Level 2		Levels 3 & 4	
Berry	Low		Medium		High	
	k	r	k	r	k	r
Huffcutt	8	0.30	19	0.25	22	0.23
Salgado	53	0.20			22	0.14
Cortina	3	0.04	8	0.20	10	0.22
Berry	3	0.14	6	0.38	27	0.16

Data from Huffcutt *et al.* (1996), Salgado & Moscoso (2002), Cortina *et al.* (2000) and Berry *et al.* (2007).
k = number of correlations; r = average correlation.

- There is not that much difference between structured and unstructured interviews in terms of correlation with MA (Salgado & Moscoso, 2002).
- The correlation between MA and interview rating is much higher for medium-structure interviews than for high- or low-structure interviews (Berry, Sackett & Landers, 2007).

How can four analyses of the same data reach four different conclusions? Inspection of the k values in Table 2.4 reveals that the first three analyses did not in fact use the same data. The three earlier analyses collectively find 102 relevant studies, but two-thirds of these are included in only one meta-analysis, while only 10% are included in all three. The three analyses are effectively of three largely different sets of research data. Why? Seventeen studies were published after 1995 so Huffcutt *et al.* could not have included them. Salgado and Moscoso appear to have found more researches on unstructured interviews partly by including European studies the other reviews overlooked, partly by including research on student admissions the others did not consider relevant. Otherwise, the reason for the differences in coverage and conclusions is not clear. The most recent analysis (Berry *et al.*) was intentionally much more selective: they excluded any research where interviewers had, or might have had, access to the MA test data, so might have allowed it to influence their rating, which makes a correlation fairly uninteresting. Note that this exclusion greatly reduced the number of studies of unstructured interviews that could be included in the meta-analysis.

Reporting bias

Do meta-analyses of selection research overestimate average validity by leaving out studies that find selection methods do not work? Reporting bias covers a range of possibilities from researchers losing interest in a project that is not coming up with 'good' results, through the notorious difficulty of getting journals to publish 'negative' results, to the deliberate suppression of inconvenient findings. Russell *et al.* (1994) showed that researches reported by academics find lower average validity than researches reported by authors employed in private industry, possibly because academics have no vested interest in showing that tests 'work'.

Checks on reporting bias have been devised, based on plotting correlation against sample size. The smaller the sample, the more correlation will vary by chance. Figure 2.5 shows three funnel plots. The area of interest is correlation based on smaller samples, where more sampling error is found and

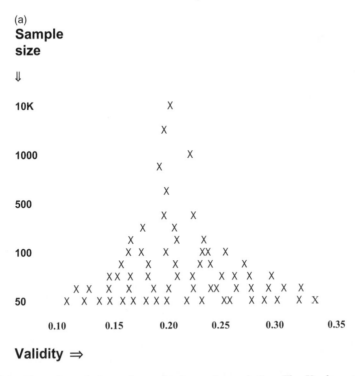

Figure 2.5   Three funnel plots of sample size and correlation. The Xs show the actual distribution of correlations in the meta-analysis. In Figure 2.5c the Ms show the presumed missing values, according to trim-and-fill analysis.

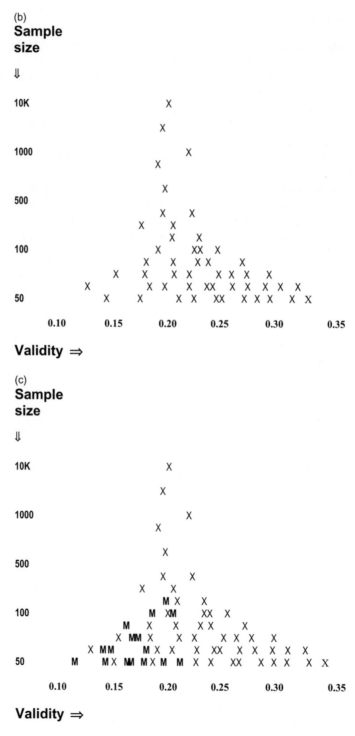

Figure 2.5 *Continued*

where a lot of selection research is also to be found. Correlations based on smaller samples should be found evenly spaced about the funnel plot, as in the lower part of Figure 2.5a. Sometimes, however, these correlations are not evenly spaced, but bunched to one side, as in Figure 2.5b, where there are more correlations in the 0.20 plus region, and fewer in the zero region. This suggests some correlations below 0.20 have somehow been overlooked. Duval's (2005) trim-and-fill procedure estimates how many correlations are 'missing', and what overall validity for the meta-analysis would be if they had been included. Figure 2.5c shows presumed missing values that have been added. Trim-and-fill has found some evidence of reporting bias in selection research, for personality questionnaires and MA tests (McDaniel, Rothstein & Whetzel, 2006a; Pollack & McDaniel, 2008), structured interviews (Duval, 2005) and ethnicity differences in work performance (McDaniel, McKay & Rothstein, 2006b). McDaniel *et al.* (2006a) noted that most earlier meta-analyses of selection research did not check for reporting bias, and suggested they should all be re-analysed.

Representativeness

Hartigan and Wigdor (1989) criticized Hunter's (1986) analysis for unrepresentative sampling of jobs: there were, for example, too few agricultural jobs. Ghiselli's (1966) original meta-analysis included few low-level, unskilled jobs. This is neither a criticism of meta-analysis, nor of Hunter's or Ghiselli's research, but an observation of a general trend in work psychology: some jobs are much more intensively researched than others. However, when meta-analysis summarizes a whole body of research and concludes that, for example, structured interviews achieve an average validity of 0.34, it is easy to assume this means for all jobs in America. Meta-analyses often give little information about type of job. Some are based largely on present employees and may not reveal so much about applicants.

Low power to detect true difference

Critics argue that meta-analysis is geared towards regarding variations between studies as noise or error, so will miss important differences, such as possible gender differences in validity. Sackett, Harris and Orr (1986) created artificial datasets in which real differences in validity of 0.10 or 0.20 were included, then checked if meta-analysis could discover this built-in moderator variable. Meta-analysis could detect a true difference of 0.20, if the number of correlations and the total sample size were very large, but could not detect a true difference in validity of 0.10 even with very large numbers. This implies that if validity of MA tests were higher for females than males, or vice versa, moderator variable analysis might fail to detect this and might dismiss the variation in validity as error.

Premature conclusions

McDaniel (McDaniel *et al.*, 2006) suggested that publication of a major meta-analysis, for example his own on interview research in 1994 (McDaniel *et al.*, 1994), tends to discourage further research in the area. If 140 researches on interview validity show that structured interviews work better than unstructured interviews, what is the point of carrying out a 141st study and how will it advance the career of the researcher who does it? If the meta-analysis reached sound conclusions, further research may not be needed. But if the meta-analysis is vitiated by reporting bias or some other deficiency, then its conclusions may be premature.

Validity generalization analysis

Ghiselli found the results of his 1966 meta-analysis disappointing:

> 'A confirmed pessimist at best, even I was surprised at the variation in findings concerning a particular test applied to workers on a particular job. We certainly never expected the repetition of an investigation to give the same results as the original. But we never anticipated them to be worlds apart.' (Ghiselli, 1966b)

Ghiselli identified two problems, both very worrying from the selector's point of view:

- Problem 1 – validity was low.
- Problem 2 – validity varied a lot from study to study.

First problem – low validity

Ghiselli's distributions of validity had averages of around 0.30 at best, which made people start asking whether it was worth using tests that contributed so little information, especially when they were getting very unpopular and starting to meet difficulties with fair employment laws. Like other early meta-analyses, Ghiselli had analysed raw correlations between test and outcome. Raw correlations may be low because there is no relationship between test and work performance, but they may only appear low through two well-known limitations of selection research: restricted range and unreliability of work performance measures.

Restricted range

Suppose researchers examine running speed and physical fitness in a group of university athletes. They might get results like those in Figure 2.6a – a very weak relationship. They might then conclude there is not much link between fitness and running speed, so that using fitness tests to select athletes would

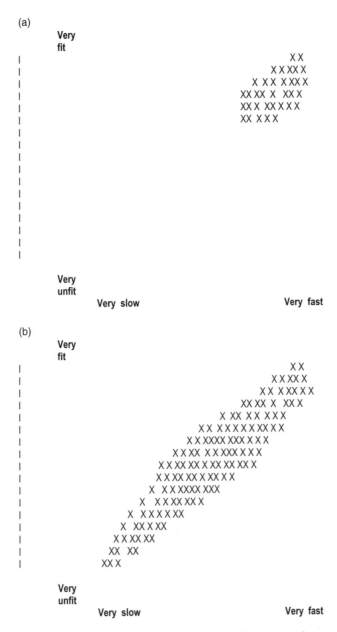

Figure 2.6 Fictitious data illustrating restriction of range, in data on the correlation between fitness and running speed.

not be very successful. This would be a mistake because it overlooks the fact that all athletes are physically fit and most can run fast. If researchers widened their sample to include all 18- to 22-year-olds, they would find a much clearer link as shown in Figure 2.6b. Including lots of not very fit people who cannot run very fast reveals the true relationship. In technical terms, in Figure 2.6a, range of fitness is restricted. Restricted range greatly reduces the correlation and may conceal it altogether. Restricted range almost always happens in personnel selection because only successful As can contribute work performance data. The researcher never knows what the work performance of unsuccessful As would be like because they never get the chance to try the job.

There are two ways of dealing with the restricted range problem. The first is *assess all and employ all*, so as to get work performance data from everyone. This is expensive and risky, so is very rarely used. During World War Two, the US Air Force did send a large unselected sample through pilot training, enabling Flanagan (1946) to calculate validity without restriction of range. The failure rate was high – 77% – but so was the correlation between test scores and success – 0.64. The other solution is easier, safer and very widely used: *statistical correction*. A simple formula allows the researcher to 'correct' the raw correlation for restriction of range, which usually increases it.

Unreliability of work performance measure

Every validity study needs an index of successful work performance (discussed in Chapter 11). Whatever is used will be less than perfectly reliable. The most widely used measure – supervisor rating – has fairly poor reliability: Schmidt and Hunter's (1977) estimate was 0.60. Two or more supervisors will not agree all that well in their rating of an employee's work performance. The next most widely used measure – training grades – is more reliable. Schmidt and Hunter's estimate is 0.80. An unreliable outcome is difficult to predict, and necessarily reduces the correlation between predictor and outcome. The usual solution is statistical correction, using a simple formula based on outcome reliability.

Validity generalization analysis (VGA)

VGA is a development of meta-analysis by Schmidt and Hunter (1977, 2004). VGA routinely corrects validity for both restricted range and outcome reliability, which can nearly double the validity correlation. Comparing rows 2 and 7 in Table 2.5 illustrates this. The corrections for restricted range and outcome reliability were devised long ago, and had been used in research long before validity generalization. It was not usual however to make both corrections, as VGA does. VGA generates therefore a very much more positive account of selection validity. An interesting aside is that other lines of research that correlate tests with 'real life' behaviour, e.g. Funder's (2007) research on personality, report raw correlations, and make no corrections at all.

Second problem – variation in validity

The correlation between general mental ability (GMA) and clerical proficiency in Figure 2.4 varies from −0.45 to 0.75. Such wide variation means that

Table 2.5 Validity generalization analysis of the data of Figure 2-4, based on data given by Schmidt & Hunter (1977).

Job	Mechanical repair worker	Bench worker	Clerk	Machine tender
Test	Mechanical principles	Finger dexterity	General intelligence	Spatial relations
1] k – number of validities	114	191	72	99
2] N – total sample size	nr	nr	nr	nr
3] r – average validity (raw)	0.39	0.25	0.36	0.11
4] Observed variance of validity	0.21	0.26	0.26	0.22
5] Estimated variance of validity	0.19	0.14	0.17	0.12
6] Observed minus estimated	0.02	0.12	0.09	0.10
7] Observed variance accounted for	90%	54%	65%	54%
8] ρ – average validity (corrected)	0.78	0.39	0.67	0.05

ρ, in line 8, is operational validity, corrected for restricted range and reliability of work performance measure.

employers can never be sure whether a selection test will work (moderately) well, or not very well, or not at all. Work psychologists initially hoped to find moderator variables (v.i.) to explain the wide variation: for example, type of job, type of organization and type of applicant. Moderator variables were found for some selection methods, but not sufficient to explain all the variation in validity. Work psychologists next turned to the very pessimistic *situational specificity hypothesis*: so many factors affect test validity, so complexly, that it is impossible to construct a model that predicts validity in any particular setting. Employers must rely on *local validation studies* to check whether their particular tests work for their particular workforce. However, there is a third possible explanation for variation in validity – sampling error.

Sampling error

The *law of large numbers* states that *large* random samples will be highly representative of the population from which they are drawn. The *fallacy of small numbers* is to suppose that *small* random samples are also representative; they are not. Correlations calculated from small samples vary a lot and most validity research has used fairly small samples. Schmidt *et al.* (1985b) suggested that one 'rogue' observation in a sample of 40 to 50 can change the correlation considerably. This can easily happen, if for example the best worker happens to be ill when tested.

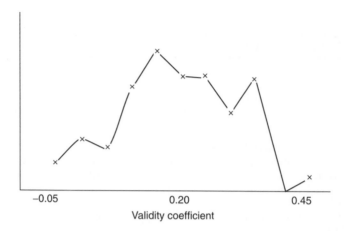

Figure 2.7   Distribution of validity coefficients for 63 sub-samples, each of 68, drawn randomly from a larger sample of 1455 US postal workers. Data from Schmidt *et al.* (1985a).

US Postal Service data demonstrate conclusively how small sample correlations vary a lot in the absence of any possible real cause (Figure 2.7). Schmidt *et al.* (1985a) randomly divided a large sample of 1455 letter sorters into 63 smaller groups of 68 each (68 because Lent, Aurbach & Levin (1971) had shown this was the average sample size in validation research). Validity of a clerical test for the whole sample was 0.22. Figure 2.7 shows the distribution of validity coefficients for the 63 mini-samples, which can only vary through sampling error. Validity ranges from −0.03 to 0.48. Most were statistically insignificant, so researchers using such small samples are more likely than not to 'miss' the link between test and work performance. Figure 2.7 shows that correlations calculated on small samples are misleading and that 68 is a small sample, too small. If the 63 correlations in Figure 2.7 vary so much just by chance, perhaps the 72 correlations for Ghiselli's clerical workers in Figure 2.4 vary as much by chance too. The other limitations of selection research – unreliability of outcome measure and range restriction – also add some more error because they vary from study to study.

Observed and expected variation in validity

VGA asks 'Can all the variation in validity be explained as error? Or is there some real variation? even after making allowance for the known limitations of selection research?' VGA compares *observed variance* with *estimated variance*. Observed variance is how much validity actually varies. Estimated variance is how much one would expect validity to vary given what is known – or can be estimated – about sources of error. Hunter and Schmidt (2004) provided computational details. *Zero residual variance* means there is no variance left when estimated variance has been subtracted from observed variance, so there is no true variation in validity. Validity is really the same in every study included in the analysis.

Table 2.5 applies VGA to the four sets of Ghiselli's data in Figure 2.4 and Table 2.3. Line 7 of Table 2.5 shows that between 54 and 90% of the observed variance in validity can be accounted for by error. For testing repair workers with tests of mechanical principles, 90% of the variation in validity can be explained, suggesting that validity does not 'really' vary much. However, for testing bench workers with finger dexterity tests, only half the variation in validity can be explained, which suggests that validity does 'really' vary. The reader may wonder why it seems to matter so much whether validity of selection methods does or does not 'really' vary. There are three reasons.

- One is practical. If the correlation between MA and work performance is always 0.50, then HR can use MA tests 'off the shelf', in the knowledge they will work.
- The second reason has more do with the standing of psychology as a science. A true science states laws; for example, 'every schoolboy knows' Boyle's law in physics, that the pressure of a gas varies inversely with its volume. Psychology has always seemed short of such general laws with which to impress the public. Perhaps the Schmidt–Hunter Law, that MA and work performance always correlate 0.50, would fill this gap. (But given the general unpopularity of MA tests, perhaps it would not).
- A third reason is identifying research needs. If VGA finds substantial unexplained variation in validity, it is worth looking for moderator variables. Newman, Jacobs and Bartram (2007) list four areas where VGA finds unexplained variation: MA tests for clerical workers, conscientiousness tests for managers, assessment centres, and interviews, especially structured interviews. By contrast, VGA of honesty tests, work sample tests and biodata find no evidence of any true variation in validity still needing to be explained.

Schmidt *et al.* (1985b) suggested researchers could – and perhaps should – have concluded as long ago as the 1920s that tests have generalized validity and that validity only appears to vary from study to study through sampling error. Why did work psychologists cling to the doctrine of situational specificity for so long? Perhaps they did not read their statistics books carefully enough and overlooked sampling error. Perhaps they were reluctant to admit that researches on samples of 50 or 60 were not very useful, especially as it is often difficult to find larger numbers. Perhaps they just wanted to carry on selling employers local validity studies.

Correcting for test reliability

Some VGAs make a third correction for (un)reliability of the selection test. From the selector's perspective, it is pointless estimating how much more accurate selection would be if tests were perfectly reliable because no test is perfectly reliable. Validity is necessarily limited by test reliability. However, researchers devising a theory of, for example, numerical ability and work performance, may find it useful to regard both as things that could ideally be measured perfectly reliably, so could legitimately correct for reliability of both before calculating their true correlation. Some analyses distinguish between estimated *true validity*, which is corrected for range restriction and unreliability of both test and criterion, and *operational validity*, which is corrected for range restriction and criterion reliability only. This book will quote operational validity rather than true validity wherever possible.

VGA extends the contribution of meta-analysis, showing that selection tests work more consistently, and work much better than people thought in the 1960s and 1970s.

Criticisms of validity generalization

Landy (2003) described VGA as the 'psychometric equivalent of alchemy. Lead was turned into gold – a collection of disappointing and contradictory validity studies were unravelled to show that we had been doing the right thing all along.' However, VGA has attracted its share of critics. Seymour (1988) dismissed it as the 'hydraulic' model of test validity. If your validity is not large enough, simply inflate it to the desired size by making corrections.

Correcting for restricted range

How much allowance for restricted range should be made? The bigger the allowance made, the bigger the consequent increase in corrected validity. Correcting for restricted range uses a formula based on the ratio of sample standard deviation (SD) to population SD. *Sample* means successful As, where researchers have the data to compute SD. *Population* might mean all As, where researchers also have the data for SD. But often population is taken to mean everyone who *might have applied*, which makes it harder to find a value for their SD.

One approach is using normative data from the test's manual. Sackett and Ostgaard (1994) presented estimates of range restriction in the Wonderlic Personnel Test, comparing SD of scores for each of 80 jobs with the overall SD of the whole database. On average, SDs for particular jobs are 8.3% smaller than the overall SD. For 90% of jobs, restriction is less than 20%. For more complex jobs, range restriction is greater, whereas for simple jobs it is much less. Ones and Viswesvaran (2003a) reported a similar analysis for the Comprehensive Personality Profile, which has a large body of descriptive data for 111 US occupations, from accountant to wrecker. Restriction of range within occupation is very small. In many validation studies, the test is not used to select, but is given for research purposes, after the people have already been selected, which explains why range of test scores is not reduced all that much.

Hunter and Hunter's (1984) VGA of the GATB database (see Chapter 6, p. 114) used a similar strategy, and also produced a fairly low estimate of range restriction, but has nevertheless proved controversial. Hunter used the SD of the whole GATB database, that is of everyone who got a job in all 515 studies, as his estimate of population SD, which generates an estimate of restriction of 20%. Critics, such as Hartigan and Wigdor (1989), objected to this. They argued that doctors and lawyers, who are at the 'top' of the GATB database, are not likely to apply for the minimum wage jobs at the 'bottom', while the people in minimum wage jobs could not apply for 'top' jobs because they lack the necessary qualifications. Hartigan and Wigdor argued that the purpose of correcting validity coefficients should not be to produce the largest possible correlation, but to give the test's user a realistic estimate of how well it will work in practice, avoiding underestimates that do not allow for known methodological limitations and avoiding overestimates based on showing how efficiently the test could reject people who would never actually apply for the job. Schmidt, Shaffer and Oh (in press) reviewed three major meta-analyses and concluded that SD of employee GMA is around 0.65 of applicant SD in all three.

Correcting for outcome reliability

How much allowance for unreliability of work performance measures should be made? Again the bigger the allowance, the bigger the resulting increase in corrected validity, which creates the worrying paradox that the less reliable the performance measure, the higher validity becomes. Assuming reliability of supervisor rating is 0.60 increases corrected validity by 29%. Hartigan and Wigdor preferred a more conservative assumption that supervisor rating reliability averages 0.80, which increases raw-to-true validity by only 12%. The most recent meta-analysis of supervisor reliability (Viswesvaran, Ones & Schmidt, 1996) favours Hunter, reporting a value of only 0.52.

There is also dispute about which type of reliability to use. The 0.60 / 0.52 value is for inter-rater reliability: how well two or more supervisors agree. Murphy and De Shon (2000) argued that difference between supervisors should not be regarded as error because different supervisors see different aspects of the worker's performance. VGA could correct instead using internal consistency reliability of supervisor rating; this is much higher – 0.86 in Viswesvaran *et al.*'s meta-analysis – so will only increase validity by 8%.

Two analyses of the GATB database

Hartigan & Wigdor reanalysed the GATB database, making different assumptions to Hunter, and reach quite different conclusions (Table 2.6). They assumed criterion reliability is 0.80, not 0.60. They did not correct for restricted range at all. These more conservative assumptions increase validity by only 12%, whereas Hunter's more generous assumptions increase it by 40%. Furthermore, Hartigan and Wigdor started from a different, lower, average raw

Table 2.6 Two analyses of the GATB database, by Hunter & Hunter (1984) and by Hartigan & Wigdor (1989).

Analysis	Hunter & Hunter	Hartigan & Wigdon
k	515	755
N	38K	76K
Uncorrected r	0.25	0.19
Performance reliability estimate used	0.60	0.80
Restricted range estimate used	0.80	1.00
Operational validity	0.47	0.22
Variance accounted for	22%	5%

validity. They used an extended GATB database in which the extra later studies show lower validity than the earlier studies used in Hunter's VGA. The combined effect of these three differences is to place their estimate of GATB's true validity at only 0.22, compared with Hunter's 0.47.

Latest development in VGA

Indirect restriction of range (IRR). Presently, VGA corrects for restriction of range using the formula for direct restriction of range (DRR). This is not actually the right formula to use because DRR does not happen all that often in selection research. Applicants are not usually selected by the test being researched, either because scores are not used to make selection decisions or because 'applicants' are not applicants at all but present employees, selected some time ago by whatever the employer was then using.

Range, especially of GMA, is often indirectly restricted because many selection criteria are linked to GMA. For example, entry to the medical profession requires successful completion of a medical degree, which tends to exclude people of lower GMA, so range of GMA scores in doctors will be restricted, even though GMA tests are not used to select. Research on GMA tests for selecting doctors will underestimate GMA's true link to medical performance because range of GMA has been restricted by use of education requirements.

A more complex correction formula for indirect range restriction, called Case III, was devised by Thorndike 60 years ago, but requires data that are rarely available. Case III also requires the variable(s) indirectly restricting range to be clearly identified, which they often are not. Applicants may have been sifted by vague concepts of the 'right background' or the 'right sort of school', which can restrict range of MA through links to social class.

The new development in VGA depends on the distinction between true GMA and GMA test score. *Classical test theory* says scores on a GMA test contain two elements: true GMA and error. Error is everything that makes the

```
        o o o                    Observed
      o o oo o oo                scores
     o o o oooo o o              on test
    oo oo ooo o oo o o
   o oo oo ooo oo ooo o o
  o o ooo o oo o ooo o o oo oo
 o  o o oo ooo oo oo oo  oooooo o o
```

```
        T TT                    True scores
      T TTT TTT
     T TT TTTTT T
    TT TT TTTTTT T T
   T T TTT TTT TT TT T T T
  T TT TT TT T TTT TTT TT T T T T
 T T T TT TTT TTTT TTT TT TTT T  T
```

Figure 2.8 Two distributions, the upper distribution showing scores on a test of mental ability, the lower the hypothetical true scores.

test less than perfectly reliable: for example, items that do not work very well, poor test administration and person tested having an 'off day'. Therefore, GMA score is always imperfectly correlated with true GMA. Note that true GMA is a hypothetical entity than can never be observed. In Figure 2.8, the lower distribution is the true GMA of the sample, while the upper distribution shows GMA test scores. Test scores are more widely scattered, by the error they contain. In Figure 2.8, the distribution of true ability is 'tighter' and range restriction is greater.

Schmidt, Oh and Le (2006) argued that IRR does not restrict range of scores on the GMA test. It cannot because IRR usually happens before the test is used. IRR restricts range on true GMA. They provided a new formula for estimating IRR from DRR and the reliability of the test in which IRR will always be greater than DRR (unless the test is perfectly reliable, which never happens). Because the test being researched on (but not used to select) is not perfectly correlated with true ability, it will always underestimate RR in true ability. Schmidt *et al.* provided an example of the two values for RR for the GATB database. Observed RR for GATB scores is 0.67 and retest reliability of GATB is 0.81, so their equation estimates RR of true GMA at 0.56, indicating considerably greater RR. Table 2.7 shows how the revised procedure compares with conventional VGA for Ghiselli's (1966b) data. True validities are 20–30% higher, reaching 0.73 for work of high complexity and breaking a new barrier – accounting for half the variance in work performance. The next few years may see a second wave of re-analyses of past data, applying corrections for IRR. (The first wave will be following McDaniel's advice and checking for reporting bias.)

What does this new correction mean? It seems to indicate how well GMA would correlate with performance as, for example, a doctor in a truly unselected sample. Not merely unselected for GMA score, but unselected for

Table 2.7 VGA of Ghiselli's (1973) data on correlation between GMA and work performance, for five levels of job complexity, using 'conventional'VGA, and VGA correcting for indirect restriction of range.

Job complexity	Conventional VGA	VGA correcting for indirect range restriction
1 (High)	0.58	0.73
2	0.58	0.74
3	0.49	0.66
4	0.40	0.56
5 (Low)	0.25	0.39

Data from Schmidt *et al.* (2006).

anything linked to GMA, such as education or social background. The resulting 0.70+ true correlations show how important individual differences in MA really are for success – a challenging conclusion, if not one likely to be warmly welcomed. But from the narrower perspective of the American or European HR manager using GMA tests to select doctors (or any other professional), how relevant is it? Pre-selection by education and social background is a fact of life; knowing how well GMA tests would work if it did not happen may not be very useful.

Key points

In Chapter 2 you have learned the following.

- Selection methods should be reliable and valid.
- Validation is necessary to ensure that the test is selecting good applicants and rejecting poor applicants.
- There are various ways to validate selection methods, some of which are more useful than others.
- Criterion validation correlates test scores with work performance scores. This is the most convincing approach since it relies on empirical evidence, but requires large numbers.
- Predictive validation is preferable to concurrent validation.
- Content validation focuses on what people need to know to do the job and does not require large numbers, but is only suitable for assessing fairly specific skills and knowledge.
- Construct validation relies on attributes people need to do the job, for example, ambition or mechanical comprehension. It is probably more useful to the psychologist trying to develop a theoretical model than to the everyday selector.
- Meta-analysis pools the results of many separate researches to generate a single overall estimate of validity.
- Meta-analysis has proved very useful, but has some problems, and may have led to premature conclusions in some areas.

- Validation research has methodological limits, including small samples, unreliable work performance measures and restricted range that create the impression of low validity; research needs therefore to be analysed carefully.
- Validity generalization analysis (VGA) is intended to generate an accurate estimate of test validity. VGA suggests that validity of MA tests may be fairly constant.
- VGA suggests that some selection tests' true relationship with work performance are higher than they appear.
- VGA makes assumptions about reliability of performance measures and restriction of range in applicants that have been questioned.
- Correcting for indirect restriction of range, using Schmidt and Hunter's new procedure, finds the true correlation of selection test (especially MA) and work performance to be even higher.

Key references

Duval (2005) describes the 'trim-and-fill' method of testing for publication bias in meta analysis.

Hunter and Hunter (1984) describe the first application of VGA to selection data, and present the first 'league table' of selection and promotion methods.

Hunter and Schmidt (2004) describe in detail methods of meta-analysis and VGA.

Landy (2003) describes the development of meta-analysis and validity generalization.

Schmidt *et al.* (1985) answer 40 questions about validity generalization analysis.

Schmidt and Hunter (1998) present an analysis of incremental validity in selection.

Schmidt, Shaffer and Oh (in press) describe the latest development in meta-analysis, correcting for indirect range restriction.

Super and Crites (1962) review early research on selection testing.

CHAPTER 3

Job description and job analysis

If you don't know where you're going, you'll end up somewhere else.

Introduction

Selectors should always start by deciding what they are looking for. In Britain, this is often done very inefficiently (but not necessarily very quickly; I once sat through a three-hour discussion of what or who we wanted in a new head of department, which succeeded only in concluding that we did not really want a psychoanalyst, but would otherwise like the 'best' candidate. I did not feel my time had been usefully spent).

Job description and person specification

Traditional British practice recommends selectors to write a job description and a person specification. Job descriptions start with the job's official title – 'Head of Contracts Compliance Unit' – then say how the job fits into the organization – 'organising and leading a team of seven implementing [a London borough] Council's contracts compliance policy' – before listing the job's main duties:

1. Devise and implement management control systems and procedures.
2. Introduce new technology to the Unit.
3. Develop strategies for fighting discrimination, poverty, apartheid and privatisation.

Job descriptions commonly fall into one of two traps. First, they list every task – important or unimportant, frequent or infrequent, routinely easy or very difficult – without indicating which is which. Second, they lapse into a vague, sub-literate 'managementspeak' of 'liaising', 'resourcing', 'monitoring', etc., instead of explaining precisely what successful applicants will find themselves doing. Many job descriptions aim to list everything employees might ever be asked to do, so they cannot subsequently say 'that's not part of my job'. Person specifications also suffer from vagueness and 'managementspeak'. Having dealt with specifics – must have HRM qualifications, must speak Mandarin Chinese – many British person specifications waste time saying applicants must be keen, well-motivated and energetic, as if any employer would be likely to want idle, unmotivated employees. American job descriptions usually focus much more sharply on KSAs – knowledge, skills and aptitudes. Ideally, the person specification indicates which selection tests to use.

Competences

Over the last 25 years, the HR world has adopted with great enthusiasm the competence approach. Competence has been defined as 'an observable skill or ability to complete a managerial task successfully'. From the selector's point of view, competences are often a very mixed bag:

- very specific skills or knowledge that workers will acquire as part of their training, but would not possess beforehand, e.g. knowing how to serve meals and drinks on an aircraft.
- more generalized skills or knowledge that organizations might wish to select for, e.g. communicating well in writing.
- aptitudes that would make it easier for a person to acquire more specific competences, e.g. flexibility, or ability to learn quickly.
- personality characteristics, e.g. resilience, tolerance.

Lists of competences are often very long, giving rise to the suspicion that statistical analysis would show that many are highly correlated. Rotundo and Sackett (2004) factor-analysed three large sets of American data; the 'Work Keys' list of seven skills, O*NET's 46 skills and DOT's 11 aptitudes, to find one or two large general factors in every dataset. One factor is general cognitive ability, and the other a motor or technical factor. Note that the data being analysed here are not test scores, but experts' ratings of what they think 400 to 500 different jobs need in way of skills and abilities. Rotundo and Sackett considered the possibility that the high intercorrelations reflect the job analyst's conceptual system, not reality, but dismissed it because the three datasets were collected in different ways. The high intercorrelations are surprising in places, given that some abilities look very specific, for example, glare sensitivity, night vision or arm–hand steadiness. Bartram (2005) described the 'Great Eight' framework of themes running through work, such as leading/ deciding, supporting/co-operating, derived from self and supervisor ratings of various lists of competences. Bartram's analysis revealed that the Great Eight are themselves quite highly correlated (average correlation 0.45), suggesting again that job or competence analysis does not succeed in differentiating work as finely as it seeks to. Lievens and Sanchez (2007) noted that some 'competency modelling' systems achieve very poor levels of inter-rater reliability, unless users are trained properly.

Job analysis methods

Job descriptions and person specifications can be drawn up by a committee in half a day. Job analysis is much more ambitious, much more detailed and has many more uses. Some methods require complex statistical analysis.

Source of information

Information about a job can be obtained from employees doing the job, from supervisors or managers or from expert job analysts. Sanchez (2000) noted employees are a good source because asking them makes the system acceptable and plausible, but less suitable in other ways; they may not understand the paperwork and may not be motivated to give accurate information. Traditional job analysis, with repeated meetings of large panels of employees or supervisors, takes up a lot of staff time, which employers are increasingly reluctant to pay for.

Analysing information

Having collected information about the work being done, the researcher faces the task of making sense of it. This can be done subjectively, by a committee, or by two types of formal statistical analysis.

Subjective

After spending a month, a week or an afternoon watching people doing the job, or talking to them, the analyst writes down his/her impressions. This is often good enough as the basis for writing a job description, but does not really merit the title 'analysis'.

Rational

Jobs are described and grouped by rational methods, that is by committee and consultation. This helps ensure the analysis makes sense to the organization, and will be accepted by them.

Statistical analysis I – factor analysis

Job analysis typically generates very large datasets. For example, Krzystofiak, Newman and Anderson (1979) had a matrix of 1,700 × 750 ratings, far too large to make any sense of 'by eye', so statistical analysis is essential. Factor analysis correlates scores for different jobs, to find factors of job performance (Box 2.7, page 34).

Statistical analysis II – cluster analysis

Cluster analysis groups jobs according to similarity of ratings (Box 3.1). Cluster analysis groups people, whereas factor analysis groups tasks. Each is useful to the selector in different ways.

Box 3.1   Cluster analysis

A typical job analysis has data from 1,700 workers and 60 scores for each, generating a $1,700 \times 60$ (= 102,000) matrix. One could try to search through this by hand to pick out people with similar profiles, but this would be very tedious and very inaccurate. Cluster analysis calculates the similarity of every possible pair of profiles, to identify groups.

An example

Some time ago, Krzystofiak, Newman and Anderson (1979) wrote a 754-item Job Analysis Questionnaire for use in a power utility (power plant) employing nearly 1,900 individuals in 814 different jobs. Employees rated how often they performed nearly 600 tasks. Krzystofiak *et al.* first factor-analysed their data and extracted 60 factors representing 60 themes in the work of the 1,900 employees. The profile for the company's Administrator of Equal Employment Opportunity showed his/her work had six themes (in order of importance): 1) personnel administration; 2) legal / commissions / agencies and hearings; 3) staff management; 4) training; 5) managerial supervision and decision making; and 6) non-line management. Knowing that a particular job has six main themes gives HR a much clearer idea how to recruit and select for it. If HR could find a test of each of the 60 factors, they would have an all-purpose test battery for every one of the 800+ jobs in the plant.

Krzystofiak *et al.* also cluster-analysed their data (Box 3.1) to sort employees into groups whose jobs were similar. One cluster comprised: Rate Analyst III, Statistical Assistant, Affirmative Action Staff Assistant and Power Production Statistician. This set of eight jobs had quite a lot in common but all came from different departments, so their similarity might easily have been overlooked. Knowing which posts have a lot in common helps plan training, staff succession, cover for illness, and so on.

Selected job analysis techniques – an overview

Over the last 30 years, job analysis techniques have multiplied almost as prolifically as personality questionnaires. New technology is beginning to allow information to be collected and pooled over the Net, without needing so many expensive face-to-face meetings. This chapter has space to describe only seven of the most widely used. In general terms, job analysis systems can be divided into *job-oriented*, *worker-oriented* and *attribute-oriented* techniques.

- *Job-oriented* techniques concentrate on the work being done: 'install cable pressurization systems' and 'locate the source of an automobile engine knock'. These tend to be job specific and are sometimes very lengthy. They are useful for planning training and staff development.

- *Content-oriented* techniques are more concerned with what the worker does to accomplish the job: 'attention to detail' and 'use of written materials'. Position Analysis Questionnaire (PAQ) and the Generalised Work Activities part of the O*NET exemplify this approach. These usually try to provide more general accounts, which apply to all jobs.
- *Attribute-oriented* techniques describe jobs in terms of traits or aptitudes needed to perform them: good eyesight, verbal fluency and manual dexterity. PAQ lists attributes as well as job content. These approaches are obviously very useful in selection.

O*NET / Dictionary of Occupational Titles (DOT)

O*NET is an electronic replacement for the former (US) DOT. O*NET (Converse *et al.*, 2004) includes for each job details of:

- Experience requirements
- Worker requirements
- Worker characteristics
- Occupational requirements, including 42 generalized work activities (GWAs), e.g. *inspecting equipment, structures or materials* and *electronic and electrical repair*
- Occupation-specific requirements
- Occupation characteristics
- DOT also included ratings of the complexity of each job, which have been widely used in research on mental ability.

O*NET's list of 46 skills are necessarily fairly general, for example, item 15 – instructing: teaching others how to do something; item 28 – installation: installing equipment, machines, wiring or programmes to meet specifications. The layperson tends to think of a skill as something more specific, for example, bricklaying or pipefitting. O*NET's list also includes six social skills, such as persuasion – persuading others to change their minds or behaviour and management skills – motivating, developing and directing people as they work, identifying the best people for the job, which seems to cover most of HR and quite a bit of general management. It would be difficult to devise a single test of such broad skills, which may limit O*NET's usefulness in selection.

Critical incident technique (CIT)

CIT is the oldest job analysis technique, devised by Flanagan (1954) to analyse failure in military pilot training during World War Two. He found the reasons that were given for failure too vague to be helpful – 'poor judgement' – or completely circular – 'lack of inherent flying ability'. Flanagan identified flying's critical requirements by collecting accounts of critical incidents, which caused recruits to be rejected. Typical incidents included trying to land on the wrong runway or coming in to land too high. CIT is open-ended and flexible, but can be time consuming. In modern CIT, hundreds or even thousands of accounts are collected and then sorted by similarity to identify the main themes in effective and ineffective performance. CIT is the basis of behaviourally anchored rating scales (BARS) (Chapter 5), and of some structured interviewing systems (Chapter 4).

Repertory grid technique (RGT)

The informant is asked to think of a good, an average and a poor worker, then to say which two differ from the third, then asked to say how. In the grid in Figure 3.1, the informant says in the first row that a good ambulance worker can be distinguished from average and poor by 'commitment', and in the second row that a good ambulance supervisor can be distinguished from average and poor by 'fairness'. Next, the analyst probes by asking the informant for specific behavioural examples of commitment, for example willingness to stay on after end of shift if there is an emergency call.

Personality-related position requirement form (PPRF)

Traditional job analysis systems tended to emphasize those abilities needed for the job. However, with the growing popularity of personality testing in selection, new systems are emerging that focus more on personality requirements. Raymark, Schmit and Guion's (1997) PPRF contained items in the format:

Elements > Sorts	Good ambulance person	Average ambulance person	Poor ambulance person	Good ambulance service supervisor	Average ambulance service supervisor	Poor ambulance service supervisor	Good ambulance service manager	••• Constructs
1	[X]	[ ]	[ ]	X			X	••• Commitment
2				[X]	[ ]	[ ]	X	••• Fairness
3	[X]			[X]	X		[X]	••• Calmness
4			[ ]			[ ]		•••
etc.								

Figure 3.1 Repertory grid technique (RGT) used in job analysis. The elements are various *role figures* (e.g. good ambulance supervisor). [ ] indicates which three elements are used to start each set.

Effective performance in this position requires the person to take control in group situation   not required / helpful / essential

Preliminary results indicate that leadership is needed in management, but not in cashiers, while a friendly disposition is needed in sales assistants, but not in caretakers. Conscientiousness, by contrast, seems needed in every job. PPRF enables selectors to use personality measures in more focused way, and to be able to justify assessing aspects of personality if challenged. Hogan, Davies and Hogan (2007) described a similar system, which also included a section on 'Derailment Characteristics':

Would job performance decline if (a person doing this job)
  becomes irritable when frustrated
  resents criticism and takes it personally

Cognitive task analysis (CTA)

Conventional JA systems might list as part of a pilot's job *to determine current location*, or for a security person *to check X-ray of baggage for suspicious items*. These are both quite complex tasks; CTA seeks to describe in greater detail the cognitive processes involved (Seamster *et al.*, 1997).

Future-oriented job analysis (FOJA)

Ford *et al.* (1999) described a project to decide what will be needed in the US soldier over the next 10 to 25 years, based on information from senior NCOs and psychologists. It listed four main attributes: cognitive aptitude (highest priority), conscientiousness / dependability, selfless service orientation, and good working memory capacity.

Position analysis questionnaire

PAQ is probably the most widely used job analysis technique. Despite its title, it is not a questionnaire, but a structured interview schedule (McCormick, Jeanneret & Mecham, 1972). PAQ is completed by a trained job analyst who collects information from workers and supervisors; however, analysts do not simply record what informants say, but form their own judgements about the job. The information PAQ collects covers nearly 200 elements, divided into six main areas (Table 3.1). Elements are rated for importance to the job, time spent doing each, amount of training required, and so on. The completed PAQ is analysed by comparing it with a very large American database. The analysis proceeds by a series of linked stages:

1. *Profile of 32 job elements.* The original factor analysis of PAQ items identified 32 dimensions which underlie all forms of work (e.g. watching things from a distance, being aware of bodily movement and balance, making decisions, dealing with the public).

Table 3.1 Position Analysis Questionnaire's six main divisions, and illustrative job elements.

PAQ division	Illustrative job elements
1. Information input	Use of written materials Near visual differentiation (i.e. good visual acuity, at short range)
2. Mental processes	Level of reasoning in problem solving Coding/decoding
3. Work output	Use of keyboard devices Assembling/disassembling
4. Relationships with other people	Instructing Contacts with public or customers
5. Job context	High temperature Interpersonal conflict
6. Other	Specified work space Amount of job structure

2. *Profile of 76 attributes.* These are the aptitudes, interests or temperament that the person needs to perform the job elements. Aptitudes include movement detection – being able to detect the physical movement of objects and to judge their direction – and selective attention – being able to perform a task in the presence of distracting stimuli. Temperament includes empathy and influencing people. The attribute profile provides a detailed person specification.

3. *Recommended tests.* The attribute profile leads naturally on to suggestions for tests to assess the attributes. If the job needs manual dexterity, the PAQ output suggests using General Aptitude Test Battery's (GATB's) pegboard test of gross dexterity. Recommendations for tests of temperament are also made, mostly for the Myers Briggs Type Indicator (MBTI; a curious choice given that the MBTI is not considered suitable for selection testing).

4. *Job component validity (JCV) data.* Based on the job's component elements, estimates are generated of the likely validity of the nine abilities assessed by GATB (Table 6.4, page 115), as well as estimates of likely average scores (Jeanneret, 1992).

5. *Comparable jobs and remuneration.* The job element profile is compared with PAQ's extensive database, to identify other jobs with similar requirements, and to estimate the appropriate salary in US$. A classic early study by Arvey and Begalla (1975) obtained PAQ ratings for 48 homemakers (housewives) and found that the most similar other job in PAQ's database was that of a police officer, followed by home economist, airport maintenance chief, kitchen helper and firefighter – all troubleshooting, emergency-handling jobs. Arvey and Begalla also calculated the average salary paid for the 10 jobs most similar to that of housewife – $740 a month, at 1968 prices.

Reliability and validity of job analysis

Reliability

Two meta-analyses of job analysis reliability have been published recently. Dierdorff and Wilson (2003) restrict their analysis to information about the job, excluding research that analyses what attributes, skills and abilities, workers need. They find inter-rater reliability higher for rating specific tasks (0.77) than for rating more generalized work activities (0.61). Voskuijl and van Sliedregt (2002) reported a meta-analysis of 91 job analysis reliabilities, over nearly 3,000 jobs. Overall reliability was on the low side, at $r = 0.59$. However, reliability was much better (ca. 0.70) for experienced professionals who got their information by observing or interviewing workers. Rating of worker attributes was less reliable (0.49) than rating of worker behaviour (0.62) or the job's worth (0.60). Dierdorff and Morgeson (2007), analysing O*NET data for 98 occupations, confirmed that agreement on the traits needed for a job is far lower (0.46) than agreement about the job's tasks (0.81) and responsibilities (0.66).

Validity

Research on validity of job analysis faces a dilemma familiar to psychologists. If results agree with 'common sense', they are dismissed as redundant – 'telling us what we already know'. If results do not agree with common sense, they are simply dismissed as wrong. Evidence for the validity of job analysis derives from showing that its results make sense, and from showing that job analysis leads to more accurate selection (page 65).

A classic analysis of the work of senior (UK) civil servants found nine factors and 13 clusters of jobs. Dulewicz and Keenay (1979) showed the results to their civil service informants, and asked if they agreed with the classification and whether they had been correctly classified. Only 7% thought the classification unsatisfactory, and only 11% disagreed with their personal classification. Banks et al. (1983) found Job Component Inventory (JCI) ratings distinguished four clerical jobs from four engineering jobs, proving JCI can find a difference where a difference ought to be. Banks et al. also showed that JCI ratings were the same for mailroom clerks in different companies, proving that JCI does not find a difference where there should not be one.

Bias in job analysis

Morgeson and Campion (1997) pointed out that job analysis relies heavily on subjective judgement, so is open to the many – they listed 16 – types of bias documented for such judgements. For example, judgements may be subject to conformity pressures, if management has definite views about the nature of the job. This could create ratings that are very reliable because everyone agrees with everyone else, but which may not be valid. Recent research has identified several biasing factors.

Gender

Dick and Nadin (2006) argued that gender discrimination in employment often starts with job analyses or descriptions, which incorporate gender-biased assumptions. They gave a 'blue collar' example of apparently objective analysis for lathe operator being written around lathes, which were designed for use by men, who tend to have bigger hands and longer arms. They gave a 'white collar' example for managers, where analysis identifies *commitment*, meaning being available at all times (because someone else looks after their children).

Personality

Cucina, Vasilopoulos and Sehgal (2005) found that job analysis can be biased by personality: conscientious people think the job needs *thoroughness and attention to detail*, while extravert people think the same job needs *general leadership*. People tend to think the job needs the traits they happen to possess.

Ability

Sanchez *et al.* (1998) cluster-analysed job analysis ratings by sales employees, and found groups who differed not only in their ratings of the importance of sales tasks, but also differed substantially in how good their own sales figures were. Sanchez *et al.* suggested that this could introduce a serious bias into job analysis. When asked to nominate sales staff to help do the job analysis, sales managers might select the less proficient, so as not to reduce the whole team's sales too much, with the potentially disastrous consequence of constructing the job analysis using the behaviour of the less successful.

Work attitudes

Conte *et al.* (2005) examined the role of job involvement in job analysis ratings in a sample of travel agents: the more involved people are with their job, the more often they see themselves meeting its more difficult tasks and the more important they see everything to be. The differences were quite large, up to $d = 0.49$.

Wording

Morgeson *et al.* (2004) found that choice of wording in job analysis makes a big difference. Describing the job in terms of abilities, as opposed to tasks, creates considerable inflation in frequency and importance ratings, even though the two sets of wording were nearly identical: *record phone messages / ability to record phone messages*. When ability wording was used, people were much more likely to claim non-existent activities, such as *checking against MLA standards.* Grouping a set of tasks into a competency inflated ratings even further.

Uses of job analysis

Job analysis has a variety of uses in selection in particular and HR work in general – so many uses in fact that one wonders how HR ever managed without it. Some uses are directly connected with selection:

1. *Write accurate, comprehensive job descriptions* which help recruit the right applicants.
2. *Select for, or train for?* Some competences can be acquired by most people by training so do not need to be selected for, whereas others may be difficult or near impossible to train so must be selected for. Jones *et al.* (2001) show that experts achieve a high degree of consensus on the trainability of the competences needed for school teaching.
3. *Choose selection tests.* A good job analysis identifies the knowledge, skills and abilities needed, allowing HR to choose the right tests.
4. *Classification.* Assigning new employees to the tasks they are best suited for, assuming they have not been appointed to a specific job.
5. *Defend selection tests.* Job analysis is legally required by the Equal Employment Opportunities Commission in the USA if the employer wants to use selection methods that create adverse impact.

Job analysis also allows more elaborate selection methods to be devised.

6. *Devise structured interview systems.* Structured interviews (Chapter 4) may be more accurate than conventional interviews, but most systems require a detailed job analysis.
7. *Write selection tests by content validation.* Job analysis allows selectors to write a selection test whose content so closely matches the content of the job that it is content valid (Chapter 2), which means it can be used legally in the USA without further demonstration of its validity.

Job analysis may be useful in other areas of HR, including providing vocational guidance, rationalizing training by identifying jobs with a lot in common, succession planning, identifying dimensions to be rated in performance appraisal and developing better measures of work performance. Additionally, job analysis may force the organization to think hard about what they are doing and why, which is often useful.

Using job analysis to select workers

Analysis by PAQ of the job of plastics injection-moulding setter in a British plant identified seven attributes needed in workers (Table 3.2), then recommended a suitable test for each attribute: for example, Raven Progressive

Table 3.2 Job analysis by Position Analysis Questionnaire, showing choice of tests for plastic injection moulding setters (Sparrow *et al.*, 1982).

Attribute	Test
Long-term memory	Wechsler Memory Scale
Intelligence	Standard Progressive Matrices
Short-term memory	Wechsler Memory Scale
Near visual acuity	Eye chart at 30 cm
Perceptual speed	Thurstone Perceptual Speed Test
Convergent thinking	Raven Progressive Matrices
Mechanical ability	Birkbeck Mechanical Comprehension Test

Matrices (RPM) for intelligence and an optician's eye chart for visual acuity (Sparrow *et al.*, 1982). Sparrow's work illustrated the use of job analysis, that is first to generate a person specification, then to choose appropriate selection tests. This may seem obvious but it is surprising how many employers even now do not do this, which places them in a very dangerous position if someone complains about their selection methods. If the employer cannot say why they are using RPM, they will find it extremely difficult to justify themselves if RPM creates adverse impact on, for example, minorities.

More ambitiously, job analysis systems can be linked to aptitude batteries. Jeanneret (1992) analysed 460 jobs for which both GATB (*see* Table 6.3, page 115) and PAQ data were available, and then asked two questions:

1. Does the PAQ profile for a job correlate with the GATB profile for the same job? If PAQ says the job needs spatial ability, do people doing the job tend to have high spatial ability scores on GATB?
2. Does the PAQ profile for a job correlate with GATB profile validity for the same job? If PAQ says the job needs spatial ability, do people with high spatial ability scores on GATB perform the job better?

The answer to both questions was 'yes'. The correlation between PAQ profile and GATB profile across jobs was 0.69. The correlation between PAQ profile and GATB validity across jobs was lower, but still positive, at 0.26. This research implies that each job needs a particular set of attributes that can be identified by PAQ and then assessed by GATB. Jeanneret and Strong (2003) reported a similar analysis for the GWA ratings of O*NET and GATB scores. For example, people doing jobs that included GWAs of operating vehicles, repairing electronic equipment or using computers tended to have higher scores on GATB Finger Dexterity.

Improving selection validity

From the selector's viewpoint, job analysis has validity if it results in more accurate selection decisions. Three meta-analyses have shown that personality testing (Tett, Jackson & Rothstein, 1991), structured interviewing (Wiesner & Cronshaw, 1988) and situational judgement tests (McDaniel *et al.*, 2007) achieve higher validity when based on job analysis.

Synthetic validation

Synthetic validation uses job analysis to identify underlying themes in diverse jobs and select appropriate tests. Synthetic validation works on the principle that validity, once demonstrated for a combination of theme X test across the workforce as a whole, can be inferred for subsets of the workers, *including sets too small for a conventional validation exercise*. Table 3.3 illustrates the principle with fictional data. A city employs 1,500 persons in 300 different jobs. Some jobs, for example, local tax clerk, employ enough people to calculate a conventional validity. Other jobs, for example, refuse collection supervisor, employ too few to make a conventional local validity study worth undertaking. Some jobs employ only one person, rendering any statistical analysis impossible. Job analysis identifies a number of themes underlying all 300 jobs; suitable tests for each theme are selected. Validity of PQ dominance score for the 25 refuse collection supervisors is inferred from its validity for all 430 persons throughout the workforce whose work requires *ability to influence others*. It is even possible to prove the validity of PQ *detail-consciousness* scale for the one and only crematorium supervisor, by pooling that individual's predictor and criterion data with the 520 others for whom detail is important. Synthetic validity also makes it possible to plan selection for new jobs: when the city takes on 10 diversity facilitators, job analysis identifies the themes in their work and the tests to use.

The combination of the PAQ and the GATB is well suited to synthetic validation because Jeanneret (1992) has shown that PAQ scores correlate with GATB scores very well and with GATB validity fairly well. This implies that

Table 3.3 Illustration of synthetic validation in a local authority (city) workforce of 1,500.

Attribute ⇒		Ability to influence	Attention to detail	Numeracy
TEST ⇒		PQ dominance	PQ detail	Numeracy test
JOB ⇓	*N*			
1 – Local clerk	200	–	XX	XX
2 – Refuse collection supervisor	25	XX	XX	XX
3 – Crematorium attendant	1	XX	XX	–
Etc.				
Total *N* involved		430	520	350
Validity		0.30	0.25	0.27
Diversity facilitator	10	XX	–	–

PAQ job analysis can predict what profile of GATB scores will be found in people doing a job successfully. PAQ can generate JCV coefficients which represent a different approach to synthetic validity. Rather than identify a single test for each competency, as in Table 3.3, JCV uses the PAQ database to generate a regression equation (Box 3.2) that indicates which tests to use for a job and what weight to give each, based on the competencies PAQ lists for that job. Hoffman, Holden and Gale (2000) used JCV estimates to create test batteries for the many jobs in the gas industry that have too few incumbents to allow conventional validation. Some job analysis systems use expert panels to match test to job theme. Scherbaum (2005) noted that synthetic validity using GATB has two drawbacks. The first is purely practical: GATB belongs to the US Employment Service and is not available to most employers. The second is more serious. All mental abilities tend to be highly intercorrelated, so selection systems based on combinations of mental abilities tend to lack differential validity: using the tests for job A to select for job B might prove to work almost as well. Synthetic validity may work better if it includes a wider range of predictors.

Box 3.2   Regression equation

GATB generates 10 separate scores. Research could correlate all 10 in turn with, for example, work performance. However, this would be misleading in the sense that GATB's 10 scores are all quite highly intercorrelated. Instead, researchers correlate a regression, which calculates the multiple correlation between all 10 GATB scores and work performance. Regression also reveals which GATB scales are most closely related to the outcome and which are redundant because they do not improve the multiple correlation.

The future of job analysis

Is job analysis always essential?

Pearlman, Schmidt and Hunter (1980) used validity generalization analysis to show that tests of mental ability predict performance equally well throughout a large and varied set of clerical jobs. They argue that there is therefore no need for detailed job analysis of clerical work. However, it would be difficult to act on Pearlman et al.'s conclusions at present. Deciding a job is clerical, and using a clerical test for selection may satisfy common sense and may be good enough for Pearlman et al., but it probably would not satisfy the Equal Employment Opportunities Commission if there are complaints about the composition of the workforce. The full detail and complexity of PAQ may be needed to prove that a clerical job really is clerical. Gibson and Caplinger (2007) described the considerable complexities of proving 'transportability' to the satisfaction of US courts and fair employment agencies.

Is job analysis becoming obsolete?

Latham and Wexley (1981) described a very long rating schedule for janitors, in which item 132 read

> *Places a deodorant block in urinal*
> *almost never – almost always*

The rest of the janitor's day was documented in similarly exhaustive detail. Management and HR professionals have begun to question this type of approach. Rapid change implies less need for task-specific skills and more need for general abilities, to adapt, to solve problems, to define one's own direction and to work in teams. Job analysis is backward looking and encourages cloning, whereas organizations need to be forward looking. Job analysis assumes that the job exists apart from the employee who holds it, whereas organizations are being 'de-jobbed', meaning employees work on a fluid set of activities that change rapidly so no job descriptions exist. Current management trends also suggest a shift to broad personal characteristics, rather than long lists of very specific skills or competences. *Total quality management* emphasizes customer service skills, self-direction, self-development and team development skills. The quest for *high-performance organizations* – a buzz word in the USA in the 1990s – lists the qualities that employees need: teamwork, customer service and leadership. This represents a shift of emphasis from very specific, and hence very numerous, skills or competences, to a few very broad abilities or traits, a shift of emphasis from the job to the person. In the USA, this may create problems since fair employment agencies insist selection must be job-related.

Key points

In Chapter 3 you have learned the following.

- It is absolutely vital to decide what you are looking for before starting any selection program. If you fail to do this, you will be unlikely to make good selection decisions and you will be unable to justify your selection methods if they are questioned or become the subject of legal dispute.
- Conventional job descriptions and person specifications are better than nothing.
- Competence frameworks are also useful, although often conceptually rather confused.
- Quantitative or statistical analysis is usually essential to make sense of large sets of job descriptive data.
- Job analysis can identify the main themes in a specific job, or whole sets of jobs, or in work in general.
- Job analysis methods include some that are fairly open-ended such as critical incident technique, and some that are more structured such as the PAQ.

- Job analysis uses subjective judgements which opens the way to some biases.
- Job analysis can improve selection systems.
- Job analysis has many other uses besides guiding selection.
- Job analysis can be used to validate tests for small samples within a larger workforce.
- Job analysis needs to look forwards as well as backwards.

Key references

Converse *et al.* (2004) describe some applications of the O*NET system.

Dick and Nadin (2006) argue that job analysis may be affected by implicit gender bias.

Dierdorff and Wilson (2003) describe a meta-analysis of job analysis reliability.

Jeanneret and Strong (2003) describe how GATB scales can be linked to O*NET's GWAs.

McCormick *et al.* (1972) describe the original research on the PAQ.

Morgeson *et al.* (2004) describe how the wording of job analysis systems affects ratings.

Raymark *et al.* (1997) describe a job analysis system specifically geared to personality requirements and assessment.

Rotundo and Sackett (2004) show how skills and competencies in job analysis systems are highly intercorrelated.

Scherbaum (2005) reviews current thinking on synthetic validity.

Useful websites

www.onetcenter.org. O*NET site.
www.occupationalinfo.org. *Dictionary of Occupational Titles*.
www.paq.com. PAQ Services Inc.
www.job-analysis.net. US job analysis site.

CHAPTER 4

The interview

'I know one when I see one'

Introduction

Interviews have been used for a long time. The Examination for promotion to Lieutenant in the Royal Navy at the beginning of the nineteenth century was an interview with three captains (Rodger, 2001). Interviews are used very widely today; the Cranfield Price Waterhouse survey (Dany & Torchy, 1994) confirmed that 80 to 100% of European employers interview prospective staff, the exception being Turkey where only 64% of employers use interview. Interviews are similarly popular in North America. Lievens, Highhouse and DeCorte (2005) found that managers place more weight on interview information than on psychological test results.

Interviews vary widely. They can be as short as three minutes or as long as two hours. There may be one interviewer, or several, in a panel or board. In campus recruitment, As often go through a series of interviews. Dose (2003) suggested that serial interviews may not work that well because interviewers fail to exchange information. In France, it is apparently quite common for As to be interviewed by everyone who will work with them. Phone interviews are increasingly widely used as a preliminary screen, or for call-centre work or when a face-to-face interview is difficult (e.g. overseas As). Videoconference interviews have the same advantages as phone interviews and provide some visual information, but are not liked by As (Chapman, Uggerslev & Webster, 2003).

In the past, interviews were often rather casual affairs. The interviewer had no job description or person specification. If asked what he/she was looking for, the interviewer might say 'someone who will fit in here' or 'the right sort of person'. The interviewer had no prepared questions, took no notes and made no ratings or quantitative assessment of candidates. This sort of interview probably still happens quite often, but most large employers have been forced to ask themselves if their selection methods are reliable, valid and fair. The traditional casual unstructured interview was very often none of these, so the need to select efficient staff and avoid unfair employment claims has caused many employers to do their interviewing more systematically. In particular, *structured interviewing* has become very popular.

Different interviews seek to assess different attributes of candidates. Reviewing 47 studies, mostly in the USA, Huffcutt *et al.* (2001) found personality dimensions, especially conscientiousness, most frequently assessed (35%), followed by applied social skills (28%) and mental ability (16%); interviews are less often used to assess knowledge and skills (10%), interests and preferences (4%), organizational fit (3%) or physical attributes (4%). Interviewers are given between three and 18 dimensions to assess, with an average of seven. As Huffcutt *et al.* noted, it is slightly odd that interviews are so widely used to assess personality and mental ability, given that tests of both are widely available, possibly more accurate, and certainly more economical to use. On the other hand, the interview may be particularly well suited to assess social skills since it is itself a social encounter.

The interview is primarily a *self-report*, in which As tell interviewers about their abilities, achievements, potential, and so on. The interview also gives As the opportunity to *demonstrate* specialized knowledge, or ability to be fluent, friendly, persuasive, and so on. It is much easier to circle *true* against *I am forceful with others* on a personality questionnaire than to create an effective impression of forcefulness on the interviewer or to provide convincing examples of past forcefulness.

Reliability and validity

Reliability

Conway, Jako and Goodman (1995) analysed 160 researches and concluded that interviewers agree well ($r = 0.77$) if they see the same interview, but less well ($r = 0.53$) if they see different interviews with the same A. The difference arises because As do not perform consistently at different interviews. Conway *et al.* argued that 0.53 is the better estimate of interview reliability in practice because inconsistency of applicant behaviour is an inherent limitation of the interview. Conway *et al.* also found that interviews are more reliable if based on a job analysis and if the interviewers are trained.

Validity

People talk about 'the validity of the interview' when perhaps they should really talk about validity of interviews for *assessing sales potential* or for *assessing intellectual ability*. Huffcutt *et al.*'s survey has shown that the interview is used to assess a wide variety of skills, abilities and traits; the very popularity of the interview may derive from its versatility. In practice, selection interviews are usually used to make a simple decision – to hire or not – and are often validated against a global assessment of how well the person does the job. In this context, perhaps it is possible to talk about 'the validity of the interview'.

Research on interview validity has been reviewed frequently from Wagner (1949) to Posthuma, Morgeson and Campion (2002). Most earlier reviews concluded that interviews were not a very good way of choosing productive workers and rejecting unproductive ones, a fact which took a long time to begin to penetrate the consciousness of line managers or HR departments.

Dunnette (1972) reported the first meta-analysis of interview validity; 30 validity coefficients in the American petroleum industry had a very low average (0.13). Hunter and Hunter (1984) obtained a similarly low average validity (0.11), rising to 0.14 when corrected for unreliability of the work per-formance measure and to 0.22 when also corrected for restricted range (see Chapter 2 for more detail of these corrections).

Three subsequent much larger meta-analyses present a more complex, and in places, more favourable picture. Wiesner and Cronshaw (1988) analysed 160 validities from research in Germany, France and Israel as well as the USA. Huffcutt and Arthur (1994) set out to replicate Hunter and Hunter's earlier analysis of the interview as a selection test for entry-level jobs based on 114 samples. McDaniel et al.'s (1994) review covers 245 correlations from a total of 86,000 persons. Table 4.1 gives average raw validities between 0.20 and 0.26, for all interviews, rising to 0.37 to 0.47 for operational validity. As Wiesner and Cronshaw remarked, the interview may not be quite such a poor predictor as many work psychologists had assumed. However, the first row of Table 4.1 is probably an overestimate of the validity of the typical interview because it includes research using structured interview systems, which differ radically from the traditional or unstructured interview. The second row shows that the interview as generally practised in Britain, the unstructured interview, achieves lower overall validity of only 0.11 to 0.18, rising to 0.20 to 0.33 when corrected to operational validity.

Validity for different characteristics

Attempts to identify which characteristics interviews can assess accurately are limited by the point already noted that the outcome measure is usually a global rating of work performance. Huffcutt et al.'s (2001) meta-analysis showed that interview ratings of some attributes (e.g. creativity) correlate better with supervisor ratings of overall job performance. However, this is not the same as showing that interviews are better at assessing creativity than persuasiveness because creativity and persuasiveness in the workplace are

Table 4.1 Summary of three meta-analyses of interview validity, by Wiesner and Cronshaw (1988), Huffcutt and Arthur (1994) and McDaniel et al. (1994).

	Wiesner & Cronshaw		Huffcutt & Arthur		McDaniel et al.	
	k	r / ρ	k	r / ρ	k	r / ρ
All interviews	150	0.26 / 0.47	114	0.22 / 0.37	160	0.20 / 0.37
All unstructured	39	0.17 / 0.31	15	0.11 / 0.20	39	0.18 / 0.33
one to one	19	0.11 / 0.20			19	0.18 / 0.34
board	19	0.21 / 0.37			15	0.18 / 0.33

r = uncorrected correlation; ρ = operational validity.

not being assessed, only overall performance. McDaniel *et al.*'s meta-analysis reported that *psychological interviews* that try to assess personality were less successful than *situational interviews* that ask hypothetical questions about 'what would you do if ...' or *job-related interviews* that assess training, experience and interests.

Interviews are sometimes used to assess what is variously referred to as 'organizational fit', 'chemistry' or 'the right type'. Sometimes this may be just a code word for interviewers' prejudices or reluctance to explain themselves, but it could refer to legitimate organization-specific requirements which interviews could be used to assess. Rynes and Gerhart (1990) reported that interviewers from the same organization agree about A's fit, showing that the concept is not idiosyncratic. However, fit could not be related to objective data such as grade-point average, but was related to appearance, which suggests an irrational element.

DeGroot and Kluemper (2007) analysed vocal attractiveness in the interview, measured objectively by spectral analysis, using a fairly complex formula: (speech rate + pitch variability) − (pitch + pause). Vocal attractiveness secures a better interview rating in people applying for retail sales jobs; they also find vocal attractiveness linked to performance rating in successful As. This suggests 'a nice voice' may be a real asset in some types of work (and something the interview is well suited to assess).

Reasons for poor validity

Why is the conventional unstructured interview apparently such a poor predictor of work performance?

Interviewer motivation

Anyone who has spent a day interviewing knows how one's attention can start to wander by the late afternoon. Brtek and Motowidlo (2002) showed that college students watching videotaped interviews can be more accurate if they try. Being told they would have to explain their ratings to the researchers makes them pay more attention to the interview.

Applicant anxiety

McCarthy and Goffin (2004) found a correlation of −0.34 between applicant anxiety and interview rating, implying that interviews may 'miss' some good As because anxiety prevents them from performing well.

Office politics

Bozionelos (2005) described how a UK business school used an interview to appoint four favoured As, even though they lacked published work or PhDs (usually essential qualifications for an academic). Bozionelos suggested that the interview is particularly easy to 'fix'. During the interview, the interviewers can encourage favoured As by smiling and eye contact, while provoking unfavoured As by aggressive or offensive comments. In the post interview discussion, interviewers can get away with vague assertions that favoured As 'performed well at interview' and accept their promises to start work on a PhD. Above all, the process leaves no record, neither of the interview, nor of the post interview discussion, so no one can find out what happened or challenge it. Other methods, such as psychological tests, by contrast, leave a paper record. Woodzicka and LaFrance (2005) confirmed that it is easy to put off interviewees; asking female As mildly sexually harassing questions resulted in reduced fluency and poorer quality answers.

Transparency

Traditionally interviewers did not tell As what dimensions the interview was intended to assess, possibly on the assumption that this would help As say the 'right things' and get a falsely high rating. Klehe *et al.* (in press) argued that 'transparency' – telling As what is being assessed – may improve interview validity, especially its ability to distinguish different dimensions. They compared structured interviews where As are told the dimensions with ones where they are not. As performed better in the transparent condition and the interview achieved slightly better discriminant validity, distinguishing better between the three dimensions being assessed.

Improving the interview

Assuming the interview is here to stay, what can be done to improve it?

Select interviewers

It seems intuitively plausible that some people will be better interviewers than others; research appears to confirm this. Some time ago, Ghiselli (1966a) found one interviewer – himself – whose accuracy in selecting stockbrokers over 17 years yielded a personal validity coefficient of 0.51. More recently, van Iddekinge *et al.* (2006) confirmed that different interviewers' decisions differ widely in accuracy. Pulakos *et al.* (1996) however questioned whether interviewers really vary. They analysed data from 62 interviewers and found a range of individual validities from –0.10 to 0.65, apparently confirming very strongly that interviewers differ. They noted however that each interviewer had done, on average, only 25 interviews and suggested that apparent variation in interviewer validity might arise from sampling error. If the 62 interviewers did another 25 interviews, the 'good' interviewers might do very much less well, while the 'poor' interviewers might, on average, 'improve'. An organization that wants to select good interviewers might need a very large sample of interviews to base its decisions on. O'Brien and Rothstein

(2008) found 16 interviewers who had each done 50 or more interviews and shows that differences between them were real and that poorer interviewers seemed overconfident and seemed to have poorer judgement. O'Brien also finds that five of the 16 had personal validities lower than zero, so weeding them out of the interview system would be definitely worth considering. However, selecting selectors could be difficult: telling senior managers they will not be allowed to do interviews because they are not very good at it might cause considerable friction.

The good judge of others

People often flatter themselves they are good judges of character. If there is such a class of person, they might be also make successful interviewers. If research could find a way to identify 'good judges of others', HR could select the selectors in advance, rather than by track record. O'Brien (2008) reviewed the extensive literature and concluded that the good judge of others cannot be identified, at least not with any certainty.

Use more than interviewer

Two meta-analyses (Wiesner & Cronshaw, 1988; McDaniel et al., 1994) compared one-to-one with panel or board interviews, with conflicting results; Table 4.1 shows Wiesner and Cronshaw found board interviews get better results, but McDaniel et al. found no difference. Conway et al. (1995) found that panel interviews are more reliable than one-to-one interviews. Many employers insist on panel interviews and equal-opportunities agencies also recommend their use.

Use the same interviewers throughout

Sharing out interviewing often means that different As, even for the same job, are interviewed by different interviewers. Huffcutt and Woehr (1999) compared 23 studies where the same interviewers interviewed all As with 100 studies where different interviewers interviewed different As, and found that using the same interviewers throughout significantly improves interview validity.

Train interviewers

Conway et al. (1995) analysed 160 studies and found that training makes interviewing more reliable. Huffcutt and Woehr (1999) compared 52 studies where interviewers were trained with 71 studies where they were not, and found that training significantly improves interview validity. Using untrained interviewers makes it difficult to defend selection decisions if they are challenged.

Take notes

Some interviewers refrain from taking notes on the argument that it distracts the applicant. On the other hand, an increasing number of organizations require interviewers to make notes, which the organization keeps in case of subsequent dispute. Huffcutt and Woehr (1999) compared 55 studies where interviewers did not take notes with 68 studies where they did, and found that taking notes significantly improves interview validity. Van Dam (2003) analysed adjectives written spontaneously by eight interviewers for 720 As, using the five-factor model (*see* Chapter 7). All five personality factors feature, with 'a preference for' agreeableness and extraversion. Employment recommendation was linked to low neuroticism, high openness and high conscientiousness. Middendorf and Macan (2008) reported that As prefer interviewers to take notes, but do not think the interview any fairer or more accurate when they do.

RESEARCH AGENDA

- Continue the search for the 'good judge of others'
- More on what interviewees think about interviewer note taking
- Whether note taking improves interview validity
- Whether note taking interferes with the conduct of the interview.

Structured interviews

The most prominent attempt at improvement is structured interviewing, which has developed rapidly since 1980. Structured interviewing does not mean following the 'seven-point plan', or agreeing who asks what before the interview starts. That is no more than good interviewing practice. Structured interview systems change every part of the interview.

- Interviewers' questions are structured, often to the point of being completely scripted.
- Interviewers' judgements are structured by rating scales, checklists, and so on.
- Some systems – but not all – forbid the interviewer asking any follow-up, probing or clarifying questions.
- The traditional last phase of the interview – asking As if they have any questions – is sometimes dropped, on the grounds that As could bias the interviewers by asking foolish questions.

Most structured interviewing systems start with a detailed job analysis, which ensures that the questions and judgements are job-related. Structured interviews are seen as legally safer, being closely job related, and not allowing the interviewer to wander off into irrelevant and possibly dangerous areas. Some structured interview systems also ensure every interview is the same, which avoids one source of possible complaint. Structured interviews are beginning to be used in Britain, in local government, in the financial sector, for sales, in manufacturing and in the hotel industry. There are several structured interview systems in current use, devised in the USA, Canada and Germany:

- situational interviews (Latham *et al.*, 1980)
- patterned behaviour description interview (Janz, 1982)
- multimodal interview (Schuler & Moser, 1995)
- empirical interview (Schmidt & Rader, 1999).

Situational interviews are developed from critical incidents (Chapter 3) of particularly effective or ineffective behaviour:

> *The employee was devoted to his family. He had only been married for 18 months. He used whatever excuse he could to stay at home. One day the fellow's baby got a cold. His wife had a hangnail or something on her toe. He didn't come to work. He didn't even phone in.*

The incidents are rewritten as questions:

> *Your spouse and two teenage children are sick in bed with a cold. There are no friends or relatives available to look in on them. Your shift starts in three hours. What would you do in this situation?*

The company supervisors who generate the incidents also agree benchmark answers for good, average and poor workers:

- *I'd stay home – my spouse and family come first (poor).*
- *I'd phone my supervisor and explain my situation (average).*
- *Since they only have colds, I'd come to work (good).*

At the interview, the questions are read out, the applicant replies, and is rated against the benchmarks. The questions are said to be phrased to avoid suggesting socially desirable answers. The situational interview looks forward, asking As what they would do on some future occasion.

Patterned behaviour description (PBD) interviews also start by analysing the job with critical incidents, but differ from the Situational interview in two ways. The PBD interviewer plays a more active role than the Situational interviewer, being 'trained to redirect [As] when their responses strayed from or evaded the question'. The PBD interview looks back, focusing on actual behaviour that occurred in the past; a typical question reads as follows:

> *Balancing the cash bag [day's accounts] is always the bottom line for a cashier position, but bags can't always balance. Tell me about the time your experience helped you discover why your bag didn't balance.*

Taylor and Small (2002) reported a meta-analysis comparing forward-oriented or hypothetical questions with past-oriented or experience-based questions, and found that the two do not differ significantly in validity. They suggested that the two types of questions may assess different things. Situational questions – they argued – assess what people know (i.e. ability), whereas behaviour description questions describe what people have done, so also reflect typical performance (i.e. personality). Questions about past work behaviour are not suitable for people with no employment experience such as school leavers or new graduates.

Multimodal interview, devised in Germany, has eight sections, including an informal rapport-building conversation at the beginning, self-presentation by A, standardized questions on choice of career and organization, behaviour description questions, situational questions and realistic job preview.

Empirical interview. Present good performers are interviewed to identify themes in effective performance (e.g. teamwork). Next, an expert panel develops around 120 possible interview questions, which are then tested in interviews with 30 outstanding and 30 unsatisfactory performers. Questions that best distinguish good from poor employees are retained. The empirical interview does not favour any particular type of question – past behaviour, future behaviour, etc; any question that works is used, even apparently vague ones like '*How competitive are you?*'. The same empirical approach is used to develop biodata (Chapter 9) and some personality questionnaires (Chapter 7). The empirical interview has some other novel features. Applicants are interviewed by telephone, the interview is tape-recorded and scored later by someone else. (It is strange how seldom interviews are recorded, given how difficult it is to remember everything the As say, or to take accurate and detailed notes.)

Validity of structured interviews

Two analyses (Wiesner & Cronshaw, 1988; Huffcutt & Arthur, 1994) found validity for structured interviews twice that for unstructured (Tables 4.1 and 4.2). The third (McDaniel *et al.*, 1994) finds a smaller difference, possibly because they defined structure differently. Wiesner and Cronshaw found structured interviews work equally well whether there is one interviewer or several, but McDaniel *et al.* – analysing a larger number of studies – found that one-to-one structured interviews achieved slightly higher validity.

After 1994, it was generally accepted that structured interviews are superior to unstructured. However, two re-analyses of McDaniel's data by Duval (2005) and Oh *et al.* (2007) threw doubt on this. The trim-and-fill technique (described in Chapter 2) indicates 'substantial publication bias' towards 'good' results for structured interviews, suggesting that 19 studies with poorer results have been somehow overlooked. By contrast, trim-and-fill finds no evidence of 'missing' studies of the unstructured interview. Duval's revised validity estimates found no difference between structured and unstructured interview validity. Oh *et al.* further re-analysed the data correcting for both publication bias and indirect range restriction (described in Chapter 2) and found struc-

Table 4.2 Summary of three meta-analyses of structured interview validity, by Wiesner and Cronshaw (1988), Huffcutt and Arthur (1994) and McDaniel *et al.* (1994).

	Wiesner & Cronshaw		Huffcutt & Arthur		McDaniel *et al.*	
	k	r / ρ	k	r / ρ	k	r / ρ
All interviews	150	0.26 / 0.47	114	0.22 / 0.37	160	0.20 / 0.37
All structured	48	0.34 / 0.62	33	0.34 / 0.57	106	0.24 / 0.44 0.20 / 0.37[a]
one to one	32	0.35 / 0.63			61	0.25 / 0.46
board	15	0.33 / 0.60			35	0.20 / 0.38

[a] Re-analysed by Oh *et al.* (2007) to take account of publication bias.
r = uncorrected average correlation; ρ = operational validity. Huffcutt & Arthur distinguish four levels of structure; the value for structured interviews is the highest level while the value for unstructured is the lowest level.

Table 4.3 Meta-analysis of empirical interview research.

	k	r	ρ
Supervisor rating	33	0.19	0.40
Production records	5	0.29	0.40
Sales	41	0.15	0.40
(Low) absenteeism	7	0.10	0.19
Tenure	21	0.28	0.39[a]

Data from Schmidt and Rader (1999).
r = raw validity; ρ = operational validity.
[a] Corrected for restricted range only.

tured interview validity lower, at 0.45, than unstructured, at 0.56. McDaniel, Rothstein and Whetzel (2006a) appeared to apologize for having persuaded many practitioners to 'create fairly laborious structured interview systems' and for discouraging further research comparing structured and unstructured interviews.

Schmidt and Rader (1999) reported an analysis of 107 researches on the empirical interview. Table 4.3 shows that the empirical interview achieves good validity for the conventional supervisor rating criterion. Table 4.3 also shows that the empirical interview can predict other aspects of work performance: output, sales and tenure – staying with the organization. Only absence is less well predicted. As Schmidt and Rader noted, no other previous research had shown the interview able to predict sales, output or absence.

The re-analysis of McDaniel *et al.*'s 1994 data created great uncertainty in one of the most important areas of selection research. It might be difficult to resolve the issue. A further meta-analysis that tries to collate every study in

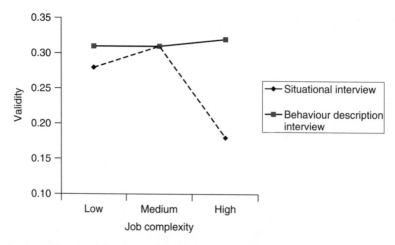

Figure 4.1 Validity of Situational and behaviour description interviews for jobs of high, medium and low complexity. Data from Huffcutt *et al.* (2004).

the three original meta-analyses, and to include research since 1994, would be worth doing. Note, however, that the number of unstructured interview validities in Table 4.1 is not that great, and if McDaniel *et al.* (2006a)'s point about premature meta-analytic conclusions is correct, it may not have increased much. If most employers have gone over to structured interviewing, partly to avoid fair employment problems, it may be difficult to obtain further data on unstructured interviews.

Accumulating research on structured interviewing now makes it possible to compare different types. Huffcutt *et al.* (2004) compared 31 studies of the Situational interview with 20 studies of the Behavior Description Interview and found overall relatively little difference, corrected validities being 0.44 and 0.50, respectively. However Figure 4.1 suggests that the Situational interview may be less suitable for highly complex jobs.

Schmidt and Zimmerman (2004) argued that structured interviews achieve good validity, simply because they are much more reliable, and noted that correcting unstructured interview validity for its very low reliability increases it to almost the same level as structured interview validity. This has an important practical implication: pooling three or four unstructured interviews might achieve acceptable reliability, and match the structured interview's validity. This could be useful for the smaller employer who cannot afford to devise a structured interview system, or does not have sufficient employees.

Interview or spoken questionnaire?

Very structured interviews, such as Latham's Situational Interview, blur the distinction between interview and paper-and-pencil test. If interviewers read from a script and do not interact with As, are they really needed? Why not print the questions in a question book and have As answer them in writing? This would be much quicker and cheaper. Schmidt and Rader give one answer – interview format does not give people time to prepare a carefully thought-out answer, which might not be entirely frank.

Resistance

The structured interview deprives interviewers of most of their traditional autonomy. They have to follow a script, have to use rating scales and are not allowed to chat with As or tell them about the organization. Sometimes they are virtually reduced to being a substitute for a written test. This may mean interviewers will start to deviate from their prescribed role, unless they are closely monitored. In many organizations, the managers who give the interviews are more powerful than HR, who bring in structured interviewing and try to maintain its quality. This suggests that structured interviewing systems may not always achieve such good results in practice. Harris (2000) reports that structured interviews in a large UK city council proved very unpopular with recruiters, being seen as inflexible, mechanical and over-structured.

'Cribbable?'

Day and Carroll (2003) confirmed that telling As the interview questions in advance will secure them better ratings in situational and behaviour description interviews. Structured interviews have set lists of questions, and set marking schemes, which creates the risk of 'cribs' being generated – guides to what to expect and what to say, especially when the interview is used for promotion. Devising new questions requires elaborate data collection and analysis, so will not be easy.

RESEARCH AGENDA

- Re-compare structured and unstructured interview validity by [1] re-analysing all available data on validity of structured and unstructured interviews, [2] reopening research on 'traditional' interviews
- Whether structured interviews work well in practice or whether validity decays through misuse
- Whether structured interviews achieve higher validity simply through greater reliability
- Which features of structured interviews need to be retained, and which could be dispensed with
- Whether use of prompts affects reliability and validity
- Whether asking every A exactly same questions increases reliability and validity
- Whether excluding interviewee questions improves reliability and validity.

Construct validity of the interview

Convergent validity

Several studies, most recently van Iddekinge *et al.* (2004) and Mussel, Berhmann and Schuler (2008), have found that interviews seem to have poor convergent / divergent validity. Assessments of the same dimension in different interviews agree poorly, while assessments of different dimensions within the same interview agree too well. This suggests that interviews may be assessing 'interview performance' rather than the set of dimensions their users think they are assessing. A similar problem arises with assessment centres (Chapter 10). To the extent that interviews 'work' – are able to predict work performance – it could be argued that this lack of convergent validity does not matter. It does matter in two ways. Employers should be wary of offering feedback based on the dimensions the interview is supposed to be assessing. Employers might find it difficult to defend their interview system if its validity is questioned.

Construct validity

Research comparing interview ratings with other assessments, usually psychological tests, gives some indication what the interview is actually assessing (which is not necessarily what it is intended to assess).

Mental ability

Two meta-analyses (Huffcutt *et al.*, 1996; Salgado & Moscoso, 2002) have reported the 'true' correlation between interview rating and tested mental ability is around 0.40, suggesting that the interview makes a moderately good disguised mental ability test. This is quite surprising; most applicants, interviewers, HR managers and laypeople do not see interviews as mental ability tests. However, Berry *et al.* (2007) argued that 0.40 is an overestimate, based on correcting for restricted range, where range has not in fact been restricted. Their more careful re-analysis found a lower true correlation of 0.27. Chapter 2 noted that four meta-analyses of mental ability and interview structure (Huffcutt *et al.*; Salgado & Moscoso; Cortina *et al.*; Berry *et al.*) found differing results, so it is not clear whether the link with mental ability is stronger for structured interviews, or for unstructured.

Job knowledge

Structured interviews correlate quite well with paper-and-pencil job knowledge tests. Critics might say this is not surprising because some structured interviews seem little more than oral job knowledge tests.

Table 4.4 Meta-analysis of construct validity of unstructured and structured interviews.

Type of interview	Unstructured		Structured	
	k	r / ρ	k	r / ρ
Job knowledge	*		8	0.27 / 0.53
Situational judgement	*		6	0.22 / 0.46
Grade point average	28	0.06 / 0.13	5	0.08 / 0.17
Social skill	6	0.22 / 0.46	5	0.34 / 0.65
Neuroticism	16	0.17 / 0.38	10	0.04 / 0.08
Extraversion	19	0.16 / 0.34	7	0.10 / 0.21
Openness	16	0.14 / 0.30	6	0.04 / 0.09
Agreeableness	18	0.12 / 0.26	6	0.06 / 0.12
Conscientiousness	18	0.13 / 0.28	13	0.08 / 0.17

Data from Salgado & Moscoso (2002).
r = raw correlation; ρ = true correlation, corrected for restricted range and reliability of both measures.
*Insufficient data.

Personality

Salgado and Moscoso's meta-analysis also reported data for personality. Table 4.4 shows that ratings in unstructured interviews correlate with the five main factors in personality to some extent. Interview ratings, for instance, reflect As' extraversion and anxiety, whether or not the interview is intended to assess these attributes. Table 4.4 shows that structured interview ratings are less affected by personality. Subsequently, Roth *et al.* (2005) reported two further studies correlating personality with structured interview rating in 500 persons and concluded that there is a weak relationship with *extraversion* and *conscientiousness*, but none with *agreeableness, neuroticism* or *openness*.

Social skill and situational judgement

Structured interviews correlate surprisingly highly with the applicant's social skill and situational judgement, which suggests structured interviews may not entirely succeed in excluding irrelevant considerations from the interviewers' decisions.

Incremental validity

Can the interview improve on prediction made by other methods? Schmidt and Hunter (1998) argued that unstructured interviews will give little or no incremental validity over mental ability tests, because unstructured interviews are highly correlated with mental ability (although Berry *et al.*'s reanalysis suggested the correlation is not so high). Cortina *et al.* (2000) provided empirical confirmation; they found that an unstructured interview adds little to tests of conscientiousness and mental ability. Schmidt and Hunter concluded that structured interviews, by contrast, will have some incremental validity over mental ability tests because both have good predictive validity, but are not so highly correlated. Cortina *et al.* (2000) confirmed that a structured interview has considerable incremental validity over tests of mental ability and conscientiousness.

Truthfulness of interview information

Interviews are mostly self-reports, where interviewees describe their achievements, their abilities, their strengths, and their weaknesses. The question therefore arises: *Do interviewees always tell the truth about themselves?* Several lines of research are relevant.

Impression management (IM)

There is a growing body of research on ploys that As might use in the interview to try to create a better impression (Table 4.5). Ellis *et al.* (2002) analysed promotion interviews for firefighters, and found virtually everyone used IM tactics. The most commonly used are self-promotion and opinion conformity; excuses and flattery on the other hand were hardly ever used. Barrick, Shaffer and DeGrassi (2008) reported a meta-analysis showing that people who seek to ingratiate and self-promote in the interview do succeed in getting much better ratings. This may be a source of error, but not necessarily; ingratiators and self-promoters may, at some level, be better performers in the workplace. Silvester *et al.* (2002) showed that the type of explanation people offer for past failures affects the impression they create. Admitting the failure was the candidate's fault – I failed the exam because I did not revise hard enough – was better received than blaming other people. Opinion conformity is arguably more difficult than most IM because As must know, or try to guess, the interviewer's beliefs and values, in order to agree with them.

It could be argued that at least some IM techniques in Table 4.5 come under the heading of what interviewees are expected to do. One sometimes hears interviewers complaining an applicant 'didn't make an effort' – to describe his/her achievements at sufficient length and with sufficient enthusiasm. However, 'making an effort' can shade imperceptibly into untruth, from genuinely thinking one did more than one really did, through claiming most or all responsibility for something that others did some or most of, to describing entirely fictitious achievements. It has been suggested that structured interviews may make IM more difficult because all As are asked same questions and have less opportunity to control the interview's agenda. Barrick *et al.*'s meta-analysis confirms this, although even structured interview ratings correlate 0.30 with interviewees' IM use.

Table 4.5 Some Impression Management (IM) tactics used in interviews, with examples.

Assertive IM	
Self-promotion	Positive descriptions of oneself 'people look to me for leadership'
Entitlements	Claiming responsibility for success, even when it was really someone else's work 'I helped make the reorganization a great success'
Enhancements	Saying an achievement was bigger than it appears 'The increase in sales I achieved was one of the biggest for some years'
Overcoming obstacles	How A got round barriers to success 'I realized that we were not getting bids out quickly enough, and reorganized the system to use e-mail'

Defensive IM	
Excuses	Claiming to have no responsibility for failures 'We lost that bid because the IT system let us down'
Apologies	Admitting being responsible for a failure 'I got the projections for that scheme wrong which is why it did not make a profit'
Justification	Accepting responsibility for failure but trying to minimize it 'We lost the XYZ bid, but it was not a particularly large project and would not have made much money'

Ingratiation	
Flattery	'I have always greatly admired your work on ...'
Opinion conformity	Saying things the interviewer will agree with 'I think it is very important to keep oneself in good shape'

Non-verbal behaviour
Smiling, eye-contact, nodding, hand gestures, and so on.

Faking good

Levashina and Campion (2006) noted that there has been little research on faking good in the selection interview (in sharp contrast to the flood of research on faking PQs, described in Chapter 7). They suggested that some features of interviews will make them harder to fake, but others may make faking easier. The longer the interview, the more difficult it might be to avoid contradicting oneself, especially if the interviewer presses hard for examples of claimed abilities or achievements. The more interviewers there are, the more time they may have to detect inconsistencies, think of probing questions, and notice hesitation or non-verbal 'giveaways'. On the other hand, features of the structured interview, designed to ensure consistency and prevent bias, may make faking easier, especially the absence of follow-up or probing questions, and not being allowed to see A's CV or application form. Allen, Facteau and

Facteau (2004) found students unable to fake good in a structured interview assessing organizational citizenship (Box 4.1), even if they are helped by being told what is being assessed. Van Iddekinge, Raymark and Roth (2005) found a structured interview assessing vulnerability, altruism and self-discipline could be faked to some extent, but the change in scores was much less than for a PQ.

Box 4.1   Organizational citizenship

This means volunteering to do things not in the job description, helping others, following rules willingly, and publicly supporting the organization. Generally assessed by supervisor's rating.

Interviewee lying

One step on from faking good or impression management is outright lying. Ekman's research suggested interviewers may not be able to detect this (Ekman & O'Sullivan, 1991). Of five sets of experts who ought to be good at detecting lies – Secret Service, CIA, FBI, National Security Agency, Drug Enforcement Agency – only one did better than chance. Weiss and Feldman (2006) described an ingenious experiment, where students attend for research on personality and are unexpectedly offered an interview for a tutoring job. After the interview, they are told there is not really a job after all, and asked to watch a recording of the interview, and pick out anything they said that was not true. Most (81%) admitted to telling at least one lie, with an average of just over two per person, in a 10–15-minute interview. The examples given suggest most were exaggerations rather than outright untruths. This interesting, if rather unethical, experiment merits replication.

RESEARCH AGENDA

- How truthful As are in selection interviews
- How good interviewers are at detecting untruths
- How far untruthful As can improve their ratings, and whether this affects interview validity.
- More data on the frequency of different types of IM, in different types of interview, in different sectors and different cultures.
- More data on how interviewers and interviewees view IM tactics, and how they affect interviewers' judgements.

Interview coaching

Students at British universities are often offered 'how to be interviewed' courses; books offering the same proliferate. There is not much research on the effectiveness of interview coaching. Maurer *et al.* (2001) found that coaching gets people better ratings in interviews for US fire and police services. Coaching seems to work by teaching people to be more organized, thinking about their answers, even making notes, before answering. Note however that Maurer's research described a highly structured interview which asks only factual questions. Taking a long time to answer and making notes might not secure a good rating in more traditional interviews.

RESEARCH AGENDA

- How many interviewees are coached
- How far coaching can improve interview ratings
- Whether coaching affects validity
- What effect coaching has in unstructured interviews

How the interviewer reaches a decision

Ideally, the interviewer will listen carefully to everything A says and reach a wise decision based on all the information available. Research has documented a number of ways in which interviewers depart from this ideal.

Interviewers make their minds up before the interview

Barrick *et al.*'s (2008) meta-analysis of 45 studies found that application form and CV/résumé have a big effect on interview rating. Some structured interview systems do not allow interviewers to see any other information about As.

Interviewers make up their minds quickly

A frequently cited study by Springbett (1958) showed that interviewers make up their minds after only four minutes of a 15-minute interview, although his methodology was not very subtle and his sample very small. Raymark *et al.* (2008) analysed a considerably larger sample of interviewers and found only a quarter said they had reached a decision within the first five minutes. Assessing personality and ability took longer than assessing physical attributes or social skill, which are more 'visible' so perhaps easier to assess. Applicants who tried to ingratiate themselves were judged quicker. Rosenthal's 'thin slices' research may also be relevant. Ratings of teachers made after seeing very short (2–10 seconds) video clips were the same as the ones made after a whole term of classes. This may be bias, but it could be argued that in some jobs, making a strong first impression is important (Ambady & Rosenthal, 1992).

The interviewer simplifies the task

Defenders of the interview argue that a good interviewer can see complex patterns in the information, which mechanistic methods, like checklists and weighted application blanks, miss. However, research casts some doubt on interviewers' claim to be doing something so complex that no other method can replace them. Research suggests that:

1. Human experts do not perform better than a system.
2. Human experts do not use information as complexly as they claim.

1. Expert vs. System. Over fifty years ago, Meehl (1954) reviewed 20 studies comparing mechanistic systems against human experts and concluded that a system always predicted as well as an expert, often better. Research since 1954 has not disproved Meehl's conclusion (Grove *et al.*, 2000).

2. Does the expert use information complexly? Research on how experts make decisions mostly uses the policy-capturing paradigm. The researcher constructs sets of cases in which information is systematically varied, asks experts to assess each case, then deduces how the experts reached their decisions. If the expert accepts one set and rejects another, and the only feature distinguishing the two sets is exam results, it follows that the expert's decisions are based on exam grades. Experts claim they do not think as simplistically as this; they say they use configurations, e.g. exam grades are important in young candidates but not for people over 30 – an interaction of age and grades. Policy capturing finds experts rarely use configurations, even simple ones. Hitt and Barr (1989) found HR managers using cues complexly, but not wisely, making 'different attributions when comparing a black, 45-year-old woman with 10 years of experience and a master's degree with a white, 35-year-old man with 10 years of experience and a master's degree'. (Unwise, because they should not base decisions on gender, age or ethnicity.)

Bias in the interview

The interview provides an ideal opportunity for the exercise of whatever bias(es) the interviewers have because they cannot help knowing every A's gender, ethnicity, age, social background and physical attractiveness, and because they often are not required to justify their decisions. (Whereas selectors can use psychological tests or biographical methods, without seeing As, or knowing their gender, ethnicity, and so on.)

Are interviewers biased against women?

Huffcutt *et al.* (2001) find that unstructured interviews do create some adverse impact on females, whereas structured interviews do not. The research reviewed is nearly all North American, so one cannot safely assume that similar results will be found in other countries, given how widely attitudes to gender vary.

Are interviewers biased by race?

Huffcutt *et al.*'s (2001) meta-analysis showed that unstructured interviews do create some adverse impact on non-white Americans, especially interviews that assess intellectual ability and experience. Huffcutt *et al.* also concluded that structured interviews do not create adverse impact on minorities, which is one reason why they are popular in the USA. However, Bobko and Roth (1999) disagreed and said that structured interviews do create some adverse impact on African Americans ($d = 0.23$). Roth *et al.* (2002) pointed out that adverse impact computations for interviews are often made in organizations where the interview is used after As have been screened already (e.g. by tests). Pre-screening by tests will tend to restrict the range of ability of those interviewed and possibly lead to an underestimate of the adverse impact of the structured interview. Roth *et al.* corrected for this restriction of range and found that structured interviews created fairly large adverse impact, d ranging from 0.36 to 0.56. Prewett-Livingston *et al.* (1996) found that interviews show own-race bias, where whites favour whites, blacks favour blacks, Hispanic Americans favour other Hispanic Americans, and so on.

Audit studies

There is an extensive literature in the USA and UK on discrimination using the audit method (Riach & Rich, 2002). For example, a white A and an Asian A apply for a real job and attend a real interview, and both are matched exactly in age, experience, qualifications, and so on, so the conclusion can be drawn that lower hiring rates for Asian As indicate deliberate discrimination. Such discrimination is usually found. Psychologists see fatal flaws in these studies. How can one be sure how white and Asian As behave comparably at an interview? The 'applicants' are carefully trained, sometimes professional actors, but interviews are inherently unpredictable, so it is impossible to be completely prepared. Moreover, audit 'applicants' may have expectations that minority As will be discriminated against, which may subtly affect their behaviour. Medical research has shown how pervasively expectations affect people, so great care is taken that no one knows which is the active drug and which is the placebo. This 'double blind' is not possible when audit studies go as far as interview, although it can work at the application form stage.

Are interviewers biased against older applicants?

Morgeson, Reider, Campion and Bull (2008) reviewed 16 laboratory studies of age discrimination in employment interviews and five field studies, and found age discrimination in real interviews much less than in simulated interviews. They suggested laboratory studies make age more salient, and provided less other relevant information.

Are interviewers biased by accent?

George Bernard Shaw once remarked that no Englishman can open his mouth without making other Englishmen despise him. An early Canadian study (Kalin & Rayko, 1978) found As with foreign accents got less favourable ratings.

Are interviewers biased by appearance?

Most people can agree whether someone is conventionally 'good-looking' or not. Barrick et al.'s (2008) meta-analysis of 17 studies found a large (0.52) correlation between attractiveness and interview rating. The effect is very strong (0.81) in unstructured interviews, but almost absent (0.17) in highly structured interviews.

Are interviewers biased by weight?

Fikkan and Rothblum (2005) reviewed extensive evidence of consistent negative stereotypes of overweight people as lacking in self-discipline, lazy, having emotional problems, or less able to get on with others, and find overweight people discriminated against in every aspect of employment, including selection. Discrimination on grounds of weight may contravene disability discrimination laws. Kutcher and Bragger (2004) found interviewers biased against overweight applicants; they used actors, whose apparent body weight in the overweight condition was increased by make-up and padding. However, the bias was only found in unstructured interviews, not in structured ones. Hebl and Mannix (2003) reported the extraordinary finding that merely sitting next to an overweight person reduces an applicant's chance of getting the job. Rudolph et al. (2008) provided an estimate of effect size of being overweight on hiring decisions across 25 studies of $d = 0.52$, which does not seem to vary much for different types of job.

Are interviewers biased by height?

Height was formerly an explicit consideration in hiring decisions. Judge and Cable (2004) suggested that 'What was once explicit may now be implicit.' They reviewed four longitudinal researches on height and earning power, including one in the UK, and found a correlation of 0.31–0.35. (The issue of correction does not arise with income and height because both can be measured with perfect reliability.) The link is found in both men and women despite the average difference in height. The link is slightly stronger in sales and management but present in all types of work: blue-collar, clerical, craft, service, professional/technical. Height might be genuinely useful in sales and management if it helps people persuade and influence others. On the other hand, it is difficult to see how it could be relevant in clerical work. Judge and Cable offered a model: height leads to increased self-esteem and social esteem, which contributes to success. It is not clear whether the effect is a positive preference for taller people or a bias against shorter people.

Are interviewers biased against homosexual As?

Hebl *et al.* (2002) sent people to apply for jobs at local stores, some identifying themselves as gay. The 'gay' As got a more negative reception – shorter interview or less-friendly interviewer – but were not actually discriminated against in terms of getting job offers. Hebl *et al.* avoided creating expectations in 'applicants', with an ingenious way of identifying some 'As' as homosexual without their knowing; As were given a hat to wear, which either said 'Proud to be Gay' or 'XYZ University', but did not know which. Interviews had to be discarded if people commented on the hat, or 'As' saw reflections of themselves.

RESEARCH AGENDA

- Gender, ethnicity or age bias in interviews in countries outside North America
- Whether structured interviews reduce interviewer bias
- Whether interviews create adverse impact, correcting for indirect range restriction

---

Law and fairness

Terpstra, Mohamed and Kethley (1999) noted that unstructured interviews are the most frequent source of dispute in USA. They estimated how many complaints one would expect for any selection method, given its frequency of use. Unstructured interviews are complained about twice as often as would be expected, whereas structured interviews are only complained about half as often as would be expected. Terpstra *et al.* found another even more compelling reason to commend structured interviews to employers. When structured interviews are the subject of complaint, the employer always won the case, whereas with unstructured interviews, 40% of employers lost their case. Williamson *et al.* (1997) analysed 130 American court cases and found two interview features that helped employers defend themselves against claims of unfairness. The first is structure: the use of standard sets of questions, limiting interviewer discretion and ensuring all interviews are the same. The second is objectivity and job-relatedness, the use of objective, specific, behavioural criteria, as opposed to vague, global, subjective criteria, also an interviewer who is trained and who is familiar with the job's requirements. The use of multiple interviewers, or panel interviews however made no difference to whether employers won their cases. Clearly structured interviewing is much better in terms of achieving fairness and avoiding losing fair employment claims.

Key points

In Chapter 4 you have learned the following.

- Interviews vary in form, and in what they seek to assess.
- Conventional unstructured interviews have poor reliability, and poor validity.
- Interviewees try to present themselves in a good light, and may sometimes even fail to tell the truth about themselves.
- Interviews can be improved by selecting interviewers, training interviewers, and using multiple interviewers.
- Structured interviews are based on job analysis, and control interview format and questions, while providing detailed rating systems.
- Research indicates structured interviews are highly reliable.
- Earlier research suggested structured interviews achieve better validity than unstructured, but re-analysis has thrown some doubt on this.
- Structured interviews may be more like orally administered tests.
- Research suggests question format in structured interviews is not critical.
- Interview ratings correlate with mental ability, personality and social skill.
- Interviewers do not always reach decisions very efficiently or rationally.
- Interviewers' thought processes may be less complex than interviewers suppose.
- Interviewers may be biased by many factors including gender, ethnicity, age, appearance, weight, or accent.
- Unstructured interviews have been the subject of many fair employment claims, many of which have been successful; structured interviews have been the subject of fewer claims, fewer of which proved successful.

Key references

Bozionelos (2005) describe a case study of interview 'fixing'.

Fikkan and Rothblum (2005) review research on weight bias in selection.

Latham *et al.* (1980) describe the first structured interview technique, the Situation Interview.

Levashina and Campion (2006) discuss the fakability of the interview.

Morgeson *et al.* (2008) review research on age discrimination in the employment interview.

Riach and Rich (2002) describe 'audit' studies of discrimination in interviews.

Salgado and Moscoso (2002) analyse research on the interview's construct validity.

Schmidt and Rader (1999) describe a structured interview technique, the empirical interview.

Williamson *et al.* (1997) analyse US fair employment cases involving interviews.

Useful websites

hr-guide.com. Includes 2000 interview questions in 24 areas.
bdt.net. Devoted to Janz's behaviour description interviewing.

CHAPTER 5

References and ratings

The eye of the beholder

Introduction

References and ratings work on the principle that the best way of finding out about applicants is to ask someone who knows them well – former employers, school teachers, or colleagues. They have seen A all day every day, perhaps for years, and can report how A usually behaves, and what A is like on 'off days'. The traditional way of doing this is the reference request; more recent developments include peer rating and '360° feedback'.

References

The Cranfield Price Waterhouse survey (Table 1.6, page 20) finds references widely used throughout Western Europe. Similarly, most American employers take up references on new employees. References are cheap, and universally accepted, because everyone has always used them. However the information is not always forthcoming; even fifty years ago Mosel and Goheen (1958) reported a return rate of only 56% for skill trades and 64% for managerial and professional posts. References may be structured – checklists, ratings – or unstructured – 'Tell me what you think of John Smith, in your own words'.

Uses of the reference

References can collect information on most headings listed in Table 1.2 (page 11): for example, mental and other ability, personality, knowledge or skill. References also have the unusual, and potentially valuable, feature of getting straight to the point. They can ask directly about work performance: Was Smith a good worker? Was Smith punctual? Most other selection tests can only infer from what As are like to what their work performance is likely to be. Table 5.1 summarizes a survey of American HR professionals which shows references used for fact checking, direct enquiry about work performance (with an emphasis on attendance), and for personal qualities but not for ability, general or specific (Bureau of National Affairs, 1995). Taylor *et al.* (2004) suggested that references may be particularly suitable for getting information on organizational citizenship (Box 4.1, page 86). Some employers use references at the sifting or shortlisting stage; others wait until they have

Table 5.1 Survey of 1331 US HR professionals about information sought in reference requests.

Dates of employment	96%
Salary history	45%
Qualifications for a particular job	56%
· Eligibility for rehire	65%
Overall impression of employability	49%
Work habits (absence, punctuality)	41%
Human relations skills	37%
Personality	24%
Driving record	42%
Credit history	25%

Data from Bureau of National Affairs, 1995.

chosen someone to appoint, and use the reference as a final check on qualifications, honesty, and so on.

Telephone references

A 1998 SHRM survey of American employers (SHRM, 1998) found over 80% used telephone referencing. Telephone referencing has several possible advantages, apart from speed; referees can be asked for examples or for clarification. Hesitation or tone of voice may be informative. One apparent advantage may really be a major snag. Some people prefer phone referencing because they think it leaves nothing for lawyers to 'discover' later, but lack of written trace is actually risky, making it hard to prove what was or was not said. Also phone conversations can be recorded. Many organizations' rules forbid either giving or seeking phone references, but Andler and Herbst (2002) suggested that these rules are often broken. They presented quite detailed scripts for getting information, including the distinctly unethical ploy of telling the referee the applicant would not get the job unless the referee gives the information requested.

Discussion so far has assumed that employers use references to evaluate potential employees, but references may have another purpose. The employer can refuse a reference or give a bad one, and so block the employee's chance of getting another job. To be certain of getting a good reference, the employee must avoid doing anything that might offend the employer. On this argument, the reference system is used by employers to control present and past staff, not to assess new staff.

Reliability

American research suggests that references lack reliability. Referees agree among themselves very poorly about As for (US) civil service jobs, with 80% of correlations lower than 0.40 (Mosel & Goheen, 1959). Recent research

(Taylor *et al.*, 2004) has confirmed that references have very poor inter-referee reliability. Some very early British research looked at reliability from a different slant. The Civil Service Selection Board (CSSB) in the 1940s collected references from school, university, armed services and former employers (Wilson, 1948); CSSB staff achieved moderately good inter-rater reliability (0.73) in assessments of As based on references alone. CSSB used five or six references, which will tend to increase reliability. Note that Wilson is addressing a different issue: whether the panel agree about what the five or six referees collectively are saying about A, not whether the five or six agree with each other.

Validity of references

American research

Mosel and Goheen reported extensive research on the Employment Recommendation Questionnaire (ERQ), a structured reference developed by the US Civil Service, which covered ability, character and reputation, skill, knowledge, human relations, and so on. For some jobs in the civil service and armed forces ERQ had zero validity (Mosel & Goheen, 1958), while for other jobs ERQ achieved limited validity ($r = 0.20$ to 0.30 uncorrected). Goheen and Mosel (1959) also compared 109 ERQs with a more searching field investigation which 'interrogated' up to six people who know A well (but are not necessarily nominated by A). In seven cases, the investigation uncovered serious disqualifying facts, such as gross incompetence or alcoholism, none of which had been mentioned in the written reference. Reilly and Chao (1982) concluded that reference checks give fairly poor predictions of supervisor ratings (uncorrected $r = 0.18$) and turnover (uncorrected $r = 0.08$). Shortly afterwards, Hunter and Hunter's (1984) review calculated average validity of reference checks against four outcomes, again finding low average correlations (Table 5.2). Hunter and Hunter's account is rather sketchy by later standards for reporting meta-analyses, and does not list the studies included, so one does not know how much this analysis overlaps with Reilly and Chao's. These early analyses generally made no corrections for outcome reliability or restricted range, so may underestimate validity.

European research

References for UK naval officer training by head teachers correlate moderately well (0.36, corrected for restricted range) with training grade in naval college (Jones & Harrison, 1982). Jones and Harrison argued that head teachers are more likely (than, say, former employers) to write careful and critical references because they know they will be writing Naval College references for future pupils and because their own credibility is at stake. Moser and Rhyssen (2001) reported a low validity (0.20 uncorrected) for telephone references for German sales staff and supervisors.

Table 5.2   Hunter and Hunter's (1984) meta-analysis of reference check validity.

Outcome ⇓	k	N	r
Supervisor rating	10	5,389	0.26[a]
Promotion	3	415	0.16
Training success	1	1,553	0.23
Tenure	2	2,018	0.27

[a] The correlation for supervisor rating is corrected for reliability of supervisor rating. No correction for restricted range is made.

Construct and incremental validity

There are few data on how references relate to other tests or what they can add to them. Taylor *et al.* (2004) found assessments of conceptually distinct attributes – consciousness, agreeableness and customer focus – are highly correlated (0.68–0.77) suggesting that references may lack divergent validity. Taylor *et al.* suggested that references cover typical behaviour, not best behaviour, so might have incremental validity on tests of skill and ability. Zimmerman, Triana and Barrick (2008) found that a structured reference had near-zero correlation with GMA and consequently achieved incremental validity over a GMA test.

Free-form references

Early researches (e.g. Wiens *et al.* 1969) showed that more favourable reference letters tended to be longer, which might not be very useful in practice because one needs to know how long a reference the referee usually writes. Colarelli, Hechanova-Alampay and Canali (2002) collected 532 letters describing 169 As for psychologist posts at a US university and made global ratings of the favourability of each letter. These proved to have near-zero (0.19) inter-referee reliability and zero validity when correlated with number of publications (a key index of work performance in academics). It is much more difficult to assess the validity of the free-form reference, as it is complex and unquantified. There is obviously much more to reference letters than global favourability. Most HR managers are familiar with the complexities of hinting at weaknesses in an ostensibly favourable reference (e.g. 'perfectionist' means 'never gets anything finishes'). Private languages of this type are easily misunderstood. Loher *et al.* (1997) attempted a content analysis of reference letters, but could find no relations between the types of words used or the types of evidence given, and the overall impact of the reference. It is difficult to see how free-form references can be validated by the conventional quantitative validation paradigm. This does not necessarily mean they are not useful; perhaps subtler ways of assessing validity need to be developed.

Reasons for poor validity of references

Referees may lack the time or motivation to write careful references. Some referees may follow a hidden agenda to retain good staff and 'release' poor staff, by writing deliberately untrue references.

Leniency

Numerous researches report that most references are positive, called the 'Pollyanna effect' after the little girl who wanted to be nice to everyone. Early research by Mosel and Goheen found ERQ ratings highly skewed; hardly any one was rated poor. More recently Grote, Robiner and Haut (2001) presented two parallel surveys of US psychologists; the first set of psychologists say they disclose negative information in references they write, but the second set complain they are rarely given any negative information in references they receive. It is not hard to see why this happens. Referees are usually nominated by applicants who obviously chose someone likely to give them a good reference. These days many employers fear an unfavourable reference may result in a libel suit. But if referees are reluctant to say anything negative, references will remain a poor source of information. Murphy and Cleveland (1995) noted that performance appraisal has a similar problem – pervasive leniency – and suggest some reasons why. Managers can observe employees' shortcomings, but have no incentive to communicate them to others, and many reasons not to, including fear of creating ill feeling, and not wanting to admit they have poor employees because this reflects on their own management performance. Murphy's argument implied that references could be an excellent source of information, if only referees could be persuaded to communicate it.

Idiosyncrasy

Baxter *et al.* (1981) searched medical school files to find 20 cases where the same two referees had written references for the same two applicants (Figure 5.1). If references are useful, what referee 1 says about applicant X ought to resemble what referee 2 says about applicant X. Analysis of the qualities listed in the letters revealed a different, and much less encouraging, pattern. What referee 1 said about applicant X did not resemble what referee 2 said about applicant X, but did resemble what referee 1 said about applicant Y. Each referee had his/her own idiosyncratic way of describing people, which came through no matter who he/she was describing. The free-form reference appears to say more about its author than about its subject. Differences in reference writing may reflect personality (of author not applicant); Judge and Higgins (1998) showed that happier people write more favourable references.

Improving the reference

Various attempts have been made to improve the reference, with mixed results.

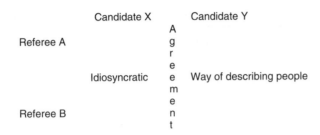

Figure 5.1 Schematic representation of the study by Baxter *et al.* (1981) of letters of reference.

Library of descriptions of work

Uhrbrock (1950) assembled a large set of 540 phrases describing work performance, which could be used to construct reference systems. They are ordered from least favourable – *is disloyal* – to most favourable – *keeps quality of work exceptionally high, day in day out*. Many are purely evaluative – *is a complete failure* – but enough are specific and verifiable: *often absent, a clock watcher, can talk intelligently on almost any topic, has foresight in anticipating future developments.*

Forced-choice format

Carroll and Nash (1972) used pairs of statements equated for social desirability:

- *has many worthwhile ideas / – completes all assignments*
- *always works fast / – requires little supervision*

This format is intended to limit leniency. Scores predicted performance ratings four months after hire quite well in university clerical workers.

Keyword counting

Peres and Garcia (1962) factor-analysed data from 625 reference letters and found five factors distinguishing good from poor As (Table 5.3). Many years later, Aamodt, Bryan and Whitcomb (1993) used Peres and Garcia's lists in selecting trainee teachers; they found counting mental agility keywords predicts mental ability, while counting urbanity keywords predicts teaching performance ratings. The keyword method may partially solve the leniency problem, by allowing a referee who wants to be really positive to say someone is intelligent not just once, but several times. Keyword counting needs freeform references; the documented idiosyncrasy of reference writers means HR will need a baseline for each referee. However, text scanning software makes keyword counting techniques much more feasible.

Table 5.3   Examples of words relating to five factors in letters of reference.

Co-operation	Mental agility	Urbanity	Vigour	Dependability
Good-natured	Imaginative	Talkative	Hustling	Precise
Accommodating	Ingenious	Chatty	Active	Persistent
Congenial	Insightful	Forward	Energetic	Methodical
Likeable	Knowledgeable	Bold	Self-driving	Tenacious
Co-operative	Intelligent	Sparkling	Vigorous	Determined

Data from Peres & Garcia (1962).

For each heading, give your overall assessment of A on the scale: 5] very good   ... 1] very poor. Then give examples of A's behaviour or achievements which form the basis of your assessment.

Interpersonal Sensitivity. *Listens well, encourages contributions from others and responds constructively. Can establish co-operative relationships with others and defuse potential conflicts. Can build useful relationships and alliances with others. Shows awareness of diversity and is sensitive to issues of gender, ethnicity, disability, and social exclusion.*

Rating:
Evidence:

Drive. *Able to set well defined and challenging goals for his/her work. Shows unflagging energy and enthusiasm across a wide range of varied employment or extracurricular activities, Shows determination in overcoming obstacles. Always meets deadlines.*

Figure 5.2   Extract from a competence based reference request.

Competence-based references

References can use the organization's competence framework and ask for behavioural evidence of, for example, resilience or time management. Figure 5.2 shows part of a typical request of this type. There seems no research on whether competence-based references work better.

Relative percentile method

McCarthy and Goffin (2001) described the Relative Percentile Method, a 100-point scale, where the referee says what percentage of persons score lower than the applicant on, for example, responsibility. McCarthy and Goffin estimated the method's validity at 0.42. The technique may work by allowing referees to be lenient – the mean percentile given was 80 – but also to differentiate at the top-end of the scale, giving someone they consider really responsible 95 rather than 85.

Personality-based structured references

Taylor *et al.* (2004) described a telephone reference covering conscientiousness, agreeableness and customer focus. The reference was structured using items taken from Goldberg's bank (Chapter 7) and a comparison format similar to McCarthy and Goffin's: How organized is [A] compared to others you have known? Pooled referees' rating predicted work performance rating 0.25, rising to 0.36 when corrected for reliability of work performance measure. The reference check is the final stage of selection, after two interviews, so restriction of range is likely, but could not be corrected for. The reference also predicted turnover to a more limited extent (0.16). Zimmerman *et al.* (2008) reported a similar study, achieving an operational validity of 0.37. Both researches averaged across three referees, which would increase validity through better reliability; Zimmerman *et al.* argued that even allowing for this the structured reference achieves better validity than the traditional unstructured. Note that both Taylor *et al.* and Zimmerman *et al.* used items from personality questionnaires, so may achieve better results by using questions selected – by the PQ development – to be relevant to the traits assessed.

Law and fairness

In the USA, employers find that the law seems to have placed them in a very difficult position with references. Little and Sipes (2000) noted that more and more Americans are suing employers over unfavourable references, which has resulted in more and more employers providing only *minimal* references. These give dates of employment, job title, possibly salary, but refuse to express any opinion about performance at work. This greatly reduces the value of the reference as a selection assessment. It also deprives good applicants of the opportunity to let employers know about their virtues. People dismissed for sexual abuse of children or violent behaviour at work can get another job, and do the same again, because the next employer is not warned about them. American courts have also introduced the concept of *negligent referral* – failing to disclose information to another employer about serious misconduct at work. This means employers risk being sued by the employee if they write a bad reference, and being sued by the next employer if they do not! To try to preserve the reference system, most states in the USA have passed immunity laws that restore 'privilege' to reference letters, meaning that employees cannot sue if the information is given in good faith, even if it proves not entirely correct. These laws require employers to show references to employees so they can make corrections or include their version of events. An SHRM survey in 2004 (SHRM, 2005) found only 2% of employers had had trouble with defamation claims, compared with 4% who had had trouble with negligent hiring claims or from not warning others about problem employees.

In Britain, the 1994 case of *Spring v Guardian Assurance* (Parry, 1999) made it possible to sue if a reference was inaccurate, whereas previously one had to prove also malice: that the referee knew the reference was inaccurate – a virtually impossible task. A number of libel cases involving references have been tried since. The last few years have also seen Data Protection Acts that give people right of access to personal data held on them by organizations. At the time of writing, no one knows for certain how this will affect reference letters; it has been suggested that the employer who *writes* the reference is not obliged to show it to the candidate, but that prospective employers who *receive* it are. This implies everyone can gain access to their references, which in turn implies that American style minimal references may be increasingly used in Britain. There is little or no research on bias in references, nor on adverse impact.

RESEARCH AGENDA

The reference is one of the most under-researched areas in personnel selection. There is barely enough research to justify a meta-analysis of validity. Little research has been attempted on the widely used free-form reference. Promising leads, such as forced-choice format, are not followed up. Sample sizes are often barely adequate. This generates a lengthy research agenda.

- More current information on what references actually ask about
- More data on validity of references, including validity for a wider range of outcomes: task, performance, organizational citizenship, counterproductive behaviour
- More data on construct validity, including correlation with other selection tests
- More data on incremental validity of references over other selection tests
- Some data on reliability, acceptability or validity of competence based references
- more research on improvements to the reference, including forced-choice format, relative percentile format
- Reasons for pervasive leniency, and how to persuade referees to be more frank
- More research on free-form references, including keyword counting, and use of private languages
- Data on the frequency of use of phone references
- Whether telephone references are lenient, reliable or valid
- Whether referees allow bias – for example, gender, ethnicity or liking – to affect what they write
- Whether references create adverse impact on protected minorities.
- More research on structured references, clarifying whether better validity is achieved by pooling across referees
- Whether referees chosen by A give more favourable or less valid references than referees chosen by the employer

---

Ratings

In personnel selection, ratings can be used both as the predictor, and as the outcome or criterion measure. Ratings used as predictor, in selection, are usually made by external referees (vs.), or by A's peers. Criterion or outcome

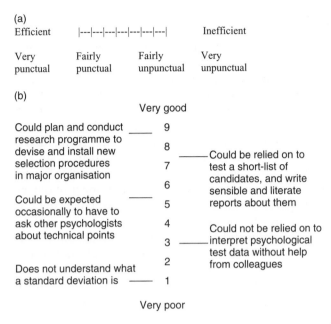

Figure 5.3 Rating formats. (a) Graphic rating scales. (b) (Invented) example of behaviourally anchored rating scale (BARS), for rating occupational psychologists.

ratings, of work performance, were traditionally made by supervisor or manager, but from the 1990s ratings by co-workers, subordinates and customers have been used as well (360 degree feedback or multi-source appraisal). Rating systems usually contain half a dozen scales, often many more. However, it is generally a mistake to multiply rating scales, because factor analysis (Box 2.7, on page 34) usually shows that a large number of ratings reduce to a much smaller number of factors. Figure 5.3a shows the conventional graphic rating scale; different formats vary the number of scale points, or supply anchors for each point – for example, very, fairly or slightly. Figure 5.3b also shows behaviourally anchored rating scale (BARS) format, which aims to make each point of the scale more meaningful to the rater, and the ratings less arbitrary. BARS aims to reduce leniency and to increase inter-rater agreement. BARS require a lot of research, and tend to be job specific, which makes them expensive.

Peer assessments

Like the reference check, peer ratings may describe personality, ability, or competencies, or may go straight to the point and rate work performance. Norton's (1992) meta-analysis found that it does not seem to make any difference to validity.

Agreement

Conway and Huffcutt (1997) meta-analysed research on inter-rater reliability of ratings of targets by peers and subordinates at work, made as part of '360 feedback' or multi-source performance appraisal. Some ratings are 'cognitive' – job knowledge, diagnosing problems, etc; some are interpersonal – human relations skill, communication; some are a mix of work performance and personality – drive and effort. One person's view of the target agrees fairly poorly with another's: an average uncorrected correlation of 0.37 for peers and 0.30 for subordinates. However, the consensus of four peers can achieve a reliability of 0.70, and the consensus of seven 0.80. The advantage of peer rating is that most targets can be rated by a number of others. Peers, subordinates and supervisors all agree moderately well (0.57 to 0.79, corrected), suggesting the ratings do contain some useful information (but note the reputation issue – v.s.). Murphy and DeShon (2000) made the point that different people see different sides of the target person, so would not be expected all to say the same about him/her. And if they did all say the same, what would be the point of asking more than one person? Others' ratings agree much less well with the target's self-rating – 0.26 to 0.31, corrected.

Reputation

When psychologists talk about inter-observer reliability, they assume the observations are independent. But, this may not be the case when people rate colleagues at work. A person's virtues and shortcomings may have been discussed at length, so a shared view of Smith's merits may have emerged, may even have been forged by Smith's friends or enemies. Chapter 12 outlines some ways in which the targets themselves can try to shape a shared consensus of their merits. In this context, high levels of agreement cease to be impressive.

Validity of peer ratings

An early meta-analysis by Reilly and Chao (1982) calculated average validities for three outcomes (Table 5.4), finding fairly large correlations, especially for promotion. A later meta-analysis of peer rating and work performance by

Table 5.4 Meta-analysis of peer rating and work performance.

Outcome	k	r
Training	10	0.31
Promotion	5	0.51
Performance ratings	18	0.37

Data from Reilly and Chao (1982).
r = uncorrected correlation.

Table 5.5 Summary of Norton's (1992) meta-analysis of peer rating and work performance.

⇓ Moderator ⇓		k	r	ρ		k	r	ρ
Use	Research	17	0.44	0.56	Administrative	10	0.28	0.37
Time together	Long	54	0.52	0.69	Short	11	0.15	0.20
Criterion	Objective	43	0.55	0.73	Subjective	22	0.29	0.39

ρ = Correlation corrected for reliability of both peer rating and outcome measure but not for restricted range.

Norton (1992) covered 56 validities and 11,000 people. The results were at first sight impressive: an uncorrected average validity of 0.48, rising to 0.58 when corrected for reliability of work performance measure. However, all the samples were present employees (and mostly military, but results for military and non-military did not differ). Norton also reported some powerful moderator variables (Table 5.5), which clearly imply peer rating will not be very useful in selection.

- ratings made for research only were far more accurate than ratings used to make decisions about people.
- ratings made after long acquaintance were far more accurate, whereas ratings made after short acquaintance correlated with work performance fairly poorly.

Norton's third moderator showed peer ratings predicted objective indices of work outcome better than subjective. Perhaps outcomes like sales figures or training grades are clearly visible to the rest of the group, which tends to make the high correlation trivial; peers may not be predicting the target's work performance, but may simply be reporting known facts.

Conway, Lombardo and Sanders (2001) reported a meta-analysis of nine studies comparing peer rating and objective measures of work performance (production, profit, absence of demerits). They found much lower validity than Norton, a correlation of only 0.28, barely increased to 0.29 by correcting for reliability of work performance measure. The difference may arise because Conway *et al.* only included correlations between peer rating and actual work outcomes, whereas Norton included correlations between peer rating and measures of skill, ability and personal characteristics. Conway *et al.* also found 14 studies comparing subordinates' rating with objective work performance measures, and found another fairly weak relationship. Zazanis, Zaccaro and Kilcullen (2001) reported that peer ratings predict success in Special Forces training in the US Army quite well, whereas ratings by army staff assessors do not predict success at all. Fleenor and Brutus (2001) note that 360-degree ratings are sometimes used for internal promotions; however, there seems to be no research on validity.

There are several theories why peer assessments can predict performance:

1. Less error. Traditional references rely on two or three opinions, where peer assessments may use a dozen or more. Multiple ratings have the advantage of ironing out idiosyncrasies: the rater who is racially biassed, or does not like people who wear bow ties will be submerged in the larger number of more sensible people.
2. Best vs. usual performance. When supervisors are present, people do their best. If they try less hard when supervisors are not there, their peers can observe this.
3. No place to hide. In military research, the group may be together, 24 hours a day, faced with all sorts of challenges – physical, mental, emotional – so they can get to know each other very well and may find it hard to keep anything hidden.

Peer rating and promotion

Peer rating seems promising for promotion decisions. Hunter and Hunter (1984) placed it at the top of their promotion 'league table'. There are however two problems. Table 5.5 shows that peer ratings collected for 'administrative' purposes (i.e. used to make decisions about people) have considerably lower validity than ratings collected for research only. Jawahar and Williams (1997) showed that administrative ratings are more lenient than ratings used only for research, which will restrict range and reduce validity. Second, peer rating is unpopular, especially if used to promote people rather than to 'develop' them (McEvoy & Buller, 1987). It is perhaps significant that so much research is done in a military setting, where people are more accustomed to doing whatever they are told without question. In some workforces, especially ones that are strongly unionized, peer rating might be rejected altogether.

Peer rating in selection

Is there any way of using peer rating in selection? One in five assessment centres include it (Spychalski *et al.*, 1997), although no data on its separate contribution to validity seem to exist. Even the longest ACs only last three days, which falls within the short duration of acquaintance in Norton's meta-analysis, where peer ratings achieve very poor validity. Employers will find it difficult to gain access to an A's former colleagues in another organization. Andler and Herbst (2002) suggested asking each A for names and phone numbers of two subordinates and two peers, then in turn asking these people for names of others who know A well. Andler and Herbst did not report any research showing whether their suggested techniques secure valid information.

Construct and incremental validity

There is not much research. Mount, Barrick and Strauss (1994) found that ratings by co-workers and customers have incremental validity on self-report by personality questionnaire.

Convergent / divergent validity

Peer ratings of a target's conscientiousness should agree with conscientiousness in a PQ completed by the target (convergent validity), but not with other ratings of the target (e.g. extraversion or agreeableness (divergent validity)). Early research (Becker, 1960) based on Cattell's 16PF did not find this, indicating poor convergent and divergent validity.

RESEARCH AGENDA

- Data on construct validity of peer ratings
- Data on incremental validity over other selection methods
- Data on convergent / divergent validity of peer ratings
- Third, hopefully definitive, meta-analysis of peer rating, distinguishing outcomes more clearly
- Whether peer ratings are used in promotion and whether they predict work performance

---

Key points

In Chapter 5 you have learned the following.

- References can be free-form or structured.
- References are rarely a very useful source of information, generally lacking reliability or validity.
- References may be improved by forced-choice format or keyword counting, but there is not yet sufficient research to be certain.
- American research shows references rarely contain any negative information.
- The traditional free-form reference is difficult to analyse quantitatively.
- Telephone references seem a grey area; it is unclear how widely they are used.
- The nature or purpose of the reference seems unclear.
- Laws in the USA and the UK seem to have placed employers in a difficult position, so that the future of the reference is in doubt.
- References may have the potential to communicate valuable information, if the right format can be identified. Some variations on the reference request may have promise.
- Peer ratings agree with work performance very well.
- Ratings by peers seem unlikely to be useful in selection, and to have limited practical value in promotion.

Key references

Baxter *et al.* (1981) document the problems of idiosyncrasy in reference writers.

Conway *et al.* (2001) report a meta-analysis of peer rating and work performance.

Grote *et al.* (2001) describe American research on the consistent favourability of references.

Little and Sipes (2000) describe the dilemma the law seems to have placed American employers in with references

McCarthy and Goffin (2001) describe research on the Relative Percentile Method which appears to get better results with references.

Mosel and Goheen (1958) described early US public sector on the validity of structured references.

Murphy and Cleveland (1995) review research on performance appraisal which has much in common with reference research.

Parry (1999) reviews recent legal development affecting references in the UK.

Taylor *et al.* (2004) describe a successful structured reference system.

CHAPTER 6

Tests of mental ability

'a ... man of paralysing stupidity ...'

Introduction

In Orwell's *Nineteen Eighty Four*, the main character Winston Smith has a neighbour, dismissively characterized as 'A fattish man of paralysing stupidity, a mass of imbecile enthusiasms ... At the ministry he was employed in some subordinate post for which intelligence was not required'. Orwell clearly thinks that some jobs need intelligent people (while other jobs do not). Tests of mental ability (MA) are widely used in personnel selection. They also have a multifaceted history of controversy and unpopularity going back to the 1960s.

- In 1969, Arthur Jensen published an article on *How Much Can We Boost IQ and Scholastic Achievement*, which stated the evidence on heritability of MA more forcefully than people in the USA were used to, or cared for. The original researches were then reread more carefully, and their defects noted.
- Jensen raised the issue of ethnicity differences in MA, notorious for its ability to 'generate more heat than light'.
- Jensen argued that remedial education, on which the American government was spending very large sums, was achieving little or nothing.
- The Civil Rights Act of 1964 led within a few years to many American employers abandoning MA testing because of adverse impact problems that have still not been resolved.

In the 1990s, controversy about MA tests was revived by Herrnstein and Murray's (1994) *The Bell Curve*, which covered much the same ground as Jensen a quarter of a century earlier – heritability, ethnic differences, remedial education – and which has been at least as widely publicized. *The Bell Curve* added one new controversial element: the existence of an 'under-class' of persons whose employment prospects are limited by low MA.

Overview of mental ability tests

General mental ability, aptitude and achievement

An *achievement test or job knowledge* test assesses how much someone knows about a particular body of knowledge (e.g. gasfitting or Microsoft EXCEL).

An *aptitude* test assesses how easy it would be for someone to acquire knowledge they do not presently possess (e.g. of computer programming). A test of *general mental ability* (GMA) or general intelligence seeks to assess how good the individual is at understanding and using information of all types.

Tests of GMA

GMA tests are the most controversial level of ability testing for a variety of reasons, some outlined at the beginning of the chapter. MA test questions vary in content – verbal, numerical, abstract. Questions vary in difficulty. Questions vary in universality. Few people in Britain, however bright or dull, know the distance from Denver to Dallas, whereas adding 5 to 6 should be possible for anyone whose culture uses numbers. Table 6.1 illustrates the test writer's dilemma: seeking to write a test of ability to use information in general but having to assess this ability through specific questions. Some tests deal with this problem by including many and varied problems, others by trying to find problems that depend as little as possible on learned information.

Because the questions in Table 6.1 vary so much, 'common sense' would expect ability to answer one to have little to do with ability to answer another. For example 'common sense' says knowing what a word means (question 1) depends on education and home background, whereas complex reasoning and mental arithmetic (question 7) require mental speed. The questions in

Table 6.1   Ten varied questions typical of mental ability tests.

1. What does the word 'impeach' mean?
          preserve   *accuse*   *propose*   *give a sermon*
2. What number comes next? 2 4 9 16 25
                    29   36   45   100
3. How far is it from Dallas to Denver in miles?
                    50   300   600   2,000
4. How much is 5 plus 6?
                    11   12   56   1
5. Big is to little as tall is to …
          short   *height*   *long*   *thin*
6. What is the rate of income tax for incomes over £40,000 a year?
                    25%   40%   75%   90%
7. How many players are there in a football team?
                    16   15   11   5   7
8. Ø is to Ø   as ⊕ is to …
                    ♦   ⊕   ∇   ∏   ⊕
9. Who wrote *The Pickwick Papers*?
10. Divide the largest number by the next to smallest number, then multiply the result by the next to largest number:
                    20   15   11   14   5   2

Table 6.1 are fictitious, but results with similar questions in real tests show fairly high positive correlations. This reflects what Spearman discovered 100 years ago, and from which he developed the theory of general intelligence, or *g*: people who are good at one intellectual task tend to be good at others. Spearman's model is convenient and very simple, which makes it attractive to HR who only need assess one thing. More elaborated accounts of MA are discussed in the section on aptitude batteries.

Practice effects

Hausknecht *et al.* (2007) meta-analysed a large number of studies where people have done the same test twice, or even three times, and found quite large practice gains ($d = 0.24$ for the first retest, and 0.51 for the second). Repeated testing with the same test, or an alternate form, gives people a considerable advantage and could distort results where some As have done the test before and some have not. Organizations, such as the US Army, that have their own tests can prohibit retesting, but most employers cannot prevent it. Indeed, professional practice guidelines in the USA and the UK say that people should be offered a retest, apparently on the assumption that the first tests may not have 'done justice' to people through unfamiliarity, test anxiety, and so on. Lievens, Reeve and Heggestad (2007) analysed large-scale MA testing for entry to medical school in Belgium, and suggested that retests predict performance poorly and that retest gain is largely a memory effect. This implies that retests should be discouraged. Perhaps an ideal arrangement, from a purely psychometric perspective, would be a single carefully arranged and thorough assessment, at say age 18 or 21, with results made available to all employers. Something like this happens in education in the USA, with Scholastic Assessment Test, and used to be done for secondary school admission in Britain, the infamous 11+ exam, which was in part a GMA test. Folk memories of 11+ might prevent the idea being accepted today.

Bias in testing

Problems arise when one identifiable section of the people tested does worse than another, and it is claimed that items were selected to favour one group. For example, question 7 in Table 6.1 might be easier for men, assuming women have less interest in football. Most tests are checked for *differential item functioning* based on gender and ethnicity.

Computerized testing

Computerized forms of existing paper-and-pencil tests usually give similar results. Computerized testing can be tailored to the applicant's (A's) performance. If A does well, the questions get harder; but if A does poorly, the questions get easier, until A reaches his/her own limit. Computerized testing can make tests more secure by item banking or item generation. In item *banking*, a subset of items is randomly selected for each A from a much larger pool of items of known difficulty. In item *generation*, the test programme creates items at the time of testing, which is easily done for some types of material, e.g. select a pair of two-digit numbers at random, for A to multiply. Banking and generation make it difficult to construct 'cribs' to the test. Computer tests can also give much more control over timing than the overall time limit of the paper-and-pencil test. Sophisticated computerized tests can simulate 'real time' events.

Internet testing

Computerized tests can be completed over the Internet and many electronic recruiting systems – discussed in Chapter 1 – include online assessment of ability. Testing people over the Internet poses a number of problems. Is the person doing the test really John Smith or someone else? How can HR stop people applying several times under different names and so giving themselves unfair practice on the test? How can they prevent people using calculators or reference books? How can they stop people copying the test and producing scoring keys? How can they prevent unauthorized use of the test by unqualified users? Tippins *et al.* (2006) note that unproctored (unsupervised) Internet testing seems to be widely used. A common approach is using unsupervised Internet testing as a screening test, then retesting shortlisted As under supervision. It is important to remember that Internet tests, just like traditional paper-and-pencil tests, should (a) be reliable, (b) be valid, (c) have useful normative data, and (d) – ideally – not create adverse impact.

Biological testing

Mental ability can be estimated from reaction time, or speed of response of the brain or nervous system. These techniques may avoid item bias problems, but are not yet sufficiently well developed to be used in selection.

RESEARCH AGENDA

• Frequency of impersonation and other cheating in internet testing

---

Interpreting test scores

Ability tests produce raw scores, which mean very little in themselves. The raw score must be interpreted by comparing it with *normative data* (e.g. scores for 1,000 apprentices), which tells the tester whether the score is above average or below, and how far above or below average. Several systems are used to interpret raw scores.

1. *Mental age and intelligence quotient (IQ)* were used for early tests; a person with a mental age of five does as well on the test as the average five-year-old. IQ was originally calculated by dividing mental age by actual (chronological) age and multiplying by 100.
2. *Percentiles* indicate what percentage of the norm group scores lower than the candidate. Percentiles are easy for the layperson to understand.

Box 6.1   Percentiles

For a sample of 466 British health service managers, a raw score of 7 on the Graduate Managerial Assessment – Numerical translates to a percentile of 30, meaning that someone who scores 7 gets a better score than 30% of health service managers.

---

3. *Standard scores* are based on standard deviations and the normal distribution. In Figure 6.1, candidate A's raw score is 1.6 SDs above average, while candidate B's is 0.4 SDs below average. The simplest standard score system is the z score in which A's z score is +1.6 and B's is –0.4. All other standard score systems are variations on z scores, designed to be easier to use by eliminating decimals and signs. Standard scores can be misleading if the distribution of scores is not normal.

Box 6.2   z Scores

Raw score is converted to z score using the formula $z = $ (raw score – sample mean) / sample SD. On the AH4 test candidate Smith's raw score is 98, while the normative sample's mean and SD are 75.23 and 14.58. Calculating z gives a value of +1.6, which shows that Smith scores 1.6 SDs above the norm group mean. Jones's raw score is 66, which gives a z of –0.40 which means Jones scores 0.4 SDs below the norm group mean.

Norms

The normative sample should ideally be large, relevant and recent. Comparing As with 2,000 people who have applied for the same job within the last three years is clearly better than comparing them with 50 people doing a roughly similar job in Czechoslovakia in the 1930s. Normative data, even for long-established and widely used tests, tend to be far from ideal. Most normative data are occupational – for example, bank managers or mechanics – but a few tests have norms based on a representative sample of the general population.

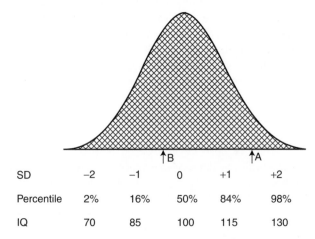

SD	−2	−1	0	+1	+2
Percentile	2%	16%	50%	84%	98%
IQ		70	85	100	115	130

Figure 6.1   Distribution of mental ability scores, showing mean, standard deviations, percentiles, and IQs.

The validity of mental ability tests

Early validation research was described in a narrative review by Super and Crites (1962). Ghiselli (1966, 1973) reported the first meta-analysis of GMA and work performance. His distributions of validity had generally rather low averages – around 0.30 (Figure 2.2 on page 31). Hunter and Hunter (1984) re-analysed Ghiselli's data, correcting for unreliability and range restriction, as described in Chapter 2. They concluded that GMA achieved corrected, or operational, validities higher than 0.40 for work performance (Table 6.2).

General aptitude test battery (GATB)

The next major meta-analysis of MA data used the very large GATB database. GATB is an aptitude battery used by the US Employment Service since 1947, and which had accumulated 515 validation researches by the early 1980s. GATB measures 10 abilities (Table 6.3). The GATB database includes mostly 'ordinary' jobs rather than higher-level ones. Hunter and Hunter (1984) showed that an uncorrected average validity of 0.25 for GMA rose to 0.47 when corrected for unreliability and range restriction, confirming their re-analysis of Ghiselli's data. (But recall that Chapter 2 described Hartigan and Wigdor's (1989) re-analysis of the GATB database, which made different assumptions to Hunter, and reached quite different conclusions, in Table 2.6, on page 50.) VGA also shows that validity of ability tests does not vary as much as Ghiselli thought his distributions showed. Schmidt and Hunter (2004) argued that validity of ability tests does not 'really' vary at all. The apparent variation is noise or error produced by the known limitations of validation research (Chapter 2).

Table 6.2 Correlation between general mental ability and work performance, for nine general types of work.

	N	r	ρ
Manager	10K+	0.29	0.53
Salesperson	1–5K	0.34	0.61
Clerk	10K+	0.30	0.54
Protective (police and fire)	1–5K	0.23	0.42
Skilled trades and crafts	10K+	0.25	0.46
Vehicle operator	1–5K	0.15	0.28
Service (hotel and catering)	1–5K	0.26	0.48
Sales assistants	1–5K	–0.06	0.27
Unskilled and semi-skilled	10K+	0.20	0.37

r = uncorrected average, from Ghiselli (1973). ρ = operational validity, corrected for restricted range and reliability of work performance measure, from Hunter & Hunter (1984). Ghiselli gives no information on number of validities in the meta-analysis, nor of exact pooled sample size. It is not clear how a negative correlation for sales assistants 'corrects' to a positive correlation.

Table 6.3 General Aptitude Test Battery, which measures nine abilities, using eight paper-and-pencil and four-apparatus tests.

	Ability	Test(s)
G	General	Vocabulary, 3-D Space, arithmetic reasoning
V	Verbal	Vocabulary
N	Numerical	Computation, arithmetic reasoning
S	Spatial	3-D space
P	Form perception	Tool matching, form matching
Q	Clerical perception	Name comparison
K	Motor co-ordination	Mark making
F	Finger dexterity	Assemble, disassemble
M	Manual dexterity	Place, turn

Validity for different types of work

Hunter and Hunter's re-analysis of Ghiselli's data showed operational validity higher than 0.40 for most types of work, except semi-skilled and unskilled workers, vehicle operation and sales assistants (Table 6.2). Table 6.4 summarizes 10 subsequent meta-analyses for specific types of work. For most, operational validity is around 0.40 to 0.60, which tends to confirm Schmidt and Hunter's (2004) argument that GMA correlates well with performance in all types of work. There are, however, some exceptions.

- Funke *et al.* (1987) found GMA tests one of the poorest predictors of achievement in science and technology, lagging behind creativity tests and biographical measures.

Table 6.4   Summary of 10 meta-analyses of general mental ability and work performance, for 12 types of work.

Type of work	k	N	r	ρ	Source
Science and technology	11	949	0.15	0.16	Funke *et al.* (1987)
Pilots	26	15,403	0.16	nr	Martinussen (1996)
Sales (rated)	22	1,231	0.23	0.40	Vinchur *et al.* (1998)
Sales (objective)	12	1,310	0.02	0.04	Vinchur *et al.* (1998)
First-line supervisor	75	5,143	nr	0.64	Schmidt *et al.* (1979)
Clerical	194	17,539	0.24	0.52	Pearlman *et al.* (1980)
Computing / accounts	58	5,433	nr	0.49	Schmidt *et al.* (1979)
Shorthand / typing / filing	65	3,986	nr	0.61	Schmidt *et al.* (1979)
Police officers	7	828	0.12	0.25[b]	Hirsh *et al.* (1986)
Firefighters	24	2,791	0.19	0.42	Barrett *et al.* (1999)
Skilled crafts (utility)	149	12,504	0.25	0.38[a]	Levine *et al.* (1996)
Skilled crafts (oil refinery)	37	3,219	nr	0.32	Callender & Osburn (1981)
Soldiers (non-commissioned/enlisted)	9	4,039	0.47	0.65	McHenry *et al.* (1990)[c]

[a]Calculated from true validity using test reliability of 0.80.
[b]Calculated from true validity using test reliability of 0.88.
[c]General soldiering proficiency.
nr = not reported; ρ = operational validity.

- Hirsh, Northrop and Schmidt (1986) found low correlations with performance in police work.
- Vinchur *et al.* (1998) found that GMA correlates with rated sales ability, but not with actual sales figures.
- Martinussen (1996) found GMA tests fairly poor predictors of performance as a pilot.

The poor results for science and technology, and pilots could be a 'pre-screening' effect, if earlier stages in selection for these types of work had excluded low GMA scorers. Correcting for restriction of range allows for people who applied for the job but were not successful, but not necessarily for people who were never in a position to apply at all. The poor results for sales and police may indicate that supervisor rating is a poor criterion, a point developed in the section in different outcomes, and in Chapter 12. There are some gaps in the coverage of types of work: unskilled and casual work, teaching (as opposed to teacher training), agriculture, mining, and railways. There is not a great deal of research on professional and technical work.

Job knowledge tests. Dye, Reck and McDaniel (1993) reported a VGA for job knowledge tests, which shows an overall corrected validity of 0.45, rising to 0.62, where the test content is closely related to the job.

Validity in different countries

People sometimes ask if it is safe to extrapolate from American research to other countries, with different ideas about work and selection. Salgado *et al.* (2003) reported a VGA across the European Community, which finds an operational validity for job performance of 0.62, a little higher than in the USA. Coverage of individual European countries was, however, uneven. The UK, France, The Netherlands, Germany and Spain contributed a lot of data; Belgium, Ireland, Portugal and Scandinavia contributed a handful of studies, while Austria, Italy, Greece and Luxembourg contributed none. Salgado and Anderson (2003) compared the UK, France, The Netherlands plus Belgium, Germany and Spain and find no difference in MA test validity. Salgado *et al.* (2003) then analysed the European data by 10 types of work and found validity higher for managerial, engineering and sales jobs, but very low for police work (confirming Hirsh *et al.*'s earlier American analysis). There are, as yet, few data on GMA and work performance from remoter, possibly more culturally different, parts of the world. On a more local scale, the EC data need to be updated to include the 'new accession' EC members, mostly from the former communist block.

Validity for different outcomes

Most research uses supervisor rating to define success at work. Supervisor ratings correlate poorly with measures of actual output where these exist (Bommer *et al.*, 1995). It is fairly easy to make a plausible case that supervisor rating might correlate with GMA through paths other than good work. For example, one could argue that brighter people will be less trouble to supervise, or be more interesting and agreeable company, or be better at seeming to do good work without actually doing so. Vinchur *et al.*'s meta analysis showed that GMA correlates with supervisor rating but not with sales figures, which is consistent with the hypothesis that some salespersons are good at creating a favourable impression on their supervisor, but not so good at actual selling. Hirsh *et al.* suggested that the supervisor rating criterion does not work well for police work because supervisors rarely see officers 'in action'. This makes it important to find, or do, research showing how well GMA predicts other aspects of work performance.

Work samples

Schmitt *et al.*'s (1984) review located three researches using work samples, in which the worker performs key tasks and is observed by an expert. GMA test validity was as high as for supervisor rating.

Output

There was an important gap in Schmitt *et al.*'s review: there were not enough studies correlating mental output with countable output to calculate a correlation. Nathan and Alexander's (1988) meta-analysis of clerical work located 22 validities for production quantity, which gave an overall validity only slightly lower than for supervisor rating.

Work quality

Nathan and Alexander's clerical work meta-analysis found only six studies of production quality, which achieved zero validity.

Training success

Hunter (1986) analysed an enormous set of US military data, for nearly half a million persons, and found a high corrected correlation between GMA and training performance. Note, however, that training success in the USA is often defined by scores in timed multiple-choice exams, which are very similar in form to MA tests, so problems of shared method variance arise.

Leadership

Recently, research has started examining links between GMA and less task-oriented aspects of work performance. Judge, Colbert and Ilies (2004) reported a meta-analysis of GMA and leadership in 151 samples with a total N of 40K. Raw correlation was 0.17, rising to 0.27, when corrected for unreliability and range restriction. Just over half the samples were students, the rest business and military but results were much the same for both. In 14 studies where leadership was defined by objective effectiveness rather than perceived effectiveness, the link was higher: a corrected correlation of 0.33. Judge *et al.* remarked that the link between GMA and leadership is weaker than the link with personality, and perhaps weaker than many expect.

Counterproductive behaviour and organizational citizenship

One tends to suppose that 'bad behaviour' at work – breaking the rules or being unco-operative – will have more to do with personality than MA. However, Dilchert *et al.* (2007) reported a follow-up of 1799 police officers, linking MA tested as part of the selection process, to later records of counterproductive behaviour such as use of excessive force, racial abuse or 'at-fault' car accidents. They found a definite link: a raw correlation of –0.19, rising to an operational validity of –0.33. They suggested that persons of lower MA are less able to foresee the consequences of their behaviour. The US Army's Project A – which found a strong link between MA and work performance (Table 6.3) – also looked at three motivational or 'will-do' aspects of work: effort and leadership, personal discipline, and physical fitness and military bearing. They found positive, but lower, correlations with MA, ranging from

0.16 to 0.31 corrected (McHenry *et al.*, 1990). Alonso (2001) found a modest correlation with organizational citizenship (0.24). Marcus (2008) found a low correlation (0.19) between lower GMA and lateness.

Organizational performance

Gottfredson (1997) and Schmidt (2002) argued that organizations that employ large numbers of low GMA people will suffer 'dramatic declines in quantity and quality of work performed', placing US international competitiveness in danger. Numerous studies show that people with lower GMA get poorer supervisor ratings or poorer training grades, which implies that organizations that employ many such people may tend to perform poorly. However, there is no empirical demonstration of this at the organizational level. Gottfredson cited the Washington DC police, described in the press as having very lax selection standards and as being very inefficient. Press reports are a useful starting point, but detailed study of the functioning of organizations that employ large numbers of less able people is needed. Within a given sector, organizations with lower levels of GMA in their workforce should, on Schmidt and Hunter's hypothesis, prove less successful. Commercial organizations may be expected to be less profitable, and more likely to go out of business. Non-commercial organizations may make more mistakes, attract more complaints or work very slowly. The hypothesis may be easier to confirm in the commercial sector.

Research might also usefully analyse work histories of able and less able persons in similar jobs. If less-able employees on average get poorer ratings from supervisors, they will presumably be less likely to be promoted, may tend to become dissatisfied, and to leave, willingly or unwillingly. Research is also needed on the way less able employees do their work, perhaps making more mistakes, perhaps slower to complete a given task, and so on. Hunter and Schmidt (1996) speculated that careers of low-ability workers will depend on their level of organizational citizenship. Less able workers who are, however, good citizens will be tolerated by supervisors because they are obviously trying hard, and may be moved to easier work. The less able worker who is also a poor citizen is – they suggest – more likely to be terminated. Career success has been researched for managers, defining success by salary or promotion achieved by middle age. Eight studies find a 'moderate' correlation of 0.27 between GMA and salary (e.g., Ng *et al.*, 2005).

Job complexity

Meta-analysis allows researchers to check whether validity is 'moderated' by other factors, such as management style. Validity of GMA tests does not seem to be moderated by anything except job complexity as rated by the US Dictionary of Occupational Titles (Hunter & Hunter, 1984). Figure 6.2 shows that the correlation between GMA and work performance is high in very complex jobs, like management, but lower in less complex jobs, like packing and

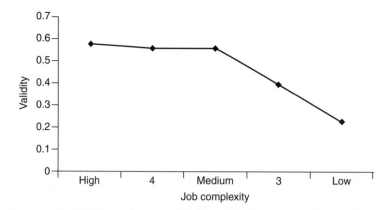

Figure 6.2   Corrected validity of GATB General + Verbal + Numerical composite with work performance, for five levels of job complexity.

handling. Salgado *et al.*'s (2003) European data also found GMA more strongly linked to performance in highly complex work.

Incremental validity

GMA tests, by and large, predict work performance fairly well. What other assessments are worth using alongside them? That will give a better prediction still? Schmidt & Hunter (1998) reviewed data on validity of other predictors and their correlation with MA, and concluded that personality tests, work samples and structured interviews will offer incremental validity on MA tests, whereas assessment centres or biodata will not. Note however that Schmidt and Hunter were not reviewing research that shows that, for example, personality tests do offer incremental validity, but research that implies they should.

RESEARCH AGENDA

More research is needed on:
- GMA and performance in unskilled and casual jobs
- GMA and work performance outside North America and Western Europe
- GMA and other aspects of work performance, including output and work quality
- GMA and non-task aspects of work performance, including counterproductive behaviour, organizational citizenship
- Mediation of the link between GMA and supervisor rating by irrelevant factors such as liking or ability to present oneself well
- GMA and performance link, at the organizational level
- Work careers of low MA persons.

---

g or aptitude battery?

As far back as 1928, Hull had argued that profiles of specific abilities will predict work performance better than tests of GMA, or *g*, on the assumption that each job requires a different profile of abilities; for example, accountants need to be numerate or architects need good spatial ability. The US military has used a succession of aptitude batteries, the latest being Armed Services Vocational Aptitude Battery (ASVAB). They calculate regression equations (Box 3.2, page 67) for different jobs, in which each aptitude score is given a different weight according to how well it predicts performance. However, during the 1980s, some American psychologists rediscovered *g* and started asking themselves whether the extra time needed to administer the whole of GATB or ASVAB adds much to their predictions (given that the various abilities assessed tend to be highly correlated).

Ree and Earles (1991) analysed ASVAB data for nearly 80,000 USAF personnel doing 82 different jobs and concluded that, while ASVAB's 10 tests include

> some seemingly specific measures of automotive knowledge, shop information, word knowledge, reading, mathematics, mechanical principles, electronic and scientific facts, as well as clerical speed … its predictive power was derived from psychometric *g*. The training courses prepared students for seemingly different job performance, such as handling police dogs, clerical filing, jet engine repair, administering injections, and fire fighting, yet a universal set of weights across all jobs was as good as a unique set of weights for each job.

Brown, Le and Schmidt (2006) replicated this finding for ASVAB and training grades. Schmidt-Atzert and Deter (1993) reported similar data for the German chemical industry. Interestingly, British military research in World War Two had earlier made the same discovery: 'We would naturally have expected the verbal and educational tests to show relatively low validities in mechanical and spatial occupations, and the mechanical spatial tests to be of value only among mechanics. But such differentiation was conspicuously small' (Vernon & Parry, 1949). Hunter (1986) has shown that using the 'wrong' equation (e.g. selecting mechanics using the electricians' equation) gives just as good results as using the right equation.

Critics argue that specific abilities are required for some jobs. Trainee military pilots with poor visuo-spatial ability tend to fail pilot training, regardless of *g* (Gordon & Leighty, 1988). Other critics argue that very broad analyses covering the entire range of MA and of work are not detailed enough to detect true differential profile validities. Baehr and Orban (1989) pointed out that Hunter's analysis lumps all managers together. They cite data showing that technical specialists and general managers, while equal in *g*, differ markedly in specific abilities. Recently, Mount, Oh and Burns (2008) have shown that perceptual speed has incremental validity on GMA in warehouse workers.

The perceptual speed test is a speed test, not a power test. The task is very simple – comparing two names – but must be performed quickly and accurately.

Mental ability and the success of teams

Selection persists in assessing the individual's character, and trying to relate it to the individual's success at work. Yet a lot of work is done by teams of people. So should not selection consider the team as a whole? Does a successful team consist of people who are all able, or will a mixture of ability be sufficient? or even better? Mixed ability teams are easier to recruit. Can one person of low ability hold everyone back? Will one very able person be able to get the group moving forwards, or will he/she be submerged and frustrated? Does the size of the team make a difference? Does the type of the work make a difference? Bell (2007) reports a meta-analysis summarizing eight studies of work team MA and team performance, which finds a fairly weak link between average ability and performance (0.26 corrected). Little evidence of more complex effects emerged; neither variability nor presence of extremes made much difference. However, seven of the eight researches studied 'physical' teams such as soldiers or assembly workers; a stronger link ($r = 0.35$, uncorrected) was found in the solitary study of 'intellectual' teams (HR staff).

RESEARCH AGENDA

- Link between average and distribution of GMA and team performance, in a wider range of work

---

Why mental ability tests predict productivity

Mental ability testing has never pretended to much in the way of systematic theory. Binet's first test was written to identify slow learners in French schools, and derived its items from the convenient fact that older children can solve problems younger ones cannot. A very large body of past research has shown there is a definite link between GMA and work performance, whereas a smaller body of current research is beginning to throw some light on why.

Occupational differences in mental ability level

Gottfredson (1997) reviewed the Wonderlic database, which gives averages for 72 varied occupations. The highest-scoring occupations are lawyer, research analyst, editor and advertising manager; the most average are cashier, clerical worker, sales assistant and meter reader; the lowest scoring are packer, material handler, caretaker (janitor) and warehouse worker. However, these data merely show that people in different jobs have different average ability levels and do not prove they need particular levels of GMA to perform successfully.

Threshold hypothesis

A widely held 'common sense' view claims that, above a certain minimum level, most people are capable of most jobs. All that ability tests can accomplish is to screen out the unfortunate minority of incompetents. This view implies a threshold or step in the relation between test scores and work performance. Mls (1935) found a clear break in truck driving proficiency at approximately IQ 80. Any Czech soldier with an IQ over 80 was equally competent to drive a truck, while all those whose IQ fell below 80 were equally unfit to be trusted with an army vehicle.

Linearity hypothesis

Linearity means work performance improves as test score increases, throughout the entire range of test scores, with no step or threshold (Figure 6.3). Several large analyses (e.g. Coward & Sackett 1990), have shown test × performance relationships are generally linear, which implies that Mls's results with the Czech army were atypical. The threshold vs. linearity issue has important fair employment implications. Linearity implies As should be placed in a strict rank order on the test, and selected in that order, because the higher the test score, the better their job performance. If the threshold hypothesis is true, all As in a broad band of scores will be equally suitable. The employer can then select to ensure a suitably diverse workforce without reducing overall efficiency.

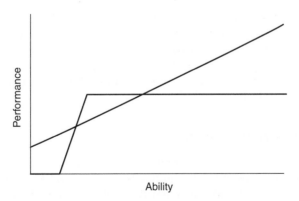

Figure 6.3 Linear vs. threshold models of the relationship between mental ability and work performance.

Test score	Appraisal rating				
	Very poor	Poor	Average	Good	Very good
Very good	7	15	20	37	21
Good	6	20	32	31	11
Average	11	18	44	20	7
Poor	13	36	33	15	3
Very poor	26	31	23	18	2

Figure 6.4   Expectancy table, showing relationship between test score, and work performance.

Setting cut-off scores

Selectors are often asked: Is this applicant appointable? In other words, what is the minimum level of MA necessary to function in this job? The commonest approach to setting cut-offs is distribution-based: do not appoint anyone who falls in the bottom one-third of existing post-holders, or more than one SD below the mean. Strictly speaking, the idea of a fixed cut-off is simplistic. The relationship between test score and performance is linear and probabilistic; the lower the score, the poorer the person's performance is likely to be. This implies any cut-off must be arbitrary. Employers with sufficiently good records may be able to construct an *expectancy table* (Figure 6.4) showing the level of work performance expected for people with different test score ranges. The employer decides the level of performance required and sets the appropriate cut-off.

Necessary but not sufficient

Table 6.5 shows few accountants had IQs more than 15 points below the accountant average, whereas quite a few lumberjacks had IQs well over their average of 85. Assuming the latter had not always wanted to be lumberjacks, the data imply they could not or did not use their high GMA to find more prestigious work. Perhaps they lacked some other important quality: energy,

Table 6.5   Average scores of accountants and lumberjacks conscripted into US Army during World War Two, and 10th and 90th percentiles.

	10th percentile	Median	90th percentile
Accountants	114	129	143
Lumberjacks	60	85	116

social skill, good adjustment, or luck. Chapter 7 shows that personality tests have incremental validity over GMA, which confirms Herrnstein's (1973) hypothesis that GMA alone is not always sufficient for success.

Do applicants need both motivation and ability?

It is plausibly argued that people need both ability and motivation to succeed in work; lazy geniuses achieve little, while energetic but dim people are just a nuisance. Sackett, Gruys and Ellingson (1998) tested this with four separate sets of data, covering 22 different jobs, and found no evidence for it; ability and motivation do not interact. Hunter, Vasilopoulos and Marton (2008) however argued that tenure – time in the job – may moderate the link. They found a multiplicative interaction between conscientiousness and GMA in law enforcement personnel who has been in the job for more than four years.

Class and education

Sociologists argue that any apparent link between occupation and GMA is created by the class system. Children from better-off homes get better education, so do better on GMA tests, which are in any case heavily biased towards the middle classes; better-off children go on to get better-paid jobs. On this argument, there is no true link between GMA and work performance; psychological tests are merely class-laden rationing mechanisms. The social class argument is countered to some extent by data from the (US) National Longitudinal Study of Youth (Wilk & Sackett, 1996). ASVAB score in 1980 predicted whether people moved up or down the occupational ladder between 1982 and 1987. Higher scorers tended to move up into work of greater complexity, while lower scorers tended to move down into work of less complexity. This implies that lower scorers have more difficulty coping with complex work, so gravitate to work more within their intellectual grasp – which would not happen if testing is just an arbitrary class-based way of keeping some people out of better jobs. Murray (1998) compared siblings, who share the same social background, but can vary a lot in GMA. The brighter sib tends to enter a more prestigious occupation, have a higher income, and to be employed more regularly.

Box 6.3   Path analysis

Path analysis is essentially a correlational analysis in which the researcher is prepared to make some assumptions about direction of cause. To take an obvious example, height might affect success as a police officer, but it is very hard to think of any way is which being successful as a police officer would make someone taller. Path analysis is generally calculated by structural equation modelling.

Mental ability, job knowledge and work performance

Some research has used path analysis (Box 6.3) to explore why GMA tests predict work performance. Hunter (1983) found that GMA did not correlate directly with supervisor ratings, but did correlate with job knowledge and work sample performance, which in turn correlated with supervisor ratings. Figure 6.5 shows that more able people are better workers primarily because they learn more quickly what the job is about. In high-level work, this may mean learning scientific method, scientific techniques and a large body of knowledge. In low-level work it may mean only learning where to find the broom and where to put the rubbish when you have swept it up. In Hunter's model, there is no direct path from GMA to work performance. Ree, Carretta and Teachout (1995) presented a path analysis for GMA, job knowledge and actual job performance. In the US Air Force, trainee pilots' *g* leads to job knowledge, in the shape of better grades in, for example navigation. Job knowledge in turn leads – less strongly – to better ratings of their flying ability in check flights.

An unemployable minority?

Over 70 years ago, Cattell (1937) made some pessimistic comments about employment prospects for people with limited MA in a complex industrial society: 'the person of limited intelligence is not so cheap an employee as he at first appears. His accident proneness is high and he cannot adapt himself to changes in method'. Gottfredson (1997) has raised the same issue, arguing

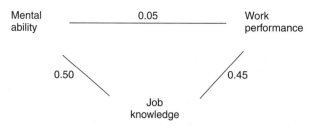

Figure 6.5   Schematic path diagram showing the paths from mental ability to work performance.

that the American armed services have three times employed low GMA recruits, once when short of recruits during World War Two, once as an idealistic experiment during the 1960s, and then by mistake in the 1970s when they miscalculated their norms. Gottfredson says 'these men were very difficult and costly to train, could not learn certain specialities, and performed at a lower average level once on a job'. Hunter and Schmidt (1996) suggested that the less able can only get minimum-wage jobs, which do not pay enough to raise a family so are only suitable as short-term jobs for young people. What is the threshold of unemployability? Cattell estimated it at IQ 85, while Gottfredson mentioned a figure of IQ 80. Hunter and Schmidt suggested that America should consider a two-tier economy in ability and fair employment law. The first tier is international, where the country must be competitive, so employers must be free to select the most able. The second tier is the domestic economy, which is not subject to foreign competition, and where reduced efficiency caused by employing the less able will cause less harm. What sectors fall into this second tier? Hunter and Schmidt mention only catering, insurance and hairdressing.

A problem with ability testing

In the USA, coaching for tests is very widespread and is provided on a commercial basis. Hausknecht et al.'s (2007) meta-analysis shows that coaching raises scores considerably ($d = 0.64$), sufficient to affect selection decisions if some As have had coaching and some have not. Barrett (1997) argued that American employers should not use a test more than once; if they do, 'the only applicants who will not receive a near perfect score would be those who couldn't afford the $1,000 or more often charged for a 'test-preparation seminar'. Barrett was suggesting that some professionals in the USA will misuse their access to test material to sell test takers an unfair advantage. Barrett also pointed out that a closed test – one used only by that employer and not accessible to outsiders – can still be compromised. The first set of people to take the test conspire to reconstruct it, each person memorizing seven items. They then give, or sell, their reconstruction to subsequent intakes.

RESEARCH AGENDA

- Ascertain frequency of fraud in use of MA tests

Law, fairness and minorities

GMA tests create adverse impact on some sections of the American population. Roth et al. (2001b) report a meta-analysis, which finds quite large differences between white and Afro-Americans ($d = 1.10$), and between white and

Hispanic ($d = 0.72$). By contrast, Americans of Chinese or Japanese ancestry score better on ability tests than white Americans (Vernon, 1982). Avolio and Waldman (1994) analysed GATB scores for 30,000 persons and reported very small age and gender differences. Hough, Oswald and Ployhart (2001) provided a detailed review of group differences in ability test scores. Ryan (2001) reviewed research on attitudes to tests – for example, anxiety, motivation or belief in ability to cope – and concludes there do not seem to be large differences between majority and minority Americans in these, so they do not seem to likely account for the difference. Differences between groups create major problems when using tests in selection and many systems of using test scores have been proposed.

Top down means selecting the highest scoring As. However, in the USA, strict application of top down will greatly reduce the number of persons from some ethnic minorities selected, and sometimes virtually exclude them altogether. This outcome is likely to prove politically unacceptable, especially in the public sector.

Top-down quota

The top-down quota is a possible compromise. The employer decides what proportion of persons appointed shall come from ethnic minorities, then selects the best minority As, even though their test scores may be lower than majority persons not appointed. This is effectively a formal quota for minorities, but one which selects the most able minority As.

Separate norms

In the 1980s, GATB used separate norms for white and African-Americans. A raw score of 300 translated into a percentile of 45 for white Americans, compared with a percentile of 83 for African Americans. Separate norms have the advantage of avoiding setting a formal quota, which often proves a focus of discontent. Both top-down quota and separate norms represent an acceptable compromise between maximizing productivity and achieving a diverse workforce. However, both became unpopular in the USA because of allegations of reverse discrimination and both were forbidden by the Civil Rights Act 1991. Neither system is formally prohibited in Britain, but both could be viewed as direct discrimination, so are considered unsafe.

Score banding

Fixed bands

Score banding means raw scores between, for example, 25 and 30, are regarded as equivalent. The principle will be most familiar to American readers in the shape of college grades and to British readers in the shape of degree classes. Banding makes scores easier to describe, at the expense of losing some information. The main problem with score bands will also be familiar to American and British readers. The difference between grade B and grade A, or a lower second and an upper second is one mark, which is bad luck for those who are short of that one mark.

Box 6.4   Standard error of difference (s.e.d.)

s.e.d. is related to standard error of measurement (Box 2.5, page 26). However, the difference between two scores contains two sources of error – the unreliability of both scores), so s.e.d. is greater.

Traditional bands are arbitrary, whereas current banding systems are based on error of difference (Box 6.4). The band is usually defined as two s.e.ds extending down from the highest scorer. The reasoning is that scores that do not differ by more than two s.e.ds can be regarded as equivalent. In Figure 6.6, the highest scorer scores 55, and two s.e.ds covers 11 raw score points, so the band starts at 55 and extends down to include 45. Within this band, all As are regarded as equal. If everyone within the band is defined as having an equal score, the employer can then give preference to minority persons, without engaging in reverse discrimination. This is called *diversity-based referral*. A number of criticisms of banding have been made (Schmidt & Hunter (1995):

Score	Majority As	Minority As	
57			
56			
55	1		↑
54	1		
53	4		
52	4		
51	6	1	
50	7		Score band
49	10	1	
48	12	2	
47	14	1	
46	16	2	
45	19	2	↓
44	25	5	
43	25	7	
42	27	10	
41	30	11	
40	25	10	

Figure 6.6 Illustration of a score band. The first column represents scores on a selection test. The second column represents number of majority As achieving that score. The third column represents number of minority As achieving that score.

- Banding fails to distinguish individual scores and average scores. It's true that two As scoring 55 and 54 are interchangeable in the sense that if they do the test again in a week's time, they might score 52 and 56. However, it is also true that research with large enough numbers will show that people who score 55 perform better than people who score 54. This follows necessarily from the fact that test and work performance are linearly related.
- The two s.e.d. criterion creates a fairly broad band, amounting to nearly one SD in test scores in the example they present. The broader the band, the less selective selection becomes.
- If the test is not very reliable, the size of the band can extend to cover most of the range of scores.
- Banding will not look very fair to an unsuccessful A who scores one point outside the band, with a score of 44, and who does not differ significantly from most of those appointed, using exactly the same reasoning and calculation as are used to define the band.

Sliding bands

This takes the error of measurement argument one stage further, by moving the band once the top scoring As have been appointed. In Figure 6.6, the top-scoring A, who scores 55, is selected, whereupon the band slides so that its upper limit is now 54 and its lower limit 44. The band now includes 30 new As scoring 44, who were previously one point outside it. Five of these are minority As who can benefit from diversity based referral. The guiding principle is that the employer should not exclude As who do not differ reliably from those who are appointed. Score bands tend to be fairly broad to start with; sliding makes them even broader, and selection even less selective.

Bands, fixed or sliding, have been criticized as a 'fudge', complicated and ingenious, but a fudge none the less. They are one way to try to achieve two apparently not very compatible goals: appointing the best, while also creating a suitably diverse workforce. However, the legal position is uncertain (Henle 2004). Score banding is accepted by American courts, but giving preference to minority persons within bands may not be legal.

Ways of reducing adverse impact

The 'holy grail' of American selection psychologists is an assessment of GMA that does not cause adverse impact. Modifications to conventional tests have been tried in the hope of achieving this.

- Computer rather than paper administration reduces adverse impact (Carey, 1994).
- Video presentation creates less AI than paper form (Chan & Schmitt, 1997).
- Questions 1 to 8 in Table 5.1 use the usual multiple choice format, but question 9 requires As to *construct* their own answer, by writing 'Charles

Dickens'. Research by Edwards & Arthur (2007) found that constructed response format reduces AI for African Americans.

Non-entrenched items do not require As to know anything such as vocabulary or general knowledge, but use entirely 'new' material. The Siena Reasoning Test (SRT) contains items along the lines of 'A SPON is heavier than a PLIN; a PLIN is heavier than a CRUN. Is a SPON heavier than a CRUN?' The SRT creates less AI and correlates equally well with supervisor rating in small groups of white and non-white production workers (Ferreter *et al.*, 2008).

Note, however, that these are mostly one off demonstrations, that need replication, and that many used college students, not real As. Some proposed solutions to adverse impact in ability testing do not seem to work.

- Several studies reviewed by Sackett, Schmitt, Ellingson & Kabin (2001) suggested that giving people more time to complete the test will not reduce AI, and may even increase it.
- 'Culture free' tests such as Raven's Progressive Matrices do not reduce adverse impact.

Other approaches are more far-reaching:

- Assessing various office abilities by a telephone work sample created less adverse impact than conventional paper-and-pencil tests (Schmitt & Mills, 2001).
- Short-term memory tests such as digit span or serial rote learning (Box 6.5) predict work performance fairly well (operational validity of 0.41), and create less adverse impact, according to a meta-analysis by Verive and McDaniel (1996).

Box 6.5   Short-term memory tests

Digit span is the ability to repeat back lists of random numbers. Serial rote learning is the ability to remember arbitrary pairings of words or numbers (e.g. KR = 21, LM = 33, etc).

Stereotype threat is the hypothesis that African Americans feel threatened by GMA tests because they know people expect them to score lower. Research with student samples has reported that the gap between white and African-American can be narrowed by telling them the test assessed problem solving, not intelligence, or widened by asking people about race before starting the test. Does this imply that AI with GMA tests could be reduced by telling As tests 'really' assess problem solving? Misleading As is unethical and tends to be self-defeating. Will people believe that ASVAB or the Wonderlic Test have suddenly ceased to be tests of MA? Most stereotype threat research uses laboratory studies with college students. Will stereotype threat affect test scores in real job As, who are strongly motivated to do well? Stricker and Ward

(2004) found asking people about ethnicity before starting the test had no effect when it was a 'real' educational test. No research has examined stereotype threat in 'real' selection. It would be unethical to tell some 'real' minority As they were doing a test of GMA, in the expectation they might score less well than those told it was a test of, for example, sales aptitude. It would probably break the law to keep asking people about race during selection. (Employers collect this information once, for equal opportunities monitoring, but should keep it separate from the main selection process).

A dissenting voice

Schmidt (2002) thought the search for an ability test that does not create adverse impact on American minorities is mistaken and doomed to failure. He argued that average differences in work performance are found between majority and some minorities (see Chapter 12), so a valid predictor of work performance will find a corresponding difference between majority and minority. A predictor that did not find a difference would not reflect differences in work performance, hence, lack validity.

Outside the USA

Adverse impact of MA tests has been documented in Israel, on Israelis of non-European origin (Zeidner, 1988) and in The Netherlands. De Meijer *et al.* (2006) find large (ca. $d = 1.00$) differences between native Dutch As for police work, and immigrants from Caribbean, North Africa, Surinam and Turkey. However, the differences are much smaller in the second generation, and are linked to proficiency in Dutch, which suggests a short-term acculturation effect. Information about ethnicity differences in test scores in Britain is conspicuous by its absence.

RESEARCH AGENDA

• Use modified format MA tests with real As

Other ways of assessing mental ability

Mental ability tests have advantages of economy, reliability and validity. However, they also have problems of adverse impact and considerable unpopularity. Are there any other ways of assessing MA?

Self-report

Assessing GMA by direct self-reports has rarely been suggested, which makes an interesting contrast with personality where self-report is the method of choice. Furnham and Dissou (2007) found that self-ratings of GMA correlate with tested GMA, but not well to be used as a substitute. Note however that their research was not done in a selection context, where people might not be unbiased or even honest. Chapter 4 noted that interviews assess intelligence to some extent, although not necessarily intending to.

Others' report

Conway *et al.* (2001) found 22 studies correlating peer ratings with GMA test scores, which achieved an average correlation of 0.15, rising to 0.32 when correcting for reliability of both. Note however that peers were not rating the targets specifically for ability but for work performance in general. Others' reports have been shown to correlate slightly better with tested intelligence, up to 0.40 where several observers' ratings are aggregated (Borkenau & Liebler, 1993). Again, these researches were not done in an employment context, where finding observers able and willing to provide accurate and truthful information might be difficult.

Demonstration

Schmidt and Hunter (1998) noted that several types of demonstrated evidence, besides tests, may be useful measures of GMA: assessment centres, biodata, work samples, structured interviews and job knowledge tests. Use of recorded evidence of educational achievement is discussed in Chapter 11. In the USA, authentic assessment is popular in education. People are assessed from portfolios of intellectual accomplishments, on the topic of their choice, in the form of their choice. This is promising because it is likely to prove acceptable, but could be very time-consuming, and possibly not very reliable.

DNA testing

Research has already identified genes associated with high and low MA. It may soon be possible to assess MA from a sliver of skin or drop of saliva. DNA testing would bypass entirely many problems of measurement, such as item bias, test anxiety, or motivation. However, DNA testing can only assess the genotype, the person's inborn potential, unaffected by culture, upbringing, education and training, or social disadvantage, which limits its value in selection. DNA testing of MA is certain to be very controversial. If DNA testing is a 'medical examination', its use in selection is already restricted by disability discrimination laws in UK and USA.

Key points

In Chapter 6 you have learned the following.

- Mental ability tests are the centre of considerable controversy.
- There are various ways of presenting and interpreting test scores.

- There are quite large practice and coaching effects
- Mental ability tests can break the '0.30 barrier', and can achieve corrected correlations with performance around 0.50.
- The relationship between MA is continuous and linear: the brighter someone is, the more likely their work performance is to be good.
- There are some areas of work where the link between GMA and work performance is not so strong.
- The link between GMA and work performance is fairly simple. There are no known moderator variables, except job complexity.
- VGA indicates there may not be much variation in validity left to explain, once error is allowed for.
- Research on MA in teams finds a correlation between team average, and team performance.
- It is not clear that multiple aptitude batteries achieve better validity than single tests of GMA.
- Research on why MA tests predict work performance is less well developed, but suggests that MA leads to improved job knowledge, which on turns leads to better work performance.
- Mental ability tests create large adverse impact on some ethnic minorities in the USA.
- Attempts to solve the adverse impact problem in the USA include trying to identify features of MA tests that will reduce adverse impact.
- Attempts to deal with the adverse impact problem in the USA include score banding which defines a range of scores as equivalent, thus allowing selection within the band to be based on achieving diversity.

Key references

Bell (2007) reviews evidence on mental ability and team performance.

de Meijer *et al.* (2006) present data on ethnicity differences in MA test data in The Netherlands.

Dilchert *et al.* (2007) report quite large relationships between mental ability and counterproductive work behaviours.

Edwards and Arthur (2007) describe a typical piece of research seeking to develop an MA tests that reduces adverse impact.

Gottfredson (1997) argues that mental ability genuinely predicts work performance, and presents data on occupational differences.

Hausknecht *et al.* (2007) review research on coaching and practice effects with mental ability tests.

Henle (2004) reviews the legal position of score banding systems in the USA.

Ree and Earles (1991) present data suggesting that general mental ability predicts work performance as efficiently as differential aptitude batteries.

Salgado *et al.* (2003) present European data on validity of mental ability tests.

Schmidt (2002) argues forcefully for the predictive power of mental ability in the workplace.

Schmidt and Hunter (1998) analyse the likely incremental validity of various other selection tests over mental ability tests.

Useful websites

psychtesting.org.uk. British Psychological Society's Psychological Testing Centre, which includes a list of UK test publishers.
apa.org/science/testing.html. American Psychological Association's site which has information about American test publishers.
buros.unl.edu/buros. Buros Institute which reviews commercially available tests.

CHAPTER 7

Assessing personality by questionnaire

Do you worry about awful things that might happen?

Introduction

Guilford (1959) defined personality as 'any distinguishable, relatively endur-ing way in which one person differs from another'. In practice, most psycholo-gists exclude mental abilities and physical attributes from the definition. There are up to eight different models of personality (Cook, 1993):

- trait   five to ten traits,
- factor   16 statistical abstractions,
- social learning   bundles of habits,
- motives   profile of needs,
- phenomenological   the way one sees the world,
- self   the way one sees oneself,
- psycho-analytic   system of defences,
- constitutional   inherited neuropsychological differences.

Most work psychologists adopt the trait or factor models. Traits are mecha-nisms within people that shape how they react to classes of event and occa-sion. A trait summarizes past behaviour and predicts future behaviour. People who are assertive have asserted themselves often in the past and can be expected to do the same in the future. Factors are similar to traits, but are derived by statistical analysis. Both models offer a convenient view of person-ality, with 5, 10 or at most 20 broad characteristics common to everyone (not just in the UK or USA, but throughout the entire world, according to some views). Simplicity and universality make this an attractive model for selectors.

✦ *Mischel's criticisms*

Some psychologists have questioned the trait and factor model; Mischel (1968) reviewed evidence, much of it by no means new even 40 years ago, that seemed to show that behaviour was not consistent enough to make general statements about personality meaningful. Consider the trait of honesty, which a whole industry in the USA undertakes to assess people for. In the 1920s, the Character Education Inquiry (Hartshorne & May, 1928) found seven sets of measures of honesty correlated very poorly, which implies it is not very informative to describe someone as 'honest' unless one specifies when, where, with what and with whom. Mischel reviewed similar evidence for other traits that often feature in job descriptions: extraversion, punctuality, curiosity, persistence and attitude to authority. Mischel favoured a habit model of personality, which is much more specific and idiosyncratic, and does not lend itself to convenient all-purpose assessments.

Measuring personality

There are many approaches to assessing personality, categorized here by the nature of the information used.

Self-report	personality questionnaire (PQ),
Other report	reference, peer rating,
Demonstration	assessment centre exercises,
Recorded	achievements, previous jobs held, qualifications and degrees,
Involuntary	graphology.

The *method variance* problem (Chapter 2) means assessors should ideally measure every trait by two different types of measure – *multi-trait multi-method measurement*. This is not always easy in practice and does not always seem to work, as research on assessment centres (Chapter 9) has found. This chapter covers the most widely used method: the PQ. PQs are what most people think of as 'personality tests'. Table 7.1 shows some typical PQ items. PQs phrase their items as questions, or as statements. Some simply present lists of trait words – for example, *ambitious*, *bossy* or *careful*. Table 7.1 also illustrates three PQ formats. Some PQs use *endorsement* format, which is quicker and easier; others use *rating* format, which generates a wider range of scores. *Forced-choice* format equates the attractiveness of the alternatives, usually to try to limit faking. PQs have a number of advantages for the selector:

- Like all self-reports, PQs are self-contained: all the information needed is provided by the applicant (A).
- PQs are very accessible: HR staff can use them after a few days training.
- PQs are fairly cheap: although some PQs cost as much as £50 a time to use, they are still very economical because As can be tested in groups, or over the Internet.
- PQs generate a lot of information, very quickly. Even a long PQ, with several hundred items, can be completed within an hour. Elliott, Lawty-Jones and Jackson (1996) timed people completing the Eysenck PQ, and found they answer on average 15–16 questions a minute, one every 4.3 seconds.

Table 7.1 A selection of PQ items and formats.

Endorsement format items

1. I am always punctual.	True	False
2. I keep my office tidy at all times.	True	False
3. Do you enjoy meeting new people?	Yes	No
4. Do you often long for excitement?	Yes	No
5. I am sometimes troubled by unusual thoughts.	True	False
6. I got on better with my mother than with my father.	True	False
7. Do you think some minorities make too much fuss about their 'rights'?	Yes	No
8. I believe there is a life after death.	True	False
9. I have a satisfying sex life.	True	False
10. I suffer a lot from indigestion.	True	False
11. Do you sometimes hear voices?	Yes	No
12. I never use bad language	True	False
13. As a child I always did what I was told	True	False
14. Dogged	[tick if the word applies to you]	

Forced-choice format items

15. On your day off would you rather paint a picture OR paint your house?
16. Would you rather be Dr Crippen OR Jack the Ripper?
17. Which of these words do you prefer?   Profit   Prophet

Rating format

18. I wait to find out what important people think before offering an opinion.						
Never	5	4	3	2	1	*Always*
19. I feel tired at the end of the day						
Never	5	4	3	2	1	*Always*
20. Energetic						
Very	5	4	5	2	1	*Not at all*

- Questions 4 and 5 in Table 7.1 suggest that PQs may tap thoughts and feelings, as well as behaviour, so PQs may get qualitatively different information, perhaps really 'get inside A's head'.
- PQs can be administered and scored by computer, which can generate a 10-page report on the A within minutes.
- PQs do not create serious adverse impact on ethnic minorities, unlike mental ability tests. This is a major factor in their recent popularity in HR work in the USA.

Box 7.1   *T* scores

The *T* score is a form of standard score in which the mean is set at 50 and the SD at 10. A raw score is converted into a *T* score using the formula $T = 50 + (10 \times ((\text{raw score} - \text{mean})/\text{SD})$. *T* scores give the same information as *z* scores (page 113) but avoid decimal points and minus signs.

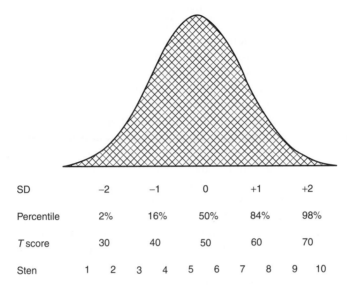

SD		−2	−1	0	+1	+2		
Percentile		2%	16%	50%	84%	98%		
T score		30	40	50	60	70		
Sten	1 2	3	4	5 6	7	8	9	10

Figure 7.1   A normal distribution of PQ scores illustrating *T* scores and stens.

Interpreting PQ scores

A raw score on a PQ, like a raw score on a mental ability test, means little, until it is related to a population – people in general, bank managers, bus drivers or students. Several variations on the standard score theme (Chapter 6) are used to interpret raw scores (Figure 7.1), including *T* scores (Box 7.1) and sten scores (Box 7.2).

Box 7.2   Sten scores

The sten is a form of standard score in which the mean is set at 5.5 and the SD at 1.5. The effect is to divide the distribution into 10 bands, each covering half a standard deviation.

Keying and validation

There are four main ways of writing PQs (*construction*) and showing that they work (*validation*).

1. *Acceptance or face validity*. People accept the PQ's results as accurate. This is a very weak test of validity because people are easily taken in by all-purpose personality profiles – the so-called *Barnum* or *horoscope* effect.
2. *Content*. The PQ looks plausible. The first ever PQ, Woodworth's Personal Data Sheet of 1917, intended to assess emotional fitness in US Army recruits,

gathered its questions from lists of symptoms in psychiatric textbooks to ensure that item content was plausible and relevant.

3 *Empirical*. The questions are included because they predict. The PQ is *empirically keyed* using *criterion groups* of people of known characteristics. The California Psychological Inventory developed its Dominance scale from answers that distinguished college students nominated as leaders from those seen as mere followers.

4 *Factorial*. The questions have a common theme. After choosing the questions, the author tests their fit by correlation and factor analysis (*see* Box 2.7 on page 34). Factor analysis estimates how many themes or factors the PQ covers: Cattell found 16 factors in his 187 questions. Some questions do not relate to any theme and are discarded. In practice, development of a new PQ almost always includes factor analysis however the questions are chosen. Critics argue that the factorial approach may produce very narrow scales, that get close to asking the same question 10 times, which ensures high item–whole correlations, high alpha coefficient and one clear factor, but at the possible expense of any generality of meaning. The technical term for a factor obtained by asking very similar questions is *bloated specific*.

The Five Factor Model (FFM) has become very popular. It is argued that analyses of PQ and rating data reliably find five separate personality factors (Table 7.2). The 'big five' are said to emerge reliably in many different cultures: the USA, Britain, Germany, The Netherlands, Israel, Russia, Japan and China, so may represent a truly global model of personality. Most recent analyses of personality and work behaviour have used the FFM. Earlier researches have

Table 7.2 The big five personality factors.

Big five factor	Alternative titles	Alternative titles (reversed)
Neuroticism	Anxiety	Emotional stability
	Emotionality	Emotional control
		Resilience
		Adjustment
Extraversion	Surgency	Introversion
	Assertiveness	
	Ascendancy	
Openness	Culture	Dogmatism
	Intellect	Closedness
	Flexibility	
Agreeableness	Likeability	Antagonism
	Friendly compliance	Psychoticism
Conscientiousness	Will to achieve	Negligence
	Dependability	
	Prudence	
	Ego control	
	Super ego strength	

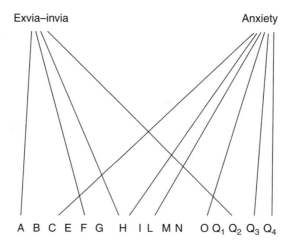

Figure 7.2 Higher-order factors, exvia-invia and anxiety, in Cattell's 16 personality factors.

been fitted into the FFM. The five factors were originally thought to be uncorrelated, but Mount *et al.* (2005) meta-analysed US normative data for four major FFM PQs and found quite substantial intercorrelations. Two superfactors emerge, provisionally called α, comprising openness and extraversion, and β, comprising agreeableness, conscientiousness and (low) neuroticism. Another snag with the FFM is that plausible cases can be – and have been – made out for three, four, six, seven, eight or nine factor models.

Hierarchical models

The Eysenck Personality Inventory measures only two factors, while Cattell found 16 factors. However, there is no real disagreement between Eysenck and Cattell. Cattell's 16 factors intercorrelate to some extent; analysis reveals higher-order factors – exvia/invia and anxiety – which resemble Eysenck's extraversion and neuroticism (Figure 7.2). Some PQs explicitly adopt a hierarchical format, distinguishing separate *facets* within each factor; for example, FFM conscientiousness may be divided into competence, order, dutifulness, achievement striving, self-discipline and deliberation.

Reliability

Viswesvaran and Ones's (2000) meta-analysis found average retest reliabilities for PQ scales between 0.73 and 0.78. This level of reliability is consistent with some scores changing considerably over fairly short periods of time. Changes exceeding 0.5 SD, that is five *T* points or one whole sten (Figure 7.1), may be expected to occur in one in three retests, and changes over one whole SD in 1 in 20 retests.

Contextualization or frame of reference

Most PQs assess personality in general, but selectors do not need to know what someone is like at home, and probably should not enquire. A PQ may give misleading results in selection if people describe how they behave outside work. Robie *et al.* (2000) described a contextualized PQ, which inserts *at work* into every question: *I take great care with detail at work*. Hunthausen *et al.* (2003) reported that a contextualized PQ achieved better results selecting airline customer service supervisors. Robie *et al.* found that contextualization raised scores – perhaps because people really are more careful at work – so new normative data will be needed.

Using PQs in selection

Opinion on the value of PQs in selection has shifted over time. In the 1960s and 1970s, they were widely dismissed as useless. Since 1990 they have grown steadily more popular, and new PQs have proliferated. But does validation research justify this new optimism? PQs try to answer five main questions:

1. Has A got the right personality for the job?
2. Will A do the job well?
3. Does A have a good 'attitude'?
4. Will A behave badly in the workplace?
5. Will the team work well?

Questions 1 and 2 look similar, but differ subtly; question 1 is answered by comparing bank managers with people in general; question 2 is answered by comparing successful and less successful bank managers.

Question 1 – the right personality?

The A-S-A model argues that certain personalities are attracted to psychology (Attraction), that certain personalities are selected to become psychologists (Selection) and that certain personalities find that psychology does not suit them (Attrition). Some employers seem to want a book of perfect personality profiles for manager, salesperson, engineer, and so on. PQ manuals meet this demand to some extent by giving norms for different occupations. The perfect profile approach has several limitations however:

- Sample sizes are often too small and cross-validation information is rarely available. Ideally, a perfect profile for a cost accountant will be based on two or more large, separate samples.
- Most perfect profiles are derived from people doing the job, taking no account of how well they do it.
- A perfect profile may show how people have changed to fit the job's demands, not how well people with that profile will do the job.

- Using perfect profiles encourages *cloning*, that is selecting as managers only people who resemble as closely as possible existing managers. This may create great harmony and satisfaction within the organization, but may make it difficult for the organization to cope with change.

Question 2 – will he/she do the job well?

The second, more important, question is whether PQs can select people who will do their job well, defined by supervisor rating, sales figures or training grades. A very early meta-analysis (Ghiselli & Barthol, 1953) was moderately favourable, reporting average correlations of up to 0.36 (Table 7.3). However, Ghiselli and Barthol only included studies where they thought the trait is relevant to the job; for example, sociability is needed for sales staff, but not for machinists. More reviews appeared in the 1960s and 1970s; Lent *et al.* (1971) found that only 12% of validity coefficients were significant, while Guion and Gottier (1965) found only 10%. These reviews, and Mischel's 1968 criticism of the trait model, led to the general feeling that PQs had no useful place in selection. Guion and Gottier concluded that 'it is difficult to advocate, with a clear conscience, the use of personality measures in most situations as a basis for making employment decisions'.

Since 1990, numerous meta-analyses have been calculated, most also using validity generalization analysis, and most fitting PQs into the FFM (Hough, 1992, 1998; Barrick & Mount, 1991; Tett Jackson & Rothstein, 1991; Salgado, 1998; Vinchur *et al.*, 1998; Hurtz & Donovan, 2000). Salgado's analysis covers European research, which sometimes gets left out of American reviews. Hurtz and Donovan asked whether forcing scales that were not designed to assess the big five into the FFM might lower validity, so limit their meta-analysis to true big five measures; it makes no difference.

Barrick, Mount and Judge (2001) summarized all these various meta-analyses in a 'meta-meta-analysis' (Table 7.4). Conscientiousness has the largest

Table 7.3 Validity of personality tests for selection for eight types of work (Ghiselli & Barthol, 1953).

Type of work ⇓	k	N	r
Supervisors	8	518	0.14
Foremen	44	6433	0.18
Clerical	22	1069	0.25
Sales assistants	8	1120	0.36
Salespersons	12	927	0.36
Protective	5	536	0.24
Service	6	385	0.16
Trades and crafts	8	511	0.29

Correlations were not corrected in any way. Correlations were only included in the analysis if the trait was considered relevant to work performance.

Table 7.4 Meta-meta-analysis of the big five and job performance.

	k	N	r	ρ
(Low) neuroticism	224	39K	0.06	0.11
Extraversion	222	39K	0.06	0.11
Openness	143	23K	0.03	0.04
Agreeableness	206	36K	0.06	0.09
Conscientiousness	239	48K	0.12	0.20

Data from Barrick *et al.* (2001).
r = raw correlation; ρ = operational validity, estimated from true validity on the basis of correction for test reliability of 0.80.

Table 7.5 Meta-meta-analysis of the big five and job performance, for four broad classes of work.

	(Low) N	E	O	A	C
Sales	0.04	0.08	−0.02	0.01	0.19
Management	0.07	0.15	0.06	0.07	0.19
Police	0.10	0.09	0.02	0.09	0.19
Skilled	0.12	0.04	0.04	0.07	0.17

Operational validity, estimated from true validity, on the basis of correction for test reliability of 0.80.
Data from Barrick *et al.* (2001).

correlation with work performance, followed by (low) Neuroticism; values for extraversion, openness and agreeableness do not differ significantly from zero. Critics (Morgeson *et al.*, 2007) note that even making corrections for reliability and restricted range, PQs do not correlate with work performance better than 0.20; they cannot even reach the *0.30 barrier*, let alone break it. Meta-analyses of PQ validity find a lot of variance unaccounted, implying there are moderator variables to be discovered. Schmidt, Shaffer and Oh (in press) applied the indirect range restriction correction (see Chapter 2) to meta-analyses of PQ validity, and found that it makes little difference, increasing operational validity by only 4%. There is much less restriction of range on PQ scores within occupations than is found for mental ability scores.

Different occupations

Barrick *et al.*'s meta-meta-analysis (Table 7.5) found some small differences between five broad classes of work:

- (low) Neuroticism correlates better with success in police work and skilled and semi-skilled work.
- Extraversion correlates better with success in management.

Some individual meta-analyses also reported occupational differences.

- Hough (1998) and Vinchur *et al.* (1998) both found extraversion correlates with sales performance.
- Two meta-analyses suggested a role for agreeableness in some types of work. Hurtz and Donovan's analysis found agreeableness and openness correlate with performance more strongly for customer service work. Mount, Barrick and Stewart (1998) found that agreeableness correlates better with performance in work where co-operation and teamwork are important (as opposed to work which simply involves interacting with clients, e.g. hotel work.)
- It has been argued that high conscientiousness could be a drawback in some jobs, encouraging indecision and bureaucracy. UK data reported by Robertson *et al.* (2000) found no correlation with rated performance in managers and a negative correlation with rated promotability.

Different aspects of work performance

Barrick *et al.* (2001) distinguished supervisor rating, training grades and objective performance such as sales (Table 7.6). Extraversion did not relate much to overall work performance, but did relate to training performance. Perhaps extraverts like new experiences, or meeting new people, (or getting away from work for a day or two!). Openness correlated with training performance; perhaps open-minded people like gaining new knowledge and skills. Conscientiousness correlates with all three performance measures, leading Barrick *et al.* to suggest it may be 'the trait-oriented motivation variable that industrial-organizational psychologists have long searched for'. (But they will need to keep searching if they want correlations larger than 0.20!).

A few more specialized meta-analyses have appeared subsequent to Barrick *et al.* Hogan and Holland (2003) argued that meta-analysis should not pool different PQs because this submerges good PQs in a larger number of inferior ones; they provided a meta-analysis, restricted to Hogan Personality Inventory data, which shows broadly similar results to Barrick *et al.*'s meta-meta-analysis, except that (low) Neuroticism correlates better than usual with work

Table 7.6 Meta-meta-analysis of the big five and three aspects of work performance.

	N	E	O	A	C
Supervisor rating	0.10	0.10	0.04	0.09	0.23
Objective	0.08	0.10	0.02	0.11	0.17
Training	0.07	0.20	0.21	0.10	0.20

Operational validity, estimated from true validity, on the basis of correction for test reliability of 0.80.
Data from Barrick *et al.* (2001).

Table 7.7   Personality and specialized work performance.

	N	E	O	A	C
Leadership – business	−0.14	0.23	0.21	−0.04	0.05
Leadership – government and military	−0.22	0.15	0.05	−0.04	0.16
Expatriate performance	−0.09	0.15	0.05	0.10	0.15
Entrepreneurship	−0.14	0.10	0.15	−0.07	0.19

Data on leadership from Judge, Bono, Ilies & Gerhardt (2002).
Data on expatriate performance from Mol *et al.* (2005).
Data for entrepreneurship from Zhao & Seibert (2006).
r = calculated from uncorrected d values.

performance. Bartram (2005) correlated PQ data with eight dimensions of managerial performance and found low correlations with FFM, the highest being 0.18 (uncorrected) between extraversion and interaction / presentation skills.

More specialized job performance

Table 7.7 summarizes research on FFM and expatriate performance, leadership, and entrepreneurship.

Expatriate work

Some expatriate workers have difficulty adjusting to a different culture and working effectively. Mol *et al.* (2005) meta-analysed 12 studies linking expatriate performance to the FFM, and found modest correlations with extraversion and conscientiousness, even more modest correlations with agreeableness and (low) neuroticism, but – perhaps surprisingly – none with openness.

Entrepreneurship

Entrepreneurs found, own and run their businesses (whereas managers work for someone else). Zhao and Seibert (2006) meta-analysed 23 studies comparing the two, and found entrepreneurs higher on extraversion, openness and conscientiousness, but lower on neuroticism and agreeableness. More detailed analysis finds the difference in conscientiousness is for achievement, not dependability. The multiple correlation between all five factors and entrepreneurial status is fairly high at 0.37.

Stress tolerance

Many jobs require ability to cope with pressure, of various sorts. While a number of stress-tolerance scales exist (Ones & Viswesvaran, 2001), no research seems to have been reported on their ability to predict coping with pressure.

Leadership

For some jobs, the ability to lead others is critical. Judge *et al.* (2002) meta-analysed leadership and the FFM, and found modest estimated true correlations for (low) neuroticism and extraversion. In civilian management, openness correlated positively, while in military and government, conscientiousness correlated positively (Table 7.7).

Combat effectiveness

Hough (1998) found (low) neuroticism correlated with combat effectiveness in US military samples. Salgado (1998) confirmed this in European military samples. Meta-analyses of conscientiousness and combat effectiveness disagree; Mount and Barrick (1995) reported 0.47 correlations in 10 studies, whereas Hough reported much lower correlations between achievement and dependability and combat effectiveness.

PQs seem generally fairly poor at answering the question 'Will he/she do this job well?'. Possibly questions about ability are better answered by ability tests. Some 15 years of intense interest and research activity do not generally seem to have produced results that are very much more impressive than those reported in the 1960s and 1970s, and which led many to dismiss PQs as not helpful in selection. It can be argued that even low validities can secure a worthwhile increase in performance when cumulated across a large workforce, especially when the assessment is quick and cheap to make.

The FFM as a whole

Multiple correlation assesses the power of all FFM factors collectively to predict work performance. If the five were as uncorrelated as originally supposed, the multiple correlation would be higher than any single correlation. Most researchers have not reported multiple correlation, but Ones *et al.* (2007) generated estimates for previous MAs, from factor validities, and estimates of FFM intercorrelations. This gives a value of 0.27 for overall job performance for Barrick *et al.*'s meta-meta-analysis, which still fails to break the 0.30 barrier. Ones *et al.*'s estimates of FFM intercorrelations may be too low, at an average of 0.15; Mount *et al.* (2005) found higher intercorrelations (average 0.29), which will reduce the multiple correlation.

Incremental validity

Two meta-analyses both suggest that PQs will have considerable incremental validity over mental ability tests. Both conscientiousness and mental ability correlate with work performance, but not with each other, so it follows logically that conscientiousness will have incremental validity on mental ability (and vice versa). Schmidt and Hunter (1998) estimated the incremental validity of the conscientiousness factor at 18%, and list the combination as one of the four most useful. Salgado's (1998) review of European data confirms this and concludes that neuroticism too will have incremental validity.

Question 3 – has he/she got a good attitude to work?

Interest in personality and work has shifted somewhat since 1990, from performance, defined by output or supervisor rating of proficiency, to a broader set of outcomes, best summarized by 'attitude', as in 'you have a bad attitude' or 'he has an attitude problem'. Employers usually prefer employees who are keen, hardworking, co-operative and helpful. In the USA, broadening of the concept of work performance is also motivated by equal opportunities concerns. Emphasizing ability, assessed by written tests and defined by training grades and supervisor ratings, creates large adverse impact problems. Emphasizing 'attitude' at work, and measures that assess it, such as PQs, may reduce adverse impact. Ability and proficiency are sometimes called 'can-do' aspects, while motivation and attitude are called 'will-do'.

Analyses of this area have used a range of terms – commendable behaviour, organizational citizenship, job dedication, 'getting along' – which overlap in meaning, and are likely to correlate, without however being synonymous. Some analyses (Mount & Barrick, 1995; Hurtz & Donovan, 2000; Hogan & Holland, 2003) are based on supervisor ratings and divide scales into different categories: for example, dedication or quality. This may not distinguish different aspects of 'attitude' from each other or even from task performance all that clearly because all supervisor ratings tend to be highly correlated. Other analyses (Hough and Project A) also use recorded data, such as 'letters of recommendation, letters of reprimand, disciplinary actions, demotions, involuntary terminations'.

Table 7.8 shows that 'attitude' aspects of work performance are linked to conscientiousness, like task aspects. Links to neuroticism and agreeableness may be stronger for attitude than task. Results for extraversion seem more variable. Table 7.8 may show that extraversion is linked to attitude to co-workers (citizenship, getting along, interpersonal facilitation) but not to attitude to the job itself (dedication). Validation of the US military's PQ, called Assessment of Background and Life Experiences (ABLE), showed ABLE correlated with three *will-do* criteria – *effort and leadership, personal discipline, physical fitness and military bearing* – better (0.16, uncorrected) than two *can-do* criteria – *technical proficiency* or *general soldiering proficiency* (Hough *et al.*, 1990; McHenry *et al.*, 1990). Mount and Barrick (1995) reported a meta-analysis for *conscientiousness* and various *will-do* criteria: reliability, effort (defined as hard work, initiative, motivation, energy and persistence) and quality, finding fully corrected or 'true' correlations of 0.40 to 0.50. They pooled all the *will-do* criteria and find an overall true validity of 0.45, against 0.22 for pooled *can-do* criteria.

RESEARCH AGENDA

- Drawing a clearer distinction between types of evidence defining attitude: self-report, other report or recorded.

Table 7.8   Meta-analyses of FFM and 'attitude' aspects of work performance.

	(Low) N	E	O	A	C
	r / ρ	r / ρ	r / ρ	r / ρ	r / ρ
Commendable behaviour	0.15 / nr	0.08[e] / nr	*	0.08 / nr	0.23 / nr
Job dedication	0.09 / 0.13	0.03 / 0.05	0.01 / 0.01	0.06 / 0.08	0.12 / 0.18
Interpersonal facilitation	0.10 / 0.16	0.06 / 0.10	0.03 / 0.05	0.11 / 0.17	0.11 / 0.16
Getting along	0.19 / 0.31	0.01 / 0.01[a] (0.10 / 0.15)[c]	0.02 / 0.03[b] (0.08 / 0.12)[d]	0.12 / 0.19	0.14 / 0.21
Organizational citizenship	0.12 / nr	0.06 / nr	nr	0.13 / nr	0.19 / nr

Data for *commendable behaviour* from Hough Barge & Kamp (2001). [e]potency facet of extraversion.
Data for *job dedication* and *interpersonal* facilitation from Hurtz & Donovan (2000).
Data for *getting along* from Hogan and Holland (2003). Extraversion split into sociability.[a] / ambition.[b]; openness split into intellectance.[c] / school success.[d]
Data for *organizational citizenship* from Borman *et al.* (2001), excludes studies which used self-reports of OC.

Question 4 – will he / she behave badly at work?

PQs can be used like the driving test: not to select the best, but to exclude the unacceptable. Using personality measures to screen As has a long history. Anderson's (1929) survey of staff at Macy's department store in New York found 20% of the employees fell into the 'problem' category – for instance, suffer chronic ill-health, are in constant trouble with fellow employees or cannot adjust satisfactorily to their work. Zickar (2001) described an unfortunate episode in American work psychology in the 1930s and 1940s, when some employers used PQs to try to exclude workers who would join trades unions, working on the curious assumption that desire to join a union was a sign of maladjustment. Some research has looked at fairly specific forms of misbehaviour – absence, theft or violence; other research groups diverse behaviours together as *deviance* or *counterproductivity*. Counterproductive behaviours (CPBs) include breaking rules, illegal activities, theft, drug use, lateness and violence.

Violence and aggression

In 1979, the Avis car-rental company were sued when an employee raped a customer and was found to have a record of similar offences. Avis should, it was claimed, have discovered the man was dangerous. *Negligent hiring* claims have become common in the USA. Hershcovis *et al.* (2007) reported an MA of workplace aggression and personality, restricting itself to trait anger and negative affectivity. Trait anger correlates well with aggression, especially aggression directed at people rather than the organization (0.43 true validity). Negative affectivity, which has some overlap with FFM neuroticism, correlates less strongly with aggression; Hershcovis *et al.*'s analysis suggested it may overlap with trait anger. Note that their definition of aggression appears to be fairly broad, extending to rudeness and 'retaliation'.

Absence is a major problem for many employers, so the possibility of selecting people less likely to be absent is attractive. Two meta-analyses reach different conclusions. Salgado (2002) summarized 8–10 studies and found virtually no correlation with any of the big five. Ones, Viswesvaran and Schmidt (2003) summarized 28 studies using honesty tests (HTs) and found moderate validity (Table 7.9). They also found that personality-based HTs predict absence moderately well (0.36 operational validity), whereas 'overt' HTs do not. This finding is odd for two reasons. Overt and personality-type HTs work equally well when correlated with counterproductivity, but not apparently when related to absence. Second, HTs seem to be measuring a composite of conscientiousness, agreeableness and neuroticism, but Salgado found no links with any of these. Ones *et al.* said that Salgado was unable to distinguish voluntary from involuntary absence – a notorious problem with absenteeism research.

Turnover

Employers often view leaving their employ as CPB, if only because it costs them time and money. Reasons people leave include furthering their career, or to escape a boring and unpleasant job. Zimmerman's (2008) meta-analysis suggested poor adjustment and impulsivity also play a part.

Honesty tests (HTs) aka integrity tests

Numerous surveys indicate that employee theft is a widespread problem in the USA; it has even been suggested that it contributes to 30% of company failures. HTs, a form of PQ, became popular in the USA, especially in the retail sector, after use of the polygraph (or lie detector test) was restricted in 1988. Table 7.10 shows some typical HT questions, some tapping attitudes related to honesty, others seeking admissions of past dishonesty. HTs have been validated against polygraph assessments or till shortages, or even low takings (on the assumption that low takings means the person is stealing). Marcus, Funke and Schuler (1997) meta-analysed the construct validity of HTs, finding positive correlations with conscientiousness (0.29) and agreeableness (0.31), and negative correlations with neuroticism (−0.28) and openness (−0.15). This suggests HTs are measuring an undifferentiated construct. HTs divide into overt or clear purpose measures, which ask directly about dishonest attitudes and behaviour, and covert or personality measures, which seek to assess for instance honesty via conscientiousness or adjustment. Covert tests are generally produced by psychologists. Ones, Viswesvaran and Schmidt (1993)

Table 7.9 Summary of meta-analyses of correlations between FFM PQs, honesty tests (HTs) and misbehaviour in the workplace.

	(Low) N	E	O	A	C	HT
	r / ρ	r / ρ	r / ρ	r / ρ	r / ρ	r / ρ
Aggression to co-workers	0.22 / 0.25					
Aggression to organization	0.24 / 0.26					
Absence	0.03 / 0.04	0.05 / 0.08	0.00 / 0.00	0.03 / 0.04	-0.04 / -0.06	0.14 / 0.20
Accidents	-0.04 / -0.08	-0.02 / -0.04	0.05 / 0.09	0.00 / -0.01	-0.03 / -0.06	nr / 0.52
	-0.18 / -0.27	0.01 / 0.02	0.29 / 0.43	-0.26 / 0.38	-0.19 / -0.28[a]	
Property damage						nr / 0.69
Theft						0.36 / 0.52
Substance abuse	-0.07	0.06[a]		-0.04	-0.28	
Turnover	-0.16 / -0.20	-0.03 / -0.04	0.09 / 0.10	-0.22 / -0.27	-0.18 / -0.22	
Law abiding behaviour	-0.41 / nr	0.29[a] / nr			0.58 / nr	
Counterproductive behaviour (CPB)						0.33 / 0.47
CPB (self-report)						0.41 / 0.58
CPB (record & other report)						0.22 / 0.32
Deviant behaviour	-0.04 / -0.06	0.01 / 0.01	0.10 / 0.11	-0.13 / -0.20	-0.16 / -0.26	
Interpersonal deviance	0.20 / 0.24	0.02 / 0.02	-0.07 / -0.09	-0.36 / -0.46	-0.19 / -0.23	
Organizational deviance	0.19 / 0.23	-0.07 / -0.09	-0.03 / -0.04	-0.25 / -0.32	-0.34 / -0.42	

Data on *aggression* from Hershcovis et al. (2007).
Data on *substance abuse* from Hough et al. (1990).
Data on *law abiding behaviour* from Hough et al. (2001).
Data for FFM and *absence, accidents* and *deviant behaviour* from Salgado (2002).
Data for *accidents* from Clarke & Robertson (2007).
Data on *interpersonal and organization deviance* from Berry, Ones & Sackett (2007). ρ is 'true' validity, corrected for reliability of both measures, but not range restriction.
Data for *honesty tests* from Ones et al. (1993), Ones & Viswesvaran (1998c) and Ones & Viswesvaran (2003).
Data on *turnover* from Zimmerman (2008).
[a] potency aspect of Extraversion only.

Table 7.10 Some questions of the type found in 'overt' honesty tests (HTs).

1] Attitudes and beliefs

Employees who take things from work are criminals who should be punished.
Most people will steal things from work if they can be sure they won't get caught.
Some people who are caught shoplifting aren't really dishonest.
Employers who don't treat their staff right deserve to get ripped off by them.
Lots of people take days off work sick when they aren't really ill.

2] Admissions

Have you taken anything from your place of work over the last five years?
I have never sold things to my friends or family for less than the right price.
How much money do you spend on alcohol in a typical week?
I bet on horse racing or sporting events quite frequently.

reported a meta-analysis of 665 HT validities, covering no less than 576,460 persons. The analysis produced some surprising results:

- HTs predict CPBs very well, achieving an operational validity of 0.47. Validity for self-reported CPBs is higher than for recorded CPBs, suggesting either possible method variance problems, or that records of CPBs may be unsatisfactory.
- Mainstream psychological tests are no more successful than overt HTs. This is disturbing for professional psychologists who have been warning the public for years that writing psychological tests is a specialized task best left to the experts (i.e. psychologists).
- HTs also predict work performance very well, achieving an operational validity of 0.34.
- HTs are surprisingly versatile; they can predict accidents at work, and property damage, as well as training performance and output (Ones & Viswesvaran, 1998c, 2001).
- HTs work for all levels of employee, not just for lower-paid workers as is sometimes supposed.

Critics (Sackett & Wanek, 1996; Berry, Sackett & Wiemann, 2007) have expressed some cautions about the validity of HTs:

- Many HTs are validated by including questions asking people to admit past dishonesty, and using these questions as criterion for the rest of the measure. This is obviously a very weak form of validation – in effect asking people twice if they will admit to dishonesty. Perhaps the correlation should be a lot higher than 0.30 to 0.40.
- The number of studies that use behavioural measures of dishonesty is considerably smaller than 665, and the number that use actual theft as the outcome fewer still. Only seven studies, with a total of 2,500 persons, used actual theft, and these achieved much poorer results, a corrected validity of only 0.13.

- While there are several dozen HTs on the market, Ones *et al.*'s meta-analysis was based largely on only six or seven, so the value of the rest remains unproved.

McDaniel, Rothstein and Whetzel (2006a) reported trim-and-fill analyses (Chapter 2, p. 39) for reporting bias for four sets of validity data presented by four unnamed American test vendors. Two of the four datasets appear to report less evidence of limited validity than trim-and-fill indicates might be expected. McDaniel *et al.* suggested this 'calls into question past meta-analyses that have relied primarily on test vendor data', specifically mentioning Ones *et al.*'s (1993) meta-analysis of HTs. It would seem advisable in future to include source of data as a moderator variable in all meta-analyses, given that two studies (McDaniel *et al.*, 2006a; Russell *et al.*, 1994) have strongly suggested it may be important. This may however be difficult for HTs, as independent researchers may not have sufficient access to test material, scoring details, and so on, to carry out any research. Pollack and McDaniel (2008) noted that some test publishers impose confidentiality restrictions on test users, which could prevent research from being published. Campion (Morgeson *et al.*, 2007) stated that some HT publishers exhibited gross publication bias, not wanting even to hear about studies that found negative results.

The very high (and uncorrected) correlations for law-abiding behaviour reported by Hough (1992) may be slightly misleading. Some studies compared criminals with non-criminals, and calculated correlations from the difference between them. Finding personality differences between delinquents and non-delinquents is not very surprising and may have problems of direction of cause. Convicted criminals might experience some difficult plausibly presenting themselves as honest, and the fact of having been convicted might remove any incentive to do so. However, other studies were more relevant, reporting quite large correlations between PQ scores when joining the army, and subsequent Absence Without Leave. The high correlations reported by Berry *et al.* (2007) may result, in part, from shared method variance because both personality and deviance are, for the most part, self-reports. Correlations for HTs may have been affected by reporting bias.

PQs seem more strongly linked to tendencies to misbehave at work, with a pattern of high neuroticism, low agreeableness and low conscientiousness. This is confirmed by the HT data, given that HTs reflect neuroticism, agreeableness and conscientiousness. However, these stronger links will not necessarily translate into better predictions of work behaviour, given that a lot of research has used concurrent validation and self-reported misbehaviour. More research showing that PQs can predict today who will misbehave in future is still needed.

RESEARCH AGENDA

- Research testing 'real' As and linking personality to 'real' CPB.

Alternatives to the FFM

Narrower traits than the big five?

Some researchers argue that specific traits give better predictions of work behaviour than the big five. Both Hough (1992, 1998) and Vinchur *et al.* (1998) found it useful to split extraversion into potency / ascendancy and affiliation, and conscientiousness into achievement and dependability. Hough (1998) argues that *conscientiousness* becomes a very broad factor indeed in some accounts of the big five, covering achievement striving, competence, dutifulness, order, self-discipline and deliberation, and that it contains elements that are potentially opposites. Achievement suggests 'self-expansive striving and setting goals to master the environment', whereas dependability suggests 'self-restrictive caution, conventionality, and adapting to goals set by others'. Results for sales (Table 7.11) seem to confirm this; achievement correlates quite well with sales, but dependability does not. Vinchur *et al.* found this difference especially marked for studies using sales figures, rather than ratings of sales ability.

Dudley *et al.*'s (2006) meta-analysis compared the conscientiousness factor and its four component narrower traits: achievement, dependability, order and cautiousness. For predicting overall work performance, the narrow traits offer little incremental validity, but dependability in particular is very strongly linked to job dedication. Type of work also makes a difference. The narrow traits of dependability and caution gave considerable incremental validity for skilled and semi-skilled work, but not for managerial, sales or customer service jobs.

Broader than the big five?

Frei and McDaniel (1998) meta-analysed 39 studies of customer service orientation and reported an average raw validity of 0.24, which corrects to 0.49. Customer service orientation means being pleasant, courteous, co-operative

Table 7.11 Sales performance, and broad and narrow personality traits.

Meta-analysis	Vinchur	Hough	
Criterion	Rating	Sales figures	Sales effectiveness
Extraversion	0.09	0.12	
Affiliation	0.06	0.08	0.19
Potency	0.15	0.15	0.25
Conscientiousness	0.11	0.17	
Achievement	0.14	0.23	0.27
Dependency	0.10	0.10	0.06

Data from Hough (1998) and Vinchur *et al.* (1998).
Correlations are not corrected in any way.

and helpful in dealing with customers, and is reckoned as an increasingly important attribute, given the importance of service industries. The higher correlation may reflect the fact that customer service orientation is a very broad trait, covering conscientiousness, agreeableness, and neuroticism. HTs (v.i.) also assess also very broad traits.

Question 5 – will the team work well?

Chapter 6 noted that selection research remains focused on the individual employee, even though a lot of work is done by teams, where personality could be especially important. Bell's (2007) meta-analysis found 11 studies of work team performance and FFM; Bell analysed average personality, variation in personality and extremes. Table 7.12 shows team performance linked to team's average PQ score for all five factors. In particular, higher levels of conscientiousness and agreeableness are linked to better performance. Earlier analyses (e.g. Table 7.4) showed agreeableness does not correlate with performance at the individual level, but Bell's findings showed it becomes important in teamwork. Bell found weaker effects for variability, where more variation in conscientiousness and openness is linked to poorer performance. Perhaps the most striking results are for extremes – the 'bad apple' effect. The higher the minimum score for conscientiousness and agreeableness, the better the group works. This suggests that one single low-scoring person, on either conscientiousness or agreeableness, can hold back the entire group. Perhaps the low scorer creates tension within the group, or sets poor standard of work that others follow, or simply demoralizes and demotivates everyone.

A separate approach to personality and teamwork argues that certain combinations of personalities create a more effective team. The Belbin Team Role Self-Perception Test assigns people to one of eight team roles, e.g. shaper, or company worker, and argues that an effective team needs the right mix of roles. If everyone wants to take charge and no one wants to be company

Table 7.12 Meta-analysis of links between team personality and team performance.

	(Low) N	E	O	A	C
k	4–5	5–7	4–5	7–9	8–10
N teams	207–354	227–492	176–323	301–495	301–525
	r / ρ	r / ρ	r / ρ	r / ρ	r / ρ
Team average	0.18 / 0.21	0.14 / 0.18	0.20 / 0.25	0.28 / 0.34	0.28 / 0.33
Team variability	−0.04 / −0.05	0.05 / 0.06	−0.11 / −0.13	−0.07 / −0.08	−0.13 / −0.16
Extreme – max	0.11 / 0.13	0.11 / 0.13	0.14 / 0.17	0.11 / 0.14	0.12 / 0.14
Extreme – min	0.00 / 0.00	0.04 / 0.04	0.07 / 0.09	0.30 / 0.37	0.22 / 0.27

Data from Bell (2007).
ρ is correlation corrected for reliability of both PQ and performance measure, but not restricted range.

RESEARCH AGENDA

- More research on team personality and performance, with wider range of jobs
- Links between team personality and other aspects of work performance including attitude and CPBs
- Exploration of how low scorers affect team functioning

worker, the team may fail. Aritzeta, Swailes and Senior (2007) reviewed research showing that balanced teams are more effective.

Complexities of PQ validity

Moderator variables

Hochwarter, Witt and Kacmar (2000) found the link between conscientiousness and work performance moderated by organizational politics. In some workplaces, people see a lot of favouritism, backstabbing, pursuit of private agendas, and so on, while in others, people see things being done more openly and fairly. Data from four fairly large and diverse samples found conscientiousness correlated with performance in people who experience a lot of organizational politics, but not in people who did not. Hochwarter *et al.* suggested that in an open and fair environment everyone works conscientiously, but when such standards are lacking, only those who have their own internal standards can work effectively.

Interactions between personality factors

Witt *et al.* (2002) hypothesized that conscientiousness will predict work performance better in people high on agreeableness. They argued that a conscientious but disagreeable person will not get on with colleagues, but be 'micromanaging, unreasonably demanding, inflexible, curt, and generally difficult to deal with'. Their hypothesis is confirmed for five of seven varied samples.

Interaction with mental ability

Schmidt, Shaffer and Oh (in press) offer the interesting suggestion that more intelligent people may be better able to modify their personality to fit their work. For example, an introvert person can behave extravertedly when required, or high neuroticism scorers can better control their neurotic impulses. This implies that PQs may predict work behaviour better in less intelligent people.

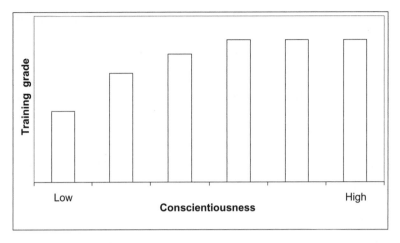

Figure 7.3 Conscientiousness and training grades in US federal law enforcement trainees. Data from Vasilopoulos *et al.* (2007).

Non-linear relationships

It is often suggested that the link between personality and work performance may not be linear, so may not be detected by correlation. Vasilopoulos, Cucina and Hunter (2007) found a non-linear relationship between personality and training performance in a large sample of police officers; Figure 7.3 shows low scores on conscientiousness are associated with poor training performance, but high scores on conscientiousness do not go with higher grades.

RESEARCH AGENDA

- More on moderator variables, both other aspects of personality and external factors.
- Whether mental ability moderates link between personality and work performance.

The problem of faking

PQs are not *tests*, but *self-reports*. A test has right and wrong answers, but a self-report does not. Many PQs look fairly transparent to critics and laypeople, who argue that no one applying for a job as a manager is likely to say true to *I am poor at organizing myself*. PQs, argue the critics, are easily faked. For many uses of PQs, this does not matter; the tester can rely on the principle of rational self-disclosure: a person seeking career advice, or help with personal problems, can be assumed to be motivated to be frank when completing a PQ. It might be unwise to rely on the same assumption when people complete PQs to get a job they really want, or really need. This implies that PQs may be less useful in selection. Some experts, however, disagree and argue that:

- most people tell the truth when completing PQs in job applications,
- it does not matter if they do not because 'faking' does not reduce PQ validity, and
- faking is not a real problem.

Assertion 1 – people tell the truth on PQs when applying for jobs

Can people fake?

In directed faking studies, people complete the PQ with instructions to give answers that will create a good impression, or secure a job they really want. A meta-analysis (Viswesvaran & Ones, 1999) showed that people find these directions easy to follow and can achieve large increases in scores (Figure 7.4). Conscientiousness, which predicts work performance best of the big five, can be improved by nearly one whole SD. HT scores also improve a lot in directed faking studies (Ones & Viswesvaran, 1998b). Directed faking research shows people can fake PQs, but does not prove they actually do when applying for jobs.

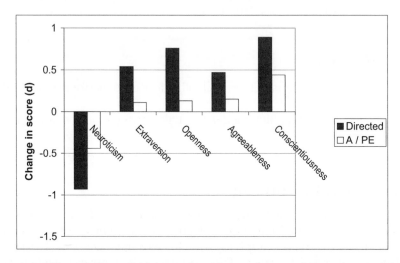

Figure 7.4   Effect of directed faking and applicant status on PQ measures of the big five. Baseline represents averages for unfaked big five or present employees. Data for directed faking from Viswesvaran & Ones (1999). Data for applicant / present employee comparison from Birkeland *et al.* (2006).

Do people fake?

There are several lines of evidence on 'real life' frequency of faking in selection. Surveys (e.g. McDaniel *et al.* 1997) report that some people say they would fake good on a PQ or have faked good, but more say they would not or have not. But, do people tell the truth about the telling the truth? Books and websites exist in the USA advising people how to fake PQs in selection.

Applicant / present employee (PE) comparisons

PEs – it is argued – have got the job so have less need to fake the PQ. Birkeland *et al.* (2006) meta-analysed 33 studies comparing As and PEs, and found As score higher on conscientiousness and lower on neuroticism (Figure 7.4). This strongly suggests some As fake good, but suggests also that directed faking research overestimates faking good in job applications. (One could question the argument that PEs will not fake; it may depend whether the results could affect their career or reputation, a point not addressed in Birkeland *et al.*'s meta-analysis.)

Applicant / research comparison

The ideal research sees the same set of people complete the PQ twice, once for research or their own enlightenment, and once in a real application for a real job. Two studies have achieved this in slightly different ways, but both suggest that up to one-third of As fake.

1. Griffith, Chmielowski and Yoshita (2007) contacted people who had completed a conscientiousness scale when applying for temp work, and asked them to complete it again, this time 'as honestly as possible'. Faking was defined as a change in score greater than error of measurement. Griffith *et al.* found that 31% had faked in selection. This study needs replication as it started with 143 As of whom only 60 agreed to complete the second phase.
2. Stewart *et al.* (2008) used a slightly unethical 'bogus job' method. Students who had completed a PQ for research were later contacted, ostensibly by someone else, and told they had been identified as possible candidates for corporate recruiting and asked to complete the same PQ. Changes larger than error of measurement defined those who faked; 14% increased their conscientiousness score.

RESEARCH AGENDA

- Replication of Griffith *et al.* and Stewart *et al.*, with larger samples and higher return rate.

Assertion 2 – faking does not reduce PQ validity

Available evidence strongly suggests some As fake good on PQs. Laypeople tend to see this a serious problem: it seems intuitively obvious that untrue answers will not predict work performance. Some researchers (e.g. Ones & Viswesvaran 1998b) assert however that faking does not reduce PQs' validity, so is not a problem. Four lines of research are relevant.

1. *Faking and factor structure.* Some research has suggested faking may change the factor structure of PQs (i.e. may change what the PQ is measuring), which tends to invalidate it altogether. Schmit and Ryan (1993) found that faked NEOs acquired a sixth 'ideal employee' factor, while Ellingson, Sackett and Hough (1999) found that faking weakened the factor structure of ABLE. However, these were directed faking studies, which generate larger effects; Bradley and Hauenstein (2006) compared the factor structure of two PQs in As, and PEs tested for research purposes only, and found no difference.

   Two lines of research depend on lie scales, which seek to detect people who are faking good, and which are discussed further on page 165.

2. *Comparing fakers and non-fakers.* With very large samples, researchers can divide fakers from non-fakers, using the lie scale, and compute separate validities for each. Hough *et al.* (1990) concluded that validity coefficients in US Army recruits who faked ABLE were no lower than in those who did not; Burns and Christiansen (2006) suggested that validity was in fact slightly reduced.

3. *Correcting for faking.* Some research has 'corrected' PQs for faking good, usually by partialling out lie scores, and concluded that this does not affect validity (Christiansen *et al.*, 1994). Unfortunately, lie scores do not seem to be good indicators of actual faking (v.i.), but are at least partly real assessments of aspects of personality – high conscientiousness and low neuroticism – that relate to work performance. So these two lines of evidence are not conclusive.

4. *Applicant / PE comparisons.* If PEs do not need to fake because they have already got the job, whereas As do fake because they want to get the job, validity of PQs may differ for the two populations. If As' PQ data are less trustworthy, validity may be lower in As. Three meta-analyses have compared As and PEs (Hough, 1998; Ones *et al.*, 1993; Tett *et al.*, 1999) with conflicting results. Ones *et al.* and Tett *et al.* found that validity is higher in As than in PEs, implying faking good does not reduce validity. Tett *et al.* assembled 83 studies of PEs, but could find only 12 of As. Hough found no difference between concurrent and predictive validity, for job performance (but found concurrent validity much higher for CPB). Concurrent validation usually means testing PEs, whereas predictive validation includes research with As.

Faking does matter in selection?

Some research casts doubt on the comforting conclusion that faking does not matter. Ellingson *et al.*'s (1999) sample completed ABLE twice, once honestly, once faking good. Ellingson used the unfaked ABLEs to decide who *ought* to get the job, and the faked ABLEs to see who *actually* would get the job. Where one in three fake and one in three are appointed, 40% of those who 'ought to have' got the job did not, seeing it go to someone who faked good. Stewart *et al.* (2008) reported a similar analysis with similar results; they noted the interesting point that people who improve when completing the PQ for selection do not always maximize their score; some people whose conscientiousness is 'really' low fake an increase that still leaves them below average, and far below the point of getting an offer. Campion (Morgeson *et al.*, 2007) offered another argument why faking does matter: 'The fact that some candidates fake means that other candidates are denied jobs' – honest applicants should not be penalized. Note however that no one has yet produced conclusive proof that faking PQs reduces validity. Hough *et al.*'s analysis used social desirability scales, which are very poor at detecting faking. Studies that use directed faking or that identify faking by increases greater than error of measurement have produced inconclusive results, or have not researched 'real' work performance. Large sample sizes are needed to prove differences between correlations.

Assertion 3 – faking is not a real issue

'Faking' covers a range of possibilities, from having a positive self-image to deliberate lying. Dipboye (Morgeson *et al.*, 2007) described some PQ answers as aspirational: *I am a good leader* may really mean *I would like to be good leader*. Is this faking? Zickar and Robie's (1999) analysis of faking rating format PQs suggested that people use the extreme answers more: *I am polite to others – always*, rather than *usually*. Is this faking, or just being a bit more emphatic?

Several authors have argued that PQs are not intended to be a literal description of real behaviour. They are rather a way of 'negotiating an identity' (Hogan, Barrett & Hogan, 2007). Most people have a favourable self-image so will present a generally favourable view of themselves. It is further argued that civilized life requires a degree of dissimulation; only criminals and small children make no attempt to conceal negative feelings or unacceptable urges. It has even been suggested that faking good is an aspect of emotional intelligence: knowing what people want to hear and being prepared to say it. There are several snags with this argument. There are jobs where saying what people want to hear is important, but there are lots more where it is not remotely appropriate. Research finds no correlation at all between faking good scores and work performance (Ones, Viswesvaran & Reiss, 1996). A PQ is an unnecessarily long and complicated way of determining if someone is a good liar. The whole argument has an air of desperation about it. Marcus (in press) offers a more reasoned version of the fakers-may-be-good-applicants argument and suggests self-presentation is a better name than faking. Marcus argues that most As see their role as presenting themselves in the best possible light, and suggests this is easier on PQs than in interviews or group exercises. He also notes that motivation affects most selection tests, not just PQs; people do better if they try hard, and worse if they are anxious.

Several features of PQs confirm that they probably do not generate accurate accounts of real behaviour. They are full of vague adverbs of frequency: for example, *sometimes, usually* or *generally*. If PQ writers wanted to know how often As lose their temper, they could at least specify *once a month, once a week or several times a day*. The speed with which people complete PQs also suggests answers are not literal descriptions of behaviour. If people can find an answer to *I generally complete tasks on* time in 1.5 seconds, they cannot be reviewing all the tasks they have completed in the last year, and calculating what proportion were finished on time. They must be answering at some more generalized level, along the lines of *I see myself as someone who* finishes tasks on time. Actually, a big problem with PQs is that we do not really know quite what people are telling us when they answer them.

Faking is not a real issue for many PQ items, in the sense that it is very hard to prove someone's answer is not true. Some PQ items can be confirmed by observation, such as items 1 and 2 in Table 7.1. Some could be verified in theory, but probably not in practice, such as item 6: the person's mother and father could tell you, if you can find them, if they are willing to discuss intimate family matters with a stranger, if they can remember events and feelings from many years ago. Many PQ items appear verifiable, but are not, such as item 3; it is easy to see if Smith meets a lot of people, but only Smith knows if he enjoys it or not. A quick check of the 60 items of the shorter version of the NEO PQ finds only one question where one could definitely prove an answer was untrue. In this respect, faking a PQ is not 'as bad as' someone claiming to have a medical degree when they have not.

Act frequency. Buss and Craik (1983) suggested assessing personality by visible, verifiable behaviours, not thoughts and feelings. The more often someone gives orders to others, the more dominant they are. The more often they apologize, the more submissive they are. So far, act frequency data have mostly been collected by self-report, which turns act frequency into a variant of the PQ. It may however lend itself well to 'at work' forms of PQs and may make warnings of verification (v.i.) more plausible.

Dealing with faking good in PQs

There are many lines of defence against faking good. Some modify the way the test is administered.

Warnings

Dwight and Donovan's (2003) meta-analysis distinguished warnings that faking can be detected, which have little or no effect, from warnings that faking will have consequences (e.g. not getting the job), which reduce faking somewhat (d = 0.30). Warning is potentially a quick and easy solution to faking, but creates some problems. It might not survive against well-informed coaching. Zickar and Gibby (2006) thought people will soon realize warnings are empty threats. Vasilopoulos *et al.* (2005) identified another possible problem: their warning said friends, family, teachers and past employers would be used to verify PQ responses, which reduced faking more in less intelligent As. Perhaps brighter As could work out which PQ items are verifiable, and avoid faking them. A PQ that incidentally assesses MA could start creating adverse impact on some minorities – the very problem selectors in the USA hope to avoid by using PQs.

Elaboration

Schmitt and Kunce (2002) found that asking As to give examples reduces faking good (of biodata) considerably. Someone who claims to have led work-groups is asked to describe the groups and the projects they worked on. Elaboration will lose the speed and convenience of the PQ.

Administer by computer

It is sometimes claimed that people are more honest about themselves when giving information to a computer. Feigelson and Dwight's meta-analysis (2000) found people slightly more willing (d = 0.11) to reveal sensitive or embarrassing information to a computer than on paper, but none of the research derives from As or employees.

Response speed

It can be argued that faking good takes longer than honest completion: A must first retrieve the 'real' answer, then decide it is not the right one to give, then choose a different, 'better' one. Speed of answering is easily measured with computer administration. Holden and Hibbs (1995) have shown that response speed reflects other factors besides faking: question length, question format (true/false or rating) and reading speed, so detecting faking by response speed may prove complex. Elliott *et al.* (1996) reported that faking the Eysenck PQ, to look like either a librarian or a stockbroker, took no longer than normal completion. This suggests that people completing PQs can access a stereotype as quickly as an accurate self-description. So perhaps people who are faking do not have to decide their own answer then reject it; perhaps they can go straight to 'the best answer for a managerial job'. Robie *et al.* (2000) reported that people can be coached to avoid taking longer. A related approach is limiting the time allowed to answer each question. Holden, Wood and Tomashewski (2001) tried restricting response time to as little as 1.5 seconds, reading the items aloud, so response time does not include reading time. It does not prevent faking.

Other approaches alter the way the test is written, to try to reduce faking.

Forced choice

Making As choose between statements equated for desirability, like items 15 to 17 in Table 7.1, is intended to prevent them from giving inflated estimates of how 'good' their personality is. Martin, Bowen and Hunt (2002) found that students can fake a junior manager profile on a rating format PQ, but not on the parallel forced-choice version. However, Putka and McCloy (2004) sounded a note of caution. The US Army's new forced-choice PQ – Assessment of Individual Motivation (AIM) – resisted faking successfully, until it was used with real recruits, when scores rose considerably ($d = 0.85$), and no longer predicted success so well. This suggests that techniques that deal with faking in laboratory tests, or with students or PEs, may not survive when used 'for real', with real As. The US Army is developing AIM, after they abandoned their earlier PQ – ABLE – because of faking good.

Forced-choice format usually creates a subtle problem – interdependence between scales (Meade, 2004). On the Allport-Vernon-Lindzey Study of Values (AVL), the six scores must total 180; the test's instructions advise using this as a check on accuracy of scoring. This happens because within each forced choice, one answer scores for, e.g. social interest, while the other scores for, e.g. aesthetic interest. However, if all six scores must total 180, the person who wants to express a strong preference for one value must express less interest in one or more others; it is impossible to get six very high (or six very low) scores on AVL (whereas this is entirely possible on conventional PQs like NEO). Forced-choice PQs cannot usually conclude that Smith is more interested in dominating others than is Jones – a *normative* comparison, the one selectors usually want to make.

Heggestad *et al.* (2006) developed a complex forced-choice format, illustrated in Table 7.13. Each item is a set of four statements, from which As choose one *most like self* and one *least like self*. Each statement relates to a different FFM factor. Two statements are positive and two are negative. Figure 7.5 shows how conventional and forced-choice forms of a PQ fared in directed faking. Forced choice was partly successful in preventing people from improving the whole profile when faking. However, it was not successful from the selector's point of view because people focused their faking good on raising their conscientiousness scores and lowering their neuroticism scores – the two that actually relate to work performance and which the selectors would probably be basing their decision on. These results suggest that people may be quite good at 'seeing through' PQs. They can not only spot the right answers to give, they can also work out which aspects of personality are more important to the employer, when forced choice prevents them from raising every score.

Table 7.13 Set of four statements, comprising one question in Heggestad *et al.*'s forced-choice format, with scoring system.

	Positive / negative	Factor	Person A's response and score	Person B's response and score
I avoid difficult reading material	–	O	Least 2	Least 1
I only feel comfortable with friends	–	E	1	Most 0
I believe that others have good intentions	+	A	Most 2	1
I make lists of things to do	+	C	1	1

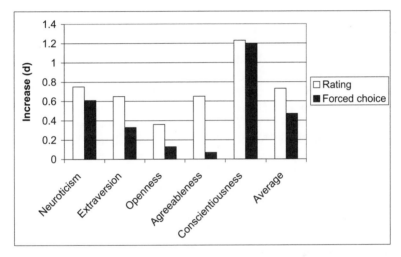

Figure 7.5 Increase in FFM scores from normal to faked, for rating and forced-choice format. Values are *d* scores. Data from Heggestad *et al.* (2006).

Lie scales

Lie scales, aka social desirability scales, aka faking good scales, aka good impression scales, are the traditional solution to faking good. People who deny common faults or claim uncommon virtues (e.g. items 12 and 13 in Table 7.1) may identify themselves as faking good. However, most lie scales turn out to be more complex. Typically, lie scores correlate with other scores on the PQ; Ones *et al.*'s (1996) meta-analysis found correlations of –0.37 with neuroticism and 0.20 with conscientiousness. This suggests that lie scales measure real aspects of personality as well as faking good. Ones *et al.* found a few researches that compared self-reported lie score with others' ratings of neuroticism and conscientiousness – which are entirely independent of the target's faking good – and still found correlations with social desirability scores on the PQ. Zickar and Drasgow (1996) used large military samples to show that lie scales were not very good at detecting directed faking; a cut-off score on the lie scale that made 5% false positives (saying an honest completion was faked) detected only 28% of directed fakings. Two recent studies (Quist, Arora & Griffith, 2007; Stewart *et al.*, 2008) identify 'real fakers' – people whose scores rose by more than error of measurement when completing the PQ for selection – and find that lie scales generally missed them.

Correcting for faking

Some PQs use the lie scale to 'correct' other scores. MMPI's *K* key assesses defensiveness, then adds varying proportions of *K* to other scores to estimate the shortcomings people would have admitted if they had been more frank. Cronbach (1970) expressed scepticism: 'if the subject lies to the tester there is no way to convert the lies into truth'. Ellingson *et al.* (1999) compared faked and unfaked ABLEs from the same sample, so could answer the question: do correction keys succeed in turning lies back into truth? At one level, the answer was 'yes'. Faked ABLEs were 'better' than unfaked on average, but the corrected faked ones were no 'better' than the unfaked. At another level, however, the answer was 'no'. Faking changed the rank order of As (compared with a rank order based on unfaked completion), and so changed who 'got the job'. Correcting for faking did not change the rank order back, so did not ensure that the 'right' people were appointed after all.

Perhaps the simplest solution to faking is changing how decisions are made. Mueller-Hanson, Heggestad and Thornton (2003) argue that faking good means high scores are ambiguous; the A might be genuinely 'good', or might be a faker. By contrast, low scores are easier to interpret; they indicate – very crudely speaking – a 'poor' A. This suggests PQs can be used to select out the unsuitable, but may not be so good at selecting in strong As. If PQs are used this way, they are better used early on, in the sifting phase, rather than at short list, which is easy with Internet assessment.

Faking good is not a new problem: Zickar and Gibby (2006) noted that the first directed faking study was published in 1934, the first forced-choice PQ in 1939, and the first lie scale in 1942.

RESEARCH AGENDA

- Whether PQs achieve validity by excluding low scorers, i.e. that who haven't got it and can't or won't fake it.
- What happens if fakers are excluded, in terms of validity, and subsequent work performance.
- Replication of Griffeth *et al.* with larger *N* and higher 'return rate' and in range of different jobs.
- What answers to PQ questions really mean?

PQs, law and fairness

PQs have encountered surprisingly little trouble with the law, especially compared with mental ability tests.

Gender differences

There are gender differences in many PQ scores (Hough, Oswald, & Ployhart, 2001); men tend to report being more forceful and competitive while women tend to report being more caring, as well as more anxious. Gender differences create a dilemma for HR. Using separate norm tables for men and women is prohibited in the USA by the Civil Rights Act of 1991, and thought inadvisable in Britain because calculating scores differently for men and women could be seen as direct discrimination. On the other hand, using pooled gender norms may create adverse impact. Using a cut-off score of $T = 60$ on dominance to select managers risks excluding more women than men. However, there have been few complaints against PQs in the USA on grounds of adverse impact, partly because the male/female differences are smaller than majority–minority differences in ability tests, and partly because PQs are not usually used with mechanistic cut-offs. Isaacson and Griffith (2007) found some suggestion that males fake PQs more than females.

Ethnicity

Comparing majority and minorities in the USA suggests PQs will not create the major adverse impact problems found with tests of mental ability. Project A (White *et al.*, 1993) found that African Americans score higher than whites on ABLE scales of dependability, achievement and adjustment. Some European data are now available. Ones and Anderson's (2002) analysis of college students in Britain found few white–Afro differences, while white–Asian and –Chinese differences 'favoured' minorities, showing them to be more conscientious. (In theory, this means white As could claim adverse impact; in practice, problems generally arise when minorities get 'poorer' scores.) However, in The Netherlands, te Nijenhuis, van der Flier and van Leeuwen (1997) found some immigrant groups score higher on neuroticism and lower on extraversion.

Age

Large age differences are found in some PQ scales; extraversion, measured by the Eysenck PQ, falls steadily and considerably ($d = 0.88$) between 18 and 65 (Cook *et al.*, 2007).

HTs, like PQs, create little adverse impact; Ones and Viswesvaran (1998a) analysed gender, age and ethnicity differences in a meta-analysis, covering 725,000 persons. Women, the over 40s, Hispanic Americans and Native Americans all score slightly more honest.

Disability

The Americans with Disabilities Act prohibits health-related enquiries before a job offer is made, which has two implications for PQs. First, questions that could be seen as health-related enquiries, such as item 10 in Table 7.1, have been deleted from some scales. Second, health includes mental health, so scales with psychiatric-sounding names, such as neuroticism, become suspect for selection use (whereas reversed *N* called *emotional stability* is more acceptable).

Privacy

Questions 7, 8 and 9 in Table 7.1 may be too intrusive to use in selection. In the *Soroka v Dayton-Hudson* case, an applicant claimed that PQ items about politics and religion were contrary to the Constitution of the State of California (Merenda, 1995); the case was settled out of court, so no definitive ruling emerged.

The potential danger of multi-score PQs

Most PQs come as fixed packages. The 16PF assesses all 16 factors every time it is used. One cannot decide to use only dominance, ego strength, and shrewdness, or to leave out suspicion and guilt proneness. This is just an inconvenience to researchers, but a serious problem for selectors. Suppose job analysis has identified dominance, ego strength and shrewdness as the (only) personality characteristics needed for the job. The other 13 scores are not job-related and should not be used in making the decision. If selectors do use them, the employer could have serious problems defending the selection system in the event of complaints. PQs that assess weakness and poor adjustment can be particularly dangerous: someone applying for a clerical job will be justifiably annoyed to find their psychopathic deviance or level of fantasy aggression have been assessed. Lewis Goldberg offers an extensive bank of scales, from which a job-specific PQ can be generated, linked to job analysis, to avoid assessing anything irrelevant. Goldberg's bank, which contains analogues to many popular PQs, has another unusual feature: it is in the public domain, and can be used by everyone without restriction or payment, through his IPIP website (address at end of chapter).

Key points

In Chapter 7, you have learned the following.

- Personality is a vaguer and more diffuse concept than ability, and there are many models of personality.
- Personality is most conveniently assessed by PQ.
- PQs are written by a variety of methods, which generally overlap to some extent, including internal analysis by statistics and external analysis, comparing group of people of known characteristics (empirical keying).

- The FFM is widely accepted, but may not give the best prediction of work behaviour; other models exist.
- PQs have limited value in predicting how well people can do a job.
- PQs may prove slightly more successful predicting 'attitude' aspects of work behaviour, although most correlations are still lower than 0.30.
- PQs may also be more successful at predicting avoidance of deviant or problematic behaviour at work.
- Preliminary results suggest that the relationship between team personality and team performance may be complex, and that low scorers may be able to hold back the entire group.
- PQs are self-reports, not tests, and can be faked.
- Directed faking research shows that most people can fake; the proportion who actually do fake in selection is less clearly documented.
- Faking may affect the outcome of selection.
- Faking can be limited but not eliminated by warnings and forced-choice format.
- Gender differences are often found with PQs, but ethnicity differences do not seem to be a major problem.
- PQs have been criticized as unduly intrusive in some of their questions.

Key references

Barrick *et al.* (2001) present a meta-meta-analysis of PQ validity.

Bell (2007) presents a meta-analysis of personality and team performance.

Berry *et al.* (2007) review research on honesty tests.

Cook (1993) gives a general introduction to personality theory and research.

Griffith *et al.* (2007) describe the error of measurement approach to detecting faking.

Guion and Gottier (1965) present an early, and not very optimistic, review of personality test validity.

Heggestad *et al.* (2006) describe a complex forced-choice format PQ.

McDaniel *et al.* (2006) describe the application of trim and fill technique to detecting selective reporting of PQ validity data.

Morgeson *et al.* (2007) discuss the issues of validity and fakability of PQs. The same issue also contains articles by Ones *et al.* and Tett & Christiansen offering counter-arguments.

Ones *et al.* (1993) present a meta-analysis of honesty test research.

Zickar (2001) describes the use of PQs to try to screen out 'thugs and agitators'.

Zickar and Gibby (2006) give an interesting historical account of the faking issue.

Useful websites

ipip.ori.org/ipip. Goldberg's bank of PQ scales.

Alternative ways of assessing personality

What year was the Bataan death march?

Introduction

Murphy (Morgeson *et al.*, 2007) thinks that the PQ is 'not salvageable' as a selection method, which creates an urgent need for a replacement. This chapter will consider alternatives, using the five headings of types of information outlined in Chapter 1.

Self-report

Chapter 1 considered the application form and CV, which raise the same issue as PQs: Can the selector believe the information the applicant supplies? Applicants (As) who claim qualifications or experience they have not got can be found out if the employer checks up, whereas PQs are generally hard to verify. Chapter 8 will consider biodata and weighted application blanks, which can be faked, but do tend to collect more readily verifiable information.

Projective tests assume that people project their personality into what they see in drawings or patterns, or how they complete sentences or stories.

Thematic Apperception Test (TAT) uses pictures chosen for their vagueness and suggestive content (Figure 8.1). People describe 'what led up to the event shown in the picture, what is happening, what the characters are thinking and feeling, and what the outcome will be', and are supposed to project into the story their own 'dominant drives, emotions, sentiments, complexes and conflicts'. The TAT is most often used to assess need for achievement, or ambition. McClelland (1971) argued that need for achievement is unconscious and cannot be assessed by PQ.

Defence Mechanism Test (DMT) is a variant on the TAT, using a picture showing a hero figure and a hideous face. The picture is made more ambiguous by being shown at first for only a fraction of second. Various defence mechanisms can be inferred from responses to the DMT; for example, seeing the hideous face as an inanimate object is coded as repression because the person is pushing emotion out of the picture.

The *Rorschach Ink Blot* test asks people what they see in 12 ink blots (Figure 8.2). Various scoring systems are used, for example, inanimate movement

Figure 8.1   A picture similar to those used in the Thematic Apperception Test.

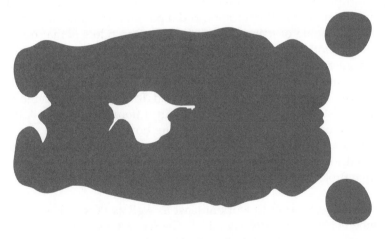

Figure 8.2   A blot similar to those used in Rorschach test.

(seeing objects, rather than people or animals, moving) indicates inner tension and feelings of helplessness, and may be a sign of poor response to stress.

Sentence completion. The Miner Sentence Completion Scale is written for select-ing managers, and assesses, for example, attitude to authority or competitive motivation, by how people complete '*My last boss was ...*' or '*I don't like people who ...*'.

Projective tests are *self-reports* because they use what A says, but have ele-ments of *involuntary* assessment because they may discover things A does not

Table 8.1   Meta-analysis of projective and PQ measures of entrepreneurial performance.

	k	N	r
TAT	8	915	0.16
Miner Sentence Completion	7	463	0.20
PQ	5	803	0.19

Data from Collins *et al.* (2004). Correlations not corrected in any way.

mean to reveal. Kinslinger (1966) reviewed early US personnel research, using Rorschach, TAT and sentence completion tests, and found generally fairly poor results. However, three small-scale meta-analyses have since found more promising results.

1. Reilly and Chao (1982) found an average uncorrected validity of 0.28 in six studies published since Kinslinger's review; removing an outlier (an unusually high value) of 0.68 reduced average validity to 0.18.
2. Martinussen and Torjussen (1993) meta-analysed 15 studies of the DMT in mostly military pilot selection and reported an uncorrected validity of 0.20. The rationale of using the test for selecting pilots is that defence mechanisms bind psychic energy, so it is not available for coping with reality in an emergency. However, Martinussen and Torjussen did discover one worrying moderator variable: the DMT works in Scandinavia, but not in Britain or The Netherlands. Martinussen and Torjussen thought the test may be administered or scored differently in different countries. A test becomes very much less useful if one isn't sure how to use it.
3. Collins, Hanges and Locke (2004) reported a meta-analysis of measures of need for achievement and entrepreneurial performance. Table 8.1 shows two projective tests achieve validity as good as a PQ.

Projective tests seem to work at least as well as PQs. A key issue, therefore, is whether they are as easily faked. There is extensive research in the clinical field, which seems to produce mixed results, but little or none in the selection context.

Interview

Chapter 4 examined the interview, which is another mixed method, largely self-report but with elements of demonstration evidence when used to assess knowledge or social skill. Chapter 4 showed that one in three selection interviews are used to assess personality, especially conscientiousness, and that they are moderately successful, to the extent that they correlate with PQs (Table 4.4, page 83). Some structured interview systems have been written specifically to assess personality. Trull *et al.* (1998) described a 120-question system for assessing the five-factor model (FFM). Chapter 4 showed structured interviews may be able to select better employees, so they may prove successful also at assessing personality. As yet, no workplace data have been reported. Nor have any data on faking good.

RESEARCH AGENDA

- More research on projective test validity
- Fakability of projective tests used for selection
- Validity and fakability of structured interviews used to assess personality.

Other reports

Reference checks were discussed in Chapter 5. They do not achieve very good validity in selection, possibly through pervasive leniency. Research has not analysed their relative success in assessing personality, compared with other attributes such as work performance, background, and so on.

Other reports can be collected in various formats: ratings, other form PQs and Q sorts.

Ratings

Others' ratings of a target person have been studied in several contexts. In the workplace, there are peer ratings, and 360-degree feedback ratings by peers and subordinates. There is also an extensive body of social psychological research by Funder (2007).

Other form PQs

PQs can be reworded to describe other people rather than oneself. *I enjoy meeting new people* becomes *[Smith] enjoys meeting new people*. Other form PQs do not seem to have been used in selection. Some leadership questionnaires collect reports from followers as well as from the leader him/herself.

Q sort technique

This technique uses statements similar to PQ items, which are sorted into nine categories according to how well they describe the target. The nine categories must form a rough normal distribution, forcing the completer to differentiate and preventing undue leniency. The Q sort is usually completed by another person, often a psychologist. The California Q sort asks for interpretations of behaviour (e.g. *target habitually tests the limits, to see how much he/she can get away with*), whereas the Riverside Q sort is more descriptive and verifiable (e.g. *verbally fluent*). Q sorts do not appear to have been used in selection.

There are other possibilities, which have not been researched much, if at all. Chapter 5 noted that research has not made much progress with free form references, where sources describe targets in their own words. Research could also analyse behavioural or emotional reactions to others. It might be instructive to know that everyone always stands up when Smith enters the room, or that many people experience fear at the sight of Jones.

Other–other agreement

Several lines of research find others' views of a target agree, to a modest extent. Chapter 5 noted that Conway and Huffcutt's (1997) meta-analysis of 360-degree feedback ratings found some inter-observer agreement, especially averaging across a number of raters. Some 360-degree ratings refer to aspects of personality, especially relations with others. The analysis showed that subordinates tend to agree better on their superiors' interpersonal behaviour, perhaps because they are at the receiving end of it. Funder's research, mostly on students, also reported generally low correlations, around 0.20 to 0.30, but confirmed that others' ratings of personality do contain some information.

Self–other agreement

Connolly, Kavanagh and Viswesvaran (2007) meta-analysed some 60 studies comparing self-report and other report of personality, and found raw correlations of 0.30 to 0.45, rising to 0.46 to 0.62 when corrected for reliability of both measures. They found relatives agree with target slightly better than work colleagues, except for conscientiousness, but work colleagues' reports still correlate 0.27 to 0.41. Their analysis did not distinguish between rating and PQ format. Funder's research showed that others' ratings of a target show some agreement with the target's self-rating. More 'visible' traits, such as sociability, are easier to rate accurately than less visible ones, such as tendency to worry. The longer others have known the target and the closer the relationship, the better other and self-ratings agree. Funder has also shown that others' reports, especially two or more others, predict the target's behaviour better than the target's self-report.

Conclusions

As noted in Chapter 5, other people who have known targets for a long time may be uniquely well placed to describe accurately their personality. It is interesting to note that a lot of personality research chooses to define someone's personality by self-report plus two or more reports from others, preferably 'knowledgeable others'. However, Chapter 5 also noted problems with other reports in the selection context. People who know the target well – former co-workers, family and friends – will tend to be inaccessible and/or unlikely to be motivated to provide a frank account. Defamation may also be a problem; if people can be sued for writing a bad reference, could they also be sued for rating Smith 1 out of 7 for trustworthiness, or checking true for *seldom completes tasks on time*? Research suggests that 360-degree feedback could generate useful data on personality, which might be accessible to HR for promotions and internal selection, although no research on their use appears to have been reported. Other employers' 360-degree feedback, needed for external selections, is likely to prove inaccessible.

Others' reports can be useful where the target person is too important to be asked to complete a PQ. American research has assessed the personality of US Presidents, all the way back to Washington, by asking historians to complete other form assessments. Rubenzer, Faschingbauer and Ones (2000) correlated other form FFM PQs with ratings of presidential 'greatness', which can be seen as an index of job performance; 'greater' presidents were more open, more extravert, but less agreeable. Conscientiousness showed how correlation based on small samples can fluctuate; including a certain recent President changed an insignificant 0.06 to a definitely positive 0.17.

Expert opinion

The limited amount of research on 'expert opinion' reported by Reilly & Chao (1982) did not yield a very high validity. Judge *et al.* (1999) used three California cohort studies to study career success longitudinally. Personality in childhood and adolescence was assessed retrospectively using ratings made by experts from detailed case histories, then related to occupational status and income when the cohort had reached their fifties. Conscientious and extravert people were more successful, while anxious people tended to be less successful. Less agreeable people were more successful, suggesting perhaps that it does not pay to be too nice to others if you want to get ahead. (Recall that 'greater' US Presidents are less agreeable.) The five personality factors combined correlated 0.54 with career success. Studies using conventional PQs, meta-analysed by Ng *et al.* (2005), found much weaker links between the big five and career success. Long-term follow-up studies are particularly valuable because they avoid direction of cause problems. Judge *et al.*'s cohort were assessed as they were before they entered employment, which excludes the possibility that being successful in work makes people less agreeable.

Background checks

Some types of background check are said to include trying to find out what As' friends and neighbours think about them, but there is no research on how often this is done, nor whether it contributes any useful information.

RESEARCH AGENDA

- How accurate reference checks are for personality
- Validity of others' reports of personality in selection and promotion
- Acceptability and fakability of others' reports of personality
- Extent of use and validity of background checks of 'lifestyle'.

Demonstration evidence

Demonstration by paper-and-pencil test

Cattell devised two personality measures that are paper-and-pencil, but not (entirely) self-report. The Motivation Analysis Test (MAT) (Bernard, Walsh & Mills, 2005) uses some novel item formats (#1 and 2 in Table 8.2), based on the assumption that peoples' motives shape the information they acquire, or the estimates they make. An aggressive person knows about machine guns, while a fearful person overestimates the risk of rabies, or knows the date of the Bataan death march. No data on the use of the MAT in selection have been reported. The Objective-Analytic Battery is more ambitious, assessing 10 factors, using seven or eight tests for each. The O-AB is only half objective, for many components are actually self-reports. Kline and Cooper (1984) concluded that many O-AB subtests measure ability, rather than personality. The O-AB is very time-consuming, taking an estimated seven times longer to complete than the self-report 16PF.

Conditional reasoning (CR)

James (Bing *et al.*, 2007) described a conditional reasoning test of aggression, intended for use in selection. Aggressive people have justification mechanisms, which cause them to draw different conclusions in a test that resembles a verbal reasoning measure. In question 3 in Table 8.2, answer [b] reveals a degree of paranoia and hostility, whereas answer [a] is sensible, and answer [c] is simply wrong. James's research showed scores predict deviant behaviour in the workplace very well, uncorrected correlations averaging 0.42. The

---

Table 8.2   Five sample items from personality tests.

1. Which of the following is not a type of machine gun?
    uzi   sterling   sten   gresley
2. What is the probability of catching rabies in Britain?
    1 in 100   1 in 1,000   1 in 10,000   1 in a million
3. Far Eastern cars are cheaper than British cars because
    a – labour costs in the Far East are lower
    b – British car manufacturers like overcharging people
    c – it costs more to ship cars to Britain
4. You are given a task you do not feel trained or qualified to do. What do you do?
    a – complete the task as best you can
    b – complain
    c – ask colleagues for help
    d – ask for the task to be given to someone else
5p. Imagine that you get a paper published in a very prestigious journal
Say in your own words what is the single most likely cause of this.
        To what extent was this due to luck?   totally 1 2 3 4 5 6 7 not at all
        To what extent was this due to you?   totally 1 2 3 4 5 6 7 not at all
5n. Imagine that you apply for a job you really want and do not even get shortlisted

CR test does not correlate with a conventional PQ measure of aggressiveness, but the combination of PQ aggression ('overt' aggression) and CR aggression ('implicit' aggression) successfully predicts higher levels of counterproductive behaviour. However, meta-analysis of a larger database by Berry, Sackett and Tobares (2007) found poorer results, with raw validities of 0.15–0.24 for CPBs, and only 0.14 for work performance. Berry *et al.* were unable to compute operational validities, but estimate them at 0.25–0.32 for CPBs and 0.19 for work performance, as good as conventional PQs. James argues the justification mechanisms are unconscious, so the aggressive person cannot 'control or manipulate or lie'. LeBreton *et al.* (2007) described a series of studies intended to show that the CR test is not fakable. Mean scores for As, present employees and students are the same; scores do not rise in directed faking. However, they also found that if people are told it is a test of aggression, and to give aggressive answers, they can achieve very high (aggressive) scores. If people can identify aggressive answers and give them, could they not equally easily spot them and not give them?

Situational judgement

Lahuis, Martin and Avis (2005) described a situational judgement test written specifically to assess conscientiousness, using questions like question 4 in Table 8.2, but have no data on its validity or relationship to other measures of conscientiousness. Further research, described in Chapter 11 shows SJTs in general, not written specially to assess personality, have low correlations with agreeableness, conscientiousness and neuroticism.

Attributional style

Research on depression has shown that depressed people tend to see good things happening by chance or others' actions, while bad things happen through their own faults. Questions 5p and 5n illustrate an attributional style test, which has proved successful selecting insurance salespeople (Corr & Gray, 1995). ASQ measures might prove fairly easy to coach for.

Implicit Association Tests (IATs)

IATs were first devised to assess racism. IAT starts by asking people to make very simple decisions: press the left key if the word is pleasant, and the right key if it is unpleasant, then press the left key if the name is Asian, and press right key if name is white. These simple decisions take about half a second to make. In the second phase of IAT, the person gets a mix of names to sort by race and words to sort by pleasantness. The person does this twice – first pressing left key for own race and pleasantness, and right key for other race and unpleasantness, then – and this is the crucial part of IAT – pressing left key for own race or unpleasantness, and right key for other race or pleasantness. Having to remember that the left key stands for Asian and nice, while the right key stands for white and nasty, slows some people down so they take around a 1/10th second longer for each decision. The test detects their implicit association between white and nice. IAT can predict behaviour towards other race persons, is reasonably reliable, and not readily faked. IAT can be adapted to assess aspects of personality (Steffens & Konig, 2006). The two interleaved lists are for self/other, and e.g. extravert/introvert. Siers & Christiansen (2008) reported some preliminary workplace data for IAT measures of extraversion, conscientiousness and neuroticism. They concluded that IAT has promise, but needs a lot of research on reliability, convergent validity (e.g. link to PQ measures) and discriminant validity (can IAT distinguish e.g. extraversion from conscientiousness?). Their results indicate IAT measures of personality may also reflect self-esteem and mental ability, which could be a problem. They suggested that IAT may prove coachable, which would limit its value in selection.

RESEARCH AGENDA

- Reliability, and validity (predictive, construct, discriminant) of CRT, ASQ and IAT
- Fakability and coachability of CRT, ASQ and IAT.

Behavioural demonstration

Lievens *et al.* (2006) used expert panels to assess the suitability of various assessment centre exercises for revealing personality. Figure 8.3 shows that written exercises may have limited scope for assessing personality, but group discussions, especially competitive ones, may prove very versatile. Gosling *et al.* (1998) found that people in a group discussion did not do anything 'prototypical' of *neuroticism* or *openness*, whereas *extraversion, conscientiousness* and *agreeable* could be coded from behaviour such as 'laughs out loud' or 'yelling at someone'.

AC exercise ⇓ Personality ⇒	N	E	O	A	C
Competitive group	√	√	√	√	√
Co-operative group	-	√	√	√	√
Oral presentation	√	-	-	-	√
Role-play	-	√	-	√	-
Case analysis	-	-	-	-	√
In tray	-	-	-	-	√

Figure 8.3 Links between six generic assessment centre exercises, and FFM, according to experts. √ indicates experts rated that exercise likely to reflect that personality factor. Data from Lievens *et al.* (2006).

Numerous other behavioural assessments have been proposed (Cattell & Warburton, 1967; Borkenau *et al.*, 2001). Many of these pre-date the FFM, but can usefully be fitted into it.

Neuroticism

The Office of Strategic Services (OSS Assessment Staff, 1948) used deliberately stressful exercises to assess the ability to remain calm under pressure, for selecting secret agents during World War Two. For example, As try to explain to hostile and bullying interrogators their unauthorized presence late at night in a government office. Clinical psychology provides behavioural tests of fear of snakes or of public speaking.

Extraversion

Tell a joke to the group, or sing a song to them. Be persuasive, fluent and forceful in a group discussion.

Open-mindedness

Evaluate three ways of spending a budget to reduce drug use in young people and generate a fourth one. Tell the group a dramatic story about each one of three TAT cards.

Agreeableness

The OSS used a construction task, in which A supervises two 'assistants' who are deliberately obstructive in contrasting ways. This checks whether A remains agreeable even when others behave in a way that might reasonably elicit less agreeable behaviour.

Conscientiousness

Hartshorne and May's (1928) Character Education Inquiry (CEI) included some very ingenious behavioural tests of honesty, giving people opportunities to lie, steal or cheat. Their battery was intended for children, but could be adapted to adults. However, the CEI tests concealed their purpose, and their very existence, in a way that would not be possible in selection (nor ethical).

There is no shortage of ideas for demonstrated assessments of the FFM, but there are some major practical problems.

The 'personality sphere'

Behavioural assessment of extraversion should cover the whole concept of extraversion, which requires demarcation of the relevant personality sphere. McFall and Marston (1970) developed a set of 16 representative examples of assertive behaviour.

Reliability

Mischel (1968) noted that CEI's honesty tests intercorrelated so poorly as to cast doubt on the existence of a trait, but they were mostly one-item tests, which are inherently unreliable. A one-item PQ would be similarly highly unreliable. Choosing a representative set of behaviours by adequate sampling of the personality sphere, as in the McFall and Marston study, will serve the two purposes of ensuring that the assessment covers the whole concept of assertiveness and of generating a reliable score.

Length

McFall and Marston listed 16 aspects of assertiveness. However, assertiveness is just one of six facets of extraversion, so 96 behavioural tests might be needed to assess the whole of extraversion, and no less than 480 to cover the entire FFM. How long will this take? Problems of applicant motivation and fatigue are likely to arise. Note also that McFall and Marston's behavioural tests are shorter than many: the assessee hears a brief description of a situation and line of dialogue (e.g. someone attempting to jump the queue in front of the assessee), then speaks his/her reply. Some behavioural assessments, such as group discussions, last 30 minutes or more. A 480-item test is by no means a preposterous idea: some PQs are longer (e.g. the MMPI with 550 questions).

Missing the point?

Assertiveness is a highly visible behaviour, by its very nature: assertion that is not noticed is not assertion. The same tends to be true of much of extraversion, which is all about how people behave with other people. The same however is not true for much of the neuroticism factor. Five of the six NEO neuroticism facets are primarily emotions: anxiety, hostility, depression, self-consciousness and vulnerability. What does a behavioural test of vulnerability look like? Vulnerability is defined by the NEO Manual – in part – as 'feel(ing) unable to cope with stress, becoming dependent, hopeless, or panicked when facing emergency situations'. The OSS behavioural tests covered this; so to some extent does the pressure of competitive group discussions in assessment centres. But what about the rest of the definition of vulnerability: 'low scorers perceive themselves as capable of handling themselves in difficult situation', whereas high scorers see themselves as not capable. Logically, the fact that someone performs badly in an exercise says nothing about what they see or feel, and vice versa. The only source of information about how people feel – anxious, depressed, vulnerable, hostile – is what they say, which 'takes us back to where we came in', the self-report or PQ. In the short NEO PQ, six of the 12 neuroticism items start with 'I feel ...' . HR's problem is that people may not readily admit feelings of inadequacy, self-doubt, resentment or hopelessness when applying for jobs.

A related issue arises with *agreeableness* and *conscientiousness*. Agreeable persons are nice to others because they like people and want to be nice to them. There are individuals who are nice to people because it suits their purposes, but they are not truly agreeable. It would be very difficult to tell the two apart by behavioural tests. Similarly, part of *conscientiousness* is having principles and standards, and feeling that one must adhere to them, which could be difficult to distinguish by behavioural tests from conforming through fear or expedience.

Ethics and acceptability

The OSS tests probably pushed As further and harder than many employers would want to do today, for fear of complaints or damaging the organization's reputation (problems that tend not to arise in wartime). However, if a job does involve a lot of stress and conflict, the employer should avoid taking on people who will not be able to cope. Demanding behavioural tests can be justified by careful job analysis, and so long as As are warned what to expect.

Rating

Behavioural demonstrations usually need raters, to say how calm or persuasive or friendly the person was. Assessment centre research (Chapter 10) finds that trained raters can achieve reasonable reliability, but may have some difficulty differentiating different aspects of personality.

Can vs. will

Behavioural demonstrations show what people *can* do, but not necessarily what they *will* do. People who can, for example, control their temper under provocation, in a role play, may not be willing or able to make the effort, day in day out, when actually 'on the job'. Only reports from others who have worked with or lived with the As can tell HR how well As customarily do control themselves. (It is of course worth knowing which As can control themselves, and worth recalling that PQs do not tell HR even that much.)

Comprehensive assessment of the whole of personality by behavioural demonstration begins to look a very large undertaking. However, more focused behavioural assessments of relevant aspects of personality are more feasible. A careful job analysis can narrow down the requirement from emotional stability to resilience, and then from resilience to dealing with difficult customers, at which point a behavioural test begins to look manageable.

RESEARCH AGENDA

A behavioural test of personality will need to establish construct validity, by showing it can both relate to other measures of personality – self-report, including PQ, and other report – as well as correlating with outcomes, such as work performance. It is probably better to start with tests of fairly specific aspects of personality, and work up to a more general assessment, such as the FFM.

Recorded evidence

When deciding whether it is safe to release violent offenders from prison, information from prison files about aggressive or threatening behaviour, and from school records about disruptive behaviour in childhood help make accurate predictions (Quinsey *et al.*, 1998). Barthell and Holmes (1968) used American high school yearbooks to show how poorly adjusted persons had done less at school, in sport, drama, organizing societies, and so on. Similar information is often used in selection, but is obtained from self-reports – for example, application form or interview. Job As usually know that it is 'better' – in terms of getting a job – to have participated in many extracurricular activities at school and college. The high school yearbook provides the employer with recorded information on who actually was. In some countries, military records might be useful; military service often subjects people to very testing experiences and allows constant scrutiny by peers and authority. In the USA and Britain too few people join the armed forces for this to be a widely useful source of data. A wealth of potentially useful information exists in computerized credit systems; personality may be revealed by how well people regulate their finances and how they choose to spend their money. Guion (1965) noted that some employers did use credit data to assess As. Using credit information in selection is illegal in some US states. In Britain, credit agencies do not permit their information to be used for assessing job As.

Some more 'science fiction' possibilities exist. There are presently an estimated half a million CCTV cameras in public places in London. Face recognition software may make it possible to identify everyone, especially if the UK government achieves its planned national ID database. Mobile phones allow their owners' movements to be plotted accurately and continuously. Information from CCTV and mobile phone tracking is already used in criminal investigations. These systems could be developed into an unfakeable continuous input to an assessment system that could allow employers to find out how As spend their time, and who their friends and 'associates' are. As Cervantes (1607/1950) said: 'Tell me the company you keep and I'll tell you what you are'. Some background investigations in selection do presently seek out this type of information. Universal surveillance might do the same job more thoroughly and more cheaply. Orwell (1949/1984) foresaw universal continuous surveillance, extending into people's homes, and predicted that it would change behaviour: 'You had to live – did live, from habit that became instinct – in the assumption that every sound you made was overheard, and, except in darkness, every movement scrutinised'. An 'expression of quiet optimism' was advisable at all times.

RESEARCH AGENDA

Some specific issues could be researched immediately
- Whether credit rating or activities outside work or school, college and military records can be linked to work performance
- How As will react to being assessed by credit record, outside work activities and past records

Involuntary evidence

Some involuntary evidence relating to personality uses psychophysiological methods. Another major theme is handwriting.

Absolute threshold

Eysenck (1967) suggested a biological basis for neuroticism and extraversion, in the brain and nervous system. The central nervous system and brain of the extravert reacts less strongly to sensory input, which is why the extravert tends to seek excitement and company, whereas the introvert is more likely to seek quiet and solitude. Because the introvert's nervous system reacts more strongly, the introvert's absolute sensory thresholds are lower: the introvert can hear sounds or see light too faint for the extravert to detect. Absolute thresholds are difficult to test, so this is probably not usable in selection.

Box 8.1   Electro-dermal activity (EDA)

Changes in the skin, preparatory to sweating, increase its electrical conductivity. Increase in EDA may indicate fear (or, as part of the polygraph, lying). Also referred to as galvanic skin response (GSR).

Response to threat

Psychopaths react physically far less, on EDA (Box 8.1), to the threat of an electric shock, so employers could screen out some potentially disruptive As. The obvious problem is that employers cannot inflict pain on As as part of the selection process. The less obvious problem is a high false positive rate, wrongly identifying 10% of the general population as psychopaths.

Graphology

'... a hail-fellow-well-met who liked to eat and drink; who might attract women of the class he preyed on by an overwhelming animal charm. I would say in fact he was a latent homosexual ... and passed as a man's man ... capable of conceiving any atrocity and carrying it out in an organised way' – a graphologist's assessment of Jack the Ripper based on what might be one of his letters (Figure 8.4). No one knows who really wrote the letter or committed the murders, so no one knows if the graphologist is right.

Table 1.6 (page 20) shows graphology widely used in personnel selection in France, but nowhere else. If handwriting accurately reflects personality, it will make a very cost-effective selection method because As could be assessed from their application forms. Graphologists usually ask people to write pen pictures of themselves, so assessment is not solely based on handwriting. (The content of the letter in Figure 8.4 reveals quite a lot about the writer's mentality; the author enclosed half a human kidney and claims to have eaten

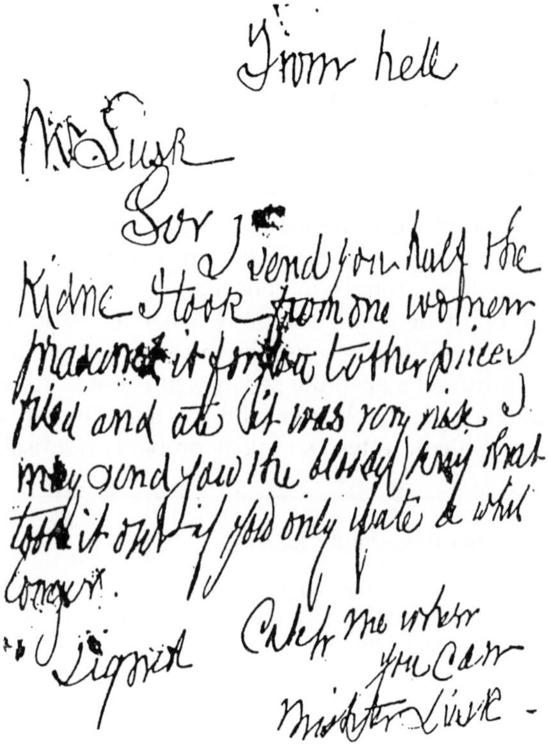
From hell
Mr Lusk
Sor
I send you half the Kidne I took from one women prasarved it for you tother piece I fried and ate it was very nise I may send you the bloody knif that took it out if you only wate a whil longer.
signed Catch me when you can Mishter Lusk

Figure 8.4 A letter attributed to Jack the Ripper.

the other half.) Neter and Ben-Shakhar (1989) reviewed 17 studies comparing graphologists and non-graphologists, rating neutral and *content-laden* scripts (such as pen pictures). With content-laden scripts, the non-graphologists, who know nothing about analysing handwriting, achieve better results than graphologists, suggesting they interpret *what* people write, not *how* they write it, and interpret it better than the graphologists. With neutral scripts, neither group achieves better than zero validity, suggesting either there is no useful information in handwriting or that no one presently knows how to extract it.

Language

Fast and Funder (2008) described some promising research on word choice and personality. They collected interview data from 200 students, along with self-report and reports by two 'knowledgeable' others. The interview was quite searching, but had no consequences, such as a job offer. Fast and Funder used a computer program to search the interview transcripts for possibly revealing patterns of word use. They reported two. Students who used a lot of 'certainty' words – for example, *guarantee, completely* or *definite(ly)* – were described by self and others as smart, thoughtful, confident and well-liked. The second set of results however showed a possible limit to the technique. Students who used a lot of sexual words – for example, *gay, nude* or *stud* – tended to be seen, by others especially, as extravert, neurotic, self-centred, self-dramatizing and unconventional. However, choice of word is not entirely 'involuntary' and most people would 'know better than' to use words like *boob* or *butt* in a job interview.

DNA

One involuntary method may have considerable potential, which probably will not be realized. Personality has a substantial heritable element, which implies research will eventually identify particular genes associated with the differences between people described as personality. It may eventually be possible to assess some aspects of personality by DNA testing. This will bypass entirely the faking problem in personality assessment. DNA testing could probably assess the basic dimensions of 'temperament', but not the finer detail of personality shaped by background and experience. It will be interesting to see whether a DNA account of personality will bear any resemblance to the big five, or Cattell's 16 factors, or any other current model. Chapter 6 noted that DNA testing may already be illegal in selection.

Key points

In Chapter 8 you have learned the following.

- Projective tests may be useful in selection.
- Others' reports of a target's personality are also useful, but may not be accessible in selection.
- Some paper-and-pencil tests of personality exist, and may be useful.
- Behavioural demonstration of personality seem more feasible for more visible aspects of personality such as extraversion, or for more closely specified aspects of personality, such as dealing with conflict.
- Recorded evidence of personality has some limited scope.
- Involuntary evidence has limited scope, except possibly for language use.

Key references

Bernard *et al.* (2005) describe Cattell's Motivation Analysis Test.

Borkenau *et al.* (2001) attempt an assessment of the FFM by purely behavioural tests.

Cattell & Warburton (1967) describe 612 very varied tests of personality.

Collins *et al.* (2004) review projective tests of achievement motivation.

Connolly *et al.* (2007) meta-analyse research on agreement between self and other reports of personality

Fast and Funder (2008) link language use to personality

Funder (2007) describes social psychological research on others' judgement of personality.

Judge *et al.* (1999) describe a longitudinal study of career success in which success as adult is predicted by personality and mental ability in childhood.

Lievens *et al.* (2006) provide data on expert rating of how well different elements of assessment centres can assess personality.

Neter and Ben-Shakhar (1989) analyse research on the value of graphology as a selection method.

Steffens and Konig (2006) describe implicit association tests for the five-factor model.

CHAPTER 9

Biodata and weighted application blanks

How old were you when you learned to swim?

Introduction

Over 80 years ago, Goldsmith (1922) devised an ingenious new solution to an old problem: selecting people who could endure selling life insurance. She took 50 good, 50 poor and 50 middling salesmen from a larger sample of 502, and analysed their application forms. She identified factors that collectively distinguished good, average, and poor: for example, age, marital status, education, (current) occupation, previous experience (of selling insurance) or belonging to clubs. Binary items – married/single – were scored +1/–1. Scoring age was more complicated: the best age was 30–40, with both younger and older age bands scoring less well. Non-linear scoring systems have remained a feature of some biographical measures. Low scorers in Goldsmith's sample almost all failed as insurance salespersons. The small minority of high scorers formed half of a slightly larger minority who were successful (Figure 9.1).

Goldsmith had turned the conventional application form into a *weighted application blank* (WAB). The principle is familiar to anyone with motor insurance. The insurance company analyses its records to find what sort of person makes more claims: for example, people who drive sports cars, people who live in London or people who run bars. Insurers do not rely on common sense, which might suggest that younger drivers, with faster reflexes, will be safer. They rely on their records, which show that young drivers on average are a poorer risk. If insurers can calculate premiums from occupation, age and address, perhaps HR can use application forms as a convenient but powerful way of selecting employees.

There are two main forms of biographical predictor: the WAB and biodata. Both start by analysing past applicants (As) to identify facts or items that are linked to an outcome. Both can be purely, even mindlessly, empirical. Items can be included if they predict the outcome, regardless of whether they 'make sense' or not. Both approaches need very large numbers, and both must be cross-validated before being used (i.e. items must be shown to work in both of two separate samples). As a consequence, both are expensive to set up, but cheap to use thereafter. Both approaches are backward

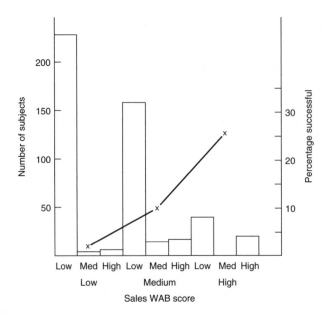

Figure 9.1   Results from the first published weighted application blank (WAB). Data from Goldsmith (1922).

looking; they will find 'more of the same' (e.g. more managers like present successful managers). This may be a problem in times of rapid change. Both are *self-reports*.

Weighted application blanks

WABs were often used to select department store staff. Mosel (1952) found that the ideal saleswoman was between 35 and 54 years old, had 13 to 16 years' formal education, had over five years' sales experience, weighed over 160 pounds, lived in a boarding house, was between 4'11" and 5'2" high, had between one and three dependants, was widowed, had lost no time from work during the last two years, and so on. More recently, Harvey-Cook and Taffler (2000) used biographical methods to predict success in accountancy training in Britain, which had a very high dropout rate. They found a surprisingly traditional set of predictors: school and university grades, being head boy/girl at school, and going to a public (i.e. private) school. Some WAB items are familiar to HR managers: (absence of) frequent job changes, being born locally, owning a home, being married, belonging to clubs and organizations, or sport. Some make sense when you know they work, but need a very devious mind to predict – 'doesn't want a relative contacted in case of emergency', as a predictor of employee theft; some are bizarre – no middle initial given (employee theft again).

Biodata

The classic WAB has tended to be supplanted since the 1960s by *biodata* or *biographical inventory*. Table 9.1 gives some typical biodata questions. Biodata uses questionnaire format with multiple-choice answers and loses the invisibility of the WAB because it is clear to As they are being assessed.

Biodata items can be divided into *hard*, which are verifiable, but also often intrusive like item 6 in Table 9.1, and *soft*, which cause less offence, but are easier to fake like item 5. Some items are *controllable*, while others are not. People choose their exercise patterns but not their parents' ages. Some employers avoid non-controllable items because they look unfair. Some biodata contain questions about attitudes (item 8) or what other people think of you (item 9).

Table 9.1   Some typical biodata items.

1. How old was your father when you were born?
   1] about 20   2] about 25   3] about 30   4] about 35   5] I don't know.

2. How many hours in a typical week do you engage in physical exercise?
   1] none   2] up to 1 hour   3] 2–3 hours   4] 4–5 hours   5] over 5 hours

3. In your last year at school, how many hours in a typical week did you study outside class hours?
   1] none   2] up to 2 hours   3] 2–4 hours   4] 5–8 hours   5] over 8 hours

4. How old were you when you first kissed someone romantically?
   1] 12 or under   2] 13 or 14   3] 15 or 16   4] over 16   5] never kissed anyone romantically.

5. How interested in current affairs are you?
   1] not at all   2] slightly   3] fairly   4] very   5] extremely

6. Which best describes your present height:weight ratio?
   1] definitely overweight   2] somewhat overweight   3] slightly overweight   4] just right   5] under weight

7. How often did you play truant from school?
   1] never   2] once or twice a year   3] 3 to 10 times a year   4] once a month   5] once a week or more

8. What do you think of children who play truant from school?
   1] very strongly disapprove   2] strongly disapprove   3] disapprove   4] unconcerned   5] can sympathise

9. My superiors at work would describe me as
   1] very lazy   2] fairly lazy   3] average   4] quite hard working   5] very hard working

10. How many times did you have to take your driving test?
    1] once   2] twice   3] three   4] four or more   5] never taken it

Biodata and personality questionnaire

Many biographical questions look very like PQ questions. What is the conceptual difference between PQ questions, like those listed in Table 7.1 (page 138), and biodata questions like those listed in Table 9.1?

1. The PQ infers from questions to trait, then from trait to work performance. Most biodata, by contrast, infer direct from questions to work performance, without any intervening variable such as dominance or conscientiousness. (Although some researchers use biographical factors or even personality traits as intervening variables in biodata.)
2. PQs have fixed keys, whereas biodata items may be rekeyed for each selection task.
3. Overall, biodata questions are more likely to be factual than personality questions, although biodata measures include many non-factual questions.
4. PQ questions are phrased to elicit a rapid, unthinking reply, whereas biodata items often sound quite clumsy in their desire to specify precisely the information they want, for example:

With regard to personal appearance, as compared with the appearance of my friends, I think that:
(a) *Most of my friends have a better appearance*
(b) *I am equal to most of them in appearance*
(c) *I am better than most of them in appearance*
(d) *I don't feel strongly one way or the other*

In a PQ, this would read more like: *I am fairly happy about the way I look – TRUE or FALSE*. Sometimes, the distinction between PQ and biodata is so fine that one wonders if the choice of title reflects more the authors' perception of what's acceptable in their organization.

Biodata keyed to personality dimensions

Mael and Hirsch (1993) described a biodata keyed to the US military's PQ, ABLE. Sisco and Reilly (2007) described similar research keying biodata to the five-factor model. Keying a biodata measure to known personality dimensions gives it psychological meaning and may ensure more generalized validity, but also raises the question why not use the PQ in the first place?

Most biographical measures are paper-and-pencil, but the method is easily adapted to computer and Internet administration, which enables it to be used at the screening stage. Van Iddekinge *et al.* (2003) described interactive voice response (IVR) administration of a biodata, where A listens to the question by telephone and answers using the telephone keypad.

Constructing biographical measures

Sources of biodata questions

Many studies used Glennon, Albright and Owens's (1963) *Catalog of Life History Items*, which listed 484 varied biographical questions. Russell *et al.* (1990) used *retrospective life experience essays*, in which Naval Academy students describe a group effort, an accomplishment at school, a disappointment and a stressful event.

Empirical keying

Traditional biographical methods were purely empirical. If poor clerical workers were underweight, or had no middle initial, or lived in Balham, those facts entered the scoring key. Purely empirical measures offend psychologists, who like to feel they have a theory. They are not happy knowing canary breeders make dishonest employees; they want to know *why*. Ideally, they would like to have *predicted* from their theory of work behaviour that canary breeders will make dishonest employees. Critics of pure empiricism argue that a measure with a foundation of theory is more likely to hold up over time and across different employers, and may be easier to defend if challenged.

Factorial keying

The first attempt to give biodata a more theoretical basis relied on *factor analysis*, to identify themes in biographical information. If the no-middle-initial question proved to be linked to half a dozen other questions, all to do with, for example sense of belonging, one has some idea why it relates to work performance, one can explain to critics why it is included and one can perhaps search for better items to reflect the underlying theme.

Rational keying

Some approaches select questions to reflect particular themes. Miner (1971) stated specific hypotheses about eliteness motivation, e.g. that status-conscious Americans will serve (as officers of course) in the Navy or Air Force, but not in the Army. Some researchers use a *behavioural consistency* approach. If job analysis indicates the job needs good organizational skills, items are written that reflect this, either on-the-job – *How often do you complete projects on time?* – or off-the-job if the organization is recruiting new employees – *To what extent do you prepare when going off on holiday?* Recently, researchers have increasingly used rational scales based on intervening constructs. Job analysis indicates that the job is stressful, so researchers seek biodata questions that tap stress tolerance. Factorial and empirical approaches can be used as well to check that the stress items do all reflect one single theme and that they do predict work performance. This approach is easier to defend, and more versatile. A biodata for stress tolerance can be used for any job that creates stress. Barrick and Zimmerman (2005) described a very short research-based biodata for predicting turnover. Less turnover should be predicted by longer tenure in previous jobs, being referred by a current employee and by 'job embeddedness' – having family and friends in the organization. These three questions predicted 'avoidable' turnover quite well (0.30).

Reiter-Palmon and Connelly (2000) compared rational and empirical construction methods and found that they work equally well, but empirical keys tend to contain more hard-to-explain items (e.g. good grades predicted by admitting to often taking feelings out on parents). Graham *et al.* (2002) found that certain types of questions seem to predict work performance better: questions that are verifiable through records, such as lateness or work, or that reflect others' opinions, like item 9 in Table 9.1. Questions that record A's own opinion of him/herself and which are not verifiable, like item 5 in Table 9.1, were less successful.

Option keying vs. linear rating

Biographical measures were traditionally scored by option keying, using tables drawn up by Strong in 1926 and revised by England in 1961. Table 9.2 illustrates the method for one of 88 WAB items from Mitchell and Klimoski's (1982) study of trainee realtors [estate agents], where the criterion of success was achieving licensed status. Columns 1 and 2 show that successful realtors are more likely to own their own home and are less likely to rent a flat or live with relatives. Column 4 assigns a scoring weight from Strong's tables. Larger percentage differences get higher weights. This technique allows for non-linear relationships.

Linear rating methods have become more popular. Linearity allows analysis by correlation and factor analysis. Mael and Hirsch (1993) argued that some apparently non-linear relations arise by chance. They cite the example of 'How many years did you play chess in high school?'. If the answer *three years* was less closely linked to work performance than the adjacent answers of *two* or *four years*, strict application of option keying would assign less weight to three than either two or four. 'The hand of reason', by contrast, suggests that the relationship is more likely to be linear and sets the scoring accordingly.

Table 9.2 A sample WAB item, and its scoring, from Mitchell & Klimoski (1982).

	Licensed	Unlicensed	Difference	Weight
Do you:				
– own your own home?	81	60	21	5
– rent home?	3	5	−2	−1
– rent apartment?	9	25	−16	−4
– live with relatives?	5	10	−5	−2

Devlin, Abrahams and Edwards (1992) compared various biodata scoring methods and found that they made little difference to biodata validity.

Biographical classification

Owens and Schoenfeldt (1979) used biodata to classify people. Scores on the Biographical Questionnaire were factor-analysed and the factor scores then cluster-analysed to group people with common patterns of prior experience. They showed that successful salesmen came from only three (of nine) biodata groups (one-time college athletes, college politicians and hardworkers) and that biodata group membership predicted survival in selling very successfully.

RESEARCH AGENDA

• Further analysis comparing methods of writing and scoring biodata

---

Validity

Two reviews offer apparently very similar overall estimates of biodata validity.

• Bliesener (1996) reported a meta-analysis of 165 biodata validities and found a mean validity of 0.30.
• Bobko and Roth (1999) also reported a meta-analysis, based in part on two earlier meta-analyses (but not Bliesener's) and in part on two large American studies. They reported a value of 0.28.

Neither analysis corrects for either restricted range or unreliability, so both represent conservative estimates of biodata validity. Biodata are evidently a fairly effective predictor. However, on closer inspection, Bliesener's value is not after all the same as Bobko and Roth's. Bliesener's overall uncorrected correlation is actually considerably higher than 0.30, at 0.39. He did something unusual in selection research: he made corrections that reduce the size of the validity coefficient. He identified five methodological shortcomings of biodata research, which he thought inflate validity. For example, concurrent designs achieve higher validity than predictive, although predictive designs offer more conclusive proof. Pure biodata achieve lower validity than biodata that include a lot of attitude or personality items. Standard scoring keys, that is the ones already written in some other research, achieve lower validity than ones written specially, which may capitalize more on chance. Correcting each individual validity coefficient for the presence of such factors reduced overall validity from 0.39 to 0.30.

Table 9.3 Summary of validity of biodata for nine work-related outcomes.

Review	R&C		H&H		S		B&H		B			G	
	k	r	k	r	k	r	k	r	k	r	r_{net}	k	r
Proficiency rating	15	0.36	12	0.37	29	0.32	26	0.32	16	0.32	0.23		
Production	6	0.46			19	0.21	10	0.31					
Objective performance									19	0.53	0.30		
Promotion			17	0.26									
Training success			11	0.30			18	0.25	49	0.36	0.22		
Absence/turnover					28	0.21	15	0.25					
Tenure	13	0.32	23	0.26			18	0.32	39	0.22	0.15		
Turnover												6	0.31
Creativity									19	0.43	0.32		

R&C: Reilly & Chao (1982); H&H: Hunter & Hunter (1984); S: Schmitt *et al.* (1984); B&H: Barge & Hough (1986); B: Bliesener (1996); G: Griffeth *et al.* (2000).
k = number of validities; r = uncorrected correlation; r_{net} = correlation corrected downwards for methodological shortcomings. 'objective performance' includes production figures, sales and absence.

Different outcomes

Biodata have been used to predict a very wide variety of work-related outcomes. Table 9.3 summarizes some of this research. (These analyses are not entirely independent because the same original researches may be included in more than one review.) Table 9.3 indicates that:

- biodata can successfully predict a wide variety of work behaviour;
- validity is higher for Bliesener's objective performance category which covers sales, production and absence; and
- validity is generally lower for predicting tenure.

Different types of work

Biodata have also been used for a wide range of types of work. Three meta-analyses (Table 9.4) found biodata achieve good validity for most occupations, with the possible exception of the armed forces, where Bliesener found validity only 0.19. Bliesener found biodata validity highest for clerical work. Validity is pooled across different criteria including training, tenure, salary, as well as supervisor rating and conventional output measures.

Several reviews and meta-analyses have been reported for specific occupations:

- Funke *et al.* (1987) reported a meta-analysis of 13 studies using biographical measures to predict research achievement in science and technology, and found an overall corrected validity of 0.47.

Table 9.4 Summary of validity of biodata for six areas of work.

Study	Mumford		Reilly		Bliesener		
	k	r	k	r	k	r	r_{net}
Managers	21	0.35	7	0.38	11	0.42	0.27
Sales	17	0.35	5	0.50	24	0.23	0.27
Factory/craftsperson	14	0.46					
Clerical	13	0.46	6	0.52	22	0.46	0.39
Armed forces	13	0.34	9	0.30	33	0.25	0.19
Science/engineering			15	0.41	16	0.41	0.33

Data from Reilly & Chao (1982), Mumford & Owens (1987) and Bliesener (1996).
k = number of validities; r = uncorrected correlation; r_{net} = correlation corrected downwards for methodological shortcomings.

- Two reviews of sales staff agree on validity of 0.28 for sales figures, but disagree on validity for rated sales ability. Vinchur *et al.* (1998) found it higher at 0.52, whereas Farrell and Hakstian (2001) found it lower at 0.33.
- Hunter and Burke (1996) reported an uncorrected validity of 0.27 in 21 studies predicting success in pilot training. They find an unexpected moderator variable in publication date. Researches reported before 1961, including many large-scale World War Two studies, achieved good validity whereas those reported after 1961 found poorer results (another example of validity appearing to decline during the twentieth century).

Bliesener's analysis found a very large gender difference. Biodata work far better for women (0.51) than for men (0.27). This may be mediated by occupation. Biodata work better for occupations where a lot of women work, such as clerical jobs, and less well for occupations where fewer women work, such as the armed forces.

Construct validity

Little is known about how biodata relate to other selection measures, nor about what they measure. Purely empirical measures, keyed to particular outcomes, may not be closely related to other measures. Mumford and Owens (1987) reviewed 21 factorial studies and listed the seven most commonly found factors: adjustment, academic achievement, intellectual/cultural pursuits, introversion/extraversion, social leadership, maturity and career development. Obviously, biodata keyed to personality will be expected to correlate with personality tests. Rothstein *et al.* (1990) reported a substantial correlation with mental ability (MA) in a single large study, but no meta-analysis has been published.

Incremental validity

Schmidt and Hunter (1998) argued that the high correlation between biodata and MA reported by Rothstein *et al.* (1990) means biodata would not achieve much incremental validity. However, some researches have reported incremental validity. Mael and Ashworth (1995) found biodata improve on MA tests in predicting attrition in army recruits. Mount, Witt and Barrick (2000) found biodata have incremental validity on MA and the big five personality factors for clerical work. McManus and Kelly (1999) found that the big five and biodata each achieve incremental validity in predicting organizational citizenship.

Validity generalization and transportability

Early research concluded that WABs and biodata did not seem to 'travel well' and tended to be specific to the organizations they were developed in. The best data on transportability come from the biodata used by the North American insurance industry since the 1930s, and dating in part back to 1919, variously called Aptitude Index Battery (AIB), Career Profile System and Initial Career Profile. Figure 9.2 shows success is closely related to AIB score and also shows how few succeed in insurance, even from the highest score bands. Figure 9.3 shows schematically the distribution of AIB scores against survival and sales, and suggests AIB is essentially a screening test, that eliminates potential failures but does not necessarily identify successes. Brown (1981) analysed AIB data, for over 12,000 sales staff from 12 large US companies. AIB was valid for all 12 companies, but proved more valid for larger, better run companies that recruit through press adverts and agencies, than for smaller

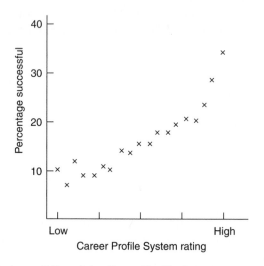

Figure 9.2   Predictive validity of the Career Profile System.

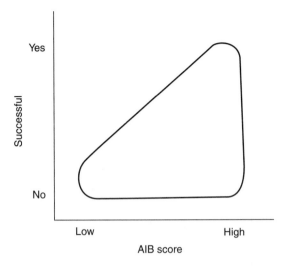

Figure 9.3   Schematic representation of the relationship between AIB score and success in selling insurance.

companies that recruit by personal contacts. AIB has been rewritten and rescored several times, but has retained some continuity.

Consortium measures

Organizations that do not employ enough people to generate their own biodata can join a consortium. Consortium measures also deal with the problem of specificity to particular jobs, outcomes or organizations. Rothstein *et al.* (1990) suggested that biodata do not 'travel well' because they are usually keyed inside one single organization, which limits their generality. The Supervisory Profile Record (SPR) derived from 39 organizations, and proved to have highly generalizable validity, being unaffected by organization, sex, race, supervisory experience, social class or education. Schmidt and Rothstein (1994) analysed SPR data for 79 separate organizations and found relatively little variation in validity from one organization, or type of supervisor, to another. Carlson *et al.* (1999) described the Manager Profile Record, developed within one organization, but used successfully in 24 others to predict salary increase and promotion. Carlson *et al.* placed more emphasis on questions having a sound rational or behavioural justification than on empirical keying.

The need for secrecy?

Early studies published their WABs in full, confident that clerks and shop assistants did not read *Journal of Applied Psychology* and could not discover the right answers to give. If the scoring system becomes known, biodata could

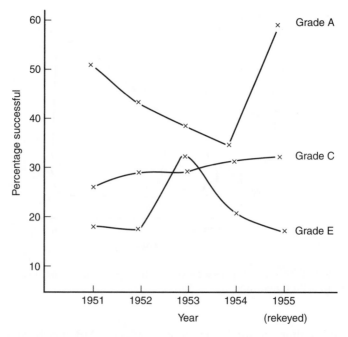

Figure 9.4   Results obtained with the Aptitude Index Battery (AIB) between 1951 and 1954. Data from Hughes *et al.* (1956).

lose predictive power. Hughes, Dunn and Baxter (1956) wrote a new form of AIB, which worked well while it was still experimental, but lost its validity as soon as it was used for actual hiring (Figure 9.4). Field managers scored the forms and were supposed to use them to reject unsuitable As; instead they guided favoured As into giving the right answers. When scoring was moved back to head office, AIB regained its validity. It is doubtful whether any selection method can be kept entirely secret these days because all come under intense legal scrutiny.

Fakability

Both WAB and biodata are self-reports. Some information is factual and could be independently verified. In practice, this rarely happens, except for details of education and previous employment. Biodata often contain a lot of attitude and personality questions, which tend to be unverifiable. Research on biodata faking has a series of parallels with research on faking PQs, discussed in Chapter 7.

- People directed to fake good can usually improve their biodata scores. Sisco and Reilly (2007) found a biodata measure of the five-factor model of personality more resistant to directed faking than a PQ.

- People directed to fake good distort their answers far more than job As (Becker and Colquitt, 1992), so directed faking studies may be misleading.
- The extent of faking by real As is uncertain. Becker and Colquitt reported that only three items of 25 were answered differently by real As. These items were less historical, objective and verifiable. On the other hand, Stokes, Hogan and Snell (1993) compared As with present employees (PEs) and found their answers much more 'socially desirable' in areas like preferred working climate, work style, or personal and social adjustment.

Research also suggests several possible ways of dealing with faking in biodata, again tending to repeat approaches tried with PQs.

- More objective and verifiable items create fewer differences between As and PEs (Stokes *et al.*, 1993).
- More complex option-keying scoring methods are less fakable than simple linear scoring systems (Kluger, Reilly & Russell, 1991). However, Stokes *et al.* (1993) found that complex scoring does not seem to prevent As from giving different responses to PEs.
- Warning people that the biodata included a lie-detection scale (which it did not) reduced faking (Schrader & Osburn, 1977).
- Bogus items were first used in biodata and have recently been resurrected in PQs. As who claimed to have used 'Sonntag connectors' (which do not exist) got better overall scores on the biodata, but their biodata score correlated less with a written job knowledge test, suggesting they were not better As (Pannone, 1984). Trick questions might not work for long in practice.
- Shermis *et al.* (1996) described a faking good scale, modelled on PQ faking good scales, consisting of 12 questions on the lines of *I have never violated the law while driving a car*.
- Schmitt and Kunce (2002) reported that elaboration reduces faking considerably: As who claim, for example, to have led several work teams are asked to give details. The reduction in faking generalizes to questions where elaboration is not asked for. Ramsay *et al.* (2006) confirmed that requiring elaboration reduces faking.

RESEARCH AGENDA

- Meta-analysis covering more recent validity research
- More research on fakability and ways of dealing with it

Biographical measures, fairness and the law

For some years, biodata were included in the list of selection methods that were 'safe' because they did not find gender or ethnicity differences. Reilly and Chao's (1982) review concluded that biodata did not, by and large, create adverse impact for minorities applying for work as bus drivers, clerical staff, army recruits or supervisors. Subsequently, Schmitt, Clause and Pulakos's (1996) meta-analysis found only fairly small Afro/white differences in biodata scores ($d = 0.20$). More recent analyses are less optimistic. Bobko and Roth (1999) re-analysed Schmitt *et al.* and concluded that the Afro / white difference is larger, at 0.33. Roth *et al.* (2001a) describe unpublished data with a white/Afro American d of 0.34, but note that As had been pre-screened on MA tests, which also create AI. Correcting for this raised white/Afro biodata d to 0.73. Sharf (1994) noted that biodata had not been challenged directly under the Civil Rights Act. Perhaps everyone thought there was no adverse impact problem. One study reported that using biodata data can reduce adverse impact. The combination of SPR and MA test, while predicting only slightly better than the MA tests alone, creates less adverse impact (Rothstein *et al.*, 1990).

Item analysis

The differences discussed previously are in total score, but it is possible also to analyse adverse impact at the question level. Biographical measures might discriminate against protected groups in subtle ways; having a city centre as opposed to suburban address in Detroit not only distinguished thieves from non-thieves, but also tended to distinguish white from non-white. Questions about participation in sport could discriminate against disabled people. Sharf (1994) thinks it is unclear whether biodata could be challenged legally question by question, so a few questions creating adverse impact may not matter. In fact, it is extremely unlikely that no gender, age, ethnicity or disability differences would be found in any of 50 to 100 biographical questions. However, if many questions show, for example, ethnicity differences, it tends to follow that total scores will also differ. Whitney and Schmitt (1997) found significant black–white differences in a high proportion (25%) of biodata questions and noted that explaining the differences in terms of, for example, different cultural values, would lead to better understanding of which items to avoid in the future. Unfortunately, they were unable to identify any systematic trends in their sample.

Privacy

As Table 9.1 shows, some biodata questions can be very intrusive. Use of biodata in the USA is complicated by the fact that the 52 states all have their own, differing laws about privacy, so questions about, for example, credit rating, are legal in some states but not in others. European employment law tends to emphasize the privacy and dignity of the applicant, which could make some biodata questions less acceptable.

Some psychologists have proposed that the *Washington Post* test for biodata face validity. Imagine headlines in the *Washington Post* (or *The Guardian*). One headline reads *Psychologists reject people for officer training because they don't like colour blue*, which sounds arbitrary and unfair. Another headline reads *Psychologists reject people for officer training because they weren't prefects at school*, which sounds much more reasonable.

RESEARCH AGENDA

• Research on acceptability of different types of biodata questions to As

---

Key points

In Chapter 9 you have learned the following.

• There are two biographical approaches: WABs which are scored from the application form and biodata which are separate questionnaires and so are more visible to As.
• Biographical measures can predict work performance, and other related aspects of workplace behaviour such as tenure, training success, promotion, absence or creativity.
• Biodata can be purely empirical, or can be guided by either a theory of, for example, eliteness motivation, or a relevant construct such as stress tolerance.
• Biodata face the same problem of quality of information being compromised by faking.
• Biodata can be written that work across a number of different organizations.
• Biodata rarely seem to attract litigation, but can look unfair or arbitrary to candidates.
• Biodata do create some adverse impact on American minorities.

Key references

Barrick and Zimmerman (2005) describe very short biodata for predicting turnover.

Bliesener (1996) presents the most recent meta-analytic review of biodata validity.

Harvey-Cook and Taffler (2000) describe a recent British biographical selection process for chartered accountants.

Hughes *et al.* (1956) describe how biodata lost validity when its scoring was compromised.

Roth *et al.* (2001) argue that biodata do create adverse impact on minorities in the USA, when pre-selection is taken into account.

Rothstein *et al.* (1990) describe the development of generic biodata, the Supervisory Profile Record.

Shermis *et al.* (1996) describe a biodata faking good scale.

van Iddekinge *et al.* (2003) describe the use of interactive voice response (IVR) technology with biodata.

Useful websites

limra.com/products/CPPlus.aspx. Life insurance industry site, giving sample biodata questions and report.

CHAPTER 10

Assessment centres

Does your face fit?

Introduction

The assessment centre (AC) was invented during World War Two, on both sides of the Atlantic more or less simultaneously. The British Army expanded rapidly and needed to recruit officers from unfamiliar backgrounds. A team of psychologists set up the War Office Selection Board (WOSB), a three-day programme of tests, exercises and interviews. In the USA, psychologists led by Henry Murray were advising the Office of Strategic Services (OSS), forerunner of the CIA, how to select spies. Murray's team identified nine dimensions to effective spying including practical intelligence, emotional stability, and maintenance of cover. Maintenance of cover required applicants (As) to pretend to be someone else throughout the assessment; the OSS programme must be unique in regarding systematic lying as a virtue.

The present shape of ACs

ACs work on the principle of *multi-dimension multi-exercise* assessment. Any single assessment method may give misleading results. Some people interview well, while others are good at tests. Whereas a person who shows ability to influence in both interview and group exercise may be more likely really to be able to influence others. The key feature of the true AC is the *dimension × exercise matrix* (Figure 10.1). AC planners identify key dimensions of work performance by job analysis, then use at least two qualitatively different methods to assess each dimension. In Figure 10.1, ability to influence is assessed by group exercise and PQ, while numerical ability is assessed by financial case study and numerical reasoning test. An assessment centre that does not have a matrix plan is not a real AC, just a superstitious imitation of one. Unfortunately, one still sometimes encounters people whose idea of an AC is any old collection of tests and exercises, begged, borrowed or stolen, included because they are available, not because they are accurate measures of important dimensions of work performance.

Dimensions – what the AC assesses

Arthur *et al.* (2003) listed 168 different dimension names in their review of AC research, and grouped them into six: *communication, consideration and*

	Influence	Numeracy	Delegation
Exercise A	XXX		XXX
Exercise B		XXX	
Test C	XXX	XXX	
Test D		XXX	XXX
In-tray			XXX

Figure 10.1 The dimension × exercise matrix underlying every assessment centre. XXX denotes influence is assessed by exercise A.

awareness of others, drive, influencing others, organizing and planning, and *problem solving.* Kolk, Born and van der Flier (2004) have an even simpler model with three broad categories: *feeling* (sociability and sensitivity to others), *thinking* (judgement and analytical skill) and *power* (tenacity and control).

Exercises – how the AC assesses

An AC includes whatever exercises are needed to assess each dimension twice. Sometimes exercises can be taken off the shelf; often they are devised specially. Spychalski *et al.*'s (1997) survey of US AC practice distinguished six main types of exercise:

- Leaderless group discussions in which the group discuss a given topic and reach a consensus, but where no one is appointed as chair. Used in most ACs. Group discussions can be co-operative or competitive.
- Role play in which A handles a dissatisfied customer, or an employee with a grievance.
- Presentation on either a specialist or a general knowledge topic. Used in about 50% ACs.
- Interview. Included in about 50% ACs.
- In-basket (or in-tray) exercise in which As deal with a set of letters, memos, and so on. (Chapter 11). Used in most ACs.
- Case analysis, usually written, of a complex problem.

ACs often include psychological tests and personality questionnaires; one in five include peer assessments. Krause and Gebert (2003) reported a survey from Germany, Austria and Switzerland which finds broadly similar results.

Assessors may be line managers or psychologists. ACs use a bewildering array of *assessor/applicant designs*. Sometimes the assessor observes and rates the same As throughout the AC; sometimes they observe and rate different As in each succeeding exercise. Sometimes assessors even rate As they have not seen, relying on other assessors' accounts. The researcher would prefer either to have every assessor rate every A on everything, or to use each assessor only once, to rate only one A, on one dimension, in one exercise. Neither is feasible in practice. This makes AC data very messy and contributes to the dimension × exercise problem, discussed later. ACs are unsatisfactory in other ways, viewed as experimental designs for assessment. For example, most have a fixed sequence, so for example, leaderless group discussion always precedes team negotiation. This is likely to create two types of order effect: assessor and applicant. If Applicant A does well in the leaderless group discussion, assessors may expect him/her to do well in the negotiation, whereas Applicant B who does poorly in the leaderless group discussion may be demoralized and do poorly for the rest of the programme. Sometimes As are rotated, so each successive group has different people; sometimes they stay in the same group throughout.

RESEARCH AGENDA

More 'analytical' research on ACs may be useful; issues such as order effects, cumulative effects, rating across and within exercises are difficult to address with real data from real ACs. Questions could be addressed by more controlled laboratory research or by using video-recorded data from 'real' ACs.

Assessors' conference. The final stage of the AC is the assessors' conference, when all information about each A is collated. The assessors resolve disagreements in ratings of exercises, then review the entire matrix, to arrive at a final set of ratings for each A. ACs sometimes use the *AT&T* model, in which assessors take very detailed notes of behaviour during the AC, but do not make any ratings until the end.

Reliability of ACs

Reliability is a complex issue. One can calculate the reliability of the entire process, of its component parts, or of assessors' ratings. Connelly and Ones (2008) found inter-rater reliability in ACs generally good, at 0.80 for overall rating, and 0.73 for specific dimensions. Wilson (1948) reported a fairly good retest reliability for the UK Civil Service Selection Board (CSSB), based on As who exercised their right to try CSSB twice. Morris (1949) described two retest reliability studies with WOSB. In the first, two parallel WOSBs were set up specifically to test inter-WOSB agreement, and two batches of As attended both WOSBs. There were 'major disagreements' over 25% of As. In the second study, two parallel Boards simultaneously, but independently, observed and evaluated the same 200 As, and achieved good agreement. Moses (1973) compared As who attended long and short ACs and were evaluated by different staff. Overall ratings from the two ACs correlated well; ratings on parallel dimensions were also highly correlated.

Validity of ACs

Like the interview, the AC is a method of assessment that can, in theory, assess whatever the organization requires. Hence, one should logically ask about

Table 10.1   Results of the AT&T Management Progress Study (Bray & Grant, 1966).

AC ratings	N	Achieved rank		
		1st line	2nd line	Middle
Potential middle manager	103	4%	53%	46%
Not potential middle manager	166	68%	86%	12%

validity of the AC for assessing, e.g. delegation. In practice, the AC, like the interview, is often used to assess general suitability for the job, and its validity computed against management's estimates, also of general suitability. When the AC tries to assess specific dimensions, there is some question whether it succeeds in doing so (see section on Dimension × Exercise Problem).

AT&T's management progress study (MPS)

The MPS was an early, and very influential, use of the AC in the USA, to promote people into middle management (Bray & Grant, 1966). People were originally assessed in 1957; on follow-up, eight years later, Table 10.1 shows the MPS achieved good predictive validity, an uncorrected correlation of 0.46.

Civil Service Selection Board (CSSB)

Since 1945, the most senior ranks of the UK Civil Service have been selected by the CSSB, whose elements include group discussions, written exercises and interviews, preceded by biodata and mental ability (MA) tests. Vernon (1950) reported a follow-up study of CSSB's early years, which showed that CSSB achieved good predictive validity (0.44 to 0.49), correcting for restricted range. Anstey (1977) continued to follow up Vernon's sample until the mid-1970s, when many were nearing retirement. Using achieved rank as criterion, Anstey reported an eventual predictive validity, after 30 years, that was very good (0.66, corrected for restricted range). All but 21 of 301 CSSB graduates in Anstey's analysis achieved Assistant Secretary rank, showing they made the grade as senior Civil servants; only three left because of 'definite inefficiency'.

Politicians

Before the 2005 British General Election, the Conservative Party used an AC to select candidates to run for election as Member of Parliament (Silvester & Dykes, 2007). Applicants were assessed on communication skill, intellectual skill, relating to people, leading and motivating, resilience and drive, and political conviction, by group exercise, competency-based interview, public

Table 10.2 Summary of three analyses of assessment centre validity.

Reviewer	Gaugler et al.			Hardison & Sackett			Arthur et al.		
Outcome	k	r	ρ	k	r	ρ	k	r	ρ
Performance	44	0.25	0.36	40	0.22	0.26			
Potential	13	0.40	0.53						
Career advance	33	0.30	0.36						
Promotion				10	0.27	nr			
Turnover				6	0.07	nr			
Training	8	0.30	0.35	10	0.31	0.35			
Sales				4	0.11	0.15			
AC dimension									
Communication							40	0.26	0.33
Consideration							37	0.20	0.25
Drive							42	0.24	0.31
Influence							47	0.30	0.38
Organizing/planning							40	0.29	0.37
Problem solving							52	0.30	0.39

Data from Gaugler et al. (1987), Hardison & Sackett (2007) and Arthur et al. (2003).
r = uncorrected validity; ρ = operational validity.

speaking exercise, in-tray and MA test. The AC achieved a modest correlation (0.25 corrected for restricted range) with the selected MPs' election success.

Meta-analyses

Two meta-analyses (Gaugler et al., 1987; Hardison & Sackett, 2007) of AC validity have been published (Table 10.2). Hardison and Sackett's analysis covers research published since Gaugler et al., so there is no overlap. An operational validity of around 0.30 may seem rather low, compared with the 0.50 or so achieved by MA tests, which are much quicker and cheaper. However, 0.30 may be underestimate. Hardison and Sackett noted that Gaugler et al.'s correction for restriction of range was very conservative. Where the original study gave insufficient information to allow any estimate of restriction, Gaugler et al. assumed that there was none; most studies gave insufficient information, so most were not corrected. Hardison and Sackett's overall validity is lower than Gaugler et al.'s estimate; they suggested that this is another effect of restricted range. Because ACs are expensive, employers increasingly use them only as the final stage of selection, after pre-screening As by biodata, tests, PQs, and so on. This means range is greatly restricted, but it is difficult to estimate exactly how much. The two meta-analyses also distinguish different criteria of success: performance ratings, rated potential for further promotion, training, and career advance. Hardison and Sackett divided career advance into promotion and turnover (Table 10.2), and found ACs do not predict turnover.

Gaugler *et al.*'s VGA uncovered several factors that moderated AC validity. AC validity was higher when:

- more assessments were included;
- psychologists rather than managers were used as assessors;
- peer evaluations were used; and
- more As were female.

AC validity was not affected by:

- ratio of As to assessors;
- amount of assessor training; and
- how long the assessors spent integrating the information.

Hardison and Sackett also found some moderators:

- validity decreases, the longer the interval between AC and outcome, but remains usefully high ($\rho = 0.22$) even with a five year interval.
- simpler ACs, with fewer dimensions and fewer exercises, achieve better validity. (Note that Gaugler *et al.* had found the opposite: validity was higher, the more assessments were included.)

Hardison and Sackett found two factors that did not affect validity:

- sector – business, military and police, or school,
- discussion of AC ratings achieved no better validity than simply averaging across assessors, suggesting the assessors' conference – a defining feature of the AC – may not be absolutely necessary.

Arthur *et al.* (2003) summarized researches that reported validity for each AC dimension separately. Validity for consideration and stress tolerance are lower. Note however that they are comparing AC rating of, for example, influence with a general performance outcome, not with a specific measure of workplace influence.

Validity of AC exercises

Nearly all AC research limits itself to overall AC rating and rarely reports data on validity of component exercises. Feltham (1988) analysed ACs for senior police officers in Britain, to show that only four components of the 13 included were needed to predict the outcome, meaning the AC could be shortened considerably. AC research has not generated data on the relative validity of different types of exercise: role play, group discussion, written task, which would be extremely useful. Vernon (1950) noted a practical problem:

most ACs are cumulative, so assessors' views of later components will be influenced by what they have seen in the earlier ones. This could be avoided by using video-recording and separate assessors.

One could argue that research on 'validity of ACs' is misguided, because every AC is different. Research should instead focus on the validity of each component of the AC, as well as the intercorrelation of components. Given this information, planners could calculate the expected overall validity of any particular AC. There is of course extensive research on validity of some AC components, such as interviews, tests and PQs, but less on the AC's defining components: group discussion, role play or simulation.

RESEARCH AGENDA

- Whether shorter and simpler ACs, with fewer dimensions and exercises, are more or less valid
- Contribution of different AC component exercises to AC validity, and/or a meta-analysis of such research
- Devise ways of estimating restricted range in multistage selection systems
- More validity research from more varied sectors of employment
- More validity research from outside North America

Reservations about AC validity

Ipsativity. One A's performance in a group exercise depends on how other As in the group behave. A fairly dominant person in a group of extremely dominant persons may look weak and ineffective by comparison. The ipsativity problem can be reduced to some extent by re-combining groups, and by introducing *normative* data from psychological tests. (Another solution might be to turn group exercises into group role plays, groups where there is only one real Applicant, and everyone else is there to play a role, for example, argumentative, overtalkative or keen but lacking in judgement. This makes the group more consistent and could get very useful information from the role players, but would make the whole process even more expensive.)

Criterion contamination can be a blatant self-fulfilling prophecy, which the uncritical observer might take for proof of validity: Smith returns from the AC with a good rating (predictor) and so gets promoted (criterion). A high correlation between AC rating and promotion is guaranteed, but proves little. Or criterion contamination can be subtler: people who have done well at the AC are deemed suitable for more challenging tasks, develop greater self-confidence, acquire more skills and consequently get promoted. Many ACs suffer from criterion contamination, because employers naturally want to act on the results of a costly assessment. The AT&T MPS is one of the few studies that kept AC results secret until calculating the validity coefficient, thereby avoiding contamination.

'Face fits'

Some time ago, Klimoski and Strickland (1977) commented on the 'curious homogeneity in the criteria used', namely 'salary growth or progress, promotions above first level, management level achieved and supervisor's ratings of potential'. These criteria 'may have less to do with managerial effectiveness than managerial adaptation and survival'. On this argument, ACs answer the question 'does his/her face fit?', not the question 'Can he/she do the job well?' Few researches on ACs have used truly objective criteria. Apparently objective criteria often involve management's opinion somewhere (e.g. promotion or training grade).

A few studies (e.g. McEvoy & Beatty 1989; Hagan *et al.* 2006) have used peer and subordinate ratings or 360-degree feedback as criterion and found these agree with AC ratings as well as supervisor ratings. This suggests that either Klimoski's criticism is unfounded, or that the peer and subordinate ratings also assess image, rather than substance. Several other lines of research use more objective criteria:

- Hagan *et al.* validate a promotion AC for department store managers against 'mystery shopper' performance. Mystery shoppers pretend to be a real customer, returning merchandise or making a complaint; they are a form of work sample, but still involve ratings. AC ratings correlated 0.35 with mystery shopper performance, which is fairly typical of AC validity levels.
- Hardison and Sackett found four studies that used a truly objective criterion – sales. Table 10.2 shows validity was much lower, which tends to confirm Klimoski's point.
- Silvester and Dykes (2007) used an objective criterion for politicians – votes, specifically 'swing', % change in vote for that constituency compared with the previous election, and report validity lower than average, but not as low as that for sales.

RESEARCH AGENDA

- More research validating AC against objective criteria

The dimension × exercise problem

The logic of the AC method implies assessors should rate As on dimensions; research suggests strongly that assessors often assess As on exercises. Figure 2.2 (page 31) showed three types of correlations in a dimension × exercise matrix:

- *convergent validity* – where the same dimension is rated in different exercises, which should be high.
- *discriminant validity* – where different dimensions are rated in the same exercise, where corrections should be lower.
- correlations for different dimensions rated in different exercises, which should be very low or zero.

However, in real ACs, what 'ought' to happen rarely does. Early research (Sackett & Dreher, 1982) found ratings of different dimensions in the same exercise correlated very highly, showing a lack of discriminant validity, while ratings of the same dimension in different exercises hardly correlated at all, showing a lack of convergent validity. The ACs were not measuring general decisiveness across a range of management exercises; they were measuring general performance on each of series of exercises. But if decisiveness in exercise A does not generalize to decisiveness in exercise B, how can one be sure it will generalize to decisiveness on the job? Two meta-analyses of AC multi-dimension, multi-exercise correlations have been reported (Born, Kolk & van der Flier, 2000; Woehr & Arthur, 2003). They reported averages for convergent validity of 0.34 and for divergent validity of 0.55/0.58; convergent validity correlations ought to be higher than divergent, not lower.

Factor analysis

If an AC is intended to assess four main dimensions, then factor analysis of AC ratings 'ought' to find four corresponding factors. What frequently emerged from conventional or *exploratory factor analysis*, however, was a set of factors corresponding to the exercises, not the dimensions. Recent research uses *confirmatory factor analysis* (CFA), part of structural equation modelling, which tests how well different models fit the data. For an AC with five dimensions and four exercises, at least five models might fit the data:

1. five dimension factors;
2. four exercise factors;
3. five dimension factors, and four exercise factors;
4. five dimension factors, with 'correlated uniquenesses' corresponding to the four exercises; and
5. four exercise factors and a general factor (of overall performance).

Model 1 is what 'ought' to be found. The ratings ought to reflect dimensions. However, attempts to fit models that include only dimensions always fail completely. Model 2 is what actually happens in many sets of AC ratings: ratings reflect exercises rather than dimensions. Model 5 is a variant of model 2, which adds an overall performance factor to the exercise factors, but does not include any dimension factors. Models 3 and 4 include both dimensions and exercise, meaning ACs are at least partly successful in assessing dimensions. Several authors have tested the fit of these models to 30 plus sets of AC data, with varying results:

- Lievens and Conway (2001) concluded that model 4, including both dimensions and exercises, fits best. Dimensions and exercises each account for 34% of variance in rating.
- Lance *et al.* (2004) disagreed and argued that Lievens and Conway's modified dimensions and exercises model exaggerated dimension variance. They concluded that model 5 – exercises plus general factor – best fits 51% of the studies. Dimensions account for 14% variance in ratings, while exercises account for 52%.
- Anderson *et al.* (2006) analysed data from Regular Commissions Boards (the successor to WOSB) and found that a dimensions and exercises model fits best, showing better convergent validity than other AC studies.
- At first research tested model fit on each set of data in turn. Bowler and Woehr (2006) incorporated all 35 datasets into a single overall six dimensions × six exercises framework, and tested model fit on a single meta-analytic dataset. They found that a six dimensions × six exercises model fits best. Dimensions account for 22% variance in ratings, while exercises account for 34%. The six dimensions are very highly correlated (average 0.79), whereas the six exercises are not (average 0.10).

These complex analyses suggest that AC ratings are dominated by exercise effects and that ACs are struggling to distinguish separate dimensions of work performance. This is a serious problem. If the AC does not succeed in assessing the six dimensions its planners intend, what is it assessing? And how does it succeed in predicting overall work performance? The dimension × exercise problem casts doubt on the AC's construct validity and could make its use hard to justify if challenged legally.

Explaining the exercise effect

Various explanations for the exercise effect have been offered. Some imply that the problem will be fairly easily be solved by changing the way the AC is run; others suggest the problem is more deep-rooted.

Overload

When assessors are given too many people to watch or too many dimensions to rate, information overload forces them to simplify the task by rating overall performance rather than aspects of it. Woehr and Arthur (2003) reported that the average number of dimensions rated in ACs is between 10 and 11, which is almost certainly too many. Howard (1997) argued that AC dimensions are a ragbag of conceptually different constructs, which the assessors simplify for themselves, by assuming they are correlated. Some are traits (energy), some learned skills (planning), some demonstrable behaviour (oral communication).

Table 10.3 Convergent validity – assessing the same dimension in different exercises – for exercises of high and low relevance to that dimension.

Relevance or trait activation potential	Low		High	
	k	Mean r	k	Mean r
Extraversion	43	0.33	31	0.40
Conscientiousness	35	0.22	39	0.31
Openness	107	0.29	6	0.33
Agreeableness	41	0.27	20	0.30
Neuroticism	15	0.34	3	0.46
Overall	241	0.29	99	0.34

Rating the unratable

Asking assessors to rate a dimension that is not manifest in observable behaviour encourages global ratings (i.e. an exercise effect). Lievens *et al.* (2006) matched AC dimensions to the five-factor model (FFM) of personality, and then divided convergent validities into correlations based on pairs of exercises suited to assessing that factor, and correlations based on pairs of exercises less well suited (having lower *trait activation potential*). Table 10.3 reveals two interesting facts. Where both exercises are well suited to revealing a factor, the correlation is higher, for all five underlying personality factors, although the difference is not large. The other interesting point is how many correlations have been computed for pairs of exercises not well suited, according to Lievens *et al.*'s expert panel, to assessing that particular factor.

Same or different raters

Poor correlations between exercises may result because *different* raters are used. Within exercise correlations may be higher because the ratings are made by the *same* rater(s). As already noted, in an ideal design, either the same raters make all the ratings or each rater is used only once. Neither is feasible in real ACs, but either could be done if everything was recorded.

The engulfing effect

Some dimensions – it is argued – are 'naturally' central to some exercises (e.g. planning/organizing to in-trays, dominance to group discussions), so ratings of these dimensions dominate, and ratings of other dimensions simply follow them. This is a plausible hypothesis, but hard to test.

True exercise effects

Perhaps performance across different dimensions 'really' is consistent because AC dimensions 'really' are positively correlated. Some pairs of AC dimensions do seem to overlap conceptually (e.g. influence and empathy). However, an average intercorrelation between AC dimensions of 0.79, reported by Bowler and Woehr (2006), does seem improbably high.

Absence of true dimension effects

Lievens (2001b) prepared video-recordings in which people showed high levels of, for example, influence, over all exercises and low levels of, for example planning, also consistently across all exercises (i.e. behaving in the way the logic of the AC expects). Observers who rated these recordings correctly reported what they saw and generated strong dimension effects in their ratings. If observers can report dimension consistency when it is present, perhaps assessors in real ACs do not report dimension consistency because it is not there.

Mis-specification

ACs do not assess the dimensions they were designed to assess, but something else, that happens to be related to job performance. The assessors are actually assessing this something else, which is why their ratings of various dimensions are highly correlated. Candidates for what ACs 'really' assess include MA, and self-monitoring, the ability to present oneself well.

Dimensions do not exist

Social learning theorists, such as Mischel (1968), would expect to find exercise effects. They do not believe in broad traits that shape behaviour consistently; they believe that behaviour is, to a large extent, shaped by the situation people find themselves in (i.e. by the particular demands of each exercise).

Solving the exercise effect problem

Three recent analyses (Born et al., 2000; Lievens & Conway, 2001; Woehr & Arthur, 2003) assess the effectiveness of various attempted solutions to the exercise effect problem.

- Convergent validity is higher when assessors have fewer dimensions to rate, consistent with the overload hypothesis. Kolk et al. (2004) confirmed this, using their very simple three-dimension model.
- Ratings by psychologists and HR specialists show more convergent validity than those from line managers or students.
- Analysis of length of training yields inconsistent results. Lievens and Conway reported that more than one day's training reduced convergent validity, whereas one might expect more training to improve it. Woehr and Arthur found that more than one day's training increased convergent

validity, but that more than five days – represented by one study only – decreased it again.

- Lievens (2001a) argued that type of training is also important; frame of reference (FoR) training seeks to give all assessors the same view of what behaviour counts as for example decision making. FoR training improves convergent validity more than training in observation skills. Schleicher *et al.* (2002) confirmed that FoR training improves reliability, convergent validity and criterion validity of an AC.
- Woehr and Arthur found that six studies where assessors rated at the end of the AC yield higher convergent validity than the larger number following the more usual practice of rating after each exercise. Melchers, Henggeler and Kleinmann (2007) noted that ACs where dimensions were rated at the end, not after each exercise, also usually used the same assessors throughout and allowed them to share information before rating, so one does not know quite what produces the improvement in convergent validity.
- Born *et al.* found seven studies where the same assessor rates both halves of the convergent validity correlation, which raises convergent validity considerably to 0.64; Born *et al.* thought this may reflect halo (i.e. may not be a true solution to the problem).
- Lievens *et al.* (2006) confirmed that ensuring that the behaviour to be rated will be visible in the exercise increases convergent validity.
- Brink *et al.* (2008) described an AC in which every exercise was recorded and rated later, which reduced the exercise effect considerably.

Other factors however make no difference:

- Ratio of assessees to assessors makes no difference; however, the researches reviewed all have fairly low ratios (two or three As per assessor), so probably did not create overload.
- Transparency – telling As what is being assessed so that they can exhibit it more clearly or consistently – does not increase convergent validity.
- Lievens and Conway find that giving assessors behavioural checklists increases convergent validity, but not significantly.

Lance *et al.* (2000b) offer a radical perspective on the dimension × exercise issue. They argue that ACs have never worked as intended: 'assessors form overall judgements of performance in each exercise ... [then] produce separate postexercise trait ratings because they are required to do so'. If assessors are 'working backwards' in this way, it is not surprising dimensions within exercises correlate highly. ACs work if the right exercises have been included, i.e. ones that 'replicate important job behaviors'. On this argument, the AC is just a collection of tests, distinguished only by including a lot of behavioural demonstration evidence such as group discussions, role plays and simulations. AC planners should abandon the dimension/trait framework, which just creates needless confusion for both assessor and researcher.

AC dimension ⇓ Personality ⇒	N	E	O	A	C
Communication	-	√	-	-	-
Consideration / awareness	-	-	-	√	-
Drive	-	-	-	-	√
Influencing others	-	√	-	-	-
Organising & planning	-	-	-	-	√
Problem solving	-	-	√	-	-
Stress tolerance	√	-	-	-	-

Figure 10.2 Links between seven generic AC dimensions, and the five-factor model of personality, according to experts. Data from Lievens *et al.* (2006).

Rupp, Thornton and Gibbons (2008) offered a different perspective. They argued that the whole dimensions × exercise issue is based on a misunderstanding. ACs were never meant to use within exercise dimension ratings, but to employ the AT&T model where overall dimension ratings are generated at the end of the AC, after reviewing all the evidence. This argument views component exercises as items in a test, not likely to yield reliable scores by themselves, but to be pooled.

Construct validity

Lievens *et al.* (2006) took a list of seven generic AC dimensions (Arthur *et al.*'s list plus stress tolerance), and linked them to the FFM of personality, using a panel of five experts (Figure 10.2). Three of the FFM factors correspond to only one AC dimension, while the remaining two correspond to two generic AC dimensions. Figure 10.2 suggests that AC research can be linked quite closely to the broader field of personality. Note however that the data of Figure 10.2 are expert opinion, not results of actual empirical research.

Two meta-analyses (Scholz & Schuler, 1993; Collins *et al.*, 2003) compare AC overall assessment ratings with ability and personality tests, with interesting results (Table 10.4).

- Both find a fairly large correlation with MA, to some extent confirming the suggestion that the AC may be an elaborate and very expensive way of assessing GMA.
- In many ACs, assessors can be biased by knowing test scores before rating applicants. However, Scholz and Schuler found four studies where assessors rated without knowing the test scores. Correlation between AC rating and GMA score was not lower, suggesting an absence of bias.
- Better AC overall ratings tend to be linked to extraversion and (low) neuroticism, but not to conscientiousness, which is surprising as conscientiousness is the personality factor most closely associated with work performance. Surprisingly, few studies have assessed conscientiousness however.
- Scholz and Schuler found correlations with the big five fairly small, while correlations for some more specific traits (e.g. self–confidence) are greater.

Table 10.4   Summary of two meta-analyses of AC construct validity.

	Collins *et al.*	Scholz & Schuler
Mental ability	0.65	0.43
Neuroticism	−0.34	−0.15
Extraversion	0.47	0.14
Openness	0.23	0.09
Agreeableness	0.16	−0.07
Conscientiousness	–	−0.06
Dominance		0.30
Achievement motivation		0.40
Social competence		0.41
Self-confidence		0.32

Scholz & Schuler corrected for reliability of both test and AC rating. Collins *et al.* corrected for restricted range and AC rating reliability but not test reliability.

Krajewski *et al.* (2007) find that AC ratings correlate much more strongly with personality in older (40+) managers than younger; perhaps older managers have had more opportunity to 'grow into' their role.

Incremental validity

Schmidt and Hunter (1998) cited Collins's estimate of 0.65 correlation between AC rating and MA (Table 10.4) and argued that the incremental validity of ACs over GMA tests will be small. However, several empirical studies have shown that ACs achieve better validity than psychological tests. Vernon (1950) found that CSSB's test battery alone had poor predictive validity. Goffin, Rothstein and Johnston (1996) found that a personality test gives considerable incremental validity over an assessment centre. Dayan, Kasten and Fox (2002) reported data for the Israeli police force, which showed incremental validity of a very thorough AC over MA tests. They suggested that Schmidt and Hunter's pessimistic conclusions may only apply to management, not to entry-level selection, and may not apply either to work where dealing with people under very difficult circumstances is crucial. Krause *et al.* (2006) reported similar incremental validity of AC over MA tests for senior German police officers.

RESEARCH AGENDA

- Meta-analysis of the intercorrelations between AC and other selection methods (from which could be computed estimates of expected incremental validity
- Review or meta-analysis of actual incremental validity achieved by different combinations of AC and other selection methods

Fairness and the assessment centre

The AC is widely regarded as fair and 'safe', meaning it creates no adverse impact on women or minorities, and will not cause legal problems. The AC has high face or content validity (Chapter 2), which may account for its popularity, and may give some protection against claims of unfairness. Fighting one's case in a committee, chairing a meeting and answering an in-tray all have clear and easily defended job relevance. However, a recent meta-analysis (Dean, Roth & Bobko, 2008) finds quite large adverse impact on African Americans ($d = 0.52$) and Hispanic Americans ($d = 0.40$). The analysis confirmed earlier findings for gender, showing women tend to do slightly better in ACs ($d = 0.19$) than men. It appears that ACs will not avoid adverse impact problems in the USA.

Key points

In Chapter 10 you have learned the following.

- AC exercises can also be sorted into six or seven broad categories.
- ACs are tailor-made, so can assess a range of dimensions by a range of exercises.
- ACs have a conceptual matrix linking dimensions to exercises.
- AC dimensions can be sorted into six or seven broad categories.
- ACs achieve fairly good validity, allowing for restriction of range.
- ACs are very complex, making it difficult to analyse how they work.
- AC validity may have an element of circularity because they tend to compare what management think of As during the AC with what management thinks of As subsequently 'on-the-job'.
- The small number of studies that have used 'objective' criteria may find lower validity.
- ACs are intended to assess dimensions as exhibited in a number of exercises (convergent validity), but appear in practice to assess global proficiency in a series of exercises.
- AC construct validity research shows ACs correlate quite strongly with mental ability, and to a lesser extent with personality.
- ACs create adverse impact on minorities in the USA, but none by gender.

Key references

Anderson (2006) describes recent research on the present version of the long established WOSB.

Anstey (1977) describes a long-term follow-up of the British CSSB.

Bowler and Woehr (2006) present a six dimension by six exercise framework for AC research, and describe some research on model fitting.

Bray and Grant (1966) describe the classic AT&T Management Progress Study.

Dean *et al.* (2008) present a meta-analysis of ethnicity and gender differences in AC ratings.

Feltham (1988) describes a British AC for selecting senior police officers.

Gaugler *et al.* (1987) present an early meta analysis and VGA of AC validity. (Hardison & Sackett's later meta-analysis has not yet been published in English).

Hagan *et al.* (2006) describe an AC for department store managers, validated against 'mystery shopper' performance.

Lance *et al.* (2000) argue that ACs do not work as planned; and should be regarded as collections of work sample tests.

Lievens and Conway (2001) present a detailed structural equation modelling account of the AC convergent/discriminant validity problem (suitable for those interested in statistics).

Silvester and Dykes (2007) describe an AC used to select would-be Conservative MPs before the 2005 election.

Thornton and Rupp (2006) provide a detailed account of AC practice.

Woehr and Arthur (2003) discuss ways of solving the discriminant/convergent validity problem.

CHAPTER 11

Emotional intelligence and other methods

Success in work 80% dependent on emotional intelligence?

Introduction

There are six miscellaneous selection tests that do not fit neatly into any other main category: emotional intelligence, education, work samples, self-assessments, physical tests and drug-use testing. Education is probably the oldest of these, having been used in Imperial China for many centuries to select public officials. Work samples can be traced back to Munsterburg's work in 1913 for the Boston streetcar system. Formal physical tests have replaced more casual physical assessments since the 1970s to conform with fair employment legislation. Drug-use testing was introduced in the USA as part of President Reagan's 1986 Drug Free Workplace policy. The most recent arrival, emotional intelligence (EI), can also be dated very precisely, to Goleman's (1995) book.

Emotional intelligence

Being able to understand others and get along with them, it is claimed, is both a vital skill in work, and one which very intelligent people often lack (what might be termed the 'geek hypothesis'). Since 1995 this gap has been filled by EI. Numerous measures have appeared; training schemes have been developed; EI has even been added to the school curriculum. EI is said to bring many benefits: finding better leaders, creating better teamwork, finding people who cope better with stress, even finding people who have morally superior values. EI is seen as trainable, so less fixed than general mental ability (GMA). EI appeals to people who do poorly on conventional GMA tests.

Assessing EI

There are actually two quite different types of EI measure, illustrated by the fictitious questions in Table 11.1. The first type, in questions 1 to 3, is a real 'test', with right and wrong answers. It resembles a GMA test, but all the questions concern dealing with people. It may have a time limit. The main EI test is the Mayer-Salovey-Caruso Emotional Intelligence Test (MSCEIT). The

Table 11.1   Some sample (fictitious) questions for assessing emotional intelligence.

1. Someone you are talking to doesn't look you in the eye. What is a likely explanation of this?
   a] *he/she is not telling the truth*
   b] *he/she respects you*
   c] *he/she likes you*

2. Look at these three pictures of the same person. In which one does she look happy?
   A   B   C

3. What mood might be helpful when generating a lot of new ideas in a group?
   fear   *very helpful* 5 4 3 2 1 *not at all helpful*
   anger   *very helpful* 5 4 3 2 1 *not at all helpful*
   contentment   *very helpful* 5 4 3 2 1 *not at all helpful*

4. I take the lead in groups.
   always   often   sometimes   occasionally   never

5. I find it difficult to control my moods.
   always   often   sometimes   occasionally   never

6. People listen to what I
   always   often   sometimes   occasionally   never

second type of EI measure, in questions 4 to 6, may look familiar. There are no right and wrong answers; there is no time limit; people are reporting their own thoughts, feelings and behaviour. This is an EI questionnaire, sometimes described as a 'mixed' EI measure. It looks very much like a personality questionnaire. Looking at the list of what a typical EI measure covers, the feeling of familiarity gets a lot stronger; the (British) Emotional Intelligence Questionnaire covers self-awareness, emotional resilience, motivation, interpersonal sensitivity, influence and persuasion, decisiveness, conscientiousness and integrity. The EIQ assesses at least three of the big five personality factors (conscientiousness, neuroticism and extraversion). Van Rooy and Viswesvaran's (2005) meta-analysis found that all EIQs intercorrelate (0.71 corrected), suggesting they all measure roughly the same thing, but they did not correlate with EI tests (0.14 corrected) indicating EIQs and EI tests were indeed different.

Validity of EI measures

Construct validity

Van Rooy and Viswesvaran (2005) and Bludau and Legree (2008) reported meta-analyses of correlations between EI tests and EIQs, and GMA and personality. Table 11.2 confirms that EI tests, principally the MSCEIT, correlate with GMA, but not with personality, whereas EIQs correlate with the big five,

Table 11.2   Meta-analysis of construct validity of EI tests and EIQs.

EI tests

	k	N	r	ρ
GMA	18	3,872	0.25	0.34
	32	5,602	0.23	0.26[a]
(low) Neuroticism	11	2,643	0.07	0.08
Extraversion	11	2,643	0.07	0.09
Openness	11	2,643	0.11	0.14
Agreeableness	10	2,529	0.15	0.18
Conscientiousness	9	2,353	0.05	0.06

EIQs

	k	N	r	ρ
GMA	28	8,514	0.11	0.13
(low) Neuroticism	27	6,800	0.34	0.40
Extraversion	25	6,367	0.30	0.36
Openness	25	6,367	0.25	0.32
Agreeableness	24	6,238	0.22	0.27
Conscientiousness	26	6,339	0.28	0.33

Data from Van Rooy & Viswesvaran (2005) and [a]Bludau & Legree (2008).
ρ = Correlation corrected for reliability of both measures.

but not with GMA. However, even the fully corrected correlations remain modest, indicating the measures are not interchangeable, and that EI measures may have something new to contribute.

Predictive validity

Several reviews of EI validity research have appeared recently (Van Rooy & Viswesvaran, 2004; Zeidner, Matthews & Roberts, 2004; McEnrue & Groves, 2006). Zeidner *et al.* found only a handful of studies of EI and work performance, mostly unsatisfactory in one way or another: very small sample size, no attempt to control for GMA or personality, or incompletely reported. Van Rooy and Viswesvaran (2004) reported a meta-analysis of 19 workplace studies of EI and found an average validity of 0.22, rising to 0.24 when corrected for criterion reliability. This analysis pooled EI test (an early version of MSCEIT) and EIQs, there being insufficient studies to analyse them separately. Grubb and McDaniel (2007) confirmed that the Bar-On Emotional Quotient Inventory, a widely used PQ format measure, is easily faked; students directed to complete the EQI as if applying for a job increased their total 'EQ' by nearly one whole SD (d = 0.88). Advocates of EI argue that EI is important at a different stage of career from other predictors: GMA gets you into management, but EI determines whether you reach the top. This is an interesting hypothesis, which could be tested using the career success paradigm, correlating EI with how far people have got by age 50. Research would also need to exclude the possibility that high EI scorers rise to the top by their mastery of office politics rather than genuine talent. Critics (e.g. Landy, 2005) note some defects in EI research. A lot is based on the publishers' databases, which are 'proprietary', i.e. not open to anyone else. Chapter 7 noted that research by people who do not have a commercial interest in a test carries a lot more weight. EI research also uses 'fishing expeditions', correlating all four, or seven or 15 EI scores with multiple outcome measures, but quoting only the significant findings.

Team performance

EI should be closely related to team performance. Bell's (2007) meta-analysis finds only two studies of EI and work team performance, which yield a low (corrected) validity of 0.10. A slightly larger number of lab studies of team performance yielded a slightly larger average validity (0.20 corrected). Research so far has not found evidence of a strong link between EI and team performance.

Incremental validity is the key test of the value of any new measure. It is especially relevant for EI measures, given that they resemble rather closely tests (of GMA and personality) everyone has been using for years. Brody (2006) notes that some EI researches control for GMA, some control for personality, some for neither, but few control for both. Van Rooy and Viswesvaran (2004) estimated the likely incremental validity of EI on GMA at only 0.03. Estimates of incremental validity of EI on PQ measures of the five-factor model (FFM) are higher, ranging from 0.06 to 0.29. Landy noted that research is also needed comparing EI with existing concepts of tacit knowledge, and with situational judgement tests. To date, a handful of studies suggest EI may not add very much to prediction of success in education or employment.

The 'predictors' fallacy

Goleman made the famous claim that success at work is '80% dependent on emotional intelligence and only 20% on IQ'. It is true that GMA tests account for only 25% of the variance in work performance; it follows logically that something else accounts for the other 75%. But it does not follow logically that the something else is EI. Nor is it very likely; accounting for 75% of the variance requires EI to correlate with work performance 0.87, far higher than any test or set of tests has ever achieved. Landy suggested that one basis for the popularity of EI may be the feeling that 'We can't perfectly explain behaviour so we need more predictors'. He also points to the snag with EI measures: 'But shouldn't these new predictors actually improve prediction?'.

Adverse impact

EI is popular in part because it is thought it will avoid all the problems created by GMA tests, especially adverse impact on ethnic minorities. Meta-analysis of 36 studies finds women score slightly higher on EI (Van Rooy & Viswesvaran, 2003). Information on ethnicity is sparser; research on students by van Rooy, Alonso and Viswesvaran (2005) using an EIQ finds Afro and Hispanic Americans score higher than white Americans, suggesting adverse impact may not be a problem.

EI measures have not so far proved all that useful in selection. Some critics dismiss them – 'faddish and confused idea massively commercialised' (Furnham 2006). However, being able to get on with others at work is very important, and selectors do need some way of assessing it. Re-inventing the PQ and calling it EI is unlikely to suit; the deficiencies of PQs were noted at some length in Chapter 7: low validity, fakability and lack of self-insight. Other approaches may prove more promising.

Other report

Table 5.1 (on page 95) shows the traditional reference is sometimes used to ask about human relations skills. EI may be assessable by ratings from peers or subordinates; Ford and Tisak (1983) devised a peer nomination measure for school pupils (e.g. Who in the class would be best at persuading the teacher to give less homework?). Peer ratings tend to be difficult to obtain in selection, but can be used for promotion. Other forms of some EIQs exist, where the completer describes someone else; these do not seem very widely used.

Demonstration by test

Test format measures like the MSCEIT may have more promise, but have construct validity problems. EI tests have actually been around since the 1920s, under the name 'social intelligence'. They fell out of favour precisely because they correlated so well with GMA that they didn't seem to be measuring anything new (Landy, 2005).

Behavioural demonstration

Group discussions and role plays, included in ACs or used in isolation, assess important aspects of EI. For some jobs, work samples can be devised (e.g. dealing with a query or complaint by telephone). Behavioural tests are slow and expensive. They also depend heavily on assessors' ratings, which create problems, discussed in Chapter 10. It is possible to outline some more elaborate behavioural tests of EI, and note the amount of research needed to make them work. Negotiation is important in many managerial jobs: getting the best deal for the organization. One approach could be an elaborate simulation, with a cast of role players, who respond to the negotiator's every move with the 'right' response (e.g. if A gets aggressive, clam up). But what is the 'right' response? Detailed analysis of many real negotiations will be needed to generate a plausible script, based on what actually succeeds or fails in real negotiations. Real negotiations can last a long time, so a very long script will be needed. Or else researchers can analyse separate components of negotiation process (e.g. non-verbal communication (NVC; receiving) – how good is A at recognizing wavering – and NVC (sending) – how good is A at not giving anything away by tone of voice, facial expression, and so on. It is much quicker to use a short EIQ with questions like *I am good at getting what I want* and *People say I can drive a hard bargain*.

Situational judgement (SJ) or tacit knowledge (TK)

Table 11.3 gives two typical problems from this type of measure, which can be traced back to the George Washington Social Intelligence Test in the 1920s. SJ tests also include various measures of supervisor judgement, dating back to the How Supervise measure used in the 1940s. Sternberg *et al.*'s (2000) work on TK uses a similar format. ('Tacit' knowledge because Sternberg argues that success often depends on knowing things, about, e.g. getting funding, that are not explicitly described anywhere.) Table 11.3 illustrates an important

Table 11.3   Two fictitious Situation Judgement/Tacit Knowledge type questions.

1. You would like to secure funding for a new research project on the link between mental ability and delinquency. Various colleagues have offered you advice. Rate each suggestion for how likely it is to help you secure funding.
   - a] Do a pilot study and get it published as quickly as possible, so you can cite it in the proposal.
   - b] Find out who is on the funding committee, and what their research interests are.
   - c] Write a letter to the Times saying that low intelligence is the main cause of delinquency, and that research in the area is urgently needed.
   - d] Get an article published that ridicules Professor X whose research finds no link between mental ability and delinquency.
   - e] Do not mention mental ability, but propose to study teaching methods and delinquency. (You can add in the mental ability tests later.)
   - f] Choose a different area of research.

2. One of your team at work is taking a lot of time off, because he says his partner is unwell. You need him to work harder or your team will not reach its target. What is the best thing to do? What is the worst thing to do?
   - a] Tell him to come to work on time every day or you will get him terminated
   - b] Sympathise
   - c] Seek to negotiate an agreement that he will reduce his absence by at least 50%
   - d] Wait, because his partner will probably soon get better.

difference between SJ and TK tests, and GMA tests. There is only one correct answer to 2 + 2 = (except in Orwell's *Nineteen Eighty Four*), but what of question 2 in Table 11.3? The 'right' answer today is 'negotiate' because that is what Western society values and all the books on conflict resolution recommend. It is not hard to list societies, past and present, where answer 1 would be considered the 'right' one. Answers to SJ and TK measures are defined by expert panels or sometimes by the consensus of the normative sample, which tends to make the test an exercise in conformity. (It also becomes impossible to include any 'difficult' questions.) The same issues arise with some EI measures. SJTs can be scored using two types of instruction, either *'What is the best thing to do?'* or *'What would you do?'*. The former tends to make the SJT a test of ability and nearly doubles its correlation with GMA; the latter makes it more a measure of personality and greatly increases its correlation with the FFM (McDaniel *et al.*, 2007). The type of instruction does not affect correlation with work performance. More elaborate SJTs have been devised (e.g. for police work) that use video rather than paper-and-pencil, and which 'branch' (Kanning *et al.*, 2006). Would-be police officers first choose what to do on encountering a group of football hooligans (confront/ignore/send for backup). If they choose to confront, they are presented with a further set of choices for dealing with the resulting aggression.

Criterion validity

SJ tests have been much more extensively researched than EI measures. McDaniel *et al.*'s meta-analysis (Table 11.4) showed relatively low uncorrected validity of 0.20, that rises 0.26, when corrected for reliability of work performance measure, but not restricted range.

Construct and incremental validity

Although SJTs have been used since the 1920s, not much was known until recently about what they measure, and why they predict work performance. McDaniel *et al.*'s meta-analysis also reported correlations between SJTs, GMA and personality. Table 11.4 shows SJTs correlate with GMA, and with three of the big five (whereas Table 11.2 shows EIQs correlate with all five personality factors). McDaniel *et al.* also estimated incremental validity of SJTs over GMA and FFM. They gave some incremental validity on PQ (ca. 0.07) and GMA (ca. 0.04) separately, but hardly any on the two combined (0.01–0.02). Situational judgement tests create less adverse impact on ethnic minorities in the USA, but do generate gender differences, favouring women (Weekley & Jones, 1999).

The three areas of research – EI, SJ and TK – look quite similar in some respects, but remain separate in the sense that people researching in one rarely seem to mention the others. No research checking the correlation between SJ tests and EI measures seems to have been reported. Ferris (Semadar, Robins & Ferris, 2006) noted several other related research headings, including politi-

Table 11.4 Meta-analysis of criterion and construct validity of SJTs.

	k	N	r	ρ
Work performance	118	24.8 K	0.20	0.26
GMA	95	30.8 K	0.29	0.32
(Low) neuroticism	49	19.3 K	0.19	0.22
Extraversion	25	11.4 K	0.13	0.14
Openness	19	4.5 K	0.11	0.13
Agreeableness	51	25.5 K	0.22	0.25
Conscientiousness	53	31.3 K	0.23	0.27

Data from McDaniel *et al.* (2007).
ρ = correlation corrected for reliability of work performance measure, or of GMA or FFM measure, but not for range restriction.

RESEARCH AGENDA

- More validity data for EI measures
- Validity data that check for overlap with measures of personality and MA
- Separate analysis of the validity of EIQs and EI tests
- Further exploration of the relationship among EI, SJ, TK, political skill, and so on.

cal skill, self-monitoring and leadership self-efficacy, and suggested the umbrella term social effectiveness.

Education

Employers in Britain often specify a university degree; professional training schemes almost always do. American employers used to require high school graduation, but few do now. Early analyses of American college grade point averages (marks from exams and course work) found weak relationships with work performance (Reilly & Chao, 1982). Roth *et al.* (1996) meta-analysed 71 studies relating grades to work performance, and find a corrected validity of 0.33. However, Figure 11.1 shows validity decays very rapidly, falling from 0.45 one year after graduation to 0.11 six years after. The US military finds high school completion useful for predicting completion of basic training: people who 'drop out' of school also tend to 'drop out' of training (Sackett & Mavor, 2003).

Education tests have fallen foul of American fair employment laws in a big way. Some US minorities do less well at school, so more fail to complete high school. Roth and Bobko (2000) reported an analysis of ethnicity differences in GPA for 7,000 students at an American university, and found a large

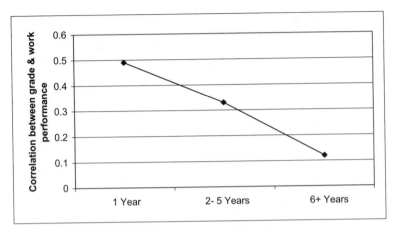

Figure 11.1 Correlation between college grades and work performance, as a function of time since graduation. Data from Roth *et al.* (1996).

difference that would create major adverse impact. The difference increases sharply from first to third year, where it amounts to $d = 0.78$. Adverse impact means the employer has to prove the job really needs the educational level or qualifications specified. This has often proved difficult. Meritt-Haston and Wexley's (1983) review of 83 US court cases found that educational requirements were generally ruled unlawful for skilled or craft jobs, supervisors and management trainees, but were accepted for police and academics. Chapter 1 described systems of setting minimum qualifications, including education, designed to select suitable As without excluding people, especially minorities, who could do the job. Berry, Gruys and Sackett (2006) used the large and representative National Longitudinal Survey of Youth to check whether education makes a good substitute for tested mental ability. They confirmed that GMA and years of education are highly correlated (0.63). Nevertheless, using amount of education (not grades) turns out to be a poor substitute for testing MA. The widely used high school diploma requirement only excludes the lowest 5 to 10% in tested MA. Even requiring the equivalent of a PhD, achieved by only 2% of people, only excludes the lower 70% of the MA distribution. However, Berry *et al.* did find that selection by education creates less adverse impact on minorities than ability tests.

Overqualified?

HR are often wary of people with degrees who apply for 'ordinary' jobs. Bewley (1999) reported a survey during the recession of the early 1990s, which found 80% of American firms unwilling to employ overqualified applicants (As). Hersch's (1991) survey suggested a possible reason: overqualified employees tend to be less satisfied with their job, and to be thinking of leaving.

RESEARCH AGENDA

• Research on how widely held the overqualification hypothesis is
• More research on the link between overqualification and work performance

Work sample tests

A work sample test familiar to most adults is the driving test. It does not try to infer ability to drive from reaction time, or eye–hand co-ordination, or personality, or past behaviour. It places you in a car and requires you to drive it from A to B. Work samples are widely used for skilled and semi-skilled jobs. Work samples are observed and rated, using checklists (Figure 11.2). Work samples can usually achieve good inter-rater reliability; Lance *et al.* (2000) quoted 0.81 to 0.98. A specialized type of work sample is the simulation (e.g. of flying or nuclear power plant operation). These can assess thoroughly – and safely – As' ability to cope with emergencies.

Validity

Roth, Bobko & McFarland (2005) reported a new meta-analysis of work sample research, not so much because there has been a lot of new research – they found only 54 validities – but because they considered previous analyses lacking in detail, or over-inclusive. Roth *et al.* excluded job knowledge and situational judgement tests as not being true work samples. Average raw validity was 0.26, rising to 0.33 when corrected for reliability of work performance measure. This is, as they note, well below Hunter & Hunter's widely cited (1984) estimate of 0.54. Virtually all the studies use present employee samples, not applicant samples, so may suffer restricted range, and may underestimate validity for As. Roth *et al.* found an interesting moderator variable – date: validity tended to be higher before 1982 than after. Recall that

---

• Remove inner tube
• Inflate and submerge in water to detect (all) punctures
• Mark (all) punctures
• Deflate tube and dry thoroughly
• Roughen tube with abrasive
• Spread adhesive and wait 30 seconds
• Peel cover off patch
• Line up carefully and press firmly on to puncture
• Dust with talc
• Do not check whether patch is firmly stuck down
• Check outer cover for damage or continued presence of nail, etc.

Figure 11.2   (Part of) checklist for work sample test, repairing a puncture.

GATB validity and AC validity also seem to have fallen over time (Chapters 2 and 10).

Construct and incremental validity

Schmidt and Hunter (1998) reported a correlation of 0.38 between work samples and GMA. Roth *et al.*'s (2005) meta-analysis confirmed Schmidt and Hunter's estimate, finding work samples correlate with GMA moderately (0.32) and situational judgement tests slightly (0.13). There are little or no data for any other measure. Schmidt and Hunter concluded the incremental validity of work sample tests over GMA test will be high (0.12), one of the highest values they cited. The combination of work sample and GMA tests is one of the three that Schmidt and Hunter recommended employers to consider using. Roth *et al.* (2005) offered an estimate for incremental validity of work samples over GMA tests, which is lower than Schmidt and Hunter's, at 0.06, but warned that their estimate makes a lot of assumptions and is not very safe.

Domain validity

Work samples can achieve domain validity in some circumstances. If HR can list every task in the job and devise work samples to match, HR can then make statements along the lines of 'X has mastered 80% of the job's demands'. X is being compared with job requirements, not with other As. This avoids many problems. HR do not need large samples; X may be the one and only person who does that job but HR can still say X has mastered 80% of it. People who have only mastered 60% are given more training until they have mastered enough to be allowed to start work. Unfortunately, few employers can afford to describe their jobs in sufficient detail, and very many jobs do not lend themselves to such detailed and specific descriptions. The American military have succeeded in listing all critical tasks for US Marines, and devising matching work samples (Carey, 1991).

True work samples can only be used if the person has already mastered the job's skills. It is clearly pointless (and dangerous) giving a driving test to someone who cannot drive. Two variations on the work sample theme can be used with inexperienced As.

Trainability tests

Trainability tests assess how well As can learn a new skill. The instructor gives standardized instructions and a demonstration, then rates A's efforts using a checklist: for example, *does not tighten chuck sufficiently* or *does not use coolant*. A meta-analysis of trainability test validity (Robertson & Downs, 1989) found that they predicted training success much better (0.39 to 0.57, uncorrected) than job performance (0.20 to 0.24).

IBT/1

From: V Wordy MICE CEMH FIME
               (Engineering Director)

To: I Prior
               (Assistant General Manager)

I am in receipt of your memorandum of 15th November concerning the necessity for more rapid progress on the revised layout of Number 4 component assembly area and am fully cognisant of the urgency of this matter myself. My strenuous efforts in this respect are not however being assisted by the calibre of some of the personnel allocated to myself for this purpose. A particular obstacle with which I am currently faced lies in the persistent absenteeism of certain members of the workforce who appear to have little interest in contributing an effort commensurate with their present rates of pay. The designated complement of shop-floor workers for Assembly Area 4 under the new establishment of 5th October is just adequate for the Area's requisites on the strict understanding that the full complement are in fact present and available for work as opposed to, for example, absenting themselves for lengthy smoking breaks in the male toilet facilities. Efforts on the part of myself and my foreman to instil a sense of purpose and discipline into a workforce sadly lacking any semblance of either attribute have not so far, I am sorry to say, received what I would consider adequate backing from the management. I would like to bring to your attention for your immediate executive action a particularly blatant case which fully merits in my estimation the immediate dismissal of the employee concerned. Yesterday our revised November schedule called for us to be securing the transfer of Number 111 lathe from its former position to its new location.

Figure 11.3   A sample item from an in-tray test.

In-tray or in-basket tests

These tests are a management work sample; As deal with a set of letters, memos, notes, reports and phone messages (Figure 11.3). A's performance is usually rated both overall and item-by-item. Overall evaluation checks whether As sort items by priority, and notice any connections between items. Some scoring methods are objective (e.g. counting how many decisions As make); others require judgements by the scorer and focus on stylistic aspects. Schippmann, Prien and Katz (1990) reviewed 22 validity studies, which they considered too diverse for meta-analysis; they concluded that criterion validity is generally good. Several studies (e.g. Bray & Grant 1966) reported that in-trays have incremental validity – and do not just cover the same ground as tests of verbal or GMA. Brannick, Michaels and Baker (1989) however reported that in-tray exercises show the same feature as the assessment centres they often form part of; factor analysis of scores yields exercise-based factors, not factors corresponding to the dimensions the test is supposed to be assessing.

Limitations of work sample tests

Work samples are necessarily job-specific so a tramway system – like the Boston, Massachusetts network that used the first work sample – will need different work samples for drivers, inspectors, mechanics, electricians, and so on, which will prove expensive. Work samples are best for specific concrete skills, and do not work so well where the work is diverse or abstract or involves other people. Work samples are usually administered one-to-one, and need expert raters, which makes them expensive.

Adverse impact

Schmitt, Clause and Pulakos's (1996) meta-analysis reported that work samples create far smaller differences than paper-and-pencil ability tests: a d statistic of 0.37 for African-Americans and zero for Hispanic Americans. However, Bobko, Roth and Buster (2005) questioned the widely held belief that work samples create little or no adverse impact; previous analyses have been based on present employee samples where less able persons have been screened out. They reported some data for true applicant samples, and find considerable AI on minorities in the USA (d values of 0.70 and 0.73). Roth *et al.* (2005) tried to include ethnicity differences in their meta-analysis, but found few studies gave any data. Chapter 14 shows work samples are readily accepted by As. Work samples are less often the subject of litigation in the USA (Terpstra *et al.*, 1999), and even less often the subject of successful litigation.

RESEARCH AGENDA

- Clarification of adverse impact, using applicant samples.
- Meta-analysis of in-tray test data.

Self-assessments

Self-assessments are the simplest form of self-report. PQs ask up to 36 questions to estimate how dominant someone is; interviews last up to an hour. A self-assessment asks only for a rating on a seven point scale: *How dominant a person are you?*

Validity

Mabe and West (1982) analysed 43 studies and reported an average raw validity of 0.31, increasing to 0.36 operational validity. They concluded that self-assessments had highest validity when

- Given anonymously – not a lot of use in selection!
- People were told self-assessments would be compared with objective tests, which means either giving a test or lying to the applicants.
- Subjects were comparing themselves with fellow workers, which again tends to make them impractical for selection.

Dunning, Heath and Suls (2004) argued that workplace self-assessments are frequently wildly optimistic. They noted especially that senior managers often have an inflated view of their own abilities to enter successfully new markets, to launch new products, or to identify properties or companies to acquire. Dunning (Kruger & Dunning, 1999) also argued that self-assessments frequently show a marked lack of self-insight. People who actually score in the bottom 25% on tests of logic or grammar place themselves around the 60th percentile because they are unable to identify poor performance, in others or in themselves. While self-assessments sometimes predict performance quite well, hardly anyone seems to use them for real decisions. Perhaps employers suppose people cannot or would not give accurate estimates of their abilities.

Physical tests

Some jobs require strength, agility or endurance. Some jobs require, or are felt to require, physical size. Some jobs require dexterity. For some jobs, attractive appearance is, explicitly or implicitly, a requirement. Hunter and Burke's (1996) meta-analysis of pilot training included seven studies of reaction time and reports an uncorrected predictive validity of 0.28.

Strength

Measures of physique and physical performance often intercorrelate very highly. Hogan (1991) concluded there are only three main factors: strength, endurance and movement quality, of which movement quality is more important in sport than work. Tests of physique or strength are sometimes used in Britain, often in a fairly arbitrary or haphazard way. North American employers use physical tests much more systematically. Armco Inc. devised a battery of physical work sample tests for labourers and have extensive data on norms, correlations and sex differences (Arnold *et al.*, 1982).

Validity

Schmitt *et al.*'s (1984) VGA yielded a raw validity of 0.32 for physical tests, used mainly to select unskilled labour. Physical tests also predict whether the employer can cope with the job without finding it too demanding, or even suffering injury. Chaffin (1974) found that the greater the discrepancy between a worker's strength and the physical demands of the job, the more likely the worker is to suffer a back injury – a notorious source of lost output in industry.

Furthermore, the relation is continuous and linear and does not have a threshold, so an employer who wants to minimize the risk of back injury should choose the strongest applicant, other things being equal.

Adverse impact

Physical tests create very substantial adverse impact on women, and, in North America, on some ethnic groups. Disability discrimination laws make it essential to prove thoroughly that a job requires particular physical abilities. Terpstra *et al.*'s (1999) review of fair employment cases in the USA found that physical tests featured three or four times as often as would be expected from their estimated frequency of use. Hence, physical tests need to be carefully chosen and validated. Hoffman (1999) described a careful programme of physical testing within the American gas industry. 'Marker' jobs such as construction crew assistant were used to show that strength tests were valid predictors of ability to do work involving carrying 80-lb bags of sand or wrestling with rusted up bolts. However, many jobs had too few people doing them for conventional validation to be possible. Hoffman used the Position Analysis Questionnaire (Chapter 3) to cluster-analyse jobs into construction, customer service or clerical for instance, and to indicate the likely physical requirements of each cluster. Construction and warehousing were high; customer service was medium; clerical was low. Included in some clusters were the 'marker' jobs. This enabled Hoffman to argue that 'this job is similar in PAQ profile to the construction assistant job, for which there is a validity study, so it's reasonable to expect physical tests to be valid for this post too'. Rayson, Holliman and Belyavin (2000) described a physical testing programme for infantry soldiers in the British Army, which was less successful. The army wants to recruit women into all branches, but also sets demanding physical standards. They first listed the main generic physical tasks the infantry soldier must be able to perform. These include the 'single lift', lifting a 44-kilogram box of ammunition from the ground to the back of a truck and the 'loaded march', covering 13 kilometres carrying a 25-kilogram pack. However, the core tasks could not be used as actual work samples on grounds of safety – suppose an applicant dropped the ammunition box on his/her foot – or practicality – the tests will be used in city centre recruiting offices, while route marches need open country and take too long. Accordingly, tests of muscle strength, muscle endurance, body size, aerobic fitness, and fat-free mass were devised which were safe and practical, and which were intended to predict ability to complete the core tasks. Unfortunately, some showed differential validity: they worked well for men but not for women, which of course meant they could not be used.

Height

Chapter 4 noted that height predicts success in work rather well, better than personality, and concluded that this is probably for the most part bias. Are there any types of work where height is a true requirement? Minimum height requirements have been dropped for police officers in the USA and the UK, to avoid problems with gender differences and because it was difficult to find any evidence of a link between height and effectiveness.

Dexterity divides into *arm and hand* or *gross* dexterity, and *finger and wrist* or *fine* dexterity. Dexterity is needed for assembly work, which is generally semi-skilled or unskilled. It is also needed for some professional jobs, notably dentistry and surgery. General Aptitude Test Battery (GATB; Chapter 7) includes both gross and fine dexterity tests. Many work sample and trainability tests also assess dexterity. Ghiselli's (1966b) meta-analysis reported moderate validities of dexterity tests for vehicle operation, trades and crafts, and industrial work. Re-analysis of the GATB database (Hunter, 1986) showed that dexterity was more important, the less complex the job. Hartigan and Wigdor (1989) suggested that the GATB data actually show that dexterity predicts success only at the lowest of five levels of complexity: cannery workers, shrimp pickers or cornhusking machine operators.

Physical attractiveness

Research on interviewing (Chapter 4) shows that appearance and attractiveness often affect selectors' decisions. But is appearance or attractiveness a legitimate part of the person specification for many jobs? Acting and modelling certainly. Appearance or attractiveness is often an implicit requirement for receptionists; many advertisements, for example, specify 'smart appearance' or 'pleasant manner'. Appearance, shading into 'charisma', is probably also important for selling, persuading and influencing jobs. Discrimination laws do not allow employers to argue that they cannot employ ethnic minority persons because customers would not like it; there is no corresponding legal protection for the less attractive.

RESEARCH AGENDA

- Whether height or attractiveness are legitimate requirements for any types of work.

Drug-use testing

The 1990 (American) National Household Survey reports that 7% of adult employees use illegal drugs (while 6.8% drink alcohol heavily). In the USA, testing As for illegal drug use is widely used, but controversial. Alcohol testing is also used in the USA for some jobs. The standard method is chemical analysis of urine samples. Alternatives include paper–and–pencil tests, co-ordination tests to detect impairment, and analysis of hair samples. Hair samples are easier to collect, transport and store, and can reveal drug use over a period of months, making it more difficult to evade the test by short term abstention (Harris & Trusty, 1997).

Validity

Research on validity of drug testing as a selection method tends to focus on absence, turnover and accidents. Large-scale research in the US Postal Service (Normand, Salyards & Mahoney, 1990) has found drug users more likely to be absent, or to suffer involuntary turnover, but not to have more accidents. Critics have argued that the link between drug use and work performance is tenuous. In correlational terms, relationships were very small (0.08 at best), and account for minute amounts of variance (0.6% at best). Critics argue that this is nowhere near enough to justify the intrusion on As' privacy and civil rights. Savings achievable from reducing absence by drug testing were estimated at four to five million dollars a year, which is not a lot in one of America's largest workforces. Other critics suggest that many employers adopt drug testing programmes to project an image, of control, or of corporate responsibility and concern for social problems. Links between drug use and work performance may be mediated by some third factor, possibly ethnicity, or general deviance; people who do not wish to fit into American society use drugs, and behave differently at work, but do not behave differently at work because they use drugs. On this argument, drug use is a convenient cue for employers who wish to avoid employing 'dropouts'. Levine and Rennie (2004) thought many employers have introduced drug-use testing without having any clear idea why.

Drug-use testing in selection is legal in the USA. Levine and Rennie argued that all As testing positive should be interviewed by an experienced doctor, to check whether they are taking illegal drugs, which are not legitimate medication. Some widely used non-prescription medication can also give positive test results. Apart from considerations of fairness, refusing employment to someone taking prescription medication might violate the Americans with Disabilities Act (ADA). (But note that asking people about prescription medicine also violates ADA, so drug-use testing in selection should be done after making a job offer – so-called pre-employment testing.) Acceptability of drug testing depends on perceptions of danger (Murphy, Thornton & Prue, 1991), so people see it as fair for surgeons, police officers, or airline pilots, but not justified for janitors, farm workers or clerks.

RESEARCH AGENDA

- Whether drug use in the work affects performance
- How many people evade detection by urine test, by short abstention or cheating

Key points

In Chapter 11 you have learned the following.

- Emotional intelligence is assessed by two types of measure: questionnaire and test.
- EI questionnaires tend to overlap with personality, while EI tests overlap with mental ability.
- EI measures are far less successful at predicting work performance than claimed.
- Situational judgement tests are widely used and achieve moderately good validity.
- Educational achievement predicts work performance in the short-term but not the long term.
- Educational achievement requirements create adverse impact in the USA.
- Work sample tests assess work performance directly and avoid inferences based on abilities or personality traits.
- Work samples may be less useful than generally supposed because new meta-analysis finds validity considerably lower, while adverse impact is much higher.
- Work samples tend to be limited to fairly specific skills.
- In-basket tests are useful in selection for management.
- Self-assessments can be valid indicators of performance, but probably not in most selection contexts
- Physical ability tests will create quite large adverse impact for gender, but can be used if carefully constructed, validated and normed.
- Drug-use testing needs to be thought about carefully – who will be excluded, how and why? What will people think of it?

Key references

Berry *et al.* (2006) analyse the usefulness of educational attainment as proxy for mental ability.

Bobko *et al.* (2005) argue that work sample tests create more adverse impact that is generally supposed.

Dunning *et al.* (2004) argue that self-assessment is fundamentally flawed.

Landy (2005) gives an interesting historical account of social and emotional intelligence testing.

Levine and Rennie (2004) give a critical review of pre-employment drug testing.

Mabe and West (1982) review early research on self-assessments.

McDaniel *et al.* (2007) present a meta-analysis of the validity of situational judgement tests.

McEnrue and Groves (2006) describe four EI tests, and summarize data on content, construct and predictive validity.

Rayson *et al.* (2000) describe the problems faced by the British Army in devising physical tests for infantry soldiers.

Roth *et al.* (2005) present a new meta-analysis of the validity of work sample tests, suggesting it is lower than generally supposed.

Schippmann *et al.* (1990) present a narrative review of in-basket test validity.

Van Rooy and Viswesvaran (2004) review research on emotional intelligence and work performance.

Zeidner *et al.* (2004) offer a critical review of emotional intelligence in the workplace.

CHAPTER 12

Criteria of work performance

'the successful employee … does more work, does it better, with less supervision, with less interruption through absence … He makes fewer mistakes and has fewer accidents … He ordinarily learns more quickly, is promoted more rapidly, and stays with the company.'
Bingham & Freyd (1926)

Introduction

Bingham and Freyd (1926) summarized the criterion issue with a list of all the things employers typically want in successful new employees: for example, learn the job quickly, avoid accidents and absence or stay rather than leave. Writing so long ago, they can be forgiven for appearing to assume the successful employee is also male. Validation compares a predictor, or selection test, with a criterion, or index of the employee's work performance. A good criterion should be:

- *Reliable* – meaning either stable (over time) or consistent (between observers).
- *Valid* – In one sense this is a tautology; the criterion defines success. But critics, and courts, often question criteria of work performance.
- *Unbiased* – The criterion should not contain unfair bias against women or ethnic minorities or any other protected group.
- *Practical* – Information can be obtained at reasonable cost, by procedures management and workers accept.

Validity

The validity of a criterion of work performance can be represented by an overlapping circles diagram, just like the validity of a selection test (Figure 2.3, page 33). In Figure 12.1 the right-hand circle represents true work performance, and the left-hand circle is the criterion of work performance.

- The shaded area in the middle is the overlap, the part of true performance that the criterion succeeds in measuring.
- The unshaded area of the right-hand circle is that part of true work performance the criterion does not succeed in measuring, sometimes referred to as criterion deficiency. For example, performance standards for infantry soldiers that failed to include marksmanship or courage would be seriously deficient.

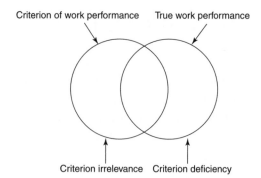

Criterion of work performance   True work performance

Criterion irrelevance   Criterion deficiency

Figure 12.1 Schematic representation of true work performance, and actual criterion.

Table 12.1 Criteria used in early validation research.

Criterion	Number of studies	% Studies
Global ratings by supervisor	213	60
Output criteria	58	16
Sales	16	5
Earnings	16	5
Accidents	13	4
Job level	13	4
Survival	10	3
Work sample	10	3
Promotion	4	1

Data from Crites (1969).

- The unshaded area of the left-hand circle covers aspects of the criterion measures, which are not part of true work performance, sometimes referred to as criterion irrelevance. Researchers are sometimes tempted to define success at work by something that is easy to quantify, but not actually very important. For example one could define the Prime Minister's success by the number of foreign heads of state entertained at 10 Downing Street, because it is easy to get that information from the Times *Court Circular* page. But is it really central to the Prime Minster's role?

Crites (1969) analysed criteria used by over 500 validation studies reported by Dorcus and Jones (1950) for the period 1914 to 1950 (Table 12.1). Rating or *subjective* criteria were used by 60% of researches, while the other 40% used a range of more *objective* criteria. Lent *et al.* (1971) confirmed that 879 of 1,506 criteria used (58%) were supervisor evaluations. The global supervisor rating was clearly the favourite criterion in early validation research. The last 15–20 years has seen an increasing emphasis on new criteria, under the headings of organizational citizenship (OC), counterproductive behaviour (CPB) and adaptability. New criteria may be predicted by different tests, which may ease adverse impact problems.

Rating or subjective criteria

Supervisor ratings

The supervisor rating criterion is very convenient to psychologists researching on selection, so long as they do not read the work of colleagues researching the same ratings under the heading of performance appraisal. Their colleagues' efforts document many problems: poor reliability, suspect validity, halo, leniency and bias. Elaborate rating formats have been devised, in the search for a system that will maximize reliability, and minimize halo and bias.

Reliability

Supervisor ratings have fairly poor reliability. Viswesvaran, Ones and Schmidt (1996) reported a meta-analysis of 40 studies covering 14,630 persons and found an average inter-rater reliability of only 0.52. Reliability over time was higher (0.81) if the same supervisor made both ratings, but not if different supervisors made successive ratings (0.50). Rothstein (1990) plotted inter-rater reliability against length of acquaintance and finds it eventually reaches 0.60, but only after 20 years. These studies imply the generally accepted estimate of 0.60 for supervisor rating reliability, often used in validity generalization analyses, is an overestimate. Rotundo and Sackett (2002) showed that different supervisors place different weight on task performance, counterproductive behaviour, and OC when making overall evaluations; these differing emphases may explain some disagreements between supervisors. As noted in Chapter 2, internal consistency reliability of supervisor rating is much higher, at 0.86. This is not necessarily a 'good' result since it tends to suggest supervisors are not successfully differentiating different aspects of performance.

Validity

Supervisor ratings are rarely criticized on grounds of their validity; for all their flaws, they have a satisfying finality about them. How do you know X is a better worker than Y? – because the supervisor says so. This is just as well because attempts to validate supervisor ratings tend to fall into circularity. One strategy is to compare supervisor ratings with 'true' ratings produced by an expert panel, but if one expert panel does not agree with another, which has given the 'true' ratings? Several lines of research suggest supervisor rating may not always be very accurate:

Comparison with objective criteria

Meta-analysis confirms that supervisor ratings and objective criteria correlate poorly (0.39), even correcting for error of measurement (Bommer *et al.*, 1995), which implies ratings and objective criteria measure different aspects of work performance.

Peer rating

Viswesvaran, Schmidt and Ones (2002) reported a meta-analysis of 31 studies comparing supervisor and peer rating of job performance. The correlation at first appears rather low, at 0.46, considering they are rating the same thing. However, Viswesvaran *et al.* noted that supervisor and peer ratings are both fairly unreliable; correcting for both sets of unreliability increases the correlation to a near perfect 0.98. Facteau and Craig (2001) used confirmatory factor analysis to show that supervisor, peer and subordinate ratings all assess the same set of 10 work performance variables. These researches suggest peer ratings could make as good a measure of work performance as supervisor ratings. An employee usually has more peers than supervisors, so peer rating would be more reliable and less idiosyncratic.

Leniency

Supervisor ratings tend to display leniency. Appraisal ratings used to decide outcomes such as promotion are more lenient ($d = 0.33$) than ratings made especially for use in selection research (Jawahar & Williams, 1997). Leniency is a big problem in validation research because it restricts range and reduces validity coefficients. Bartram (2007) showed that forced-choice format criterion may solve some of the problems of supervisor ratings. Table 12.2 gives four sample items. Supervisors first rate the target's performance for each separately, on a conventional five scale, then choose *most like* target and *least like* target. This limits leniency, and increases correlation between supervisor rating and selection test by 50%. This format needs a lengthy supervisor rating schedule: Bartram's contained 160 items. Forced choice was used in performance appraisal in the 1960s but proved unpopular (Murphy & Cleveland, 1995).

Bias

Supervisor ratings are also known to be affected by several types of bias, discussed in a later section.

Table 12.2 Examples of statements, used for supervisor rating, and forced choice (Bartram, 2007).

Allocates realistic time scales for activities	1	2	3	4	5
Successfully promotes own ideas	1	2	3	4	5
Produces memos which are easy to follow	1	2	3	4	5
Understands organizational strategy	1	2	3	4	5
Which statement is most true of target? Which is least true?					

(Bartram, 2007).

Objective criteria

The first reported validation study (Link, 1918) used an objective criterion – munitions output over a four-week period. Objective criteria divide into:

- output/production/sales;
- personnel criteria;
- training grades; and
- work samples and walk-throughs.

Output/production

In some jobs, there is a countable output: for example, units produced, breakages or spoiled work. However, output may not depend solely on how hard the worker works; a whole host of other factors may play a part: how well the machinery works, whether materials arrive in time, whether other workers do their bit, and so on. For these sorts of reasons, output criteria can have fairly low reliability. Production workers are often interdependent; each worker's output is regulated by the speed of the line, or socially by *output norms* (tacit agreements not to work too hard). The *key-stroke* criterion, or *electronic performance monitoring*, in word processing or supermarket check-outs, allows output to be measured, precisely, continuously and cheaply.

Sales

It is easier to sell a good product in an affluent area than a mediocre product in a deprived area. Researchers can address this issue by standardizing sales figures. Suppose average sales are £340 K in company A, and £430 K in company B. Sales figures in both companies into converted into z scores, using a mean of £340 K in company A, and a mean of £430 K in company B. A salesperson who sells £400 K in company A is doing well, but in company B is below average. This assumes that it is easier to sell more in company B, which may be true if the company has a better product or more prosperous customers. But suppose company B employs better sales people, which is why they sell more. In that case, standardizing the sales figures for a validity study would be very misleading. Stewart and Nandkeolyar (2006) identified another problem with sales figures. Apparently random fluctuations in sales figures turn out to be largely explained by variations in *referrals*: the more names of interested customers the salesperson gets, the more sales he/she makes.

Research

Output criteria have been used also for scientific work: for example, inventions patented or scientific papers published. The quality of scientific research can be estimated by the number of times the work is cited by other scientists. Scientists have been arguing for years whether publication and citation rates are good criteria of scientific output.

Work quality

Critics often complain that output criteria used in selection overlook quality. Three researches that did include quality criteria got worryingly poor results.

Hoffman, Nathan and Holden (1991) assessed quality in gas appliance repair work, using an inspector's error count done 'blind'; quality did not correlate at all with mental ability or job knowledge test scores, which do however predict the more usual output and supervisor rating criteria. DuBois *et al.* (1993) obtained similar results for supermarket checkout operators; mental ability tests are not related to accuracy, but do predict speed. Nathan and Alexander's (1988) meta-analysis of clerical work found tests do not correlate at all with quality. This important issue is surprisingly little researched. Bommer *et al.* (1995) found objective and subjective measures of quality agree even less well than objective and subjective measures of quantity.

Everyday vs. best performance

Work psychology distinguishes how well people can do if they really try and how well they do routinely. Objective criteria of work performance may overlook this distinction. Dubois *et al.* (1993) found that best performance in supermarket checkout operators correlates very poorly (0.11 to 0.32) with typical performance, and that ability tests correlate with best performance rather than typical. Supermarkets will usually be more interested in typical performance than best. Ployhart, Lim and Chan (2001) found similar results for leadership in Singapore army recruits. Their best performance, during a two-day assessment centre, is poorly related to their typical performance, during the three months of basic training, and shows a different pattern of correlation with personality.

Personnel criteria

These include: advancement/promotion, length of service, turnover, punctuality, absence, disciplinary action, accidents and sickness. They are easy to collect, but may be unreliable or have skewed distributions. Most personnel criteria also exhibit multiple causation: an accident is unlikely to reflect nothing but the carelessness of the person concerned; for instance, it will depend also on others' behaviour or the company safety culture. Some personnel criteria depend on subjective judgement, notably promotion/advancement. Training grades have been very widely used in American military selection research, where every one of many Military Occupational Specialists has a training course which soldiers must pass to become tank mechanics, dog handlers, military police, and so on. Training grades may involve some subjective judgement.

Work samples and walk-throughs

Until recently, validation research rarely used work samples as criterion; they are so expensive to develop that employers prefer to use them for selection. But a work sample used for selection cannot be used again as criterion; a high correlation would be trivial. Project A (Campbell *et al.*, 1990) devised a set of *hands-on work sample* criteria, designed to prove conclusively ASVAB's validity in the face of congressional criticism. Tank crews are observed and rated, in a real tank, repairing the radio, unjamming the gun and driving the tank from A to B. The work sample criteria can be used to validate less expensive (and dangerous) *walk-through* criteria, in which the soldier stands in a mock-up tank, and explains how to unjam the gun, or describes how the vehicle is driven. There is a subjective element in most work samples because they are generally rated by expert observers.

RESEARCH AGENDA

- More research on selecting for quality of work

New criteria

Organizational citizenship (OC)

Katz and Kahn (1966) noted years ago that 'an organisation which depends solely upon its blueprint of prescribed behaviour is a very fragile social system'. Many employers in Britain in the 1960s and 70s found how right Katz and Kahn were, when unions told their members to stick to the letter of their job description by 'working to rule'. The willingness to do more than one's prescribed tasks at work is called OC or contextual performance (as opposed to task performance). Coleman and Borman (2000) collected numerous example of citizenship and had them sorted by experts to identify three main themes:

- Personal support: helping others, motivating others, co-operating with others and showing consideration for others.
- Organizational support: representing the organization favourably, showing loyalty, complying with rules and procedures.
- Conscientious initiative: persisting with extra effort to complete tasks, taking the initiative and doing things to develop oneself.

Hoffman *et al.* (2007) showed that OC and task performance correlate, but are nevertheless distinctly separate concepts.

Counterproductive behaviour

There are lots of things employees do which employers wish they would not do. Gruys and Sackett (2003) listed no less than 66 separate examples of CPB, some listed in the third column of Table 12.3. Bennett and Robinson (2000) reported a survey which finds CPBs alarmingly frequent, from the employer's point of view; nearly 80% employees admit taking longer breaks than they should or not working when they should, while more serious behaviours such as theft or falsifying expenses are admitted by a quarter.

Table 12.3 Some examples of counterproductive behaviour, sorted into 11 classes, with number of CPBs in each class.

General category	N	Example(s)
Theft	10	Steal from customer
		Give away goods or services for free
Destruction of property	4	Deliberately sabotage production
Misuse information	5	Destroy or falsify records
		Lie to supervisor to cover up a mistake
Misuse time/resources	13	Work unnecessary overtime
		Use e-mail for personal purposes
Poor attendance	5	Leave early without permission
		Take sick leave when not really sick
Poor quality work	3	Intentionally do work badly or incorrectly
Alcohol use	3	Come to work with a hangover
Drug use	3	Sell drugs at work
Inappropriate verbal	8	Argue or quarrel with customers
Inappropriate physical	7	Unwanted sexual advances to customer
		Physical attack on co-worker
Unsafe behaviour	4	Endanger colleagues by not following safety procedures
		Not read safety manuals

How to obtain data on CPBs

There are three possible sources: self-report, others' report and records. All three present problems.

- *Self-reports.* Only Smith knows how often he/she is late, or aggressive or steals things, so Smith is the best source of data, but Smith may not choose to incriminate him/herself, even in an anonymous survey. One possible approach would be asking a large workforce to keep a daily diary of CPBs.
- *Others' reports.* Colleagues' or supervisors' opinions may project a generally favourable, or unfavourable, view of Smith into estimates of Smith's absenteeism, or aggressiveness. Supervisor ratings are notoriously poor at differentiating aspects of Smith's performance, and notoriously prone to halo. Some of Smith's shortcomings are very visible to supervisors and colleagues, but some are not; others may not know who steals, spreads rumours, or sabotages production.
- *Records* may be inaccessible, inaccurate or incomplete. The organization usually knows how much is stolen but often does not know who the thieves are (especially the clever ones).

The structure of CPB

There are at least four approaches to checking if various CPBs go together, meaning the person who, for example is often late, is also likely to steal, start fights or take drugs. The first three approaches use correlation and factor analysis of the three available sources of data – self-report, other report and records.

- Self-reports will have method variance problems. People who see themselves as honest will tend deny all faults, even the ones they actually have.
- Other reports may suffer from halo (or its opposite, the 'horns' effect), assuming that people who steal also cheat.
- Statistical analysis of recorded data will often be difficult because data are incomplete, or seriously skewed, or based on too small samples. Combining data from organizations, to get a large enough sample, will create its own problems. Opportunities for, e.g. theft, vary greatly; there is plenty to steal if you work in a department store, but not if you dig ditches for a living. Differences in local norms, and management's tolerance for CPB, will also make comparison across organizations very difficult.
- The fourth method, quite widely used, is *perceived likelihood of co-occurrence*. For example, Gruys and Sackett's student sample analysed the likely co-occurrence of their 11 categories: how likely is that someone who steals will also use drugs.

CPB typologies

Robinson and Bennett (1995) proposed a typology of deviant behaviours based on perceived similarity and likely co-occurrence. One dimension is *seriousness*, ranging from stealing and sabotage, through spreading rumours or 'going slow', to hiding in the back room reading a newspaper or gossiping about the manager. The other dimension is *organizational-interpersonal*. The two dimensions define four quadrants, shown in Figure 12.2. Gruys and Sackett's analysis, also based on co-occurrence, yielded two factors. The first – interpersonal–organizational – is similar to Robinson and Bennett's second dimension. The second is task relevance: things linked to work, such as absence, lateness, ignoring safety, opposed to things less linked to work, such as quarrelling with co-workers.

One dimension?

Ones and Viswesvaran (2003b) argued that CPB is a single dimension. They found six studies that correlate absenteeism with other CPBs: aggression, alcohol use, antagonistic work behaviour, destruction of property, drug misuse, misuse of information, misuse of time and resources, substance abuse, theft, and unsafe behaviour. They calculated a weighted correlation of 0.44, between absence and other CPBs, rising to 0.58 when corrected for the reliability of both measures. Table 12.4 lists three parallel analyses for other CPBs. Quite large positive correlations are found for all four, suggesting a single underlying theme. The correlation for theft is highest, leading Ones and

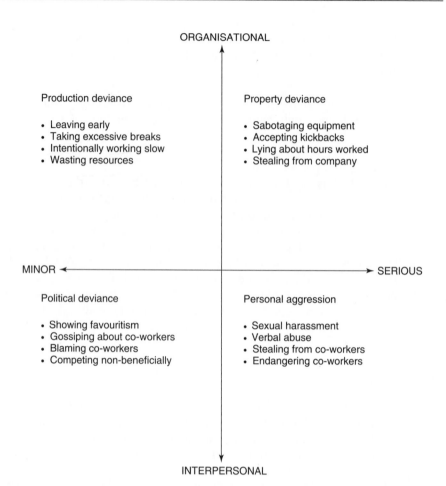

Figure 12.2   Two dimensions of workplace deviance (Robinson & Bennett, 1995).

Viswesvaran to suggest it may serve as a marker for CPBs, which would be convenient as honesty tests exist to detect theft, and according to Ones *et al.* (1993) work fairly well. Unfortunately, there are not enough researches to allow differentiation by data source, and most, but not all, seem to have used self-reports. Self-reports may overestimate consistency if they reflect self-concept rather than actual behaviour: *I am not the sort of person who steals things/picks fights/can't be trusted.*

It has been suggested that OC and CPB may actually be opposite ends of a single dimension. Dalal (2005) reported a meta-analysis of 49 correlations between OC and CPBs, which finds a low correlation of –0.27 (or –0.32 corrected for reliability of both measures). This suggests they are related but not interchangeable. However, most of the data appear to be self-reports, so shared method variance based on, e.g. self-concept may account for the correlation.

Table 12.4   Estimated correlation between four types of CPB, and all other types of CPB.

	k^a	r	ρ
Absenteeism/withdrawal	9	0.44	0.58
Antagonistic beh'r/aggression/violence	4	0.42	0.55
Substance abuse	4	0.30	0.44
Theft/property violations	5	0.44	0.62

Data from Ones & Viswesvaran (2003).
[a]Estimated – some sources are meta-analyses. ρ – correlation corrected for reliability of both measures.

RESEARCH AGENDA

• Extension of Ones and Viswesvaran's meta-analysis of CPB, differentiating data sources

---

Adaptability

Changes in work, such as new technology and globalization, require employees to be much more adaptable. Pulakos *et al.* (2002) proposed an eight-dimensional model of adaptability, and provide a measure of it, the Job Adaptability Inventory. Their dimensions include solving problems creatively, dealing with uncertainty, learning new technologies, interpersonal adaptability adaptability, cultural adaptability, handling stress and handling emergencies.

Structure of work performance

Multidimensional models of work performance

Critics argue global criteria are oversimplified and misleading because people succeed in many different ways. Therefore, validation studies need multiple criteria. Several general models of work performance have been proposed, which usually list up to a dozen separate aspects that could be used as criteria. These include Viswesvaran's 10 dimensions, and Project A's five-dimensional criterion space.

Five dimensions – Project A

The revalidation of selection tests (Campbell *et al.*, 1990) for the American armed services, adopted a five-dimensional 'criterion space':

• technical proficiency
• general soldiering proficiency

Table 12.5 Viswesvaran et al.'s (2005) 10 dimensions of effective work performance, with examples for an academic psychologist.

Dimension	(Academic) example	%
Productivity	Publications, research grants	37
Effort	Working longer than 9–5	30
Job knowledge	Understanding latest version of SPSS	29
Interpersonal competence	Getting on well with colleagues and students	44
Administrative competence	Completing student records accurately and promptly	28
Quality	Marking student essays carefully	32
Communication competence	Giving clear lectures, writing papers that are clear	20
Leadership	Motivating research staff to find more participants	17
Compliance with rules	Only parking in permitted places	34
Overall job performance		76

% column indicates frequency of use in Payne *et al.*'s (2008) survey of supervisor ratings.

- effort and leadership
- personal discipline
- fitness and military bearing.

The five dimensions were derived from over 20 work performance measures, including rating scales, using BARS format, and personnel records, as well as measures more usually used as predictors: work samples, role plays, job knowledge tests, and situational judgement tests. Project A's attempts to assess combat effectiveness of troops who had not yet seen combat faced the problem that the soldiers doing the rating had never been in combat either. But as they note, combat effectiveness is rather central to the soldier's role! (Knapp *et al.*, 2001).

Ten dimensions

Viswesvaran, Schmidt and Ones (2002) listed no less than 486 different job performance measures. Fortunately, they were able to go on to show that all this confusing variety could be reduced to ten basic categories, when sorted by experts (Table 12.5). Payne *et al.* (2008) analysed 282 researches, allocating supervisor ratings to Viswesvaran *et al.*'s headings. Their analysis found the most frequently rated specific aspect of work performance is interpersonal competence. Payne *et al.* found CPB rarely included (10%) in supervisor rating schedules.

Hierarchical models

Some models are hierarchical, suggesting different aspects of work performance may correlate to some extent, while remaining conceptually and

Figure 12.3 Possible hierarchical structure of work performance, suggested by Crites (1969).

empirically distinct. Many years earlier, Crites (1969) had suggested that success may have a hierarchical structure, like intellectual ability (Figure 12.3). At the highest level is the general factor – overall vocational success. At the intermediate level are group factors: administrative skills and drive and initiative. At the level of specific factors are individual ratings such as company loyalty, and single objective criteria, such as scrap.

The monolithic hypothesis

Viswesvaran (Viswesvaran and Ones, 2005) argued that work performance is a unitary concept, and criticized the 'Pollyanna-ish view of success' that 'every employee could be in the top 10% albeit in different dimensions of performance (evaluated by different sources)'. If work performance is 'monolithic', the criterion problem resolves itself, and HR's task becomes much easier: there really is such a class of person as the good employee. All HR need now is the perfect selection test – fast, cheap and infallible – to identify him/her. Viswesvaran's argument rested on complex statistical analyses of two sets of data: supervisor and peer ratings of work performance, and his 1993 survey of a century's work performance research. The supervisor and peer rating data analysis is described in detail in Viswesvaran, Schmidt and Ones (2005), but the larger dataset seems described in detail only in his unpublished PhD thesis.

Rating data

There is no doubt that supervisor ratings of work performance contain a very large general factor. But is this true consistency of worker performance, or halo in the supervisor's judgement? Is there any way of telling the two apart? Halo means different ratings intercorrelate strongly even though the scales are not logically related; the person who is rated polite is likely also to be rated well-adjusted, able, highly motivated, and so on. This is a pervasive feature of all ratings made by human observers, and was first noted as long ago as 1907. Some researchers try to distinguish between *illusory halo* where the rater treats dimensions as correlated when they are not, and *true halo* where the rater is correct because the dimensions being rated really are correlated. It is very difficult to establish whether dimensions 'really' are correlated or not, when they can only be assessed by ratings which exhibit halo. Viswesvaran *et al.* (2005) however proposed an analysis based on comparing supervisor and peer ratings. Ratings made the same person exhibit halo, but ratings of different things by different people – they argue – do not. Therefore, if supervisor ratings of, for example, *initiative*, correlate with peer ratings of, for example, *helpfulness*, this is not halo but a true correlation. They use this analysis to conclude there a large 'real' factor running through supervisor ratings of work performance. Schneider, Hough and Dunnette (1996) were not convinced and argued assumptions about dimensions being correlated could be shared by different raters (i.e. raters could all share same halo).

The larger dataset

Viswesvaran (1993, described by Viswesvaran & Ones, 2005) assembled 2,600 correlations between work performance measures, apparently of all types, rating, objective and 'personnel'. These data will tend to be very confused and hard to analyse. Different researches include different subsets of work performance measures. Viswesvaran used a combination of structural equation modelling and meta-analysis that can apparently bring all these separate studies together. It can combine studies of, for example, absence and theft, with separate studies of absence and drug use as if research had studied all three together in the same sample (when it had not in fact done so). Viswesvaran and Ones (2005) said that the analysis 'concluded that a general factor exists across all measures of job performance used ... over the past 100 years'. Schneider, Hough and Dunnette (1996) again expressed doubt and noted that a lot of the correlations are less than 0.25, even after correction, which they argued is more consistent with a multidimensional model. Viswesvaran (2002) has published a meta-analysis of absenteeism against four other outcomes (Table 12.6). People who are absent a lot produce less, of poorer quality and are rated as making less effort, and being harder to get on with. It could be argued that some relationships in Table 12.6 have direction

Table 12.6   Meta-analysis of absence and four other work performance measures.

Recorded absence X	k	N	r	ρ
Organizational records of productivity	7	$1.8K$	−0.17	−0.21
Organizational records of quality	12	$1.3K$	−0.37	−0.48
Supervisor rating of effort	10	$1.6K$	−0.35	−0.54
Supervisor rating of interpersonal behaviour	15	$2.8K$	−0.20	−0.33

Data from Viswesvaran (2002).
ρ = Corrected for the reliability of both measures, but not range restriction.

of cause problems. Supervisors know who is absent a lot, and it would be odd if they gave them a high rating for effort.

RESEARCH AGENDA

It is difficult to see where research should go next. The halo problem in supervisor ratings is insoluble, if Schneider *et al.*'s argument about shared halo is accepted. Collecting a sufficient quantity of 'objective' data would require very careful data collection, over a very long period, in a very large workforce. It is a sufficiently important question to make such a project worth trying.

Bias

A survey of managers by Longenecker, Sims and Goia (1987) confirmed what many employees have probably always suspected: managers allow bias to affect their ratings. In fact, many in Longenecker's survey were quite blatant about using performance appraisals to send people messages, to work harder, to show more respect, or to get a job somewhere else. Supervisor bias can also affect apparently objective criteria, if supervisors 'overlook' absence, or petty delinquency, or substandard output, in favoured workers, but officially record it for employees they don't like.

Ethnicity bias is a major concern. If some white supervisors are biased against non-white employees, the whole validation paradigm can be undermined. However, simply finding a difference in supervisor rating of, for example, white and African Americans, does not in itself prove bias because supervisors could be reporting real differences in performance.

One line of research uses a within groups design, where black and white supervisors rate the same set of black and white workers. Sackett and Dubois (1991) were able to find some suitable data in the Project A and GATB databases, and reported that both black and white supervisors rate white workers higher, suggesting a true difference in performance, not bias. However, Stauffer and Buckley (2005) re-analysed the data and disagree. They said that while it is true that both white and black supervisors rate white workers higher, there is an interaction between race of supervisor and race of worker. Figure 12.4 shows white supervisors see a much bigger difference between black and white workers than do black supervisors. This interaction suggests white supervisors 'mark down' black workers (or possibly that black supervisors ignore the poorer performance of black workers). Either way some supervisors' ratings appear to be biased by ethnicity.

Another approach compares rating of work performance, with objective measures that are – in theory – unbiased. Four successive meta-analyses of white and Afro-American differences in work performance have distinguished subjective measures, generally supervisor ratings, and a variety of objective measures (Ford, Kraiger & Schechtman, 1986; Chung-Yan & Cronshaw, 2002; Roth, Huffcutt & Bobko, 2003; McKay & McDaniel, 2006). Note however that

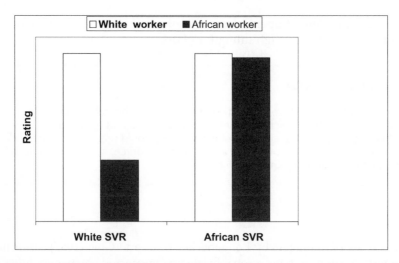

Figure 12.4   Average ratings by white and African-American supervisors, of white and African-American workers. Data from Stauffer & Buckley (2005).

Table 12.7   Four meta-analyses of differences in white and African Americans' work performance, assessed objectively and subjectively.

Assessment ⇒	Objective		Subjective	
	k	d	k	d
Ford *et al.*	53	0.21	53	0.20
Chung-Yan & Cronshaw	30	0.12	57	0.30
Roth *et al.* (quality of work)	8	0.24	10	0.20
(quantity of work)	3	0.32	5	0.09
(absence)	8	0.23	4	0.13
McKay & McDaniel	62	0.22	510	0.28

some data counted as 'objective' are based on someone's opinion, for example, who gets promoted. Table 12.7 summarizes all four analyses, which reach conflicting conclusions:

- Ford *et al.* found no difference between objective and subjective
- McKay and McDaniel found a small difference, in the direction of subjective measures showing a larger difference.
- Roth *et al.* found subjective measures show a smaller difference
- Chung-Yan and Cronshaw found subjective measures show a larger difference.

Only Chung-Yan and Cronshaw's analysis can be seen as definite evidence of possible bias. The largest and most recent analysis, by McKay and

McDaniel, found little difference between subjective and objective measures, indicating an absence of bias in supervisor ratings. However, Roth *et al.* noted the possibility that raters these days may feel pressure not to generate ethnicity differences in performance ratings. It is very easy to compute means for white and non-white employees, and a large difference might cause comment, or reflect on raters' fairness or competence as a supervisor. McDaniel, McKay and Rothstein (2006b) applied 'trim-and-fill' analysis for reporting bias to this area, and found evidence of a shortage of large differences in published research but not in unpublished, suggesting perhaps that some researchers are reluctant to publish data on ethnicity differences work performance. An earlier meta-analysis (Kraiger & Ford, 1985) of 74 studies found a small, but consistent, *own race bias*, accounting for 5% of variance in ratings. There are no published European data on these issues.

Age and gender bias

Waldman and Avolio (1986) reported a meta-analysis of links between age and work performance showing that productivity objectively measured increases with age, whereas supervisory ratings tend to decrease with age, which implies possible bias in the ratings. Bowen, Swim and Jacobs (2000) reported a meta-analysis of performance appraisal, which found no evidence of gender bias.

Worker satisfactoriness

Critics have suggested supervisor ratings really measure worker satisfactoriness not job performance. Worker satisfactoriness includes behaviours that please management, as well as, or even instead of, good job performance.

- *Ingratiation.* Measure of Ingratiatory Behaviors in Organisational Settings (MIBOS) identifies many ways to please management (besides doing good work): for example, tell them about your successes, compliment them on their successes, listen sympathetically to their problems or run errands for them (Kumar & Beyerlein, 1991).
- *Organizational fads and chairman's whims.* In the 1890s, the Royal Navy valued 'spit and polish' so highly that some ship's captains were said to try to avoid gunnery practice in case the powder smoke spoiled their paintwork.
- *Pseudo-targets.* Higher management or politicians create a set of indicators against which performance will be assessed. For example, hospital managers are judged by length of waiting list for surgery, which can have unintended consequences, as when patients needing only minor, but quick, operations are given priority over patients with more serious illness, just to get the waiting list shortened.
- *First World War mentality.* Organizations occasionally exist in which subordinates gain credit for pushing ahead with management plans that are absurdly wrong, in pursuit of aims which are completely pointless, stifling

criticism of either purpose or method with cries of 'commitment' and 'loyalty'.

Good reputation or good performance?

In many organizations, supervisors rate reputation; a good reputation can be earned by good work but many features of large organizations make it easy to earn one in other ways (Cook, 1995). Many supervisors rarely see the people they are rating, so have to rely on reputation.

- *Social reality.* A company that manufactures gearboxes has its success defined externally and unambiguously, by its sales figures. A university, by contrast, constructs its own social reality. A consensus of academics decides what issues are worth researching and teaching, and by implication whose work has merit. Where success is defined by the organization and its staff, greater scope exists for creating undeserved reputations.
- *Attributability problem.* Complex organizations and long time scales mean it is often hard to assign true responsibility for successes or failures, which opens the door for fast operators to steal the credit for successes, avoid the blame for failures and build an undeserved reputation.
- *Empire-building.* In many organizations, success is defined in terms of increasing the size of one's department or budget. Services are provided for the sake of justifying the organization's expansion.
- *Reorganizations* create a perfect form of pseudo-work, divorced from external standards. The efforts of dozens, even hundreds, of workers are centred for months on something that has no end product and often serves no useful purpose, but is an ideal environment for the person who seeks to build a reputation. Reorganizations also blur responsibility for successes and failures,
- *Cover your back.* In cautious organizations, a good reputation is built largely by not doing things: for example, not making controversial decisions, not attracting complaints or not getting bad publicity.
- *It's who you know, not what you know.* A widely voiced observation, which implies one's time may be better spent creating a network of allies and contacts than doing any actual work.
- *The non-working day.* Only part of an academic's day is spent doing core job-description activities – teaching students, and conducting research. The rest of the day gets filled up by chattering, drinking coffee, tidying up, meetings, pointless paperwork, and so on. The more of the working day is filled by non-work or semi-work, the more time there is to set about making oneself well thought of, without doing any good teaching or useful research.

RESEARCH AGENDA

- European research on ethnicity and gender bias in supervisor rating
- More research on subtler biases in supervisor ratings

Dynamic criteria

Does work performance change over time? This could have important implications for selection, and validation. Suppose people take 12 months to settle into a new job. Collecting work performance data after three months might give very misleading results. Sturman, Cheramie and Cashen (2005) presented a meta-analysis of 22 studies measuring work performance over time, on at least three occasions. They concluded work performance is very stable over time, although the longer the time interval the lower the correlation. Over a six-month interval, work performance is very stable (r around 0.90). Over a longer time span, of three years, the correlation falls to 0.50. Consistency is less for objective measures like sales, than for ratings, and less for complex jobs (managers, academics, salesperson, securities brokers) than for simpler jobs (machine workers sewing machine operators, welders and bank clerks).

Qualitative shifts in work performance would create more of a problem for selection. Murphy (1989) argued for *transition* and *maintenance* stages in work performance. In transition, the worker is still learning the job, whereas in maintenance the job is very well learned and largely automatic. Ability tests will therefore predict performance during transition, i.e. in the short term, but not in the long term. Critics argue that 'real' jobs, as opposed to simple laboratory tasks, are always sufficiently complex to ensure that automatization does not happen. Farrell and McDaniel (2001) reported an analysis of the GATB database, examining the relationship between general intelligence and job performance over time spans of up to ten years, and distinguishing between simple jobs that might become automatic and complex jobs that will not. The correlation for general intelligence generally remains positive, for both types of job, over the 10-year time span. It would be very valuable to replicate this study as a true follow-up; the GATB data are cross sectional.

RESEARCH AGENDA

- A true follow-up of validity over a long time span
- More research on qualitative shifts in work performance such as 'honeymoon' periods

---

Criteria, fairness and the law

Criterion ratings face some legal problems. They may be accused of bias, which usually means racial bias. Research reviewed earlier in this chapter suggests that may be a problem. US fair employment agencies may also find fault with ratings that are unreliable, subjective, or too general. In the important *Albemarle* case (Chapter 13), criterion ratings were ruled unsatisfactory because they were vague, and their basis unclear. In *Rowe v General Motors* supervisor ratings were again ruled unsatisfactory, because supervisors had no written instructions about the requirements for promotion, and because standards were vague and subjective. In the case of *Wade v Mississippi Co-operative Extension Service*, the court ruled that supervisor ratings of attitude, personality, temperament, and habits had to be job-related:

> *a substantial portion of the evaluation rating relates to such general character-istics as leadership, public acceptance, attitudes toward people, appearance and grooming, personal contact, outlook on life, ethical habits, resourcefulness, capacity for growth, mental alertness and loyalty to organisation. As may be readily observed, these are traits which are susceptible to partiality and to the personal taste, whim or fancy of the evaluator.*

Nor are objective criteria free from challenge. An employer cannot simply say 'high turnover' and leave it at that. It may be necessary to prove that high turnover creates problems, costs money, or results from employees' restlessness and not from the employer's behaviour.

Predictor or criterion?

Project A uses as criteria measures normally used as predictors: work samples, role plays, job knowledge tests, and situational judgement tests. This has been done before to some extent. The gist of Klimoski's criticism of assessment centre validity was that assessment centres use the opinion of one set of managers (rating AC performance) to predict the opinion of another set of managers at a later point (rating performance on the job). The same could be said of interviews, especially traditional unstructured interviews. This raises some interesting questions about the whole selection exercise. Which assessments could not be used a criterion? Personality inventories, or other generalized assessment of personality, tests of mental ability, biographical measures. Anything that assesses the individual, as a person. Anything that relies on past behaviour or achievement.

Any measures of a particular skill or competence could logically be used as criterion as well as predictor. This implies some types of selection might become conceptually little more than exercises in retest reliability. If the recruit can show good situational judgement before joining the army, he/she will presumably show as much after a year in the army. Or else the second assessment of e.g. counselling a subordinate will reflect how effective the organization's training has been. Very specific assessments that predict very specific outcomes are useful to the employer, but have limitations. Such predictor criterion relationships will lack much if any general interest, or relevance in understanding success in various sorts of work. They might also have limited shelf-life for the employer, if the job changes and different skills are required.

Key points

In Chapter 12 you have learned the following.

- Whatever criterion or measure of work performance is used w̠ imperfect.
- The most frequently used criterion is the supervisor rating, which is convenient, and inclusive, but frequently also biased.
- Objective criteria such as output, absence or sales, are complex, being shaped by many forces; they are also often unreliable.
- Increasing attention is being paid to other aspects of workplace behaviour, such as organizational citizenship, and counterproductive behaviour.
- Work performance changes over times, but remains constant enough to make selection a viable enterprise.

Key references

Cook (1995) discusses ways on which the supervisor rating criterion can be biased, or affected by irrelevant considerations.

Gruys and Sackett (2003) investigate the dimensionality of counterproductive work behaviours.

Hoffman *et al.* (1991) report research on quality as criterion in gas repair work.

McKay and McDaniel (2006) report the most recent analysis of ethnicity differences in work performance.

Murphy and Cleveland (1995) review research on performance appraisal.

Ployhart *et al.* (2001) compare typical and best performance indices.

Stauffer and Buckley (2005) detect possible ethnicity bias in supervisor ratings.

Sturman *et al.* (2005) analyse consistency of work performance over time. (Especially suitable for readers interested in statistics).

Viswesvaran *et al.* (1996) present a meta analysis of supervisor rating reliability.

Viswesvaran and Ones (2005) provide the most accessible account of the monolithic work performance hypothesis.

Minorities, fairness and the law

Getting the numbers right

Introduction

The House of Commons of the British Parliament numbers 650 Members of Parliament. Following the 2005 election, there is a 'record number' of female MPs – 128, as well as 15 ethnic minority MPs.

Once upon a time, employers could 'hire at will, and fire at will'. They could employ only fair-haired men, or red-haired women, or Baptists, or sycophants, or Freemasons, or football players. They could sack men who wore brown suits, or women who wore trousers. They might be forced out of business by more efficient competitors, who chose their staff more carefully and treated them better, but they were in no danger from the law. Employers could also indulge any racial stereotypes they happened to have: for example, do not employ Fantasians because they are all dimwits, or do not employ Ruritanians because they are unreliable. Those bad old days are long past.

Fair employment legislation has shaped selection practices in the USA for over 40 years. In 1964, the Civil Rights Act (CRA) prohibited discrimination in employment on grounds of race, colour, religion, or national origin (Table 13.1). CRA also prohibited discrimination on grounds of gender. Apparently the US government did not originally intend to include women as a *protected minority*, but the scope of CRA was broadened by hostile Senators who thought it would reduce the bill to an absurdity, and lead to its defeat. CRA was joined in 1967 by the Age Discrimination in Employment Act, and in 1990 by the Americans with Disabilities Act. US government agencies were created to enforce the new laws, including Equal Employment Opportunities Commission (EEOC) and the Office of Federal Contract Compliance Program. (Contract compliance means requiring organizations that supply the government to comply fully with fair employment laws.) In 1970 and 1978, EEOC issued *Uniform Guidelines on Employment Selection Procedures*, which go into considerable technical detail.

British law

In Britain, the Race Relations Act (1976) set up the Commission for Racial Equality, which issued its *Code of Practice* in 1984. The Sex Discrimination Act (1975) set up the Equal Opportunities Commission, which issued its Code of

Table 13.1   Key events in the development of 'fair employment' legislation in Britain and the USA.

Year	USA	UK
1964	Civil Rights Act	
1967	Age Discrimination Act	
1970	First Guidelines published	
1971	Griggs v Duke Power	
1975	Albemarle Paper Co. v Moody	
1976		
1975		Sex Discrimination Act
		Race Relations Act
1976		
1978	Uniform Guidelines published	
1984		CRE Code published
1985		EOC Code published
1988	Watson v Ft Worth Bank	
1989	Wards Cove Packing Co. v Antonio	
1990	Americans with Disabilities Act	London Underground case
		Paddington guards case
1991	Civil Rights Act	
1995		Disability Discrimination Act
1999		Disability Rights Commission
2003		Employment Equality (Sexual Orientation) Regulations
		Employment Equality (Religion and Belief) Regulations
2006		Employment Equality (Age) Regulations
2007		Commission for Equality and Human Rights

Practice in 1985. Both British codes of conduct are short documents compared with the American Uniform Guidelines, and do not give any very detailed instructions about selection. In 1995, the Disability Discrimination Act extended protection to disabled people. Discrimination on grounds of religion, belief and sexual orientation became illegal in the UK in 2003, and on grounds of age from October 2006. All UK equal opportunities agencies have recently merged into the Commission for Equality and Human Rights. In June 2008, the government announced an Equality Bill, which – if passed – will allow employers to give preference to under-represented groups, where applicants (As) are equally well-qualified.

Overview

Figure 13.1 shows how fair employment laws work in the USA. The American model has also been followed to some extent in many other countries. If selection excludes more minorities than whites, or more women then men, it creates *adverse impact* (AI). The employer can remove AI by *quota hiring* to 'get

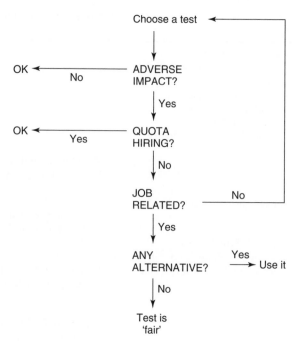

Figure 13.1   Stages in deciding whether a selection test is legally fair.

the numbers right'. Or else the employer can try to demonstrate the selection test is *job-related* (i.e. valid). The employer who succeeds in proving the selection test job-related faces one last hurdle – proving there is *no alternative* test that is equally valid but does not create AI.

Adverse impact

In Britain, 8% of the population are ethnic minority; and half are female. If Members of Parliament were selected without regard to gender or ethnicity, Table 13.2 shows there would be 325 women MPs, and 52 minority MPs.

Adverse impact is not quite what the layperson thinks of as discrimination. AI does not mean turning away minorities in order to keep the job open for white males, or otherwise deliberately treating minorities differently. Deliberate discrimination, in the USA, is called *disparate treatment*, and can be proved by the *McDonnell Douglas test*, which means essentially telling a suitably qualified minority person 'sorry – the job's gone' then offering it to a majority person. Adverse impact means the organization's recruitment and selection methods result in fewer women or ethnic minority persons being employed. The lack of women and minorities may not be intentional. Generally accepted ways of selecting staff may create unforeseen AI. For example, the case of

Table 13.2 Actual composition of the British House of Commons following the 2005 election, and expected composition, based on the assumption that MPs are selected regardless of gender and ethnicity.

	Actual	Expected	Expected (four-fifths rule)
Male	518	325	
Female	128	325	260
White	641		
Minority	15	52	42

Green v Missouri Pacific Railroad showed that excluding As with criminal records created AI because minorities were more likely to have criminal records. Indirect discrimination can occur in quite unforeseen ways. Arvey *et al.* (1975) compared employers who took a long time to fill vacancies (average of 76 days from closing date to interview) with ones who worked fast (14 days), and found the long wait halved the number of minority As who appeared for interview. The long wait creates AI and is not job-related, so it is probably illegal discrimination. All that is needed to prove AI is a statistical analysis of gender and ethnicity in the workforce, which makes it a very powerful tool in the hands of those seeking to prove discrimination.

Computing adverse impact

Are there fewer women or minority persons in the House of Commons than one would expect? Psychologists immediately think of calculating the Chi-squared statistic, but the problem with Chi-squared statistic is that it is almost impossible not to find a significant discrepancy when analysing large numbers. No employer is likely to have a perfect balance of ethnicity and gender throughout a large workforce. In the USA, the Uniform Guidelines introduced the four-fifths rule. If the selection ratio (selected / applied) for a protected minority is less than four-fifths of the highest ratio for any group, a 'presumption of discrimination' is established. Roth, Bobko and Switzer (2006) noted that the four-fifths rule can give misleading results in small samples. For example, suppose the selection ratio is really the same, at 0.50, for both men and women, and that groups of 50 men and 50 women are assessed each week. Chance variations in such small groups will result in one in seven weeks' intakes appearing to break the four-fifths rule.

> The proportion of women in the Commons is obviously far less than four-fifths the number of men; the number of minorities is significantly fewer than four-fifths of 8% of 650. Therefore 'recruitment and selection' for the Commons creates adverse impact on both women and on minorities.

If there is no AI, the employer has no problem, but if AI is demonstrated, the burden of proof shifts to the employer to prove good business reasons, which essentially means proving the selection procedure is valid. Good business reasons do not include saying customers will not like female / minority staff, so the shortage of minority and female MPs could not be justified by claiming people would not vote for them. Employers whose 'numbers are not right' are presumed guilty of discrimination until they succeed in proving their innocence. This can be difficult and expensive, so most employers prefer to avoid creating AI in the first place.

Adverse impact in Britain

Extensive data on AI in graduate recruitment in Britain were reported by Scott (1997). Table 13.3 shows overall, minority As are less successful, showing AI. However, the minorities vary considerably, with (South Asian) Indian As being as successful as white As, and Chinese As considerably more successful than the white majority. Black As experience AI at the pre-selection stage, being less likely to get a first interview. The three Indian sub-continent groups differ considerably; parallel differences are found in average education and income levels for the three groups.

Adverse impact league tables

There is a trend, especially in the USA, to try to draw up league tables of AI, using the d statistic (e.g. Ployhart & Holtz, 2008). These tables are intended to guide selectors in their choice of selection test. However, such analyses present considerable methodological problems, some obvious, others more subtle. Obvious problems include small and unrepresentative samples. It is clearly unwise to base statements about gender or ethnicity differences on any but very large and definitely representative, samples. Another problem is the multiplicity of minorities. Even excluding the 'other' categories, the UK Census distinguishes six ethnic minority groups (see Table 13.3). Getting enough data to construct meaningful d statistic tables for six white–minority comparisons will be an enormous task. (And even six categories may not be enough, given the increasing diversity of the British population. The expansion of the European Community has added an estimated 1/2 million Polish people to the UK workforce since 2004.)

Roth et al. (2001a) identified a subtler problem. Adverse impact tables are often based on present employee (PE) samples, which may be seriously misleading. To take a trivial example, showing that male and female firefighters do not differ in strength does not mean the fire brigade can be sure its physical strength test will not create AI in its next wave of As. If the PE firefighters were selected by the strength test, then all the females will necessarily be strong enough (and the question to ask is what proportion of male and female As failed the strength test). However, the problem can be subtler than this. Suppose the PEs were selected not by the strength test but by something that looks different but is nevertheless related to strength, possibly a biodata with a lot of questions about exercise, sport and fitness. The PE firefighters will not

Table 13.3   White and minority British applicants for graduate recruitment schemes (Scott, 1997).

	N	% selected for first interview	% selected for employment
White	49,370	23	3.4
Black African	648	13	1.7
Black Caribbean	162	19	1.9
Black other	88	18	2.3
All black	1,001	13	1.6
Bangladeshi	142	21	1.4
Indian	1,706	28	3.2
Pakistani	530	20	2.1
All South Asian	2,378	26	2.8
Chinese	457	26	5.4
All minorities	6,462	18	1.9

Note: The total ethnic minority figures are higher than the total for the separate groups because some employers did not differentiate between minorities.

have the same distribution of strength scores as the As, so AI estimates based on them do not tell the fire brigade what will happen when the test is used with the next wave of As. This problem of indirect selection is particularly great for mental ability (MA) tests, which have been shown to correlate positively with many other selection measures including AC ratings, interviews and work samples (Schmidt & Hunter, 1998). Another version of the same problem can arise in sequential selection systems. Suppose the employer first sifts by minimum qualification, then selects by test. An AI estimate based on the As who do the test may be misleading, if sifting for minimum qualifications has screened out many minority persons with lower levels of MA.

Combinations or composites of selection tests

Recently, American researchers have been trying to solve the AI problem by using combinations of tests. Can a combination be found that will achieve good validity but not create too much AI? Researchers have tried composites of ability and personality tests, with not very promising results. For example, Potosky, Bobko and Roth (2005) tried combining MA with a conscientiousness PQ, or structured interview, or biodata, and found no reduction at all in AI.

Actually, there is no need for empirical research to demonstrate this. It follows logically that if two groups differ a lot in scores on a test used for selecting employees, then fewer of the lower-scoring group will be selected. The effect can be diluted by using other measures that do not generate a score difference, but cannot be eliminated. The only way of eliminating AI based on MA would be to find another measure that produced an equally large difference but in the opposite direction, so the two differences cancelled each other out. This might still create problems: HR now have two differences to worry about.

Terpstra *et al.* (1999) reported a survey of 158 US Federal court cases between 1978 and 1997, which found that the most frequently challenged methods were unstructured interviews, MA tests and physical tests. By contrast, biodata, personality and honesty tests, work samples, and assessment centres were rarely the subject of court cases. A second survey (Terpstra & Kethley 2002) finds the public sector over-represented in fair employment cases, especially local (city) government, police, firefighters and teachers. Executive, managerial and administrative jobs were also over-represented, while wholesale, retail, clerical, production, craft and repair jobs were under-represented. Concern over fair employment seems focused more on better-paid and more secure jobs.

British MPs are not employees, so are not covered by fair employment laws.

Quota hiring

Employers who cannot prove good business reasons, or do not want to go through the trouble and expense of trying, must 'get their numbers right', which tends to mean quota hiring. Quotas can be hard or soft. A hard quota requires every other new employee to be from a minority, whereas a soft quota tells the HR department in effect to 'try to find more minorities'. London's Borough of Lambeth, noted for its very progressive policies, announced in 1986 a soft quota for disabled black women in its road-mending teams.

Formal quotas

Some formal quota systems for MA test scores were discussed in Chapter 6. In *top-down quota*, the employer selects the best minority As even though they do not score as high as the best white As. In *separate norming*, minority As' raw scores are converted to percentiles using a separate minority mean. In the 1980s, the EEOC favoured separate norms, but in 1986 the VG-GATB system's separate norms (*see* Chapter 6) were challenged as discriminatory and the system was shelved (Hartigan & Wigdor, 1989). The CRA of 1991 prohibited separate norms. In 1996, California voted for Proposition 209 that prohibited using group membership as a basis for selection decisions in education or public sector employment; this does not seem to have had much effect on selection. Separate norms are not viewed with favour in Britain either. Presently, *score banding* (Chapter 6) argues that people who do not differ reliably, in terms of error of measurement, should be treated as equal.

Affirmative action (AA)

Affirmative action is defined as 'the voluntary adoption of special programs to benefit members of minority groups'. Kravitz (2008) described many things employers can do to attract minority As, to make sure they do themselves justice in the selection (and to ensure they stay once employed). For example, internship (work experience) programmes with local schools show minority pupils possible careers and prepare them for selection assessments.

Diversity

Diversity means adopting a policy of employing people from many different backgrounds, who vary in gender, ethnic background, (dis)ability, and so on. Many advantages are claimed, including making recruitment easier, reducing staff costs, reducing absence and turnover, improving flexibility and creativity, improving customer service, creating a better public image, increasing sales to minority customers, and so on. Critics note that conclusive proof of all this tends to be lacking, and note that diversity can cause negative outcomes too. Sacco and Schmitt (2005) studied one aspect of diversity in a US fastfood chain, across a quarter of a million workers in over 3,000 branches, and found the 'diverse' employee, the one who was not like his/her co-workers in age, gender or ethnicity, tended to leave sooner. Liao, Joshi and Chuang (2004) found that the 'diverse' employee, in the shape of the one man or woman in an otherwise all-female or all-male workplace, tends to experience a lot of 'interpersonal deviance' (e.g. name calling or practical jokes).

RESEARCH AGENDA

- Consequences of a more diverse workforce, in terms of output, morale, and so on
- Consequences of a more diverse workforce, in terms of outcomes for individual employees.

Job-relatedness

If the test creates AI and the employer wants to continue using it, the employer must prove that the test is job-related, or valid. This is an area where work psychologists ought to be able to make a really useful contribution. However, early court cases showed that lawyers and psychologists had different ideas about demonstrating test validity. Two events made the 1970s a very bad decade for selection in general, and psychological tests in particular: the 1971 Supreme Court ruling on *Griggs v Duke Power Co.* and EEOC's 1970 Guidelines on Employee Selection Procedures.

Griggs v Duke Power Company

Before the CRA, the Duke Power Company in North Carolina did not employ Afro-Americans, except as labourers. When CRA came into effect, the company changed its rules: non-labouring jobs needed a high-school diploma or national high-school graduate average scores on the Wonderlic Personnel and Bennett Mechanical Comprehension Tests, which 58% white employees achieved, but only 6% of Afro-Americans. The Supreme Court ruled that the company's new tests discriminated – not necessarily intentionally. The Court's ruling attributed Afro-Americans' lower scores on Wonderlic and Bennett tests to inferior education in segregated schools. The Court said that 'The touchstone is business necessity. If an employment practice which operates to exclude negroes cannot be shown to be related to job performance, the practice is prohibited'. The ruling argued that high-school education and high test scores were not necessary because existing white employees with neither continued to perform quite satisfactorily. It is difficult to overemphasize the importance of the *Griggs* case:

- *Griggs* established the principle of AI. An employer could be proved guilty of discriminating by setting standards that made no reference to gender or ethnicity, and that were often well-established, 'common-sense' practice.
- *Griggs* objected to assessing people in the abstract, and insisted that all assessment be job-related. This implicitly extended the scope of the act; employers cannot demand that employees be literate, or honest, or ex-army, or good-looking, just because that is the sort of person they want working for them.
- Business necessity means job-relatedness, which means validity. Duke Power had introduced new selection methods but done nothing to prove they were valid.

The *Griggs* case illustrates another important point about law and selection. Although the CRA was passed in 1964, it was not until 1971 that its full implications became apparent. How a particular law will affect selection cannot be determined simply from reading what it says. What is crucial – and takes a long time to emerge – is how the courts will interpret the law.

EEOC's Guidelines

The American Psychological Association (APA) had previously published its *Standards for Educational and Psychological Tests*, which described ways of proving that selection procedures were valid. When EEOC drew up the Guidelines, APA persuaded them to recognize its Standards. It seemed a good idea at the time, but went badly wrong. The APA's *ideal* standards for validation became EEOC's *minimum acceptable standards*, which made proving selection methods valid very difficult.

Albemarle Paper Co. v Moody

Four years after *Griggs*, another court examined a 'hastily assembled validation study that did not meet professional standards' (Cronbach, 1980), and did not like it. Albemarle used the Wonderlic Personnel Test, validated against supervisor ratings. The court made a number of criticisms of the study's methodology:

- The supervisor ratings were unsatisfactory: *there is no way of knowing precisely what criterion of job performance the supervisors were considering, whether each of the supervisors was considering the same criterion, or whether, indeed, any of the supervisors actually applied a focused and stable body of criteria of any kind.*
- Only senior staff were rated, whereas the tests were being used to select for junior posts.
- Only white staff were rated, whereas As included minorities.
- The results were an 'odd patchwork'. Sometimes Form A of the Wonderlic test predicted, where the supposedly equivalent Form B did not. Local validation studies with smallish sample sizes often get 'patchy' results. Work psychologists accept this, but Albemarle showed that outsiders expected tests to do better.

Risk

Business necessity allows some employers to use selection methods creating AI without having to prove their validity exhaustively, if 'the risks involved in hiring an unqualified applicant are staggering'. The case of *Spurlock v United Airlines* showed America's enthusiasm for equality stopped short of being flown by inexperienced pilots. The court even agreed that pilots must be graduates 'to cope with the initial training program and the unending series of refresher courses'.

Bona fide occupational qualification (BFOQ)

This is known in Britain as *genuine* OQ. When Congress was debating CRA, a Congressman waxed lyrical about a hypothetical elderly woman who wanted a female nurse – white, black or Hispanic – but female, so Congress added the concept of BFOQ: that for some jobs, being male, or female, is essential. US courts and agencies have interpreted BFOQ very narrowly. Early on, airlines found that they could not insist that flight attendants be female as a BFOQ. Nor would the elderly woman have been allowed to insist on her female nurse. The scope of the BFOQ is limited in practice to actors and lavatory attendants.

Proving selection is job-related

Validation was discussed previously, in Chapter 2, from an exclusively psychological point of view. Now it is necessary to consider it again, adding a lawyer's perspective, using the three types of validation – content, criterion and construct – mentioned by the APA's Standards and EEOC's Guidelines. The Guidelines expressed a preference for criterion validation.

Criterion validation

Miner and Miner (1979) described an ideal criterion validation study, in which the employer should:

- test a large number of As,
- but not use the test scores in deciding who to employ,
- ensure there is a wide range of scores on the test,
- wait for as long as necessary, then collect work performance data, and
- not use a concurrent design, where test data and work performance data are collected at the same time.

It sounds quite easy – but there are several reasons why it is difficult, time-consuming and expensive in practice.

Criterion

This 'must represent major or critical work behavior as revealed by careful job analysis' (*Guidelines*). Rating criteria may be accused of bias, especially if minorities or women get lower ratings. The Guidelines list acceptable criteria as production rate, error rate, tardiness, absenteeism, turnover and training performance; note that this list does not include citizenship or 'attitude'. This could be a problem now that employers are trying to broaden their concept of work performance, primarily to reduce AI.

Sample size

The correlation between test and outcome must be significant at the 5% level – yet the typical local validation study rarely has enough people to be sure of achieving this (Chapter 2). EEOC help ensure the sample size is too small by insisting that differential validities for minorities be calculated, and by insisting that every job be treated separately.

Concurrent / predictive validity

The Uniform Guidelines favour predictive validity, which takes longer and costs more.

Representative sampling and differential validity

A representative sample contains the right proportion of minorities and women. The hypothesis of *differential validity* postulates that tests can be valid for whites or males but not for minorities or females. An employer with an all-white and/or all-male workforce cannot prove there is no differential validity without employing women and/or minorities, making this the 'Catch 22' of the Guidelines.

Some MA tests create so much AI on some minorities that the agencies, the courts and the minorities are unlikely ever to accept them, no matter what proof of their predictive validity is produced. Kleiman and Faley's (1985) review of 12 early court cases on criterion validity was not very encouraging for any employers thinking of relying on proving that their selection procedures actually predict productivity.

- Courts often appeared to suppose some tests had been completely discredited and could never be proved valid – notably the Wonderlic Personnel Test.
- Courts often examined item content or format even though this is irrelevant when assessing predictive validity.
- Courts often objected to coefficients being corrected for restricted range.
- Courts often ignored or avoided technical issues, or took a common sense approach to issues like sample size where common sense is generally wrong.
- Courts' decisions were inconsistent and unpredictable.
- Only five of the 12 employers won their cases.

Critics may say psychologists have just been hoist with their own petard. They always claimed their tests were the best way to select staff. They always insisted validating tests was a highly technical business best left to the experts. But when American fair employment agencies took them at their word, the psychologists could not deliver an acceptable validity study. Their 50-year-old bluff had been called. In fact, fair employment legislation has done work psychologists a big service, forcing them to prove more thoroughly that tests are valid and worth using, by validity generalization analysis (VGA; Chapter 2), utility analysis (Chapter 14) and differential validity research (v.i.).

Validity generalization analysis

VGAs for general mental ability (GMA) tests imply that local validity studies are pointless because GMA tests are valid predictors for every type of work. Accepting these conclusions would leave little or no scope for fair employment cases involving GMA tests, so it is not surprising that American civil rights lawyers are not keen to accept VGA (Seymour, 1988). The Guidelines say nothing about meta-analysis or VGA, for the simple reason the Guidelines have not been revised since 1978. Landy (2003) and Cascio and Anguinis (2005) both noted that few legal cases have involved validity generalization. Landy drew the pessimistic conclusion that one of these cases – *Atlas Paper Box Co v EEOC* – means validity generalization is unlikely to prove acceptable to US courts. Harpe (2008) noted that EEOC requires either a local validity study, or a transportability study using detailed job analysis to prove the two jobs really are the same. McDaniel (2007) wondered if the EEOC prefers to make employers defend every case in exhaustive detail (rather than being to rely on validity generalization), with a hidden agenda of making it so difficult that employers will find it easier to hire their quota of protected groups.

Content validation

In 1964, when CRA was passed, content validity was virtually unheard-of and not very highly regarded. Guion (1965) said: 'Content validity is of extremely limited utility as a concept for employment tests. ... [it] comes uncomfortably close to the idea of face-validity unless judges are especially precise in their judgements'. Content validation became the favourite validation strategy after the Guidelines and the *Griggs* case because criterion validation was impossibly difficult (v.s.), and the courts could not understand construct validation (v.i.). Content validation has three big advantages:

1. No criterion is required so it cannot be unsatisfactory. The test is its own justification.
2. There is no time interval between testing and validation. The test is validated before it is used.
3. Content valid tests are easy to defend in court. Every item of the test is clearly relevant to the job.

Content validation requires careful job analysis to prove that the test 'is a representative sample of the content of the job' (Guidelines). Test content must reflect every aspect of the job, in the correct proportions; if 10% of the job consists of writing reports, report writing must not account for 50% of the test. It is easy to prove job-relatedness for simple concrete jobs, such as keyboard skills tests. Some US employers have tried to use content validity methods for assessing personality or general ability, usually in the hope of avoiding AI problems. The Guidelines specifically block this: 'a content strategy is not appropriate for demonstrating the validity of selection procedures which purport to measure traits or constructs, such as mental ability, aptitude, personality, common-sense, judgement, leadership and spatial ability.'

Construct validation

'A demonstration that (a) a selection procedure measures a construct (something believed to be an underlying human trait or characteristic, such as honesty) and (b) the construct is important for successful job performance' (Guidelines). Cronbach (1980) gave the example of high-school graduation. A narrow approach might conclude that employees do not need to write essays or do sums or even to be able to read, so graduation is not job-related. The broader construct validity approach argues it is a reasonable supposition that people who do well at school differ from those who do not, in more than just academic ability. Cronbach called the 'something' *motivation* and *dependability*.

So, an employer who does not want lazy, undependable employees could hope to exclude them by requiring a high-school diploma. Cronbach's example showed very clearly why construct validation is not a promising approach. The constructs motivation and dependability are exactly the sort of abstractions that are difficult to define, difficult to measure and difficult to defend in court. In fact, general education requirements are rarely accepted by American courts (Chapter 9). Harpe (2008) noted that US employers hardly ever rely on construct validity to defend selection.

Alternative tests

The 1970 Guidelines required employers to prove no alternative test existed that did not create AI before they used valid tests that did create AI. *Albemarle Paper Company v Moody* overruled this in 1975 on the grounds that employers could not prove a negative, but in 1978 the Guidelines placed the obligation to prove a negative back on the employer. Some time ago, Reilly and Chao (1982) and Hunter and Hunter (1984) reviewed a range of alternative tests, and concluded that none achieved the same validity for selection as ability tests, except biodata and job tryouts. For promotion, a range of alternative tests are as valid as ability tests: work samples, peer ratings, job knowledge tests and assessment centres.

UK practice

The Commission for Racial Equality's (CRE) Code recommended employers to keep detailed records to compare actual and ideal composition of applicant pool and workforce. They have adopted the AI principle, and offer the four-fifths principle as guidance, but not a legal requirement. The CRE Code recommended that 'selection criteria and tests are examined to ensure that they are related to job requirements and are not unlawfully discriminatory'. The Equal Opportunity Commission's (EOC) Code similarly said 'selection tests … should specifically relate to job requirements'. The CRE's Code was particularly concerned that employers do not require better command of English or higher educational qualifications than the job needs. CRE's earlier formal Inquiries dealt with employers sufficiently ignorant or unsubtle to say things like '[we don't employ West Indians because they are] too slow, too sly, too much mouth and they skive off', then with employers whose recruitment methods appeared to keep out minorities, usually by 'word of mouth' recruiting. (At the time of writing the new Commission for Equality and Human Rights is still using the former CRE and EOC guidance on recruitment and selection.)

In the 1980s, the first cases involving psychological tests began to appear. In the 'Centurion managers' case, London Underground appointed 160 middle managers in such a rush that they did not have time to include all the tests psychologists had recommended, or to pre-test the ones they did use (CRE, 1990). The tests used, numerical and verbal reasoning, and an interview, created AI on minority As. In 1990, another case involving tests came to trial – the 'Paddington Guards' case (CRE, 1996). British Rail guards [conductors] seeking promotion to driver were tested with verbal reasoning, numerical reasoning, and clerical tests. A group of guards of Asian origin alleged unfair discrimination because the tests were not clearly job-related, but were harder for people whose first language was not English. A striking feature of the case was that British Rail had a job analysis for train drivers, done by Netherlands Railways, but did not use it to match tests to the job's needs. Both cases were settled out of court, and did not give rise to any legal rulings about test use in Britain.

Fair employment laws have not had the impact in Britain they had in the USA. The British government has not introduced *contract compliance*, although some local authorities have. English law does not provide for *class actions*, in which one person's test case can be used to enforce the rights of a whole class of others (e.g. female As). (This can be enormously expensive for US employers. In the State Farm Insurance case, the employer found guilty of gender discrimination had to pay $193K not just to the plaintiff, but to each of 812 other women as well). UK fair employment agencies have not concerned themselves with the technical detail of testing and validation, in marked contrast to the US EEOC and their Guidelines. The EOC's notes for lawyers (Equal Opportunities Commission, 2005) included the interesting observation that 'tribunals seem disinclined to tangle with technicalities of testing and may ignore evidence where experts appear on each side'.

European law

'European law' means laws passed by the European Community (EC), rather than by individual European states. The Community's Social Charter includes concerns with equal opportunities in employment, and for people 'excluded' from employment by disability or other reasons. The EC has accepted the idea of AI as discrimination by results, and several European countries – Italy, Ireland and The Netherlands – have incorporated the concept into their legislation (Higuera, 2001).

Disability

The Americans with Disabilities Act (ADA) was passed in 1990 and came into effect in 1992. ADA defines disability very broadly, to cover mental retardation, specific learning disabilities such as dyslexia, emotional or mental illness, AIDS / HIV and 'morbid' obesity, as well as physical disability, blindness and deafness. ADA does not however cover mild obesity, gambling, sexual deviations such as paedophilia, short-term illnesses or injuries, pregnancy, or common personality traits. Current (illegal) drug use is also excluded, but rehabilitated former drug users are covered. Alcoholism is covered by ADA, but employers can require employees to be sober during working hours. Simon and Noonan (1994) argued that ADA may prevent employers from refusing to hire As who smoke because nicotine is a legal drug, and smoking is a form of addiction. ADA covers discrimination against someone thought to have a disability (e.g. HIV / AIDS), but who in fact has not. So far, the commonest disabilities mentioned in ADA cases have been back trouble and emotional / psychiatric problems (Coil & Shapiro, 1996). The same survey found over half of all complaints concerned termination, while only 9% concerned hiring.

Job analysis

ADA distinguishes between *essential* and *marginal* job functions. Ability to drive is essential for a bus driver, but marginal for an office worker. If a disabled person cannot perform an essential function, the employer may refuse to make an offer. Employers may ask if As can perform an essential function, and may ask As to demonstrate their ability. Employers should not reject disabled As because they cannot perform a marginal function. This means careful job analysis is vital. ADA also implies person specifications need to be more detailed. For example, if the job needs someone who can handle stress well, the person specification should make this clear. (But employers should not make blanket assumptions, e.g. that a history of mental illness means someone cannot handle stress well.)

Medical examinations

Employers may only carry out medical examinations on people who have been offered a job, not as part of the selection process. 'Medical examination' is interpreted fairly broadly, so may cover some selection tests. The Minnesota Multiphasic Personality Inventory (MMPI), widely used in the USA to screen As for police work, was originally keyed to psychiatric diagnosis and gives its scales psychiatric names such as Schizophrenia, which tends to make it look very like a medical examination. Physical tests, of strength or stamina, may count as medical checks if they include measures of blood pressure or heart rate.

Accommodation

Employers must make *reasonable accommodation* to disabled persons, both as employees and As. This includes adapting selection methods by providing large-print question books, Braille question books, tape format, or someone to help the applicant. Time limits are sometimes changed to accommodate dyslexic As, or to allow for changes in format slowing As down. Changing the time limit for a timed test invalidates the norms, and so makes the results very hard to interpret. Research on educational testing reviewed by Geisinger, Boodoo and Noble (2002) suggested that allowing extra time can result in *over-predicting* subsequent college performance (i.e. that students do not do as well as expected); possibly they were given too much extra time. There is no workplace research on this issue. Given the diversity of disability, and the very large sample sizes needed to compare validities, no workplace research seems likely to be forthcoming. Employers may never know if allowing 50% or 100% or 200% extra time for a particular disability will make the test 'the same as for' someone without that disability. One implication of ADA may be a need for more untimed tests. ADA has the usual collection of vague, but crucial, phrases like *'reasonable* accommodation' or *'undue* hardship', whose meaning for employers will only become apparent after a series of court cases.

Britain again followed American practice, with the 1995 Disability Discrimination Act (DDA). DDA excludes addiction to any drug, including nicotine and alcohol, unless the drug is medically prescribed, and only covers mental illness if 'recognised by a respected body of medical opinion'.

Differential validity and test fairness

Ethnicity

Critics often claim tests, especially MA tests, are valid for the white majority but not for minorities. A series of meta-analyses of mostly American data in the 1970s eventually reached the comforting conclusion that differential validity did not seem to be a problem, and that tests worked equally well for white, Afro- and Hispanic Americans. However, Berry and Sackett (2008) argued that it is premature to dismiss differential validity as a problem. They noted that differences in validity have been found in both employment and educational testing. Hartigan and Wigdor (1989) found GATB validity 0.06–0.07 lower for African Americans. Three large American military studies, including Houston and Novick (1987), found correlation between test and training success 0.08 to 0.26 points lower. Berry and Sackett argued that the 1970s meta-analyses relied on comparing correlations in small samples, which has low statistical power. They located a very large set (131K) of Scholastic Assessment Test data, predicting college grades, and found validity for African- and Hispanic Americans the same as for white Americans. Similarly extensive current data for employment testing would be highly desirable. (Recall that Chapter 6 notes that GATB validity seems to have shrunk over time, so data from the 1950s and 1960s may not reflect the current picture.) Te Nijenhuis and van der Flier (2000) reported data for various immigrant groups in The Netherlands, and found little evidence of differential validity of ability tests. There are no published data on this important issue for Britain.

Gender

Rothstein and McDaniel (1992) presented a meta-analysis of 59 studies where validity coefficients for males and females could be compared. Overall, there was no difference. However, the results suggested that where the work is usually done by one gender (e.g. most machinists are male), validity is higher for the majority gender. This trend is particularly marked for low-complexity jobs, where female validity for 'female' jobs was 0.20 higher than male validity. Rothstein and McDaniel suggested the result may reflect a bias in the supervisor rating criterion. Men who enter a low-complexity, and traditionally female, occupation may be seen by the (mostly female) supervisors as somehow out of the ordinary. Saad and Sackett (2002) analysed ABLE data for nine US Army specialist jobs and find the relationship between personality and work performance the same for male and female.

Test fairness

Critics often claim tests are not 'fair', meaning minorities do not score as well as whites. The technical meaning of test fairness is quite different. Unfair means the test does not predict the minority's productivity as accurately as it predicts majority productivity. Several models of test fairness have been proposed. The most widely accepted is Cleary's model, which is based on regression lines. Figure 13.2 shows two types of unfair test, where there is differential validity.

- Figure 13.2a shows a slope difference, between the regression lines. The test predicts productivity more accurately for one group than the other.

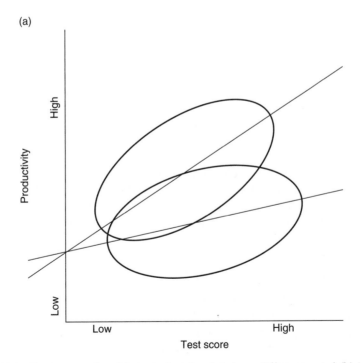

Figure 13.2   Two types of unfair test, showing (a) slope difference, and (b) intercept difference.

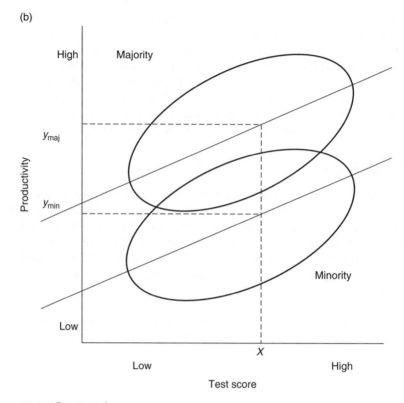

Figure 13.2 Continued

- Figure 13.2b shows an intercept difference. Minority and majority differ in test score but do not differ in productivity. Test scores under-predict minority persons' work performance; minority persons do better work than the test predicted.

Figure 13.3 shows a test which is fair, even though majority and minority averages differ. A regression line fitted to the two distributions has the same slope, and the same intercept, which means it is one continuous straight line. Test scores predict productivity, regardless of minority or majority group membership.

Alternative fairness models

Although the Cleary model is generally accepted, other models have been proposed, notably the Thorndike model. Chung-yan and Cronshaw (2002) noted that higher scorers are more likely to be accepted but to prove to be less successful employees, whereas low scorers are more likely to be rejected even though they would have been more successful employees. This happens because the correlation between score and work performance is far from

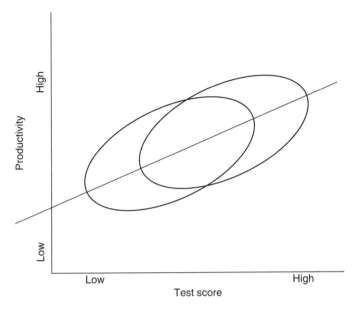

Figure 13.3   A fair test, in which test scores predict productivity equally accurately for minority and majority applicants.

perfect. Where higher scorers are mostly white Americans and low scorers are mostly minority Americans, this creates a problem. Thorndike suggests setting cut-offs for the two groups so that if 30% of minority persons would turn out to be successful employees, then 30% would be accepted.

RESEARCH AGENDA

- Large-scale investigation of differential validity in US employment testing.
- More research on possible differential validity by gender.
- Research on differential validity by gender and ethnicity in Britain, Europe, and elsewhere.

Unprotected groups

There are still sections of the population who are not covered by fair employment legislation.

Sexual orientation

A high proportion of homosexual men and women in America report discrimination in employment (Croteau, 1996), but have no legal protection.

In Britain, discrimination on grounds of sexual orientation has been illegal since 2003.

Body build

Overweight people in the USA report widespread discrimination in employment, and have no legal protection, unless 'morbidly' obese (Fikkan & Rothblum, 2005).

Social exclusion

In the UK, social exclusion and disadvantage are a concern of the present government, and have been specifically mentioned in university admission. Why not employment also? If people from certain backgrounds find it difficult to pass university entrance tests, and need special provision, might not the same be true of employment tests? Social exclusion and disadvantage may prove more difficult to define and assess than gender or ethnicity.

The ungifted

While some psychologists and employers seem happy with the idea of differences in intelligence, the government and the general population seem either unaware or unreceptive. Characterizing people as unintelligent, or explaining their behaviour as caused by low intelligence, seems increasing politically unacceptable. It seems unlikely that people of low intelligence would be listed directly as a protected minority because that implies accepting the concept, and perhaps using the tests. However, it is more possible that something closely linked to low intelligence might eventually confer protected minority status, perhaps low educational achievement.

Conclusions

Fair employment legislation is needed because discrimination in employment on grounds of gender and ethnicity is clearly unacceptable, and would be rejected by most people these days. However, fair employment law has not primarily concerned itself with overt discrimination, but with AI. In the USA, AI places the burden of proof on employers, effectively requiring them to prove they are not discriminating if there are not 50% females and X% ethnic minority persons throughout the entire workforce. It is less immediately obvious that this is entirely reasonable, or what the average person wants.

The effect of new fair employment laws typically takes some years to become apparent and does not always seem to be quite what was intended. This creates prolonged periods of uncertainty and costs employers large amounts. The CRA has often, only half-jokingly, been called 'the work psychologists' charter'. Lawyers too have done very well from it. But fair employment legislation was not meant to benefit psychologists and lawyers; it was intended to help minorities.

While it is true fair employment laws have been a burden to American employers, it could also be argued that they have indirectly helped work psychology, by forcing the profession to look much harder at issues like utility, validity and differential validity, to devise new techniques, like validity generalization or rational estimates, and to devise better selection methods.

Key points

In Chapter 13 you have learned the following.

- Fair employment law covers gender, ethnicity, disability and age.
- Most fair employment selection cases involve AI, not direct discrimination.
- Adverse impact means fewer minority persons are successful. If the success rate for minority persons is less than four-fifths that of the majority, AI is established.
- Getting the numbers right, i.e. ensuring the correct proportions of women and minorities in the workforce, can be difficult as there are legal restrictions on how employers can achieve it.
- A selection method that creates AI must be proved – in court – to be valid, which is expensive and uncertain.
- If the test is proved valid, the employer must also show there is no possible alternative that is equally valid but which will not create AI.
- American researchers are trying sets of tests to try to find a combination that will prove valid but create no AI.
- Differential validity means that a test has different validity for minority and majority persons.
- North American research on differential validity does not reach firm conclusions. Virtually no research has been reported on this issue outside the North America.
- Disability discrimination legislation means employers must not use health related enquiries as part of the selection process
- Employers must try to adapt selection tests to disabled As.
- In Britain, far fewer unfair selection cases have been brought, and the position is still much more open.
- Other countries, in Europe and elsewhere, have adopted the same basic AI model.

Key references

Cascio and Anguinis (2005) discuss legal aspects of validity generalization.

Coil and Shapiro (1996) describe the operation of the Americans with Disabilities Act.

CRE (1990) describes the Centurion Managers case, one of the few fair employment cases involving psychological tests that have been tried in the UK.

Higuera (2001) provides a European perspective on fair employment.

Hough *et al.* (2001) provide a detailed review of gender and ethnicity differences in a range of selection tests.

Kleiman & Faley (1985) review early attempts by American employers to prove in court their selection tests were valid.

Kravitz (2008) outline ways of increasing minority representation by affirmative action.

Liao *et al.* (2004) describe one of the down sides of diversity.

Potosky *et al.* (2005) describe an example of using composites of mental ability and alternative measures to reduce adverse impact.

Roth *et al.* (2001) discusses problems in assessing adverse impact.

te Nijenhuis and van der Flier (2000) present data on differential validity of psychological tests in The Netherlands.

Saad and Sackett (2002) present data on differential validity by gender in American military testing.

Terpstra *et al.* (1999) give a survey of US fair employment cases between 1978 and 1997.

Useful websites

usdoj.gov/crt/ada. Official ADA site.
eeoc.gov. US government fair employment agency.
equalityhumanrights.com. UK Commission for Equality and Human Rights.
hrhero.com. Interesting question and answer site on US fair employment.

CHAPTER 14

The value of good employees

The best is twice as good as the worst

Introduction

In an ideal world, two people doing the same job under the same conditions will produce exactly the same amount. In the real world, some employees produce more than others. This poses two questions:

- How much do workers vary in productivity?
- How much are these differences worth?

The short answer to both questions is 'a lot'. An answer to the first question is good workers do twice as much work as poor workers. An answer to the second question says the difference in value between a good worker and a poor one is roughly equal to the salary they are paid.

How much does worker productivity vary?

Hull (1928) described ratios of output of best to worst performers in a variety of occupations. He reported that the best spoon polishers polished five times as many as the worst. Ratios were less extreme for other occupations – between 1.5 to 1 and 2 to 1 for weaving and shoemaking jobs. Tiffin (1943) drew graphs of the distribution of output for various jobs, including hosiery loopers, who gather together the loops of thread at the bottom of a stocking to close the opening left in the toe (Figure 14.1). Most workers fall between the extremes to form a roughly normal distribution of output. If the distribution is normal, it can be summarized by its mean (MEANp) and standard deviation (SD_P). The standard deviation of the data in Figure 14.1 is the SD_P of hosiery looping.

Judiesch and Schmidt (2000) reviewed research on SD_P. For 95 samples of unskilled workers, SD_P is 18% of average output, indicating a substantial difference between good and poor performers. Defining 'the best' as two SDs above the mean and 'the worst' as two SDs below, Judiesch and Schmidt's 18% average for SD_P confirmed neatly that the best, at 136%, is twice the worst, at 64%. Earlier analyses had suggested that paying people piece-rate, as is common in blue-collar jobs, compressed the distribution of output, but making allowance for error of measurement, Judiesch and Schmidt concluded that this does not happen. SD_P for low-level jobs is 18% whether people are paid

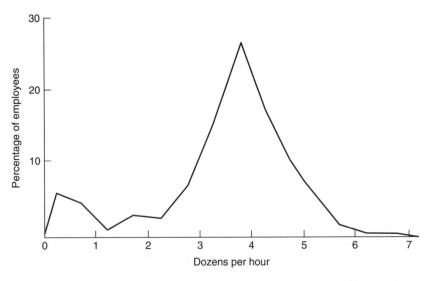

Figure 14.1   Distribution of productivity for 199 hosiery loopers (Tiffin, 1943).

by the hour or by output. SD_P is slightly higher for white-collar jobs, being 20–24% for low-level clerical jobs. SD_P is considerably higher for more complex work, being 27% for skilled craft jobs, 35% for clerical jobs that involve making decisions and 46% for professional jobs. This implies that the best:worst ratio in higher-level work will be much greater. Few professional jobs have been analysed however, probably because it is far easier to count the output of soap wrappers or bicycle chain assemblers than that of managers. It is also worth noting that many of the studies Judiesch and Schmidt analysed were very old, and the jobs involved may no longer exist in the same form, if at all.

How much is a productive worker worth?

If some workers produce more than others, an employer that succeeds in selecting them will make more money – but how much more? A lot of ingenious effort has gone into trying to put a cash value on the productive worker. Accountants can, at least in theory, calculate the value of each individual worker: so many units produced, selling at so much each, less the worker's wage costs, and a proportion of the company's overheads. In practice, such calculations proved very difficult. But if accountants cannot put a precise value on an individual production worker's output, how can they hope to do so for a manager, supervisor or human resource (HR) director?

Rational estimates (RE)

In the late 1970s, psychologists devised a technique for putting a cash value on the people doing any job, no matter how varied and complex its demands or how intangible its end products. RE technique was invented by Schmidt and Hunter, who argued that supervisors 'have the best opportunities to observe actual performance and output differences between employees on a day-to-day basis' (Schmidt *et al.*, 1979). So, the best way to put a value on a good employee is simply to ask supervisors to judge the employee's worth. REs are collected using these instructions:

> Based on your experience with [widget press operators] we would like you to estimate the yearly value to your company of the products and services provided by the average operator. Consider the quality and quantity of output typical of the average operator and the value of this output … in placing a cash value on this output, it may help to consider what the cost would be of having an outside firm provide these products and services.

Similar estimates are made for a good operator and for a poor one. 'Good' is defined as an operator at the 85th percentile, one whose performance is better than 85% of his/her fellows. 'Poor' is defined as an operator at the 15th percentile. Why 15% and 85%? Because these values correspond roughly to one standard deviation either side of the mean. Therefore, assuming the value of operators is normally distributed, the three estimates – 15th percentile, mean and 85th percentile – can be used to calculate the standard deviation of operator productivity, referred to as SD_y. SD_y summarizes the distribution in value to the employer of differences in output between employees (Figure 14.2). SD_y tells the employer how much the workers' work varies in value. SD_y is a vital term in the equation for estimating the return on a selection programme. The smaller SD_y is, the less point there is putting a lot of effort and expense into selecting staff because there is less difference in value between good and poor staff.

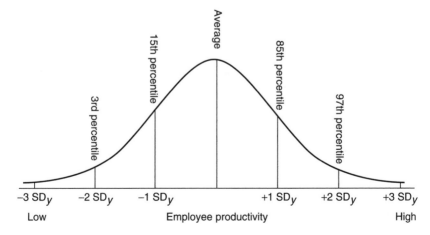

Figure 14.2   The distribution of employee productivity, showing the percentile points used in Rational Estimate technique to measure it.

A large number of supervisors make REs, then averages are calculated. Schmidt, Gast-Rosenberg and Hunter (1980) analysed REs for good, average, and poor computer programmers. The differences between average and good, and average and poor, both around $10,000, did not differ significantly, which confirms the distribution is normal. Bobko, Shetzer and Russell (1991) reported an estimate of SD_y for college professor of $55.6K – although the value varied greatly according to the way it was elicited. Yoo and Muchinsky (1998) generated estimates for 24 very varied jobs, and got a range of SD_y estimates from a low of $5.8K for window cleaners and toll collectors, to highs of $84K and $62K for stockbrokers and work psychologists. They found that the more complex the job, in terms of either data analysis or interaction with other people, the greater SD_y was, confirming Judiesch and Schmidt's (2000) finding for SD_P.

Variations on the RE theme

Other methods of estimating the distribution of employee value have been proposed.

- *Superior equivalents technique.* Army commanders estimate how many tanks with superior (85th percentile) crews would be the match in battle of a standard company of 17 tanks, with average crews. Estimates converged on a figure of nine. An elite tank company need number only nine to be the match of an average company, neatly confirming Hull's estimate that the best is twice as good as the worst (Eaton, Wing & Mitchell, 1985).
- Judiesch (2001) varied RE technique by asking supervisors for estimates of output and staffing levels for average, good and poor performers. If an average nurse can look after three patients adequately, how many could a good nurse look after? If the unit needs three average nurses, how many poor nurses would be needed to get the same work done, to the same standard? Supervisors found these estimates easier to make; they also translate more directly into savings in staffing levels (and hence money).
- Raju Burke and Normand (1990) propose a different utility model that does not require estimation of SD_y. Instead they use A – average total compensation per employee, covering salary, benefits, bonuses and direct overheads – to put a figure to costs, and SD_r, the SD of performance appraisal ratings for employees, to put a figure to differences between employees. This model assumes that performance appraisal accurately describes differences between workers, which is not always true. Leniency is a pervasive problem of performance appraisal, which would undermine Raju *et al.*'s method.

The 40–70% rule

SD_y for computer programmers worked out at 55% of salary, which prompted Schmidt and Hunter to propose a rule of thumb:

SDy is between 40 and 70% of salary.

Good and poor workers are each one SD_y from the average, so the difference between best and worst is two SD_ys. If SD_y is 40 to 70% of salary, the difference between good and poor is between 80 and 140% of salary, which generates another rule of thumb:

The value of a good employee minus the value of a poor employee is roughly equal to the salary paid for the job.

If salary for the job in question is £30,000, the difference in value between best and worst worker is roughly £30,000 too. Recall that good and poor, at the 85th percentile and 15th percentile, are far from being the extremes.

Are rational estimates valid?

Some critics think that REs are dangerously subjective and research has cast some doubt on their validity. Bobko *et al.* (1991) showed that relatively minor changes in wording the instructions, or order of presentation, generate a very wide range of SD_y estimates, from as low as $29K to as high as $101K. Another study asked supervisors to explain how they generated REs (Mathieu & Tannenbaum, 1989) and found most – especially the more experienced – based their estimates on salary. This makes some of Schmidt and Hunter's rules of thumb look suspiciously circular. If REs of SD_y are based on salary, it is not surprising to find they are closely related to salary.

Is productivity normally distributed?

Psychologists like normal distributions, if only to justify the statistical analyses they use. Schmidt *et al.* (1980) found evidence that value to the organization is normally distributed. Subsequently however, Yoo and Muchinsky (1998) found that value was not normally distributed for 15 of the 24 occupations they studied. In every case, the above average estimate (50–85) was higher than the below average estimate. This is consistent with there being more high performers than would be found in true distribution. Note however that they used the same panel to estimate for all 24 jobs so shared rating bias could explain their results.

RESEARCH AGENDA

• Estimates of the normality of productivity and value distributions using more sophisticated methods.

Calculating the return on selection

It is fairly easy to calculate the cost of selection, although many employers only think of doing so when asked to introduce new methods; they rarely work out how much existing methods, such as day-long panel interviews, cost. It is more difficult to calculate the return on selection. The formula was first stated by Brogden in 1946, but for many years had only academic interest because a crucial term in it could not be measured – SD_y, the SD of employee productivity. Until rational estimate technique was devised, there was no way of measuring how much more good employees are worth. Brogden's equation states:

$$\text{SAVING per EMPLOYEE per YEAR} = (r \times SD_y \times Z) - (C/P),$$

where:

r	is the validity of the selection procedure (expressed as a correlation coefficient).
SD_y	is the standard deviation of employee value, in pounds, dollars or euros.
Z	is the calibre of recruits (expressed as their standard score on the selection test used).
C	is the cost of selection per applicant (A).
P	is the proportion of As selected.

Or to put it in plain English, the amount an employer can save, per employee recruited per year, is:

VALIDITY of the test
times
CALIBRE of recruits
times
SD_y
minus
COST of selection
divided by
PROPORTION of As selected

Here is a worked example:

- The employer is recruiting in the salary range £40,000 p.a., so SD_y can be estimated – by the 40% rule of thumb – at £16,000.
- The employer is using a test of mental ability whose validity is 0.45, so r is 0.45.
- The people recruited score on average 1SD above the mean (for present employees), so Z is 1. This assumes the employer succeeds in recruiting high-calibre people.

- The employer uses a consultancy, who charge £750 per candidate.
- Of 10 As, four are appointed, so P is 0.40.

The SAVING per employee per year is:

$$(0.45 \times £16,000 \times 1) - (£650/0.40)$$
$$= £7,200 - £1,875$$
$$= £5,325$$

Each employee selected is worth some £5,000 a year more to the employer than one recruited at random. The four employees recruited will be worth in all £21,300 more to the employer each year. The larger the organization, the greater the total sum that can be saved by effective selection hence the estimate in Chapter 1 of $18 million for the Philadelphia police force.

Selection pays off better when:

- calibre of recruits is high;
- employees differ a lot in worth to the organization, i.e. when SD_y is high; and
- selection procedure has high validity.

Selection pays off less well when:

- recruits are uniformly mediocre;
- SD_y is low, i.e. workers do not vary much in value; and
- selection procedure has low validity.

Employers should have no difficulty attracting good recruits in periods of high unemployment (unless pay or conditions are poor). RE and other research show that SD_y is rarely low. The third condition – zero validity – may often apply, when employers use poor selection methods. But if any of the three terms are zero, their product – the value of selection – is necessarily zero too. Only the right-hand side of the equation – cost – is never zero.

Utility analysis in practice

Other authors have pointed out that some utility theory estimates of savings achieved by good selection are over-optimistic.

- Increased productivity is not all 'money in the bank'. Increased production means increased costs. Moreover, the costs of selection are incurred before the savings are made, so interest charges need to be included.
- Brogden's equation overestimates the return on selection because it assumes that everyone offered a job will accept it. In practice, some As, especially the better ones, reject the employer's offer, so the calibre of the new employees – Z in the Brogden equation – is reduced (Murphy, 1986).
- At a more individual level, selecting the most capable may have hidden costs, if such individuals turn out to be divisive, verbally abusive or a bully,

for example. This might reduce others' job satisfaction or even output, and result in people leaving the organization.

- Vance and Colella (1990) commented that utility theory makes the simplistic assumption that every worker works in isolation, whereas in reality much work is done by teams, where superhumans performing at the 95% percentile will be held back by slower mortals performing at the 50th percentile. Organizations in the Soviet Union had discovered this in the 1930s. They held up as a model a coal miner called Alexei Stakhanov who had exceeded his quota of coal many times over, and encouraged other workers to try to achieve enormous outputs. Some 'Stakhanovites' proved a liability; either they produced far more of their product than was actually needed, or else the organization had to provide extra workers to bring in extra raw materials, and carry away the Stakhanovite's output.

Do utility estimates impress management?

Macan and Highhouse (1994) reported that 46% of work psychologists and HR managers say they use utility arguments to sell projects to managers. By contrast, Latham and Whyte (1994), who admitted to being sceptical about utility theory, found managers less likely to buy a selection package from a work psychologist on the strength of utility estimates.

Proving selection really adds value

Critics of utility theory dismiss it as just another set of meaningless estimates along the lines of 'traffic congestion costs £30 million a day'. Vance and Colella (1990) complained that savings that dwarf the national debt are postulated, but no real savings from selection have been demonstrated. These critics are asking for proof that using good selection methods actually improves the organization's performance. Recently, some researches have provided proof, although it is probably still not as specific and definite as the critics would like. Huselid, Jackson and Schuler (1997) correlated general HR effectiveness with employee productivity (defined as net sales per employee), return on assets and profitability, across 293 organizations. They report weak (0.10 to 0.16) significant correlations between HR effectiveness and capability, and return on assets and profitability, but not with employee productivity. Their measures of HR effectiveness and capability were however very global, including only a few specific references to selection and recruitment in a 41-item list. Their correlation may seem very low, but 0.10–0.20 is good by the standards of this type of research; it is difficult to demonstrate any relationship between how organizations operate and how well they do. A correlation of 0.14 implies that organizations with better HR will make more money. Subsequently research in this area has burgeoned. Combs *et al.* (2006) reported a meta-analysis of 92 studies, which find correlations of the same order of magnitude as Huselid's pioneering study. Most researches are similarly global, making it difficult to identify the contribution of better selection. Combs *et al.* separated out 15 studies which correlated *selectivity* with performance, finding a correlation of 0.14. Selectivity was coded from the number of selection tests the organization used or from the number of As rejected, making it a fairly broad measure of selection.

Perhaps the most convincing data were provided by Terpstra and Rozell (1993). They correlated performance with selection practice across 201 organizations, and showed that organizations that use structured interviews, mental ability tests, biodata, analysis of recruiting source and validation of selection methods had higher annual profits, more profit growth and more sales growth. The relationship was very strong (0.70–0.80) in sectors that depend crucially on the calibre of their staff, such as service industries and the financial sector, but insignificant in sectors where capital equipment is more possibly important, such as manufacturing.

Most researches have taken a very broad view of HRM, on the argument that it is the whole pattern of HR that matters, rather than specifics like selection. Most HR managers after all spend relatively little time on selection, compared with training, performance management, employee relations, and so on. It would nevertheless be useful to retain some specificity in identifying the contribution that selection makes to organizational performance. In fact it would be useful to report even more specific analyses, looking for links between individual selection methods and organizational performance. Do organizations that use structured interviews make more money than the ones that do not? Do organizations that rely on mental ability tests show higher productivity? Research has shown which methods have higher validity in conventional validation research. But does a higher correlation between selection test and supervisor rating ultimately result in more profit for the organization? It should, but it would be useful to have confirmation. Perhaps some selection methods fail to realize their potential at the level of the 'bottom line'. Suppose that personality tests put off many good As, or mental ability tests cause legal problems, or structured interviews fail to identify people who do not stay. The test's validity will not work through into better profitability or productivity.

Wright *et al.* (2005) noted a serious flaw with this whole area of research: direction of cause. Most researches are cross-sectional, so data could be interpreted as showing that better-run companies are more profitable, and also use better HRM and selection methods. It does not follow that better HRM or selection creates greater profitability. For conclusive proof, a longitudinal study is needed, showing that increased profitability follows changes in selection.

RESEARCH AGENDA

- Research at the organizational level, linking specific selection practices to profitability and productivity
- Longitudinal study across organizations linking HR and selection to productivity

The applicant's perspective

Why the applicant's perspective matters

Some British work psychologists think they know why testing took off in Britain during the 1980s – because unemployment had dramatically increased. Employers no longer needed to worry whether As would be put off by strange new selection methods, in place of the traditional CV – reference – interview. Anderson (2004) commented how little notice selection research has taken the A's perspective, compared with the thousands of 'employer-centric' validation studies. One can list half a dozen good reasons why employers should ask themselves what As will make of their selection practices:

- Selection methods might put people off, either applying or accepting an offer.
- Disgruntled As may dissuade others from applying.
- Disgruntled As will share their negative view of the organization with all their friends, and relatives, and colleagues – a sizeable number of people.
- Some rejected As may complain, perhaps even start a court case.
- Research has even suggested some disgruntled As cease buying the organization's products or services.
- Last but not least, abstract justice requires As be treated with respect.

Applicants' preferences for selection methods

Hausknecht, Day and Thomas (2004) meta-analysed 10 surveys of liking for nine selection methods. Figure 14.3 shows clearly that traditional methods of CV / resume, reference and interview are favoured, graphology is not liked, and 'psychological tests' come inbetween. These results seem very stable across cultures, having been replicated in The Netherlands (Anderson & Witvliet, 2008), Spain and Portugal (Moscoso & Salgado, 2004), and Italy (Bertolino & Steiner, 2007), among others. Hausknecht *et al.* suggest the data show people like methods that are face-valid and that give As the opportunity to perform well. Another interpretation could be that people like the familiar – CV, reference, interview – and do not trust psychologists' contributions. These surveys lack realism to some extent because most ask students what they think of, e.g. using PQs in selection. It would be useful to get ratings from people who have just completed, e.g. a PQ in a real job application. Hausknecht *et al.* noted that little is known about what people think of assessments used for promotion. Another neglected area is length: one's impression is that people dislike very long selection systems. (This may mediate the dislike of 'psychological tests', if As see the interview as standard, making 'tests' an unwelcome extension of the ordeal.).

Stone-Romero, Stone and Hyatt (2003) reported a US survey of perceived invasion of privacy by selection tests. Traditional tests, application form and interview, are least invasive, lie detector and drug-use testing the most

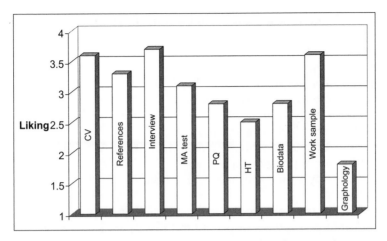

Figure 14.3 Favourability ratings of nine selection methods, across 10 surveys, Data from Hausknecht *et al.* (2004).

Table 14.1 Ten selection tests in order of perceived invasiveness of applicant privacy.

Application form	1	Least invasive
Interview	2=	
Physical ability test	4	
MA test	5	
Personality test	6	
Honesty test	7	
Work sample	2=	
Lie detector	10	
Drug-use test	9	
Background check	8	Most invasive

Data from Stone-Romero *et al.* (2003).

invasive. Psychological tests fall in between. Liking for methods and perceived invasiveness seem closely linked (*see* Table 14.1).

Models of applicant reactions

Gilliland (1993) proposed an organizational justice model of reactions to selection, which has inspired a great deal of research. Organizational justice has two main aspects:

- Distributive justice – whether jobs go to those who deserve them.
- Procedural justice – whether selection procedures are fair.

Gilliland listed nine aspects of procedural justice. Assessment should:

- be job-related,
- be face-valid,
- have perceived predictive validity,
- give As the opportunity to perform,
- be consistently administered,
- explain what is done and why,
- be done by people who are pleasant and treat As with respect,
- not ask improper questions, and
- provide opportunity for reconsideration.

Research has tended to focus on the first five or six of these. Table 14.2 shows that overall perceptions of procedural justice are shaped by job-relatedness, validity and opportunity to perform, more than by consistency or explanation. Schleicher *et al.* (2006) noted the paucity of research on opportunity to perform, which they argued is the most important procedural rule. Their data indicated people who were rejected for a real job complained afterwards of not having enough time, not being told clearly enough what to do, not being asked the right questions, and so on. Other aspects of procedural justice, including job-relatedness, seemed less salient to them. Schleicher *et al.* argued that selectors should try to make sure As do feel they have the opportunity to perform well, by allowing enough time, not relying exclusively on written tests or structured interviews, and making sure As understand exactly what they are meant to do.

Hausknecht *et al.* (2004) also meta-analysed the relationship between perceived justice and the five outcomes. Table 14.3 shows perceptions of procedural and distributive justice only weakly related to actual performance in selection. There were stronger links with how attracted As were to the organization, whether they would recommend it to others, and their intention to accept an offer. Hausknecht *et al.* found no usable research on links between perceived fairness and actual work performance, or A's withdrawal.

Table 14.2   Correlation between aspects of procedural justice, and overall procedural justice.

	k	r
Job-relatedness	7	0.50
Face-validity	11	0.60
Perceived predictive validity	9	0.56
Opportunity to perform	1	0.45
Consistency	3	0.17
Explanation	2	0.04

Data from Hausknecht et al. (2004). NB excludes data collected from students rating hypothetical selections.

Table 14.3 Correlation between procedural and distributive justice, and five outcomes.

	Procedural justice		Distributive justice	
	k	r	k	r
Attraction to organization	15	0.39	4	0.14
Intention to recommend	12	0.41	4	0.33
Intention to accept offer	12	0.25	1	0.44
Perceived performance in selection	8	0.47		
Actual performance in selection	14	0.11	3	0.26

Data from Hausknecht *et al.* (2004). NB excludes data collected from students rating hypothetical selections.

Methodological problems

A lot of research on As' perception of selection is methodologically weak. Most studies collect all the information at the same time, from the same person, which creates problems of direction of cause. For example, people who think that the organization's selection methods are unfair tend to say they are less likely to accept an offer. Do they decide not to accept an offer because they do not like the selection methods? Or do they form a dislike of the organization, so refuse the job offer, and incidentally find fault with the selection system? If researchers collected data on what people think of the selection system before they go through it, or found out whether they were successful, research would be in a stronger position to infer cause. Schleicher *et al.* (2006) asked people about selection methods twice, once after the assessment, then again three months after being told they had succeeded or failed. Rejection made people more critical of the selection's fairness. Too many studies use students, reacting to hypothetical selection, not real As for real jobs. Hausknecht *et al.* found 60% of research used students; of the remaining 40%, half, for some reason, were police officers and firefighters, leaving other sectors seriously under-represented. Hausknecht *et al.* analysed students and real As separately, and found effects are stronger in student samples. The data in Tables 14.2 and 14.3 are for 'real' samples only.

Other themes

While perceived fairness of selection is very important, there are other aspects of what As think that might usefully be researched: what As infer about the organization's likely success, or up-to-dateness, or whether they form expectations about how 'tight a ship' the organization will be. Schleicher *et al.* (2006) reported one of very few studies to allow people to say what they think about selection, in their own words. Many comments concerned opportunity to perform, especially after people were told they had been turned down.

Another theme was opportunity to interact with the assessors, which may explain why interviews are so popular. It might also be interesting to consider the perspective of not-so-good As (who nevertheless would like to get the job). They may not care much about accuracy or fairness. They may even prefer employers who use bad selection methods because they have more chances of getting a job.

Billsberry (2007) presented a completely open-ended survey of As' experiences of selection. Some accounts described experiences familiar to many: finding the shortlist includes an internal candidate who gets the job, leaving everyone else feeling – probably correctly – that they never had much chance, and were only there because the rules said five people must be interviewed. Another theme was deliberate misrepresentation, to get people to apply for, or accept, jobs which were not at all what As were led to believe. Several As mentioned failure to keep to schedule, interviewers who clearly had not read the application form, interviewers who seemed to have no idea how to conduct an interview, or made no attempt to conceal obvious, sometimes illegal, prejudices. Billberry's data suggested that many As see selection, or at least the selectors, in terms of competence. Another theme in Billsberry's cases is malice: some As feel some managers see the interview as an opportunity to score points off As, or to be deliberately offensive.

RESEARCH AGENDA

- More research on As' preferences, using real As with real experience of assessments
- More longitudinal research on how As see selection
- More open-ended exploratory research of how As view selection

---

Fit

Most US selection research follows the 'predictivist' approach, focusing on selecting the most effective workers, who will maximize the organization's productivity or profitability. Workers are viewed in much the same way as raw materials, hence the name HR. Utility theory and rational estimates exemplify this approach. Some Europeans (e.g. Herriot, 1992) prefer a different approach, seeing recruitment and selection as a social process, in which both worker and employer try to decide if the other is right for them – whether they 'fit' each other. Billsberry (2007) describes quite a few examples of As for jobs deciding during the selection process that this employer is not for them, sometimes even deciding because of the selection process. Others found the selection process well-organized and the selectors fair and friendly, and were drawn to that employer. The worker is often at a considerable disadvantage here. Someone with scarce skills and a good track record may be able to choose between several employers, and secure the job on their terms. Many workers have to take what they can get.

There is an extensive body of research on person organization fit (POF). Fit has been assessed in three ways:

- direct – asking the person how well do you fit the organization?
- indirect subjective – the person describes his/her values, then the organization's values, and similarity is computed.
- direct objective – the person describes his /her values, which are compared with what the organization, in the shape of management or a consensus, says are its values.

Direct – subjective comparisons find a closer fit than direct – objective. Some people think they share more of the organization's values than they actually do. This could be a problem when, or if, they realize the discrepancy.

Kristof-Brown, Zimmerman and Johnson (2005) and Arthur et al. (2006) reported meta-analyses of the extensive research on POF. The 'All studies' column of Table 14.4 finds POF weakly related to task performance, more strongly related to turnover and organizational citizenship, and very strongly related to (employer's) intent to hire. However, many studies collect all the data from the same source; finding employers do not intend to hire people they see as not sharing their values is not especially surprising. The 'Conservative studies' column of Table 14.4 contains only studies where the information comes from different sources. Relationships are much lower, but still present for turnover, intent to hire, job satisfaction and commitment. Note also that there is not all that much research on POF and job performance that uses independent data on performance.

POF as selection test?

POF seems to predict turnover to a worthwhile extent, so could be worth selecting for. Chapter 4 noted interviews are sometimes used to assess fit.

Table 14.4   Relationship of person – organization fit to six outcomes. Conservative studies are ones where information does not all come from the same person.

	All studies		Conservative studies	
	k	r / ρ	k	r / ρ
Task performance	17	0.11 / 0.13	9	0.03 / 0.04
Organizational citizenship	13	0.21 / 0.27	3	0.04 / 0.06
Turnover	8	0.21 / 0.24	6	0.20 / 0.23
Intent to hire	9	0.53 / 0.61	3	0.16 / 0.18
Job offer	8	0.29 / 0.32	6	0.03 / 0.03
Job satisfaction	65	0.35 / 0.44	19	0.23 / 0.29
Organizational commitment	44	0.42 / 0.51	12	0.23 / 0.27

Data from Kristof-Brown et al. (2005) and Arthur et al. (2006) (for turnover).

PQ-type measures of POF are available, but of unproven value (Hambleton, Kallieth & Taylor, 2000). Self-reports of POF might be easy to distort if used for selection. Selecting for fit could lead to cloning, which Chapter 7 noted can be dangerous. Fit could also be a code word for bias, even illegal discrimination. An alternative approach, outside the 'predictivist' perspective, might be to give As extensive, and candid, information about the organization, and rely on them to decide if they will 'fit'. Billsberry *et al.* (2005) note that POF has generally been defined in terms of values, meaning the organization's values; they suggest a less 'employer-centric' approach, allowing employees or As to say what they mean by fit, in their own words.

RESEARCH AGENDA

- More research linking fit, assessed by comparing employee's view with organization's, to work performance, and employer's intention to hire
- Exploration of As' and employees' ideas about fit

Key points

In Chapter 14 you have learned the following.

- Utility theory deals with the cost-effectiveness of selection.
- People vary in the amount of work they do, and in the value of their work to the organization.
- It is possible to estimate how people vary by various techniques including Rational Estimates.
- Estimates of how much people vary can be used to determine when selection is cost-effective, and when it is not.
- Estimates of how people vary can also be used to estimate the return on selection programmes.
- Utility estimates do not seem to impress managers all that much.
- Some evidence suggests good selection may improve organization's profitability.
- Applicants prefer some selection methods to others.
- Applicant's perceptions have been explained by an organizational justice perspective.
- Fit is related to turnover, but not to work performance.

Key references

Billsberry (2007) presents 52 case studies of applicants' experience of selection.

Combs *et al.* (2006) present a meta-analysis of research on HR practices and organizational performance.

Hausknecht *et al.* (2004) report a meta-analysis of applicant reactions to selection procedures.

Judiesch and Schmidt (2000) review research on individual differences in productivity.

Kristof-Brown *et al.* (2005) review research on person organization fit.

Schleicher *et al.* (2006) describe research on applicant reactions, using a follow-up design and collecting open-ended responses.

Terpstra and Rozell (1993) present data showing better selection may be linked to increased profitability

Vance and Collella (1990) criticize utility theory estimates as unrealistic.

CHAPTER 15

Conclusions

Calculating the cost of smugness

We find everywhere a type of organisation (administrative, commercial, or academic) in which the higher officials are plodding and dull, those less senior are active only in intrigue … and the junior men are frustrated and frivolous. Little is being attempted, nothing is being achieved.

(C. Northcote Parkinson 1958)

In some organizations, the costs of selecting ineffective staff mount indefinitely because the organization lacks the mechanism, or the will, to dispense with their services. Naturally, the morale in such organizations suffers, driving out the remaining efficient workers, until only the incompetent remain, creating the state of terminal sickness so graphically described by Northcote Parkinson. Staff wander aimlessly about 'giggling feebly', losing important documents, coming alive only to block the advancement of anyone more able, 'until the central administration gradually fills up with people stupider than the chairman'. Other diagnostics include surly porters and telephonists, out-of-order lifts, a proliferation of out-of-date notices and smugness, especially smugness. The organization is doing a good job, in its own modest way; anyone who disagrees is a troublemaker who would probably be happier somewhere else. Parkinson advises that smugness is most easily diagnosed in the organization's refectory. The terminally smug do not just consume an 'uneatable, nameless mess'; they congratulate themselves on having catering staff who can provide it at such reasonable cost – 'smugness made absolute'.

   Selectors sometimes often see their task as avoiding mistakes, minimizing error. They bring in psychologists as the final check whether the applicant selected is 'safe'. So long as the year's gone by, with no obvious disasters, and no complaints, HR have done their job. This negative approach to selection is wrong. Chapter 14 showed there is a continuous distribution of productivity from the very best to the very worst; selection is not as simple as avoiding mistakes – not employing a small minority of obvious incompetents or troublemakers. The employer who succeeds in employing average staff has not succeeded in employing good staff; the employer who finds good staff has not found excellent staff.

How to select

Chapter 2 listed six criteria for judging selection tests:

reliable	giving an consistent account of the applicant.
valid	selecting good applicants and rejecting poor ones.
fair	complying with equal opportunities legislation.
acceptable	to As as well as the organization.
cost-effective	saving the organization more than it costs to use.
easy to use	fitting conveniently into the selection process.

Validity is the most important criterion. Unless a test can predict work performance, there is little point using it. (Unreliable tests cannot achieve high validity.) Table 15.1 collates the results of the various meta-analyses and VGAs discussed in earlier chapters. The earlier analyses, by Dunnette, Vineberg and Joyner; Schmitt *et al.*; Reilly and Chao; and Hunter and Hunter, remain in some cases the main source of information. Later meta-analyses for graphology, interviewing, biographical measures, psychomotor tests, job knowledge tests, personality testing, projective tests, assessment centres, and work sample and trainability tests generally confirm the conclusions of the earlier meta-analyses. Research on personality questionnaires (PQs) confirms they generally predict job proficiency very poorly, but other research – not included in Table 15.1 – suggests that PQs may predict honesty, effort, organizational citizenship, leadership and absence of counterproductive behaviour more successfully. Note however that trim-and-fill analysis (Chapter 2) has cast some doubt on meta-analytic conclusions; re-analysis may result in downward revision of some validity estimates.

Fairness

This means fairness in the legal sense. Table 15.2 summarizes the relative merits of 10 selection methods against five criteria (subsuming reliability under validity). Ratings for fairness in Table 15.2 are primarily based on US experience. Chapter 13 noted that many other countries' fair employment agencies tend to model themselves on American practice, so American experience may be a useful guide to the shape of things to come elsewhere. As time passes, selection methods tend to acquire poorer ratings under this heading. For example, personality tests were listed as 'untested' in the Second Edition of this book, but from the Fourth Edition were listed as 'some doubts' because the US *Soroka* case had raised, but not settled, the issue of invasion of privacy. Since the Fourth Edition, new meta-analyses and distinguishing between adverse impact in applicants and present employees has thrown doubt on work samples and assessment centres, which used to be thought 'safe'. Bobko and Roth (1999) have challenged the generally accepted view that structured interviews and biodata cause no adverse impact. Consequently, no test now has a 'no-problem' rating.

Table 15.1   Summary of the operational validity of different selection tests for work performance.

	Early analyses					Later analyses			Minor analyses	
	D	R&C	V&J	H&H	S	W&C	H&A	McD		Reference
Reference										
Interview	16									
Unstructured IV		18[b]		26		47	37	47		
Structured IV		19[b]		14		31	20	33	40	Schmidt & Rader 1999
Empirical IV						62	57	44	62	Salgado et al. 2003
General MA	45			53	25					
Perceptual	34									
Psychomotor	35								42	Salgado 1994
Aptitude			28		27					
Job knowledge	51			48					45	Dye et al. 1993

	Early analyses					Later analyses				Minor analyses	
	D	R&C	V&J	H&H	S	B&M	Tett	Sal	BMJ		Reference
Personality questionnaire	08										
Neuroticism						−07	−22	−13	−11		
Extraversion						10	16	08	11		
Openness						−03	27	06	04		
Agreeableness						06	33	01	09		
Conscientiousness						23	18	15	20		
Honesty test										41	Ones et al. 1993
Customer service										50	Frei & McDaniel 1998
Projective	'little'	18[b]								16–20[b]	Martinussen & Torjussen 1993; Collins et al. 2004
Peer ratings	37[b]			49						58	Norton 1992
Graphology		'none'								21/zero[a]	Neter & Ben-Shakhar 1989

	D	R&C	V&J	H&H	S	Blies	Funk	Drak		
Biodata	34	35								
AC			24	37 43	24 41	30[b]	47	21[b]	37/26	Gaugler et al. 1987 / Hardison & Sackett 2004
Emotional intelligence									24	van Rooy & Viswesvaran 2004
Situational judgement test									26	McDaniel et al. 2007
Self-assessment									08–45	Mabe & West 1982
Physical test				32						
Education		14	25	10					33	Roth et al. 1996
Work sample test				54	38				33	Roth et al. 2005
Trainability test									20–24[b]	Robertson & Downs 1989
In-tray test									28[b]	Robertson & Kandola 1982

[a] 0.21 overall, zero for content free text.
[b] uncorrected validity.

Blies = Bliesener (1996); B&M = Barrick & Mount (1991); BMJ = Barrick, Mount & Judge (2001); D = Dunnette (1972); Drak = Drakeley, in Gunter et al. (1993); Funk = Funke et al. (1987); H&A = Huffcutt & Arthur (1994); H&H = Hunter & Hunter (1984); McD = McDaniel et al. (1994); R&C = Reilly & Chao (1982); Sal = Schmitt et al. (1984); S = Salgado (1997); Tett = Tett et al. (1991); V&J = Vineberg & Joyner (1982); W&C = Wiesner & Cronshaw (1988).

Table 15.2 Summary of 12 selection tests by five criteria.

	Validity	Legal fairness	Acceptability	Cost	Practicality
Interview	Low	Uncertain	High	Med/high	High
Structured iv	High	Some doubts	Some doubts	High	Limited (?)
References	Moderate	Some doubts	Medium	V low	High
Peer rating	High	Untested	Low	V low	V limited
Biodata	High	Some doubts	Low	High	High
Ability test	High	Major doubts	Low	Low	High
Psychomotor	High	Untested	Untested	Low	Moderate
Job knowledge	High	Some doubts	Untested	Low	High
PQ	Variable	Some doubts	Low	Low	Fair
AC	High	Some doubts	High	V high	Fair
Work sample	High	Some doubts	High	High	Moderate
Education	Moderate	Major doubts	Untested	Nil	High

Diversity–validity dilemma

Ployhart and Holtz (2008) described the problem facing HR in the USA. They want to use valid tests to select, but must also achieve a diverse, or representative, workforce. Unfortunately, validity and diversity seem, to some extent, inversely related. The most valid tests tend to create the most adverse impact. Ployhart and Holtz reviewed 16 varied attempts to solve this dilemma, such as score banding, emphasis on personality rather than ability, modifying ability tests, which were all discussed in previous chapters. They suggested using interview, situational judgement tests and biodata, either supplementing ability tests or replacing them, reducing reading and mental ability requirements as far as possible, and using face-valid methods, such as interviews, to try to ensure applicants see the selection process as fair.

Cost tends to be accorded too much weight by selectors. Cost is not an important consideration, so long as the test has validity. A valid test, even the most elaborate and expensive, is almost always worth using. Chapter 13 showed that the return on selection is often considerable, far outweighing its cost. In Table 15.2, interview costs are given as medium / low because interviews vary so much and because they are so much taken for granted that few estimates of their cost have been made. Structured interview costs are high because they have to be written specially for each job. Biodata costs are given as high or low; the cost is high if the inventory has to be specially written for the employer, but might be low if a 'ready-made' consortium biodata could be used. The cost of using educational qualifications is given as nil because the information is routinely collected through application forms. Checking what As say will cost a small amount.

Practicality means the test is not difficult to introduce because it fits into the selection process easily. Ability and personality tests are very practical because they can be given over the Internet or to groups of applicants. References are very practical because everyone is used to giving them. Assessment centres are only fairly practical because they need a lot of organizing. Peer assessments are highly impractical because they require applicants to spend a long time with each other. Structured interviews may have limited practicality because managers may resist the loss of autonomy involved. Work sample and psychomotor tests have limited practicality because candidates have to be tested individually, not in groups.

Acceptability to applicants is important, especially in times of full employment. Ratings are largely based on Hausknecht *et al.*'s (2004) meta-analysis of various surveys, which was described in Chapter 14.

Taking validity as the overriding consideration, there are seven classes of test with high validity: peer ratings, biodata, structured interviews, ability tests, assessment centres, work sample tests and job knowledge tests. Three of these have limited scope. Peer ratings can rarely be used in selection, while work sample and job knowledge tests only work for jobs where specific skills or knowledge are central. This leaves biodata, structured interviews, MA tests and assessment centres.

- Biodata do not achieve quite such good validity as ability tests, and are not as transportable, which makes them more expensive.
- Structured interviews probably have good validity but limited transportability, and are expensive to set up.
- MA tests have excellent validity, can be used for all sorts of job, are readily transportable, are cheap and easy to use, but fall foul of the law in the USA.
- Assessment centres have excellent validity, can be used for most grades of staff, but are difficult to install, expensive and may create adverse impact.
- Work samples have quite good validity but are expensive because they are necessarily specific to the job, and may create adverse impact.
- Job knowledge tests have good validity, are easy to use and are cheap because they are commercially available, but they are more likely to cause legal problems because they are usually paper-and-pencil tests.

Most other tests in Tables 15.1 and 15.2 have lower validity – but not zero validity. Tests with validities below 0.10–0.20 can be worth using if they are cheap, or if they contribute new information. Hence, the only test in Table 15.1 that can be definitely dismissed as never worth using is graphology.

- Personality questionnaires achieve poor validity for predicting work performance, but may prove more useful for predicting other aspects of the applicant's contribution to the organization.
- References have only moderate validity, but are cheap to use. Legal cautions however are tending to limit their value.

Incremental validity

The big gap in present knowledge is the validity of combinations of tests. Schmidt and Hunter (1998) made estimates based on intercorrelations of predictors, and argue that many other tests add little to mental ability tests.

Empirical research on actual incremental validity is as yet relatively thin. Chapter 7 shows that personality tests do contribute incremental validity when used with MA tests. Chapter 11 shows that in-tray exercises contribute incremental validity to tests of mental ability. There remain however a large number of possible combinations of selection methods, where no information about incremental validity is available. Do reference checks improve on personality questionnaires? Is there anything to be gained adding peer ratings to work samples and MA tests? What combination of the methods listed in Tables 15.1 and 15.2 will give the best results, and how good will that 'best' be?

Incompetence + jealousy = 'injelitance'?

The discussion has assumed that all employers genuinely want the best applicants; Northcote Parkinson thinks this is very naive: 'if the head of an organization is second rate, he will see to it that his immediate staff are all third-rate: and they will, in turn, see to it that their subordinates are fourth rate'. Such organizations suffer *injelitance* – 'a disease of induced inferiority', compounded equally of incompetence and jealousy. The 'injelitant' organization does not fill vacancies with stupid people accidentally – dull, smug people at its core deliberately recruit even duller, smugger people, to protect their own positions. And what better way is there to perpetuate incompetence than the traditional interview? Mediocrities can be selected and promoted, using the code words 'soundness', 'teamwork' and 'judgement'. And what greater threat to injelitant organizations can there be than objective tests of ability, which might introduce unwelcome, disruptive 'clever' people? Parkinson thinks injelitance is a terminal illness of organizations, which can only be cured by dismissing all the staff, and burning the buildings to the ground. He does suggest however that 'infected personnel' might be 'dispatched with a warm testimonial to such rival institutions as are regarded with particular hostility'.

The future of selection

This final section offers a number of suggestions about likely trends, under five headings.

Technical refinements

Voice recognition and transcription

Voice recognition and transcription software may soon make it possible to generate transcripts of interviews, group discussions and other AC exercises, very quickly and cheaply. This could prove useful in case of dispute about improper interview questions, for quality checks on interviewers, and to extract far more information and more accurate information from interviews and group exercises.

Computer simulations

Computers can now generate realistic moving images of people moving and talking; this is already done in computer games and in the cinema. It may be possible to generate role plays or other exercises using computer-generated 'customers', 'complainants' or 'appraisees'. These would be more convenient and economical to use, and more consistent than a human role player. The problem with simulations is not so much generating the images and sounds, but providing a plausible and realistic script, and devising software that can characterize the assessee's responses.

Short-term trends in assessment

Testing

Grade inflation, in school and university exams, may devalue educational qualifications and encourage more employers to use ability tests. Already some universities are considering whether to use tests to select students, saying the school exams do not differentiate. Some employers are saying the same about university degrees.

Attributes assessed

Assessing the applicant, as a person, rather than assessing specific abilities that are very closely job-related, may become more common. For example, employers need people who can adapt to new skills and fill a variety of roles. Some employees need to be able to cope with stress. Others need to be able to cope with aggressive or violent customers. Increasing globalization might make it necessary to assess more specifically the ability to fit into other cultures, or work 'away from home', an issue that arises already with expatriate staff. Increasing emphasis on 'security' may create a need to assess for 'security risk', which may prove very difficult for several reasons: faking good and concealment, links with ethnicity, and a low base rate, hence lots of false positives.

Changes in the law

Limits on what HR can assess people by

Brenkert (1993) argued that the 'commercial relationship does not entitle [the employer] to probe the attitudes, motives and beliefs of the person beyond their own statements, record of past actions and the observations of others'. Brenkert's argument would restrict assessment to educational achievement and work experience, results of technical and cognitive tests, 'in-tray' exercises, role playing, group exercises, as well as references and interview structured around the candidate's job knowledge. This links to the idea that HR should only assess the specific ability to carry out the job activities and should therefore only assess specific knowledge and skills. Applicants should not be assessed on any 'non-job-relevant' activities, which excludes leisure interests, lifestyle, possibly also personality. This would severely restrict most 'sifting' systems, which often rely heavily on non-work activity.

Privacy

The idea of a right to privacy is gaining ground and could have implications for selection assessments. Personality tests in particular may be especially vulnerable because they can appear very intrusive to applicants, as well as not sufficiently job-related.

Data protection

Employees now have right of access to personnel files. Applicants have right of access to interview notes, test data and (probably) references. Some organizations list specified materials, (e.g. interview notes) that should be retained in case applicants want to see them (and assessors are warned not to write down anything unsuitable). Suppose assessors were required to keep a detailed record of the whole process; this could include a record of discussions about which of two equally matched applicants gets the job and why.

Factors that might limit legal controls on selection

Globalization

Developed countries like Britain and the USA have to compete with countries where wages are lower and employers are less regulated. Organizations that find it too expensive or onerous to employ people in Europe or North America may move their operations to cheaper, less extensively regulated countries.

'Emergencies'

In wartime, people's rights tend to be suddenly and drastically curtailed. During World War Two, the British government quickly gave itself powers to direct people into any employment where they were needed. The elaborate system of fair employment legislation could disappear very quickly if it seemed to be hindering the country's ability to cope with an external threat.

Broader strategic issues

Psychological contract

Once upon a time, employees and employers had a 'psychological contract': the employee gave loyalty and commitment, in exchange, the employer provided a job for life, with training and promotion, and so on. In the hard times of the 1980s, many employees found the psychological contract 'wasn't worth the paper it wasn't written on'. When employers needed to, they broke the contract and made people redundant, in large numbers. The breaking of the psychological contract should make employees view the organization differently, perhaps more realistically. Employees might be less willing to go beyond their contractual obligations. This might reduce the scope for personality measures because individual differences in organizational citizenship might be less important, or less readily translated into differences in performance.

Power balance

In Britain, since 1979, the power of the trade unions has declined greatly, which has correspondingly increased the power of management. Organizations are free to pursue productivity and profitability. Unsatisfactory or superfluous employees can be 'released'. It could be argued that the easier it is to terminate unsatisfactory staff, the less vital effective selection becomes.

Rising unemployment

An employer who succeeds in recruiting able, productive workers needs fewer of them. If all employers use highly accurate tests to select very productive workers, the number of jobs will shrink, creating more unemployment. If employers start exchanging information, the ungifted could find themselves never even being shortlisted. This has some alarming implications:

- A steadily growing, unemployed, disillusioned and resentful underclass.
- What will all those unemployed people do? Will the government have to bring in work programs to keep them occupied and out of trouble?
- At the other end of the distribution of ability, a shrinking workforce, of more able people, works harder and longer to maximize productivity. In the process, they wear themselves out and have no time left to enjoy life.
- If fewer and fewer people produce more and more, who is going to buy it? How are they going to pay for it?

References

Aamodt M G, Bryan D A & Whitcomb A J (1993) Predicting performance with letters of recommendation. *Public Personnel Management*, **22**, 81–90.

Allen T D, Facteau J D & Facteau C L (2004) Structured interviewing for OCB: construct validity, faking, and the effects of question type. *Human Performance*, **17**, 1–24.

Alonso A (2001) *The Relationship between Cognitive Ability, Big Five, Task and Contextual Performance: A Meta-Analysis*. Unpublished Master's these, Florida International University.

Ambady N & Rosenthal R (1992) Thin slices of expressive behavior as predictors of interpersonal consequences: a meta-analysis. *Psychological Bulletin*, **111**, 256–274.

Anderson N (2004) Editorial – the dark side of the moon: applicant perspectives, negative psychological effects (NPEs), and candidate decision making in selection. *International Journal of Selection and Assessment*, **12**, 1–8.

Anderson N & Witvliet C (2008) Fairness reactions to personnel selection methods: an international comparison between the Netherlands, the United States, France, Spain, Portugal, and Singapore. *International Journal of Selection and Assessment*, **16**, 1–13.

Anderson N, Lievens F, van Dam K & Born, M (2006) A construct–driven investigation of gender differences in a leadership-role assessment center. *Journal of Applied Psychology*, **91**, 555–566.

Anderson V V (1929) *Psychiatry in Industry*. Holt, New York.

Andler E C & Herbst D (2002) *The complete reference checking handbook*, 2nd edn. Amacom, NY.

Anstey E (1977) A 30–year follow–up of the CSSB procedure, with lessons for the future. *Journal of Occupational Psychology*, **50**, 149–159.

Aritzeta A, Swailes S & Senior B (2007) Belbin's team role model: development, validity and applications for team building. *Journal of Management Studies*, **44**, 96–118.

Arnold J D, Rauschenberger J M, Soubel W G & Guion R G (1982) Validation and utility of a strength test for selecting steelworkers. *Journal of Applied Psychology*, **67**, 588–604.

Arthur W, Bell S T, Villado A J & Doverspike D (2006) The use of person–organization fit in employment decision making: an assessment of its criterion-related validity. *Journal of Applied Psychology*, **91**, 786–901.

Arthur W, Day E A, McNelly T L & Edens P S (2003) A meta-analysis of the criterion-related validity of assessment center dimensions. *Personnel Psychology*, **56**, 125–154.

Arthur W, Woehr D J, Akande A & Strong M H (1995) Human resource management in West Africa: practices and perceptions. *International Journal of Human Resource Management*, **6**, 347–367.

Arvey R D & Begalla M E (1975) Analysing the homemaker job using the Position Analysis Questionnaire (PAQ). *Journal of Applied Psychology*, **60**, 513–517.

Arvey R D, Gordon M E, Massengill D P & Mussio, S J (1975) Differential dropout rates of minority and majority job candidates due to 'time lags' between selection procedures. *Personnel Psychology*, **28**, 175–180.

Avolio B J & Waldman D A (1994) Variations in cognitive, perceptual, and psychomotor abilities across the working life span: examining the effects of race, sex, experience, education, and occupational type. *Psychology and Ageing*, **9**, 430–442.

Baehr M E & Orban J A (1989) The role of intellectual abilities and personality characteristics in determining success in higher-level positions. *Journal of Vocational Behavior*, **35**, 270–287.

Banks M H, Jackson P R, Stafford E M & Warr P B (1983) The Job Components Inventory and the analysis of jobs requiring limited skill. *Personnel Psychology*, **36**, 57–66.

Barge B N & Hough L M (1986) Utility of biographical data for predicting job perform-ance. In: L M Hough (ed.) *Utility of temperament, biodata and interest assessment for predicting job performance: a review and integration of the literature*. Army Research Inst., Alexandria, VA.

Barrett G V (1997) An historical perspective on the Nassau County Police entrance examination: Arnold v Ballard (1975) revisited. The *Industrial/Organisational Psychologist*; www.siop.org/tip/backissues/tipoct97/BARRET~1.htm

Barrett G V, Polomsky M D & McDaniel M A (1999) Selection tests for firefighters: a comprehensive review and meta–analysis. *Journal of Business and Psychology*, **13**, 507–513.

Barrick M R & Mount M K (1991) The big five personality dimensions and job perform-ance: a meta-analysis. *Personnel Psychology*, **44**, 1–26.

Barrick M R & Zimmerman R D (2005) Reducing voluntary, avoidable turnover through selection. *Journal of Applied Psychology*, **90**, 159–166.

Barrick M R, Mount M K & Judge T A (2001) Personality and performance at the beginning of the new millennium: what do we know and where do we go next? *International Journal of Selection and Assessment*, **9**, 9–30.

Barrick M R, Shaffer J & DeGrassi S (2008) *A meta-analysis of the relationship between 'peripheral' information and employment interview outcomes*. Paper presented at 23rd Annual Conference of SIOP, San Francisco.

Barthell C N & Holmes D S (1968) High school yearbooks: a nonreactive measure of social isolation in graduates who later became schizophrenic. *Journal of Abnormal Psychology*, **73**, 313–316.

Bartram D (2000) Internet recruitment and selection: kissing frogs to find princes. *International Journal of Selection and Assessment*, **8**, 261–274.

Bartram D (2005) The great eight competencies: a criterion-centric approach to validation. *Journal of Applied Psychology*, **90**, 1185–1203.

Bartram D (2007) Increasing validity with forced-choice criterion measurement formats. *International Journal of Selection and Assessment*, **15**, 263–272.

Bartram D, Lindley P A, Marshall L & Foster J (1995) The recruitment and selection of young people by small businesses. *Journal of Occupational and Organizational Psychology*, **68**, 339–358.

Baxter J C, Brock B, Hill P C & Rozelle R M (1981) Letters of recommendation: a question of value. *Journal of Applied Psychology*, **66**, 296–301.

Becker W C (1960) The matching of behavior rating and questionnaire personality factors. *Psychological Bulletin*, **57**, 201–212.

Becker T E & Colquitt A L (1992) Potential versus actual faking of a biodata form: an analysis along several dimensions of item type. *Personnel Psychology*, **45**, 389–406.

Bell S T (2007) Deep-level composition variables as predictors of team performance: a meta-analysis. *Journal of Applied Psychology*, **92**, 595–615.

Bennett R J & Robinson S L (2000) Development of a measure of workplace deviance. *Journal of Applied Psychology*, **85**, 349–360.

Bernard L C, Walsh R P & Mills M (2005) The Motivation Analysis Test: an historical and contemporary evaluation. *Psychological Reports*, **96**, 464–492.

Berry C M & Sackett P R (2008) *Toward understanding race differences in validity of cognitive ability tests*. Paper presented at 23rd Annual Conference of SIOP, San Francisco.

Berry C M, Gruys M L & Sackett P R (2006) Educational attainment as a proxy for cognitive ability in selection: effects on levels of cognitive ability and adverse impact. *Journal of Applied Psychology*, **91**, 696–705.

Berry C M, Ones D S & Sackett P R (2007) Interpersonal deviance, organizational devi-ance, and their common correlates: a review and meta-analysis. *Journal of Applied Psychology*, **92**, 410–424.

Berry C M, Sackett P R, & Landers R N (2007) Revisiting interview-cognitive ability relationships: attending to specific range restriction mechanisms in meta-analysis. *Personnel Psychology*, **60**, 837–874.

Berry C M, Sackett P R & Tobares V (2007) *A meta-analysis of conditional reasoning tests of aggression*. Paper presented at 22nd Annual Conference of SIOP, NewYork.

Berry C M, Sackett P R & Wiemann S (2007) A review of recent developments in integrity test research. *Personnel Psychology*, **60**, 271–301.

Bertolino M & Steiner D F (2007) Fairness reactions to selection methods: an Italian study. *International Journal of Selection and Assessment*, **15**, 197–205.

Bertrand M & Mullainathan S (2004) Are Emily and Greg more employable than Lakisha and Jamal? A field experiment on labor market discrimination. *American Economic Review*, **94**, 991–1013.

Bewley T F (1999) *Why Don't Wages Fall During a Recession*. Harvard University Press, Boston, MA.

Billsberry J (2007) *Experiencing Recruitment and Selection*. Wiley, Chichester.

Billsberry J, Ambrosini V, Moss–Jones J & Marsh P (2005) Some suggestions for mapping organizational members' sense of fit. *Journal of Business and Psychology*, **19**, 555–570.

Bing M N, Stewart S M, Davison H K, Green P D, McIntyre M D & James L R (2007) An integrative typology of personality assessment for aggression: implications for predicting counterproductive workplace behavior. *Journal of Applied Psychology*, **92**, 722–744.

Bingham W V & Freyd M (1926) *Procedures in Employment Psychology*. Shaw, Chicago.

Birkeland S A, Manson T M, Kisamore J L, Brannick M T & Smith M A (2006) A meta-analytic investigation of job applicant faking on personality measures. *International Journal of Selection and Assessment*, **14**, 317–335.

Bliesener T (1996) Methodological moderators in validating biographical data in personnel selection. *Journal of Occupational and Organizational Psychology*, **69**, 107–120.

Bludau T & Legree P (2008) *Breaking down emotional intelligence: a meta-analysis of EI and GMA*. Paper presented at 23rd Annual Conference of SIOP, San Francisco.

Bobko P & Roth P L (1999) Derivation and implications of a meta-analytic matrix incorporating cognitive ability, alternative predictors, and job performance. *Personnel Psychology*, **52**, 561–589.

Bobko P, Shetzer L & Russell C (1991) Estimating the standard deviation of professors' worth: the effects of frame of reference and presentation order in utility analysis. *Journal of Occupational Psychology*, **64**, 179–188.

Bobko P, Roth P L & Buster M (2005) Work sample selection tests and expected reduction in adverse impact: a cautionary note. *International Journal of Selection and Assessment*, **13**, 1–10.

Bommer W H, Johnson J L, Rich G A, Podsakoff P M & MacKenzie S B (1995) On the interchangeability of objective and subjective measures of employee performance: a meta-analysis. *Personnel Psychology*, **48**, 587–605.

Borkenau P & Liebler A (1993). Convergence of stranger ratings of personality and intelligence with self-ratings, partner ratings, and measured intelligence. *Journal of Personality and Social Psychology*, **65**, 546–553.

Borkenau P, Riemann R, Angleitner A & Spinath FM (2001) Genetic and environmental influences on observed personality: evidence from the German Observational Study of Adult Twins. *Journal of Personality and Social Psychology*, **80**, 655–668.

Borman W C, Penner L A, Allen T D & Motowidlo S J (2001) Personality predictors of citizenship performance. *International Journal of Selection and Assessment*, **9**, 52–69.

Born M P, Kolk N J & van der Flier H (2000) *A meta-analytic study of assessment center construct validity*. Paper presented at 15th Annual Conference of SIOP, New Orleans.

Bowen C C, Swim J K & Jacobs R R (2000) Evaluating gender biases on actual job performance of real people: a meta-analysis. *Journal of Applied Social Psychology*, **30**, 2194–2215.

Bowler M C & Woehr D J (2006) A meta-analytic evaluation of the impact of dimension and exercise factors on assessment center ratings. *Journal of Applied Psychology*, **91**, 1114–1124.

Bozionelos, N (2005) When the inferior candidate is offered the job: the selection interview as a political and power game. *Human Relations*, **58**, 1605–1631.

Bradley K M & Hauenstein N M A (2006) The moderating effects of sample type as evidence of the effects of faking on personality scale correlations and factor structure. *Psychology Science*, **48**, 313–335.

Brannick M T, Michaels C E & Baker D P (1989) Construct validity of in-basket scores. *Journal of Applied Psychology*, **74**, 957–963.

Bray D W & Grant D L (1966) The assessment center in the measurement of potential for business management. *Psychological Monographs*, **80** (17, whole No. 625).

Brenkert G G (1993) Privacy, polygraphs and work. In White T (ed.) *Business Ethics: a Philosophical Reader*. Macmillan, New York.

Brink K E, Lance C E, Bellenger B L, Morrison M A, Scharlau E & Crenshaw J L (2008) *Discriminant validity of a 'next generation' assessment center*. Paper presented at 23rd Annual Conference of SIOP, San Francisco.

Brody N (2006) Beyond g. In: Murphy, KR (ed.) *A critique of Emotional Intelligence: What Are the Problems and How Can They Be Fixed?* Lawrence Erlbaum, Mahwah, NJ.

Brown S H (1981) Validity generalization and situational moderation in the life insurance industry. *Journal of Applied Psychology*, **66**, 664–670.

Brown K G, Le H & Schmidt F L (2006) Specific aptitude theory revisited: is there incremental validity for training performance? *International Journal of Selection and Assessment*, **14**, 87–100.

Brtek M D & Motowidlo S J (2002) Effects of procedure and outcome accountability on interview validity. *Journal of Applied Psychology*, **87**, 185–191.

Bureau of National Affairs (1995) Hiring. *Personnel Management*, **201**, 284–285.

Burns G N & Christiansen N D (2006) Sensitive or senseless: on the use of social desirability measures in selection and assessment. In: R L Griffith & M H Peterson (eds) *A Closer Examination of Applicant Faking Behavior*. Information Age Publishing, Greenwich, CT.

Buss D M & Craik K H (1983) The act frequency approach to personality. *Psychological Review*, **90**, 105–126.

Buster M A, Roth P L & Bobko P (2005) A process for content validation of education and experience-based minimum qualifications: an approach resulting in federal court approval. *Personnel Psychology*, **58**, 771–799.

Callender J C & Osburn H G (1981) Testing the constancy of validity with computer-generated sampling distributions of the multiplicative model variance estimate: results for petroleum industry validation research. *Journal of Applied Psychology*, **66**, 274–281.

Campbell C C, Ford P, Rumsey M G, Pulakos E D, Borman W C, Felker D B, de Vera M V & Riegelhaupt B J (1990) Development of multiple job performance measures in a representative sample of jobs. *Personnel Psychology*, **43**, 277–300.

Carey N B (1991) Setting standards and diagnosing training needs with surrogate job performance measures. *Military Psychology*, **3**, 135–150.

Carey N B (1994) Computer predictors of mechanical job performance: Marine Corps findings. *Military Psychology*, **6**, 1–30.

Carroll S J & Nash A N (1972) Effectiveness of a forced-choice reference check. *Personnel Administration*, **35**, 42–46.

Carlson K D, Scullen S E, Schmidt F L, Rothstein H & Erwin F (1999) Generalizable biographical data validity can be achieved without multi-organizational development and keying. *Personnel Psychology*, **52**, 731–755.

Cascio WF & Anguinis H (2005) Test development and use: new twists on old questions. *Human Resource Management*, **44**, 219–235.

Cattell R B (1937) *The Fight for Our National Intelligence*. P S King, London.

Cattell R B & Warburton F W (1967) *Objective Personality and Motivation Tests.* University of Illinois Press, Urbana.

Cervantes M (1607/1950) *Don Quixote.* Penguin, Harmondsworth.

Chaffin D B (1974) Human strength capability and low back pain. *Journal of Occupational Medicine,* **16**, 248–254.

Chan D & Schmitt N (1997) Video-based versus paper-and-pencil method of assessment in situational judgement tests: subgroup differences in test performance and face validity perceptions. *Journal of Applied Psychology,* **82**, 143–159.

Chapman D S & Webster J (2003) The use of technologies in the recruiting, screening, and selection processes for job candidates. *International Journal of Selection and Assessment,* **11**, 113–120.

Chapman D S, Uggerslev K L, & Webster J (2003). Applicant reactions to face-to-face and technology-mediated interviews: a field investigation. *Journal of Applied Psychology,* **88**, 944–953.

Chartered Institute of Personnel and Development (2006) *Annual Survey Report 2006: Recruitment, Retention and Turnover.* CIPD, London.

Christiansen N D, Goffin R D, Johnston N G & Rothstein M G (1994) Correcting the 16PF for faking: effects on criterion-related validity and individual hiring decisions. *Personnel Psychology,* **47**, 847–860.

Chung–yan G A & Cronshaw S F (2002) A critical re-examination and analysis of cognitive ability tests using the Thorndike model of fairness. *Journal of Occupational and Organizational Psychology,* **75**, 489–509.

Clark T (1992) Management selection by executive recruitment consultancies. *Journal of Managerial Psychology,* **7**, 3–10.

Clarke S & Robertson I (2007). An examination of the role of personality in work accidents using meta-analysis. *Applied Psychology: an International Review,* **57**, 94–108.

Coil J H & Shapiro L J (1996) The ADA at three years: a statute in flux. *Employee Relations Law Journal,* **21**, 5–38.

Colarelli S M, Hechanova-Alampay R & Canali K G (2002) Letters of recommendation: an evolutionary psychological perspective. *Human Relations,* **55**, 315–344.

Coleman V I & Borman W C (2000) Investigating the underlying structure of the citizenship performance domain. *Human Resource Management Review,* **10**, 25–44.

Collins C J, Hanges P J & Locke E A (2004) The relationship of achievement motivation to entrepreneurial behavior: a meta-analysis. *Human Performance,* **17**, 95–117.

Collins J M, Schmidt F L, Sanchez-Ku, M, Thomas, L, McDaniel, M A & Le, H (2003) Can basic individual differences shed light on the construct meaning of assessment center evaluations? *International Journal of Selection and Assessment,* **11**, 17–29.

Combs J, Yongmei L, Hall A & Ketchen D (2006) How much do high-performance work practices matter? A meta-analysis of their effects on organizational performance. *Personnel Psychology,* **59**, 501–528.

Commission for Racial Equality. (1990) *Lines of Progress: an Enquiry into Selection and Equal opportunities in London Underground.* CRE, London.

Commission for Racial Equality. (1996) *A Fair Test? Selecting Train Drivers at British Rail.* CRE, London.

Connelly B S & Ones D S (2008) *Interrater reliability in assessment center ratings: a meta-analysis.* Paper presented at 23rd Annual Conference of SIOP, San Francisco.

Connolly J J, Kavanagh E J & Viswesvaran C (2007) The convergent validity between self and observer ratings of personality: a meta-analytic review. *International Journal of Selection and Assessment,* **15**, 110–117.

Conte J M, Dean M A, Ringenbach K L, Moran S K & Landy F J (2005) The relationship between work attitudes and job analysis ratings: do rating scale type and task discretion matter? *Human Performance,* **18**, 1–21.

Converse P D, Oswald F L, Gillespie M A, Field K A & Bizot E B (2004) Matching individuals to occupations using abilities and the O*NET. *Personnel Psychology,* **57**, 451–487.

Conway J M & Huffcutt A I (1997) Psychometric properties of multisource perform-ance ratings: a meta-analysis of subordinate, supervisor, peer, and self-ratings. *Human Performance*, **10**, 331–360.

Conway J M, Jako R A & Goodman D F (1995) A meta-analysis of interrater and inter-nal consistency reliability of selection interviews. *Journal of Applied Psychology*, **80**, 565–579.

Conway J M, Lombardo K & Sanders K C (2001) A meta-analysis of incremental valid-ity and nomological networks for subordinate and peer ratings. *Human Performance*, **14**, 267–303.

Cook M (1993) *Levels of Personality*, 2nd edn. Cassell, London.

Cook M (1995) Performance appraisal and true performance. *Journal of Managerial Psychology*, **10**, 3–7.

Cook M, Cripps B, Eysenck H J & Eysenck S B G (2007) *Eysenck Cripps Cook Occupational Scales: Technical Manual*. ECCOS Partnership, Dartington.

Corr P J & Gray J A (1995). Attributional style, socialization and cognitive ability as predictors of sales success: a predictive validity study. *Personality and Individual Differences*, **18**, 241–252.

Correll S J, Benard S & Paik I (2007) Getting a job: is there a motherhood penalty? *American Journal of Sociology*, **112**, 1297–1338.

Cortina J M, Goldstein N B, Payne S C, Davison H K & Gilliland S W (2000) The incremental validity of interview scores over and above cognitive ability and conscientiousness scores. *Personnel Psychology*, **53**, 325–351.

Coward W M & Sackett P R (1990) Linearity of ability–performance relationships: a reconfirmation. *Journal of Applied Psychology*, **75**, 297–300.

Crites J O (1969) *Vocational Psychology*. McGraw Hill, New York.

Cronbach L J (1980) Selection theory for a political world. *Public Personnel Management Journal*, **9**, 37–50.

Cronbach L J (1970) *Essentials of Psychological Testing*, 3rd edn. Harper and Row, New York.

Croteau J M (1996) Research on the work experiences of lesbian, gay and bisexual people: an integrative review of methodology and findings. *Journal of Vocational Behavior*, **48**, 195–209.

Cucina J M, Vasilopoulos N L & Sehgal K G (2005) Personality-based job analysis and the self-serving bias. *Journal of Business and Psychology*, **20**, 275–290.

Dalal R S (2005) A meta-analysis of the relationship between organizational citizenship behavior and counterproductive work behavior. *Journal of Applied Psychology*, **90**, 1241–1255

Dany F & Torchy V (1994) Recruitment and selection in Europe: policies, practices and methods. In: C Brewster & A Hegewisch (eds.) *Policy and Practice in European Human Resource Management: the Price Waterhouse Cranfield Survey*. Routledge, London.

Davison H K & Burke M J (2000) Sex discrimination in simulated employment contexts: a meta-analytic investigation. *Journal of Vocational Behavior*, **56**, 225–248

Day A L & Carroll S A (2003) Situational and patterned behavior description inter-views: a comparison of their validity, correlates, and perceived fairness. *Human Performance*, **16**, 25–47.

Dayan K, Kasten R & Fox S (2002) Entry-level police candidate assessment center: an efficient tool or a hammer to kill a fly? *Personnel Psychology*, **55**, 827–849.

Dean M A, Roth P L & Bobko P (2008) Ethnic and gender subgroup differences in assess-ment center ratings: a meta-analysis. *Journal of Applied Psychology*, **93**, 685–691.

DeGroot T & Kluemper D (2007) Evidence of predictive and incremental validity of personality factors, vocal attractiveness and the situational interview. *International Journal of Selection and Assessment*, **15**, 30–39.

Derous E, Nguyen H H & Ryan A M (2008) *Do applicants with an Arab-sounding name suffer more hiring discrimination?* Paper presented at 23rd Annual Conference of SIOP, San Francisco.

Devlin S E, Abrahams N M & Edwards J E (1992) Empirical keying of biographical data: cross-validity as a function of scaling procedure and sample size. *Military Psychology*, **4**, 119–136.

Dick P & Nadin S (2006) Reproducing gender inequalities? A critique of realist assumptions underpinning personnel selection and practice. *Journal of Occupational and Organizational Psychology*, **79**, 481–498.

Dierdorff E C & Morgeson F P (2007) Consensus in work role requirements: the influence of discrete occupational context on role expectations. *Journal of Applied Psychology*, **92**, 1228–1241.

Dierdorff E C & Wilson M A (2003) A meta-analysis of job analysis reliability. *Journal of Applied Psychology*, **88**, 635–646.

Dilchert S, Ones D S, Davis R D & Rostow C D (2007) Cognitive ability predicts objectively measured counterproductive work behaviors. *Journal of Applied Psychology*, **92**, 616–627.

Di Milia, L (2004) Australian management selection practices: closing the gap between research findings and practice. *Asia Pacific Journal of Human Resources*, **42**, 214–228.

Ding V J & Stillman J A (2005) An empirical investigation of discrimination against overweight female job applicants in New Zealand. *New Zealand Journal of Psychology*, **34**, 139–148.

Dorcus R M & Jones M H (1950) *Handbook of Employee Selection*. McGraw Hill, New York.

Dose J J (2003) Information exchange in personnel selection decisions. *Applied Psychology: an International Review*, **52**, 237–252.

Dubois C L Z, Sackett P R, Zedeck S & Fogli, L (1993) Further exploration of typical and maximum performance criteria: definitional issues, prediction, and white–black differences. *Journal of Applied Psychology*, **78**, 205–211.

Dudley N M, Orvis K A, Lebiecki J E & Cortina J M (2006) A meta-analytic investigation of conscientiousness in the prediction of job performance: examining the intercorrelations and the incremental validity of narrow traits. *Journal of Applied Psychology*, **91**, 40–57.

Dulewicz S V & Keenay G A (1979) A practically oriented and objective method for classifying and assigning senior jobs. *Journal of Occupational Psychology*, **52**, 155–166.

Dunnette M D (1972) *Validity Study Results for Jobs Relevant to the Petroleum Refining Industry*. American Petroleum Institute, Washington, DC.

Dunning D, Heath C & Suls J M (2004) Flawed self-assessment: implications for health, education, and the workplace. *Psychological Science in the Public Interest*, **5**, 69–106.

Duval S J (2005) The trim and fill method. In: H R Rothstein, A J Sutton & M Borenstein (eds) *Publication Bias in Meta-Analysis: Prevention, Assessment and Adjustments*. Wiley, Chichester, UK.

Dwight S A & Donovan J J (2003) Do warnings not to fake reduce faking? *Human Performance*, **16**, 1–23.

Dye D A, Reck M & McDaniel M A (1993) The validity of job knowledge measures. *International Journal of Selection and Assessment*, **1**, 153–157.

Eaton N K, Wing H & Mitchell K J (1985) Alternate methods of estimating the dollar value of performance. *Personnel Psychology*, **38**, 27–40.

Edwards B D & Arthur W (2007) An examination of factors contributing to a reduction in subgroup differences on a constructed-response paper-and-pencil test of scholastic achievement. *Journal of Applied Psychology*, **92**, 794–801.

Ekman P & O'Sullivan M (1991) Who can catch a liar? *American Psychologist*, **46**, 913–920.

Elliott S, Lawty-Jones M & Jackson C (1996) Effect of dissimulation on self-report and objective measures of personality. *Personality and Individual Differences*, **21**, 335–343.

Ellingson J E, Sackett P R & Hough L M (1999) Social desirability corrections in personality measurement: issues of applicant comparison and construct validity. *Journal of Applied Psychology*, **84**, 155–166.

Ellis A P J, West B J, Ryan A M & DeShon, R P (2002) The use of impression management tactics in structured interviews: a function of question type? *Journal of Applied Psychology*, **87**, 1200–1208.

Equal Opportunities Commission (EOC). (2005). *Discrimination in Recruitment Methods.* www.eoc-law.org.uk.

Eysenck H J (1967) The Biological Basis of Personality. CC Thomas, Springfield, IL.

Facteau J D & Craig S B (2001) Are performance appraisal ratings from different rating sources comparable? *Journal of Applied Psychology*, **86**, 215–227.

Farrell J N & McDaniel M A (2001) The stability of validity coefficient over time: Ackerman's (1988) model and the General Aptitude Test Battery. *Journal of Applied Psychology*, **86**, 60–79

Farrell S & Hakstian A R (2001) Improving salesforce performance: a meta-analytic investigation of the effectiveness and utility of personnel selection procedures and training interventions. *Psychology and Marketing*, **18**, 281–316.

Fast LA & Funder D C (2008) Personality as manifest in word use: correlations with self-report, acquaintance report, and behavior. *Journal of Personality and Social Psychology*, **94**, 334–346.

Feigelson M E & Dwight S A (2000) Can asking questions by computer improve the candidness of responding? *Consulting Psychology Journal: Practice and Research*, **52**, 248–255. .

Feltham R (1988) Assessment centre decision making: judgemental vs. mechanical. *Journal of Occupational Psychology*, **61**, 237–241.

Ferreter J M, Goldstein H W, Scherbaum C A, Yusko K P & Jun H (2008) *Examining adverse impact using a nontraditional cognitive ability assessment.* Paper presented at 23rd Annual Conference of SIOP, San Francisco.

Fikkan J & Rothblum E (2005) Weight bias in employment. In: K D Brownell, R M Puhl, M B Schwartz & L Rudd (eds) *Weight Bias: Nature, Consequences, and Remedies.* Guilford Press, New York.

Flanagan J C (1946) The experimental validation of a selection procedure. *Educational and Psychological Measurement*, **6**, 445–466.

Flanagan J C (1954) The critical incident technique. *Psychological Bulletin*, **51**, 327–358.

Fleenor JW & Brutus S (2001) Multisource feedback for personnel decisions. In: D W Bracken, C W Timmreck & A H Church (eds) *The Handbook of Multisource Feedback: the Comprehensive Resource for Designing and Implementing MSF Processes.* Jossey Bass, San Francisco.

Ford J K, Kraiger K & Schechtman S L (1986) Study of race effects in objective indices and subjective evaluations of performance: a meta-analysis of performance criteria. *Psychological Bulletin*, **99**, 330–337.

Ford L A, Campbell R C, Campbell J P, Knapp D J & Walker C B (1999) *21st Century Soldiers and Non-Commissioned Officers: Critical Predictors of Performance* (FR-EADD-99-45). HumRRO, Alexandria, VA.

Ford M E & Tisak M S (1983) A further search for social intelligence. *Journal of Educational Psychology*, **75**, 196–206.

Foster J J, Wilkie D & Moss B (1996) Selecting university lecturers: what is and should be done. *International Journal of Selection and Assessment*, **4**, 122–128.

Frei R L & McDaniel M A (1998) Validity of customer service measures in personnel selection: a review of criterion and construct evidence. *Human Performance*, **11**, 1–27.

Funder D C (2007) *The Personality Puzzle*, 4th edn. Norton, New York.

Funke U, Krauss J, Schuler H & Stapf K H (1987) Zur Prognostizierbarkeit wissenschaftlich–technischer Leistungen mittels Personvariablen: eine Metaanalyse der Validitat diagnosticher Verfahren im Bereich Forschung und Entwicklung. *Gruppendynamik*, **18**, 407–428.

Furnham A (2006) Explaining the popularity of emotional intelligence. In K R Murphy (ed) *A Critique of Emotional Intelligence: What Are the Problems and How Can They Be Fixed?* Lawrence Erlbaum, Mahwah, NJ.

Furnham A & Dissou G (2007) The relationship between self-estimated and test-derived scores of personality and intelligence. *Journal of Individual Differences*, **28**, 37–44.

Gaugler B B & Thornton G C (1989) Number of assessment center dimensions as a determinant of assessor accuracy. *Journal of Applied Psychology*, **74**, 611–618.

Geisinger K F, Boodoo G & Noble J P (2002) The psychometrics of testing individuals with disabilities. In: R B Ekstrom & D K Smith (eds) *Assessing Individuals with Disabilities in Educational, Employment and Counseling Settings*. APA, Washington DC.

Ghiselli E E (1966a) The validity of a personnel interview. *Personnel Psychology*, **19**, 389–394.

Ghiselli E E (1966b) *The Validity of Occupational Aptitude Tests*. Wiley, New York.

Ghiselli E E (1973) The validity of aptitude tests in personnel selection. *Personnel Psychology*, **26**, 461–477.

Ghiselli E E & Barthol R P (1953) The validity of personality inventories in the selection of employees. *Journal of Applied Psychology*, **37**, 18–20.

Gibson W M & Caplinger J A (2007) Transportation of validation results. In: S M McPhail (ed) *Alternative Validation Strategies: Developing New and Leveraging Existing Validity Evidence*. Wiley, New York.

Gilliland S W (1993) The perceived fairness of selection systems: an organizational justice perspective. *Academy of Management Review*, **18**, 694–734.

Glennon J R, Albright L E & Owens W A (1962) *A catalog of life history items*. American Psychological Association, Chicago.

Goffin R D, Rothstein M G & Johnston N G (1996) Personality testing and the assessment center: incremental validity for managerial selection. *Journal of Applied Psychology*, **81**, 746–756.

Goheen H W & Mosel J N (1959) Validity of the Employment Recommendation Questionnaire: II. Comparison with field investigations. *Personnel Psychology*, **12**, 297–301.

Goldsmith D B (1922) The use of the personal history blank as a salesmanship test. *Journal of Applied Psychology*, **6**, 149–155.

Goldstein I L (1971) The application blank: how honest are the responses? *Journal of Applied Psychology*, **55**, 491–492.

Goleman D (1995) *Emotional Intelligence*. Bantam, New York.

Gordon H W & Leighty R (1988) Importance of specialised cognitive function in the selection of military pilots. *Journal of Applied Psychology*, **73**, 38–45.

Gordon R A & Arvey R D (2004) Age bias in laboratory and field settings: a meta-analytic investigation. *Journal of Applied Social Psychology*, **34**, 468–492.

Gosling S D, John O P, Craik K H & Robins R W (1998) Do people know how they behave? Self-reported act frequencies compared with on-line codings by observers. *Journal of Personality and Social Psychology*, **74**, 1337–1349.

Gottfredson L S (1997) Why g matters: the complexity of everyday life. *Intelligence*, **24**, 79–132.

Graham K E, McDaniel M A, Douglas E F & Snell A F (2002) Biodata validity decay and score inflation with faking: do item attributes explain variance across items. *Journal of Business Psychology*, **16**, 573–592.

Graziano W G, Jensen–Campbell L A & Hair E C (1996) Perceiving interpersonal conflict and reacting to it: the case for agreeableness. *Journal of Personality and Social Psychology*, **70**, 820–835.

Griffeth R W, Hom P W, Gaertner S (2000) A meta-analysis of antecedents and corre-lates of employee turnover: update, moderator tests, and research implications for the next millennium. *Journal of Management*, **26**, 463–488.

Grote C L, Robiner W N & Haut A (2001) Disclosure of negative information in letters of recommendation: writers' intentions and readers' experience. *Professional Psychology: Research and Practice*, **32**, 655–661.

Griffith R L, Chmielowski T & Yoshita Y (2007) Do applicants fake? An examination of the frequency of applicant faking behavior. *Personnel Review*, **36**, 341–355.

Grove W M, Zald D H, Lebow B S, Snitz B E & Nelson C (2000) Clinical versus mechanical prediction: a meta–analysis. *Psychological Assessment*, **12**, 19–30.

Grubb W L & McDaniel M A (2007) The fakability of Bar-On's Emotional Quotient Inventory short form: catch me if you can. *Human Performance*, **20**, 43–59.

Gruys M L & Sackett P R (2003) Investigating the dimensionality of counterproductive work behavior. *International Journal of Selection and Assessment*, **11**, 30–42.

Guilford J P (1959) *Personality*. McGraw Hill, New York.

Guion R M (1965) *Personnel Testing*. McGraw-Hill, New York

Guion R M & Gottier R F (1965) Validity of personality measures in personnel selection. *Personnel Psychology*, **18**, 135–164.

Gunter B, Furnham A & Drakeley R (1993) *Biodata: biographical indicators of business performance*. Routledge, London.

Hagan C M, Konopaske R, Bernardin H J & Tyler C L (2006) Predicting assessment center performance with 360-degree, top-down, and customer-based competency assessments. *Human Resource Management*, **45**, 357–390.

Hambleton A J, Kalliath T & Taylor P (2000) Criterion-related validity of a measure of person-job and person-organization fit. *New Zealand Journal of Psychology*, **29**, 80–85.

Hardison C M & Sackett P R (2007) Kriterienbezogene Validitat des Assessment Centers: lebendig und wohlauf? In: H Schuler (ed) *Assessment Center zur Potenzialanalyse*. Hogrefe, Gottingen.

Harpe L G (2008) *Test validity: a multiple stakeholder approach, enforcement agency perspective*. Paper presented at 23rd Annual Conference of SIOP, San Francisco.

Harris L (2000) Procedural justice and perceptions of fairness in selection practice. *International Journal of Selection and Assessment*, **8**, 148–157.

Harris M M & Trusty M L (1997) Drug and alcohol programs in the workplace: a review of recent literature. In: I Robertson & C Cooper (eds) *International Review of Industrial and Organisational Psychology*. John Wiley & Sons, Chichester.

Harris M M, Dworkin J B & Park J (1990) Preemployment screening procedures: how human resource managers perceive them. *Journal of Business and Psychology*, **4**, 279–292.

Hartigan J A & Wigdor A K (1989) *Fairness in Employment Testing*. National Academy Press, Washington, DC.

Hartshorne H & May M A (1928) *Studies in the Nature of Character. I Studies in Deceit*. Macmillan, New York.

Harvey-Cook J E & Taffler R J (2000) Biodata in professional entry-level selection: statistical scoring of common format applications. *Journal of Occupational and Organizational Psychology*, **73**, 103–118.

Hausknecht J P, Day D V & Thomas S C (2004) Applicant reactions to selection procedures: an updated model and meta-analysis. *Personnel Psychology*, **57**, 639–683.

Hausknecht J P, Halpert J A, Di Paolo N T & Gerrard M O M (2007) Retesting in selection: a meta-analysis of coaching and practice effects for tests of cognitive ability. *Journal of Applied Psychology*, **92**, 373–385.

Hebl M R & Mannix L M (2003) The weight of obesity in evaluating others: a mere proximity effect. *Personality and Social Psychology Bulletin*, **29**, 28–38.

Hebl M R, Foster J B, Mannix L M & Dovidio J F (2002) Formal and interpersonal discrimination: a field study of bias toward homosexual applicants. *Personality and Social Psychology Bulletin*, **28**, 815–825.

Heggestad E D, Morrison M, Reeve C L & McCloy R A (2006) Forced-choice assessments of personality for selection: evaluating issues of normative assessment and faking resistance. *Journal of Applied Psychology*, **91**, 9–24.

Henle C A (2004) Case review of the legal status of banding. *Human Performance*, **17**, 415–432.

Herriot P (1992) Selection: the two subcultures. *European Work and Organizational Psychologist*, **2**, 129–140.

Herrnstein R J (1973) *IQ in the Meritocracy*. Allen Lane, London.

Herrnstein R J & Murray C (1994) *The Bell Curve: Intelligence and Class Structure in American Life*. Free Press, New York.

Hersch J (1991) Education match and job match. *Review of Economics and Statistics*, **73**, 140–144.

Hershcovis M S, Turner N, Barling J, Arnold K A, Dupre K E, Inness M, LeBlanc M M & Sivanathan N (2007) Predicting workplace aggression: a meta-analysis. *Journal of Applied Psychology*, **92**, 228–238.

Higuera L A (2001) Adverse impact in personnel selection: the legal framework and test bias. *European Psychologist*, **6**, 103–111.

Hirsh H R, Northrop L C & Schmidt F L (1986) Validity generalization results for law enforcement occupations. *Personnel Psychology*, **39**, 399–420.

Hitt M A & Barr S H (1989) Managerial selection decision models: examination of configural cue processing. *Journal of Applied Psychology*, **74**, 53–61.

Hochwarter W A, Witt L A & Kacmar K M (2000) Perceptions of organizational politics as a moderator of the relationship between conscientiousness and job performance. *Journal of Applied Psychology*, **85**, 472–478.

Hoffman B J, Blair C A, Meriac J P & Woehr D J (2007). Expanding the criteria domain? A quantitative review of the OCB literature. *Journal of Applied Psychology*, **92**, 555–566.

Hoffman C C (1999) Generalizing physical ability test validity: a case study using test transportability, validity generalization, and construct-related validation evidence. *Personnel Psychology*, **52**, 1019–1041.

Hoffman C C, Holden L M & Gale K (2000) So many jobs, so little 'N': applying expanded validation models to support generalization of cognitive test validity. *Personnel Psychology*, **53**, 955–991.

Hoffman C C, Nathan B R & Holden L M (1991) A comparison of validation criteria: objective versus subjective performance and self- versus supervisor ratings. *Personnel Psychology*, **44**, 601–619.

Hofstede G (2001) *Culture's Consequences*. Sage, Thousand Oaks, CA.

Hogan J (1991) Physical abilities. In: M D Dunnette & L M Hough (eds) *Handbook of Industrial and Organizational Psychology*. Consulting Psychologists Press, Palo Alto, CA.

Hogan J & Holland B (2003) Using theory to evaluate personality and job-performance relations: a socioanalytic perspective. *Journal of Applied Psychology*, **88**, 100–112.

Hogan J, Davies S & Hogan S (2007) Generalizing personality-based validity evidence. In: S M McPhail (ed) *Alternative Validation Strategies: Developing New and Leveraging Existing Validity Evidence*. Jossey-Bass, San Francisco.

Hogan J, Barrett P & Hogan R (2007) Personality measurement, faking, and employment selection. *Journal of Applied Psychology*, **92**, 1270–1285.

Holden R R & Hibbs N (1995) Incremental validity of response latencies for detecting fakers on a personality test. *Journal of Research in Personality*, **29**, 362–372.

Holden R R, Wood L L & Tomashewski L (2001) Do response time limitations counteract the effect of faking on personality inventory validity? *Journal of Applied Psychology*, **81**, 160–169.

Hoque K & Noon M (1999) Racial discrimination in speculative applications: new optimism six years on? *Human Resource Management Journal*, **9**, 71–82.

Hough L M (1992) The 'big five' personality variables – construct confusion: description versus prediction. *Human Performance*, **5**, 139–155.

Hough L M (1998) Personality at work: issues and evidence. In: M Hakel (ed.) *Beyond Multiple Choice: Evaluating Alternatives to Traditional Testing for Selection*. Erlbaum, Mahwah NJ.

Hough L, Barge B & Kamp J (2001). Assessment of personality, temperament, vocational interests, and work outcome preferences. In: J P Campbell & D J Knapp (eds) *Exploring the Limits of Personnel Selection and Classification*. Lawrence Erlbaum, Mahwah, NJ.

Hough L M, Eaton N K, Dunnette M D, Kamp J D & McCloy R A (1990) Criterion-related validities of personality constructs and the effect of response distortion on those validities. *Journal of Applied Psychology*, **75**, 581–595.

Hough L M, Oswald F L & Ployhart R E (2001) Determinants, detection and amelioration of adverse impact in personnel selection procedures: issues, evidence and lessons learned. *International Journal of Selection and Assessment*, **9**, 152–194.

Houston W M & Novick M R (1987) Race-based differential prediction in Air Force technical training programs. *Journal of Educational Measurement*, **24**, 309–320.

Howard A (1997) A reassessment of assessment centers: challenges for the 21st century. *Journal of Social Behavior and Personality*, **12**, 13–52.

Huffcutt A I & Arthur W (1994) Hunter and Hunter (1984) revisited: interview validity for entry–level jobs. *Journal of Applied Psychology*, **79**, 184–190.

Huffcutt A I & Woehr D J (1999) Further analysis of employment interview validity: a quantitative evaluation of interviewer-related structuring methods. *Journal of Organizational Behavior*, **20**, 549–560.

✓Huffcutt A I, Conway J M, Roth P L & Klehe U C (2004) The impact of job complexity and study design on situational and behavior description interview validity. *International Journal of Selection and Assessment*, **12**, 262–273.

Huffcutt A I, Conway J M, Roth P L & Stone N J (2001) Identification and meta-analytic assessment of psychological constructs measured in employment interviews. *Journal of Applied Psychology*, **86**, 897–913.

Huffcutt A I, Roth P L & McDaniel M A (1996) A meta-analytic investigation of cognitive ability in employment interview evaluations: moderating characteristics and implications for incremental validity. *Journal of Applied Psychology*, **81**, 459–473.

Hughes J F, Dunn J F & Baxter B (1956) The validity of selection instruments under operating conditions. *Personnel Psychology*, **9**, 321–324.

Hull C L (1928) *Aptitude Testing*. Harrap, London.

Hunter A E, Vasilopoulos N L, Marton N R & Cucina J M (2008). *Revisiting P=f(A×M): the roles of tenure and performance domain*. Paper presented at 23rd Annual Conference of SIOP, San Francisco.

Hunter D R & Burke E F (1996) Predicting aircraft pilot-training success: a meta analysis of published research. *International Journal of Aviation Psychology*, **4**, 297–313.

Hunter J E (1983) A causal analysis of cognitive ability, job knowledge, and supervisory ratings. In: F Landy, S Zedeck & J Cleveland (eds) *Performance Measurement and Theory*. Erlbaum, Hillsdale, NJ.

Hunter J E (1986) Cognitive ability, cognitive aptitudes, job knowledge, and job performance. *Journal of Vocational Behavior*, **29**, 340–362.

Hunter J E & Hunter R F (1984) Validity and utility of alternative predictors of job performance. *Psychological Bulletin*, **96**, 72–98.

Hunter J E & Schmidt F L (1996) Intelligence and job performance: economic and social implications. *Psychology, Public Policy and Law*, **2**, 447–472.

Hunter J E & Schmidt F L (2004) *Methods of Meta-Analysis: Correcting Error and Bias in Research Findings*, 2nd edn. Sage, Thousand Oaks CA.

Hunthausen J M, Truxillo D M, Bauer T N & Hammer L B (2003) A field study of frame-of-reference effects on personality test validity. *Journal of Applied Psychology*, **88**, 545–551.

Huo Y P, Huang H J & Napier N K (2002) Divergence or convergence: a cross-national comparison of personnel selection practices. *Human Resource Management*, **41**, 31–44.

Hurtz G M & Donovan J J (2000) Personality and job performance: the big five revisited. *Journal of Applied Psychology*, **85**, 869–879.

Huselid M A, Jackson S E & Schuler R S (1997) Technical and strategic human resource management effectiveness as determinants of firm performance. *Academy of Management Journal*, **40**, 171–188.

Isaacson J A & Griffith R L (2007) *Sex and faking: implications for selection decisions.* Paper presented at 22nd Annual Conference of SIOP, New York.

Isaacson J A, Griffith R L, Kung M C, Lawrence A & Wilson K A (2008) *Liar, liar: examining background checks and applicants who fail them.* Paper presented at 23rd Annual Conference of SIOP, San Francisco.

Janz T (1982) Initial comparisons of patterned behavior description interviews versus unstructured interviews. *Journal of Applied Psychology*, **67**, 577–580.

Jawahar I M & Williams C R (1997) Where all the children are above average: the performance appraisal purpose effect. *Personnel Psychology*, **50**, 905–925.

Jeanneret P R (1992) Application of job component/synthetic validity to construct validity. *Human Performance*, **5**, 81–96.

Jeanneret P R & Strong M H (2003) Linking O*NET job analysis information to job requirement predictors: an O*NET application. *Journal of Applied Psychology*, **56**, 465–492.

Jones A & Harrison E (1982) Prediction of performance in initial officer training using reference reports. *Journal of Occupational Psychology*, **55**, 35–42.

Jones R G, Sanchez J I, Parameswaran G, Phelps J, Shoptaugh C, Williams M & White S (2001) Selection or training? A two-fold test of the validity of job-analytic ratings of trainability. *Journal of Business Psychology*, **15**, 363–389.

Judge T A & Cable D M (2004) The effect of physical height on workplace success and income: preliminary test of a theoretical model. *Journal of Applied Psychology*, **89**, 428–441.

Judge T A & Higgins C A (1998) Affective disposition and the letter of reference. *Organizational Behavior and Human Decision Processes*, **75**, 207–221.

Judge T A, Colbert A E & Ilies R (2004) Intelligence and leadership: a quantitative review and test of theoretical propositions. *Journal of Applied Psychology*, **89**, 542–552.

Judge T A, Bono J E, Ilies R & Gerhardt M W (2002) Personality and leadership: a qualitative and quantitative review. *Journal of Applied Psychology*, **87**, 765–780.

Judge T A, Higgins C A, Thoresen C J & Barrick M R (1999) The big five personality traits, general mental ability, and career success across the life span. *Personnel Psychology*, **52**, 621–652.

Judiesch M K (2001) Using estimates of the output productivity ratio (SDp) to improve the accuracy and managerial acceptance of utility analysis estimates. *Journal of Business Psychology*, **16**, 165–176.

Judiesch M K & Schmidt F L (2000) Between–worker variability in output under piece–rate versus hourly pay systems. *Journal of Business Psychology*, **14**, 529–551.

Kalin R & Rayko D S (1978) Discrimination in evaluative judgements against foreign accented job candidates. *Psychological Reports*, **43**, 1203–1209.

Kanning U P, Grewe K, Hollenberg S & Hadouch M (2006) From the subjects' point of view: reactions to different types of situational judgment items. *European Journal of Psychological Assessment*, **22**, 168–176.

Katz D & Kahn R L (1966) *The social psychology of organisations.* John Wiley & Sons, New York.

Keenan T (1995) Graduate recruitment in Britain: a survey of selection methods used by organizations. *Journal of Organizational Behavior*, **16**, 303–317.

Keenan T (1997) Selection for potential: the case of graduate recruitment. In N Anderson & P Herriott (eds.) *International Handbook of Selection and Appraisal*. John Wiley & Sons, Chichester.

Kethley R B & Terpstra D E (2005). An analysis of litigation associated with the use of the application form in the selection process. *Public Personnel Management*, **34**, 357–375.

Kinslinger H J (1966) Application of projective techniques in personnel psychology since 1940. *Psychological Bulletin*, **66**, 134–149.

Klehe U, Konig C J, Richter G M, Kleinmann M & Melchers K G (2008) Transparency in structured interviews – consequences for construct and criterion-related validity. *Human Performance*, **21**, 107–137.

Kleiman L S & Faley R H (1985) The implications of professional and legal guidelines for court decisions involving criterion-related validity: a review and analysis. *Personnel Psychology*, **38**, 803–833.

Klimoski R J & Strickland W J (1977) Assessment centers – valid or merely prescient. *Personnel Psychology*, **30**, 353–361.

Kline P & Cooper C (1984) A construct validation of the Objective-Analytic Test Battery (OATB). *Personality and Individual Differences*, **5**, 323–337.

Kluger A N, Reilly R R & Russell C J (1991) Faking biodata tests: are option–keyed instruments more resistant? *Journal of Applied Psychology*, **76**, 889–896.

Knapp D J, Campbell C H, Borman W C, Pulakos E D & Hanson M A (2001) Performance assessment for a population of jobs. In: J P Campbell & D J Knapp (eds) *Exploring the Limits of Personnel Selection and Classification*. Erlbaum, Mahwah NJ.

Kolk N J, Born M P & van der Flier H (2004) A triadic approach to the construct validity of the assessment center: the effect of categorizing dimensions into a feeling, thinking, and power taxonomy. *European Journal of Psychological Assessment*, **20**, 149–156.

Kraiger K & Ford J K (1985) A meta-analysis of ratee race effects in performance ratings. *Journal of Applied Psychology*, **70**, 56–65.

Krajewski H T, Goffin R D, Rothstein M G & Johnston N G (2007) Is personality related to assessment center performance? That depends on how old you are. *Journal of Business and Psychology*, **22**, 21–33.

Krause D E & Gebert D (2003) A comparison of assessment centre practices in German-speaking regions and the United States. *International Journal of Selection and Assessment*, **11**, 297–312.

Krause D E, Kersting M, Heggestad E D & Thornton G C (2006) Incremental validity of assessment center ratings over cognitive ability tests: a study at the executive management level. *International Journal of Selection and Assessment*, **14**, 360–371.

Kravitz D A (2008) The diversity-validity dilemma: beyond selection – the role of affirmative action. *Personnel Psychology*, **61**, 173–193.

Kristof-Brown A L, Zimmerman R D & Johnson E C (2005) Consequences of individuals' fit at work: a meta-analysis of person–job, person–organization, person–group, and person–supervisor fit. *Personnel Psychology*, **58**, 281–342.

Kruger J & Dunning D (1999) Unskilled and unaware of it: how difficulties in recognizing one's own incompetence lead to inflated self–assessments. *Journal of Personality and Social Psychology*, **77**, 1121–1134.

Krzystofiak F, Newman J M & Anderson G (1979) A quantified approach to measurement of job content: procedures and payoffs. *Personnel Psychology*, **32**, 341–357.

Kumar K & Beyerlein M (1991) Construction and validation of an instrument for measuring ingratiatory behaviors in organizational setting. *Journal of Applied Psychology*, **76**, 619–627.

Kutcher E J & Bragger J D (2004) Selection interviews of overweight job applicants: can structure reduce the bias? *Journal of Applied Social Psychology*, **34**, 1993–2022.

LaHuis D M, Martin N R & Avis J M (2005) Investigating nonlinear conscientiousness–job performance relations for clerical employees. *Human Performance*, **18**, 199–212.

Lance C E, Johnson C D, Douthitt S S, Bennett W & Harville D L (2000a) Good news: work sample administrators' global performance judgements are (about) as valid as we've suspected. *Human Performance*, **13**, 253–277.

Lance C E, Lambert T A, Gewin A G, Lievens F, & Conway J M (2004) Revised estimates of dimension and exercise variance components in assessment center postexercise dimension ratings. *Journal of Applied Psychology*, **89**, 377–385.

Lance C E, Newbolt W H, Gatewood R D, Foster M R, French N R & Smith D E (2000b) Assessment center exercise factors represent cross-situational specificity, not method bias. *Human Performance*, **12**, 323–353.

Landy F J (2003) Validity generalization: then and now. In: K R Murphy (ed.) *Validity Generalization: a Critical Review*. Lawrence Erlbaum Associates, Mahwah, NJ.

Landy F J (2005) Some historical and scientific issues related to research on emotional intelligence. *Journal of Organizational Behavior*, **26**, 411–424.

Latham G P & Wexley K N (1981) *Increasing Pproductivity through Performance Appraisal*. Addison Wesley, Reading, MA.

Latham G P & Whyte G (1994) The futility of utility analysis. *Personnel Psychology*, **47**, 31–46.

Latham G P, Saari L M, Pursell E D & Campion M A (1980) The situational interview. *Journal of Applied Psychology*, **65**, 422–427.

LeBreton J M, Barksdale C D, Robin J & James L R (2007) Measurement issues associated with conditional reasoning tests: indirect measurement and test faking. *Journal of Applied Psychology*, **92**, 1–16.

Lent R H, Aurbach H A & Levin, L S (1971) Predictors, criteria, and significant results. *Personnel Psychology*, **24**, 519–533.

Levashina J & Campion M A (2006) A model of faking likelihood in the employment interview. *International Journal of Selection and Assessment*, **14**, 299–316

Levine E L, Spector P E, Menon S, Narayanan L & Cannon-Bowers J (1996) Validity generalization for cognitive, psychomotor, and perceptual tests for craft jobs in the utility industry. *Human Performance*, **9**, 1–22.

Levine M R & Rennie W P (2004) Pre-employment urine drug testing of hospital employees: future questions and review of current literature. *Occupational and Environmental Medicine*, **61**, 318–324.

Liao H, Joshi A & Chuang A (2004) Sticking out like a sore thumb: employee dissimilarity and deviance at work. *Personnel Psychology*, **57**, 969–1000.

Lievens F (2001a) Assessor training strategies and their effects on accuracy, interrater reliability, and discriminant validity. *Journal of Applied Psychology*, **86**, 255–264.

Lievens F (2001b) Assessors and use of assessment centre dimensions: a fresh look at a troubling issue. *Journal of Organizational Behavior*, **22**, 203–221.

Lievens F & Conway J M (2001) Dimension and exercise variance in assessment center scores: a large-scale evaluation of multitrait-multimethod studies. *Journal of Applied Psychology*, **86**, 1202–1222.

Lievens F & Sanchez J I (2007) Can training improve the quality of inferences made by raters in competency modeling? A quasi-experiment. *Journal of Applied Psychology*, **92**, 812–819.

Lievens F, Highhouse S & DeCorte W (2005) The importance of traits and abilities in supervisors' hirability decisions as a function of method of assessment. *Journal of Occupational and Organizational Psychology*, **78**, 453–470.

Lievens F, Chasteen C S, Day E A, & Christiansen N D (2006) Large-scale investigation of the role of trait activation theory for understanding assessment center convergent and discriminant validity. *Journal of Applied Psychology*, **91**, 247–258.

Lievens F, Reeve C L & Heggestad E D (2007) An examination of psychometric bias due to retesting on cognitive ability tests in selection settings. *Journal of Applied Psychology*, **92**, 1672–1682.

Link H C (1918) An experiment in employment psychology. *Psychological Review*, **25**, 116–127.

Little B L & Sipes D (2000) Betwixt and between; the dilemma of employee references. *Employee Responsibilities and Rights Journal*, **12**, 1–8.

Locke E A (1961) What's in a name? *American Psychologist*, **16**, 607.

Loher B T, Hazer J T, Tsai A, Tilton K & James J. (1997) Letters of reference: a process approach. *Journal of Business and Psychology*, **11**, 339–355.

Longenecker C O, Sims H P & Goia D A (1987) Behind the mask: the politics of employee appraisal. *Academy of Management Executive*, **1**, 183–193.

Mabe P A & West S G (1982) Validity of self-evaluation of ability: a review and meta-analysis. *Journal of Applied Psychology*, **67**, 280–296.

Macan T H & Highhouse S (1994) Communicating the utility of human resource activities: a survey of I/O and HR professionals. *Journal of Business Psychology*, **8**, 425–436.

MacFarland J (2000) Rejected by Resumix. http://www.govexec.com/dailyfed/0900/092500ff.htm.

Machwirth U, Schuler H & Moser K (1996) Entscheidungsprozesse bei der Analyse von Bewerbungsunterlagen. *Diagnostica*, **42**, 220–241.

Mael F A & Ashworth B E (1995) Loyal from day one: biodata, organisational identification, and turnover among newcomers. *Personnel Psychology*, **48**, 309–333.

Mael F A & Hirsch A C (1993) Rainforest empiricism and quasi-rationality: two approaches to objective biodata. *Personnel Psychology*, **46**, 719–738.

Marcus B (2008) *The relationship of GMA to counterproductive work behavior revisited*. Paper presented at 23rd Annual Conference of SIOP, San Francisco.

Marcus B (in press) 'Faking' from the applicant's perspective: a theory of self-presentation in personnel selection settings. *International Journal of Selection and Assessment*.

Marcus B, Funke U & Schuler H (1997) Integrity Tests als spezielle Gruppe eignungsdiagnostischer Verfahren: Literaturuberblick und metaanalytische Befunde zur Konstruktvaliditat. *Zeitschrift fur Arbeits– und Organisationspsychologie*, **41**, 2–17.

Martin B A, Bowen C C & Hunt S T (2002) How effective are people at faking personality questionnaires? *Personality and Individual Differences*, **32**, 247–256.

Martinussen M (1996) Psychological measures as predictors of pilot performance: a meta-analysis. *International Journal of Aviation Psychology*, **6**, 1–20.

Martinussen M & Torjussen T (1993) Does DMT (Defense Mechanism Test) predict pilot performance only in Scandinavia? In: R S Jensen & D Neumeister (eds) *Proceedings of the Seventh International Symposium on Aviation Psychology*. Avebury Aviation, Aldershot.

Mathieu J E & Tannenbaum S I (1989) A process–tracing approach toward understanding supervisors' SDy estimates: results from five job classes. *Journal of Occupational Psychology*, **62**, 249–256.

Maurer T J, Solamon J M, Andrews K D & Troxtel D D (2001) Interviewee coaching, preparation strategies, and response strategies in relation to performance in situational employment interviews: an extension of Maurer, Solamon, & Troxtel (1998). *Journal of Applied Psychology*, **86**, 709–717.

McCarthy J M & Goffin R D (2001) Improving the validity of letters of recommendation: an investigation of three standardised reference forms. *Military Psychology*, **13**, 199–222.

McCarthy J & Goffin R (2004) Measuring job interview anxiety: beyond weak knees and sweaty palms. *Personnel Psychology*, **57**, 607–637.

McClelland D C (1971) *The Achieving Society*. Van Nostrand, Princeton, NJ.

McCormick E J, Jeanneret P R & Mecham R C (1972) Study of job characteristics and job dimensions as based on the Position Analysis Questionnaire (PAQ). *Journal of Applied Psychology*, **56**, 347–368.

McDaniel M A (2007) Validity generalization as a test validation approach. In: S M McPhail (ed) *Alternative Validation Strategies: Developing New and Leveraging Existing Validity Evidence.* John Wiley & Sons, New York.

McDaniel M A, Douglas E F & Snell A F (1997) *A survey of deception among job seekers.* Paper presented at 12th Annual Conference of SIOP, St Louis, MO.

McDaniel M A, Rothstein H R & Whetzel D L (2006a) Publication bias: a case study of four test vendors. *Personnel Psychology,* **59**, 927–953.

McDaniel M A, Schmidt F L & Hunter J E (1988) A meta–analysis of the validity of methods for rating training and experience in personnel selection. *Personnel Psychology,* **41**, 283–314.

McDaniel MA, McKay P & Rothstein H (2006b) *Publication bias and racial effects on job performance: the elephant in the room?* Paper presented at 21st Annual Conference of SIOP, Dallas TX.

McDaniel M A, Hartman N S, Whetzel D L & Grubb W L (2007) Situational judgment tests, response instructions, and validity: a meta-analysis. *Personnel Psychology,* **60**, 63–91.

McDaniel M A, Whetzel D L, Schmidt F L & Maurer, S D (1994) The validity of employment interviews: a comprehensive review and meta-analysis. *Journal of Applied Psychology,* **79**, 599–616.

McEnrue M P & Groves K (2006) Choosing among tests of emotional intelligence: what is the evidence? *Human Resource Development Quarterly,* **17**, 9–42.

McEvoy G M & Beatty R W (1989) Assessment centers and subordinate appraisals of managers: a seven-year examination of predictive validity. *Personnel Psychology,* **42**, 37–52.

McEvoy G M & Buller P F (1987) User acceptance of peer appraisals in an industrial setting. *Personnel Psychology,* **40**, 785–797.

McFall R M & Marston A R (1970) An experimental investigation of behavior rehearsal in assertive training. *Journal of Abnormal Psychology,* **76**, 295–303.

McHenry J J, Hough L M, Toquam J L, Hanson M A & Ashworth S (1990) Project A validity results: the relationship between predictor and criterion domains. *Personnel Psychology,* **43**, 335–354.

McKay P F & McDaniel M A (2006) A reexamination of black–white mean differences in work performance: more data, more moderators. *Journal of Applied Psychology,* **91**, 538–554.

McKinney A P, Carlson K D, Mecham R L, D'Angelo N C & Connerley M L (2003) Recruiters' use of GPA in initial screening decisions: higher GPAs don't always make the cut. *Personnel Psychology,* **56**, 823–845.

McManus M A & Kelly M L (1999) Personality measures and biodata: evidence regarding their incremental predictive value in the life insurance industry. *Personnel Psychology,* **52**, 137–148.

Meade A W (2004) Psychometric problems and issues involved with creating and using ipsative measures for selection. *Journal of Occupational and Organizational Psychology,* **77**, 531–552.

Meehl P E (1954) *Clinical versus Statistical Prediction.* University of Minnesota Press, Minneapolis.

de Meijer L A L, Born M P, Terlouw G & van der Molen H T (2006) Applicant and method factors related to ethnic score differences in personnel selection: a study at the Dutch police. *Human Performance,* **19**, 219–251.

Melchers K G, Henggeler C & Kleinmann M (2007) Do within-dimension ratings in assessment centers really lead to improved construct validity? *Zeitschrift fur Personalpsychologie,* **6**, 141–149.

Merenda P F (1995) Substantive issues in the Soroka v. Dayton-Hudson case. *Psychological Reports,* **77**, 595–606.

Meritt-Haston R & Wexley K N (1983) Educational requirements: legality and validity. *Personnel Psychology,* **36**, 743–753.

Middendorf C & Macan T (2008) *Applicant reactions to interviewer note-taking.* Paper presented at 23rd Annual Conference of SIOP, San Francisco.

Miner J B (1971) Personality tests as predictors of consulting success. *Personnel Psychology*, **24**, 191–204.

Miner M G & Miner J B (1979) *Employee Selection within the Law.* Bureau of National Affairs, Washington, DC.

Mischel W (1968) *Personality and Assessment.* Wiley, New York.

Mitchell T W & Klimoski R J (1982) Is it rational to be empirical? A test of methods for scoring biographical data. *Journal of Applied Psychology*, **67**, 411–418.

Mls J (1935) Intelligenz und fahigkeit zum kraftwagenlenken. *Proceedings of the eight international conference of psychotechnics, Prague*, pp. 278–284.

Mol S T, Born M P, Willemsen M E & van der Molen H T (2005) Predicting expatriate job performance for selection purposes: a quantitative review. *Journal of Cross-Cultural Psychology*, **36**, 590–620.

Morgeson F P & Campion M A (1997) Social and cognitive sources of potential inaccuracy in job analysis. *Journal of Applied Psychology*, **82**, 627–655.

Morgeson F P, Campion M A, Dipboye R L, Hollenbeck J R, Murphy K & Schmitt N (2007) Reconsidering the use of personality tests in personnel selection contexts. *Personnel Psychology*, **60**, 683–729.

Morgeson F P, Delaney-Klinger K, Mayfield M S, Ferrara P & Campion M A (2004) Self-presentation processes in job analysis: a field experiment investigating inflation in abilities, tasks and competencies. *Journal of Applied Psychology*, **89**, 674–686.

Morgeson F P, Reider M H, Campion M A & Bull R A (2008) Review of research on age discrimination in the employment interview. *Journal of Business and Psychology*, **22**, 223–232.

Morris B S (1949) Officer selection in the British Army 1942–1945. *Occupational Psychology*, **23**, 219–234.

Moscoso S & Salgado J F (2004) Fairness reactions to personnel selection techniques in Spain and Portugal. *International Journal of Selection and Assessment*, **12**, 187–196.

Mosel J N (1952) Prediction of department store sales performance from personal data. *Journal of Applied Psychology*, **36**, 8–10.

Mosel J N & Goheen H W (1958) The validity of the Employment Recommendation Questionnaire in personnel selection: I. Skilled traders. *Personnel Psychology*, **11**, 481–490.

Mosel J N & Goheen H W (1959) The validity of the Employment Recommendation Questionnaire: III Validity of different types of references. *Personnel Psychology*, **12**, 469–477.

Moser K & Rhyssen D (2001) Referenzen als eignungsdiagnostische Methode. *Zeitschrift fur Arbeits- und Organisationspsychologie*, **45**, 40–46.

Moses J L (1973) The development of an assessment center for the early identification of supervisory talent. *Personnel Psychology*, **26**, 569–580.

Mount M K, Oh I S & Burns M (2008) Incremental validity of perceptual speed and accuracy over general mental ability. *Personnel Psychology*, **61**, 113–139.

Mount M K & Barrick M R (1995) The big five personality dimensions: implications for research and practice in human resources management. *Research in Personnel and Human Resources Management*, **13**, 153–200.

Mount M K, Barrick M R & Strauss J P (1994) Validity of observer ratings of the big five personality factors. *Journal of Applied Psychology*, **79**, 272–280.

Mount M K, Barrick M R & Stewart G L (1998) Five-factor model of personality and performance in jobs involving interpersonal interactions. *Human Performance*, **11**, 145–165.

Mount M K, Barrick M R & Strauss J P (1999) The joint relationship of conscientiousness and ability with performance: test of the interaction hypothesis. *Journal of Management*, **25**, 707–721.

Mount M K, Witt L A & Barrick M R (2000) Incremental validity of empirically keyed biodata scales over GMA and the five factor personality constructs. *Personnel Psychology*, **53**, 299–323.

Mount M K, Barrick M R, Scullen S M & Rounds J (2005) Higher-order dimensions of the big five personality traits and the big six vocational interest types. *Personnel Psychology*, **58**, 447–478.

Muchinsky P M (2004) When the psychometrics of test development meets organizational realities: a conceptual framework for organizational change, examples, and recommendations. *Personnel Psychology*, **57**, 175–209.

Mueller-Hanson R, Heggestad E D & Thornton G C (2003) Faking and selection: considering the use of personality from select-in and select-out perspectives. *Journal of Applied Psychology*, **88**, 348–355.

Mumford M D & Owens W A (1987) Methodology review: principles, procedures, and findings in the applications of background data measures. *Applied Psychological Measurement*, **11**, 1–31.

Murphy K R (1986) When your top choice turns you down: effect of rejected offers on the utility of selection tests. *Psychological Bulletin*, **99**, 133–138.

Murphy K R (1989) Is the relationship between cognitive ability and job performance stable over time? *Human Performance*, **2**, 183–200.

Murphy K R & Cleveland J N (1995) *Understanding Performance Appraisal: Social, Organisational, and Goal-Based Perspectives*. Sage, Thousand Oaks, CA.

Murphy K R & DeShon R (2000) Interrater correlations do not estimate the reliability of job performance ratings. *Personnel Psychology*, **53**, 873–900.

Murphy K R, Thornton G C & Prue K (1991) Influence of job characteristics on the acceptability of employee drug testing. *Journal of Applied Psychology*, **76**, 447–453.

Murphy N (2006) Testing the waters: employers' use of selection assessments. *IRS Employment Review*, **852**, 42–48.

Murray C (1998) *Income inequality and IQ*. AEI Press, Washington DC.

Mussel P, Berhmann M & Schuler H (2008) *Explaining the psychometric properties of structured and unstructured interviews*. Paper presented at 23rd Annual Conference of SIOP, San Francisco.

Nathan B R & Alexander R A (1988) A comparison of criteria for test validation: a meta-analytic investigation. *Personnel Psychology*, **41**, 517–535.

Neter E & Ben-Shakhar G (1989) The predictive validity of graphological inferences: a meta-analytic approach. *Personality and Individual Differences*, **10**, 737–745.

Newman D A, Jacobs R R & Bartram D (2007) Choosing the best method for local validity estimation: relative accuracy of meta-analysis versus a local study versus Bayes-analysis. *Journal of Applied Psychology*, **92**, 1394–1413.

te Nijenhuis J & van der Flier H (2000) Differential prediction of immigrant versus majority group training performance using cognitive ability and personality measures. *International Journal of Selection and Assessment*, **8**, 54–60.

te Nijenhuis J, van der Flier H & van Leeuwen L (1997) Comparability of personality test scores for immigrants and majority group members: some Dutch findings. *Personality and Individual Differences*, **23**, 849–859.

Ng T W H, Eby L T, Sorenson K L & Feldman D C (2005) Predictors of objective and subjective career success: a meta-analysis. *Personnel Psychology*, **58**, 367–408.

Normand J, Salyards S D & Mahoney J J (1990) An evaluation of preemployment drug testing. *Journal of Applied Psychology*, **75**, 629–639.

Norton S M (1992) Peer assessments of performance and ability: an exploratory meta–analysis of statistical artifacts and contextual moderators. *Journal of Business and Psychology*, **6**, 387–399.

O'Brien J & Rothstein M (2008) *Selection interviewer judgment and personal fear of invalidity*. Paper presented at 23rd Annual Conference of SIOP, San Francisco.

Oh I S, Postlethwaite B E, Schmidt F L, McDaniel M A & Whetzel D L. (2007) *Do structured and unstructured interviews have nearly equal validity? Implications of recent developments in meta-analysis*. Paper presented at 22nd Annual Conference of SIOP, New York.

Ones D S & Anderson N (2002) Gender and ethnic group differences on personality scales in selection: some British data. *Journal of Occupational and Organizational Psychology*, **75**, 255–276.

Ones D S & Viswesvaran C (1998a) Gender, age and race differences on overt integrity tests: results across four large–scale applicant data sets. *Journal of Applied Psychology*, **83**, 35–42.

Ones D S & Viswesvaran C (1998b) The effects of social desirability and faking on personality and integrity assessment for personnel selection. *Human Performance*, **11**, 245–269.

Ones D S & Viswesvaran C (1998c) Integrity testing in organizations. In R W Griffin, A O'Leary–Kelly & J M Collins (eds.) *Dysfunctional behavior in organizations Vol. 2. Nonviolent behaviors in organizations*. JAI Press, Greenwich CT.

Ones D S & Viswesvaran C (2001) Integrity tests and other criterion-focused occupational personality scales (COPS) used in personnel research. *International Journal of Selection and Assessment*, **9**, 31–39.

Ones D S & Viswesvaran C (2003a) Job–specific applicant pools and national norms for personality scales: implications for range–restriction corrections in validation research. *Journal of Applied Psychology*, **88**, 570–577.

Ones D S & Viswesvaran C (2003b) The big–5 personality and counterproductive behaviours. In A Sagie, S Stashevsky & M Koslowsky (eds.) *Misbehaviour and dysfunctional attitudes in organizations*. Palgrave Macmillan, Basingstoke.

Ones D S, Viswesvaran C & Schmidt, F L (1993) Comprehensive meta–analysis of integrity test validities: findings and implications for personnel selection and theories of job performance. *Journal of Applied Psychology*, **78**, 679–703.

Ones D S, Viswesvaran C & Reiss A D (1996) Role of social desirability in personality testing for personnel selection: the red herring. *Journal of Applied Psychology*, **81**, 660–679.

Ones D S, Viswesvaran C & Schmidt F L (2003) Personality and absenteeism: a meta–analysis of integrity tests. *European Journal of Personality*, **17**, S19–S38.

Ones D S, Dilchert S, Viswesvaran C & Judge T A (2007) In support of personality assessment in organizational settings. *Personnel Psychology*, **60**, 995–1027.

O'Reilly C A, Chatman J & Caldwell D F (1991) People and organizational culture: a profile comparison approach to assessing person–organization fit. *Academy of Management Journal*, **34**, 487–516.

Orwell G (1949/1984) *Nineteen Eighty–Four*. Clarendon Press, Oxford.

OSS Assessment Staff. (1948) *Assessment of men*. Rinehart, New York.

Owens W A & Schoenfeldt L F (1979) Toward a classification of persons. *Journal of Applied Psychology*, **65**, 569–607.

Pannone R D (1984) Predicting test performance: a content valid approach to screening applicants. *Personnel Psychology*, **37**, 507–514.

Parkinson C N (1958) *Parkinson's law*. John Murray, London.

Parry G (1999) A legal examination of two cases involving employment references. *Educational Management and Administration*, **27**, 357–364

Payne S C, Horner M T, Deshpande S S & Wynne K T (2008) *Supervisory performance ratings: what have we been measuring?* Paper presented at 23rd Annual Conference of SIOP.

Pearlman K, Schmidt F L & Hunter J E (1980) Validity generalization results for tests used to predict job proficiency and training success in clerical occupations. *Journal of Applied Psychology*, **65**, 373–406.

Peres S H & Garcia J R (1962) Validity and dimensions of descriptive adjectives used in reference letters for engineering applicants. *Personnel Psychology*, **15**, 279–286.

Piotrowski C & Armstrong T (2006) Current recruitment and selection practices: a national survey of Fortune 1000 firms. *North American Journal of Psychology*, **8**, 489–496.

Ployhart R E & Holtz B C (2008). The diversity–validity dilemma: strategies for reducing racioethnic and sex subgroup differences and adverse impact in selection. *Personnel Psychology*, **61**, 153–172.

Ployhart R E, Lim B C & Chan K Y (2001) Exploring relations between typical and maximum performance ratings and the five factor model of personality. *Personnel Psychology*, **54**, 807–843.

Pollack J M & McDaniel M A (2008) *An examination of the PreVisorTM Employment Inventory for publication bias*. Paper presented at 23rd Annual Conference of SIOP, San Francisco.

Posthuma R A, Morgeson F P & Campion M A (2002) Beyond employment interview validity: a comprehensive narrative review of recent research and trends over time. *Personnel Psychology*, **55**, 1–81.

Potosky D, Bobko P & Roth PL (2005) Forming composites of cognitive ability and alternative measures to predict job performance and reduce adverse impact: corrected estimates and realistic expectations. *International Journal of Selection and Assessment*, **13**, 304–315.

Prewett–Livingston A J, Feild H S, Veres J G & Lewis, P M (1996) Effects of race on interview ratings in a situational panel interview. *Journal of Applied Psychology*, **81**, 178–186.

Pulakos E D, Schmitt N, Whitney D & Smith M (1996) Individual differences in interviewer ratings: the impact of standardisation, consensus discussion, and sampling error on the validity of a structured interview. *Personnel Psychology*, **49**, 85–102.

Pulakos E D, Schmitt N, Dorsey D W, Arad S, Hedge J W & Borman W C (2002) Predicting adaptive performance: further tests of a model of adaptability. *Human Performance*, **15**, 299–323.

Putka D J & McCloy R A (2004). Preliminary AIM validation based on GED Plus program data. in D J Knapp, E D Heggestad & M C Young (eds.) *Understanding and improving the Assessment of Individual Motivation (AIM) in the army's GED Plus Program*. US Army Institute for the Behavioral and Social Sciences, Alexandria VA.

Quinsey V L, Harris G T, Rice M E & Cormier C A (1998) *Violent offenders: appraising and managing risk*. Washington, DC: American Psychological Association.

Quist J S, Arora A & Griffith R L (2007) *Social desirability and applicant faking behavior: a validation study*. Paper presented at 22nd Annual Conference of SIOP, NewYork.

Raju N S, Burke M J & Normand J (1990) A new approach for utility analysis. *Journal of Applied Psychology*, **75**, 3–12.

Ramsay L J, Schmitt N, Oswald F L, Kim B H & Gillespie M A (2006) The impact of situational context variables on responses to biodata and situational judgement inventory items. *Psychology Science*, **48**, 268–287.

Raymark P H, Schmit M J & Guion R M (1997) Identifying potentially useful personality constructs for employee selection. *Personnel Psychology*, **50**, 723–736.

Raymark P H, Keith M, Odle–Dusseau H N, Giumetti G, Brown, B & van Iddekinge C H (2008) *Snap decisions in the employment interview*. Paper presented at 23rd Annual Conference of SIOP, San Francisco.

Rayson M, Holliman D & Belyavin A (2000) Development of physical selection procedures for the British Army. Phase 2: relationship between physical performance tests and criterion tasks. *Ergonomics*, **43**, 73–105.

Ree M J & Earles J A (1991) Predicting training success: not much more than g. *Personnel Psychology*, **44**, 321–332.

Ree M J, Carretta T R & Teachout M S (1995) Role of ability and prior job knowledge in complex training performance. *Journal of Applied Psychology*, **80**, 721–730.

Reilly R R & Chao G T (1982) Validity and fairness of some alternative employee selection procedures. *Personnel Psychology*, **35**, 1–62.

Reiter–Palmon R & Connelly M S (2000) Item selection counts: a comparison of empirical key and rational scale validities in theory-based and non–theory-based item pools. *Journal of Applied Psychology*, **85**, 143–151.

Riach P A & Rich J (2002). Field experiments of discrimination in the market place. *The Economic Journal*, **112**, F480–F518.

Roberts B W, Harms P D, Caspi A & Moffitt T E (2007) Predicting the counterproductive employee in a child–to–adult prospective study. *Journal of Applied Psychology*, **92**, 1427–1436.

Robertson I T & Downs S (1989) Work–sample tests of trainability: a meta–analysis. *Journal of Applied Psychology*, **74**, 402–410.

Robertson I T & Kandola R S (1982) Work sample tests: validity, adverse impact and applicant reaction. *Journal of Occupational Psychology*, **55**, 171–183.

Robertson I T, Baron H, Gibbons P, McIver R & Nyfield G (2000) Conscientiousness and managerial performance. *Journal of Occupational and Organizational Psychology*, **73**, 171–180.

Robie C, Schmit M J, Ryan A M & Zickar M J (2000) Effects of item context specificity on the measurement equivalence of a personality inventory. *Organizational Research Methods*, **3**, 348–365.

Robinson D D (1972) Prediction of clerical turnover in banks by means of a weighted application blank. *Journal of Applied Psychology*, **56**, 282.

Robinson S L & Bennett R J (1995) A typology of deviant workplace behaviors: a multidimensional scaling study. *Academy of Management Journal*, **38**, 555–572.

Rodger N A M (2001) Commissioned officers' careers in the Royal Navy, 1690–1815. *Journal of Maritime Research*, June 2001. retrieved from http://www.jmr.nmm.ac.uk/server/show/conJmrArticle.52/viewPage/11.

Roth P L & Bobko P (2000) College grade point average as a personnel selection device: ethnic group differences and potential adverse impact. *Journal of Applied Psychology*, **85**, 399–406.

Roth P L, Bobko P, Switzer F S & Dean M A (2001a) Prior selection causes biased estimates of standardized ethnic group differences: simulation and analysis. *Personnel Psychology*, **54**, 591–617.

Roth P L, Bobko P & Switzer F S (2006) Modeling the behavior of the 4/5ths rule for determining adverse impact: reasons for caution. *Journal of Applied Psychology*, **91**, 507–522.

Roth P L, Huffcutt A I & Bobko P (2003) Ethnic group differences in measures of job performance: a new meta–analysis. *Journal of Applied Psychology*, **88**, 694–706.

Roth P L, van Iddekinge C H, Huffcutt A I, Eidson C E, & Schmit M J (2005) Personality saturation in structured interviews. *International Journal of Selection and Assessment*, **13**, 261–273.

Roth P L, Bobko P & McFarland L A (2005) A meta–analysis of work sample test validity: updating and integrating some classic literature. *Personnel Psychology*, **58**, 1009–1037.

Roth P L, Bevier C A, Switzer F S & Schippmann J S (1996) Meta–analyzing the relationship between grades and job performance. *Journal of Applied Psychology*, **81**, 548–556.

Roth P L, Bevier C A, Bobko P, Switzer F S & Tyler P (2001b) Ethnic group differences in cognitive ability in employment and educational settings: a meta-analysis. *Personnel Psychology*, **54**, 297–330.

Roth P L, Van Iddekinge C H, Huffcutt A I, Eidson C E & Bobko P (2002) Corrections for range restriction in structured interview ethnic group differences: the values may be larger than researchers thought. *Journal of Applied Psychology*, **87**, 369–376.

Rothstein H R (1990) Interrater reliability of job performance ratings: growth to asymptote level with increasing opportunity to observe. *Journal of Applied Psychology*, **75**, 322–327.

Rothstein H R & McDaniel M A (1992) Differential validity by sex in employment settings. *Personnel Psychology*, **7**, 45–62.

Rothstein H R, Schmidt F L, Erwin F W, Owens W A & Sparks C P (1990) Biographical data in employment selection: can validities be made generalizable? *Journal of Applied Psychology*, **75**, 175–184.

Rotundo M & Sackett P R (2002) The relative importance of task, citizenship, and counterproductive performance to global ratings of job performance; a policy capturing approach. *Journal of Applied Psychology*, **87**, 66–80.

Rotundo M & Sackett P R (2004) Specific versus general skills and abilities: a job level examination of relationships with wage. *Journal of Occupational and Organizational Psychology*, **77**, 127–148.

Rubenzer S J, Faschingbauer T R & Ones D S (2000) Assessing the U.S. presidents using the Revised NEO Personality Inventory. *Assessment*, **7**, 403–420.

Rudolph C W, Wells C L, Weller M D & Baltes B B (2008) *Weight–based bias and evaluative workplace outcomes: a meta-analysis*. Paper presented at 23rd Annual Conference of SIOP, San Francisco.

Rupp D E, Thornton G C & Gibbons A M (2008) The construct validity of the assessment center method and usefulness of dimensions as focal constructs. *Industrial and Organizational Psychology*, **1**, 121–125.

Russell C J, Mattson J, Devlin S E & Atwater D (1990) Predictive validity of biodata items generated from retrospective life experience essays. *Journal of Applied Psychology*, **75**, 569–580.

Russell C J, Settoon R P, McGrath R N, Blanton A E, Kidwell R E, Lohrke F T, Scifres E L & Danforth G W (1994) Investigator characteristics as moderators of personnel selection research: a meta–analysis. *Journal of Applied Psychology*, **79**, 163–170.

Ryan A M (2001) Explaining the black–white test score gap: the role of test perceptions. *Human Performance*, **14**, 45–75.

Ryan A M, McFarland L, Baron H & Page R (1999) An international look at selection practices: nation and culture as explanation for variability in practice. *Personnel Psychology*, **52**, 359–391.

Rynes S & Gerhart B (1990) Interview assessments of applicant "fit": an exploratory investigation. *Personnel Psychology*, **43**, 13–35.

Saad S & Sackett P R (2002) Investigating differential prediction by gender in employment–oriented personality measures. *Journal of Applied Psychology*, **87**, 667–674.

Sacco J M & Schmitt N (2005) A dynamic multilevel model of demographic diversity and misfit effects. *Journal of Applied Psychology*, **90**, 203–231.

Sackett P R (2003) The status of validity generalization research: key issues in drawing inferences from cumulative research findings. In K R Murphy (Ed.) *Validity generalization: a critical review*. Erlbaum, Mahwah NJ.

Sackett P R & Dubois C L Z (1991) Rater–ratee race effects on performance evaluation: challenging meta–analytic conclusions. *Journal of Applied Psychology*, **76**, 873–877.

Sackett P R & Dreher G F (1982) Constructs and assessment center dimensions: some troubling empirical findings. *Journal of Applied Psychology*, **67**, 401–410.

Sackett P R & Mavor A (2003). *Attitudes, aptitudes, and aspiration of American youth: implications for military recruiting*. National Academies Press, Washington DC.

Sackett P R & Ostgaard D J (1994) Job–specific applicant pools and national norms for cognitive ability tests: implications for range restriction corrections in validation research. *Journal of Applied Psychology*, **79**, 680–684.

Sackett P R & Wanek J E (1996) New developments in the use of measures of honesty, integrity, conscientiousness, dependability, trustworthiness, and reliability for personnel selection. *Personnel Psychology*, **49**, 787–829.

Sackett P R, Gruys M L & Ellingson J E (1998) Ability–personality interactions when predicting job performance. *Journal of Applied Psychology*, **83**, 545–556.

Sackett P R, Harris M M & Orr J M (1986) On seeking moderator variables in the meta–analysis of correlational data: a Monte Carlo investigation of statistical power and resistance to Type I error. *Journal of Applied Psychology*, **71**, 302–310.

Sackett P R, Schmitt N, Ellingson J E & Kabin M B (2001) High–stakes testing in employment, credentialing, and higher education: prospects in a post–affirmative-action world. *American Psychologist*, **56**, 302–318.

Salgado J F (1994) Validez de los tests de habilidades psicomotoras: meta-analisis de los estudios publicados in Espana (1942–1990). *Revista de Psicologia Social Aplicada*, **4**, 25–42.

Salgado J F (1998) Big five personality dimensions and job performance in army and civil occupations: a European perspective. *Human Performance*, **11**, 271–289.

Salgado J F (2002) The Big Five personality dimensions and counterproductive behaviors. *International Journal of Selection and Assessment*, **10**, 117–125.

Salgado J F & Moscoso S (2002) Comprehensive meta-analysis of the construct validity on the employment interview. *European Journal of Work and Organizational Psychology*, **11**, 299–324.

Salgado J F & Anderson N (2002) Cognitive and GMA testing in the European Community: issues and evidence. *Human Performance*, **15**, 75–96.

Salgado J F & Anderson N (2003) Validity generalisation of GMA tests across countries in the European Community. *European Journal of Work and Organizational Psychology*, **12**, 1–17.

Salgado J F, Anderson N, Moscoso S, Bertua C, De Fruyt F & Rolland J P (2003) A meta–analytic study of general mental ability validity for different occupations in the European Community. *Journal of Applied Psychology*, **88**, 1068–1081.

Sanchez J I (2000) Adapting work analysis to a fast-paced electronic business world. *International Journal of Selection and Assessment*, **8**, 207–215.

Sanchez J I, Prager I, Wilson A & Viswesvaran C (1998) Understanding within-job title variance in job-analytic ratings. *Journal of Business and Psychology*, **12**, 407–418.

Scherbaum, C A (2005) Synthetic validity: past, present, and future. *Personnel Psychology*, **58**, 481–515.

Schippmann J S, Prien E P & Katz J A (1990) Reliability and validity of in-basket performance measures. *Personnel Psychology*, **43**, 837–859.

Schleicher D J, Day D V, Mayes B T & Riggio R E (2002) A new frame for frame-of-reference training: enhancing the construct validity of assessment centers. *Journal of Applied Psychology*, **87**, 735–746.

Schleicher D J, Venkataramani V, Morgeson F P & Campion M A (2006) So you didn't get the job ... *Now* what do you think? Examining opportunity-to-perform fairness perceptions. *Personnel Psychology*, **59**, 559–590.

Schmidt F L (2002) The role of general cognitive ability and job performance: why there cannot be a debate. *Human Performance*, **15**, 187–210.

Schmidt F L & Hunter J E (1977) Development of a general solution to the problem of validity generalization. *Journal of Applied Psychology*, **62**, 529–540.

Schmidt F L & Hunter J E (1995) The fatal internal contradiction in banding: its statistical rationale is logically inconsistent with its operational procedures. *Human Performance*, **8**, 203–214.

Schmidt F L & Hunter J E (1998) The validity and utility of selection methods in Personnel Psychology: practical and theoretical implications of 85 years of research findings. *Psychological Bulletin*, **124**, 262–274.

Schmidt F L & Hunter J (2004) General mental ability in the world of work: occupational attainment and job performance. *Journal of Personality and Social Psychology*, **86**, 162–173.

Schmidt F L & Rader M (1999) Exploring the boundary conditions for interview validity: meta-analytic validity findings for a new interview type. *Personnel Psychology*, **52**, 445–464.

Schmidt F L & Rothstein H R (1994) Application of validity generalisation to biodata scales in employment selection. In: G S Stokes, M D Mumford & W A Owens (eds) *Biodata Handbook: Theory, Research and Use of Biographical Information in Selection and Performance Prediction.* CPP Books, Palo Alto, CA.

Schmidt F L & Zimmerman R D (2004) A counterintuitive hypothesis about employment interview validity and some supporting evidence. *Journal of Applied Psychology*, **89**, 553–561.

Schmidt F L, Gast-Rosenberg I & Hunter J E (1980) Validity generalization results for computer programmers. *Journal of Applied Psychology*, **65**, 643–661.

Schmidt F L, Oh I S & Le H (2006) Increasing the accuracy of corrections for range restriction: implications for selection procedure validities and other research results. *Personnel Psychology*, **59**, 281–305.

Schmidt F L, Shaffer J & Oh I S (in press) Increased accuracy for range restriction corrections: implications for the role of personality and general mental ability in job and training performance. *Personnel Psychology*.

Schmidt F L, Hunter J E, McKenzie R C & Muldrow T W (1979) Impact of valid selection procedures on work-force productivity. *Journal of Applied Psychology*, **64**, 609–626.

Schmidt F L, Ocasio B P, Hillery J M & Hunter J E (1985a) Further within-setting empirical tests of the situational specificity hypothesis in personnel selection. *Personnel Psychology*, **38**, 509–524.

Schmidt F L, Hunter J E, Pearlman K & Hirsh H R (1985b) Forty questions about validity generalization and meta-analysis. *Personnel Psychology*, **38**, 697–798.

Schmidt-Atzert L & Deter B (1993) Intelligenz und Ausbildungserfolg: eine Untersuchung zur prognostischen Validitat des I-S-T 70. *Zeitschrift fur Arbeits– und Organisationspsychologie*, **37**, 52–63.

Schmit M J & Ryan A M (1993) The big five in personnel selection: factor structure in applicant and nonapplicant populations. *Journal of Applied Psychology*, **78**, 966–974.

Schmitt N & Kunce C (2002) The effects of required elaboration of answers to biodata questions. *Personnel Psychology*, **55**, 569–587.

Schmitt N & Mills A E (2001) Traditional tests and job simulations: minority and majority performance and test validities. *Journal of Applied Psychology*, **86**, 451–458.

Schmitt N, Clause C S & Pulakos E D (1996) Subgroup differences associated with different measures of some common job-relevant constructs. *International Review of Industrial and Organizational Psychology*, **11**, 115–139.

Schmitt N, Gooding R Z, Noe R A & Kirsch M (1984) Metaanalyses of validity studies published between 1964 and 1982 and the investigation of study characteristics. *Personnel Psychology*, **37**, 407–422.

Schneider R J, Hough L M & Dunnette M D (1996) Broadsided by broad traits: how to sink science in five dimensions or less. *Journal of Organizational Behavior*, **17**, 639–655.

Scholz G & Schuler H (1993) Das nomologische Netzwerk des Assessment Centers: eine Metaanalyse. *Zeitschrift fur Arbeits- und Organisationspsychologie*, **37**, 73–85.

Schrader A D & Osburn H G (1977) Biodata faking: effects of induced subtlety and position specificity. *Personnel Psychology*, **30**, 395–404.

Schuler H & Moser K (1995) Die validitat des multimodalen interviews. *Zeitschrift fur Arbeits- und Organisationspsychologie*, **39**, 2–12.

Scott S J (1997) *Graduate selection procedures and ethnic minority applicants*. MSc thesis, University of East London.

Seamster T L et al (1997) *Applied Cognitive Task Analysis in Aviation*. Ashgate, Brookfield, VT.

Semadar A, Robins G & Ferris G R (2006) Comparing the validity of multiple social effectiveness constructs in the prediction of managerial job performance. *Journal of Organizational Behavior*, **27**, 443–461.

Seymour R T (1988) Why plaintiffs' counsel challenge tests, and how they can successfully challenge the theory of 'validity generalisation'. *Journal of Vocational Behavior*, **33**, 331–364.

Sharf J C (1994) The impact of legal and equal employment opportunity issues on personal history enquires. In: G S Stokes, M D Mumford & W A Owens (eds) *Biodata Handbook: Theory, Research, and Use of Biographical Information in Selection and Performance Prediction*. Consulting Psychology Press, Palo Alto, CA.

Shermis M D, Falkenberg B, Appel V A & Cole R W (1996) Construction of faking detector scale for a biodata survey instrument. *Military Psychology*, **8**, 83–94.

SHRM (Society for Human Resource Management) (1998) *SHRM Reference Checking Survey*. SHRM, Alexandria, VA.

SHRM (Society for Human Resource Management) (2005) *2004 Reference and Background Checking Survey Report*. SHRM, Alexandria, VA.

Siers B P & Christiansen N D (2008) *On the validity of implicit association test measures of personality traits*. Paper presented at 23rd Annual Conference of SIOP, San Francisco.

Silvester J & Dykes C (2007) Selecting political candidates: a longitudinal study of assessment centre performance and political success in the 2005 UK General Election. *Journal of Occupational and Organizational Psychology*, **80**, 11–25.

Silvester J, Anderson–Gough F A, Anderson N R & Mohammed A R (2002) Locus of control, attributions and impression management in the selection interview. *Journal of Occupational and Organizational Psychology*, **75**, 59–78.

Simon H A & Noonan A M (1994) No smokers need apply: is refusing to hire smokers legal? *Employee Relations Law Journal*, **20**, 347–367.

Sisco H & Reilly R R (2007) Five factor biodata inventory: resistance to faking. *Psychological Reports*, **101**, 3–17.

Sparrow J, Patrick J, Spurgeon P & Barwell F (1982) The use of job component analysis and related aptitudes on personnel selection. *Journal of Occupational Psychology*, **55**, 157–164.

Springbett B M (1958) Factors affecting the final decision in the employment interview. *Canadian Journal of Psychology*, **12**, 13–22.

Spychalski A C, Quinones M A, Gaugler B B & Pohley K (1997) A survey of assessment center practices in organizations in the United States. *Personnel Psychology*, **50**, 71–90.

Stauffer J M & Buckley M R (2005) The existence and nature of racial bias in supervisory ratings. *Journal of Applied Psychology*, **90**, 586–591.

Steffens M C & Konig S S (2006) Predicting spontaneous big five behavior with implicit association tests. *European Journal of Psychological Assessment*, **22**, 13–30.

Sternberg R J, Forsythe G B, Hedlund J, Horvath J A, Wagner R K, Williams W M, Snook S A & Grigorenko E L (2000) *Practical Intelligence in Everyday Life*. Cambridge University Press, Cambridge.

Stewart G L & Nandkeolyar A K (2006) Adaptation and intraindividual variation in sales outcomes: exploring the interactive effects of personality and environmental opportunity. *Personnel Psychology*, **59**, 307–332.

Stewart G L, Darnold T C, Zimmerman R D, Barrick M R, Parks L, & Dustin S L (2008) *Exploring how response distortion of personality measures affects individuals*. Paper presented at 23rd Annual Conference of SIOP, San Francisco.

Stokes G S, Hogan, J B & Snell, A F (1993) Comparability of incumbent and applicant samples for the development of biodata keys: the influence of social desirability. *Personnel Psychology*, **46**, 739–762.

Stone–Romero E F, Stone D L & Hyatt D (2003) Personnel selection procedures and invasion of privacy. *Journal of Social Issues*, **59**, 343–368.

Stricker L J & Ward W C (2004) Stereotype threat, inquiring about test takers' ethnicity and gender, and standardised test performance. *Journal of Applied Social Psychology*, **34**, 665–693.

Sturman M C, Cheramie R A & Cashen L H (2005) The impact of job complexity and performance measurement on the temporal consistency, stability, and test-retest reliability of employee job performance ratings. *Journal of Applied Psychology*, **90**, 269–283.

Super D E & Crites J O (1962) *Appraising Vocational Fitness by Means of Psychological Tests*. Harper and Row, New York.

Taylor P J & Small B (2002) Asking applicants what they *would do* versus what they *did* do: a meta–analytic comparison of situational and past behaviour employment interview questions. *Journal of Occupational and Organizational Psychology*, **75**, 277–294.

Taylor P, Keelty Y & McDonnell B (2002) Evolving personnel selection practices in New Zealand organisations and recruitment firms. *New Zealand Journal of Psychology*, **31**, 8–18.

Taylor P J, Pajo K, Cheung G W & Stringfield P (2004) Dimensionality and validity of a structured telephone reference check procedure. *Personnel Psychology*, **57**, 745–772.

Terpstra D E & Kethley R B (2002) Organizations' relative degree of exposure to selection discrimination litigation. *Public Personnel Management*, **31**, 277–292.

Terpstra D E & Rozell E J (1993) The relationship of staffing practices to organizational level measures of performance. *Personnel Psychology*, **46**, 27–48.

Terpstra D E & Rozell E J (1997) Why some potentially effective staffing practices are seldom used. *Public Personnel Management*, **26**, 483–495.

Terpstra D E, Mohamed A A & Kethley R B (1999) An analysis of Federal court cases involving nine selection devices. *International Journal of Selection and Assessment*, **7**, 26–34.

Tett R P, Jackson D N & Rothstein M (1991) Personality measures as predictors of job performance: a meta-analytic review. *Personnel Psychology*, **44**, 703–742.

Tett R P, Jackson D N, Rothstein M & Reddon J R (1999) Meta-analysis of bidirectional relations in personality-job performance research. *Human Performance*, **12**, 1–29.

Thornton G C & Rupp D E (2006) *Assessment Centers in Human Resource Management: Strategies for Prediction, Diagnosis, and Development*. Erlbaum, Mahwah, NJ.

Tiffin J (1943) *Industrial Psychology*. Prentice Hall, New York.

Tippins N T, Beaty J, Drasgow F, Gibson W N, Pearlman K, Segall D O & Shepherd W (2006) Unproctored internet testing in employment settings. *Personnel Psychology*, **59**, 189–225.

Trull T J, Widiger T A, Useda J D, Holcomb J, Doan B T, Axelrod S R, Stern B L & Gershuny B S (1998). A structured interview for the assessment of the five-factor model of personality. *Psychological Assessment*, **10**, 229–240.

Uhrbrock R S (1950) Standardization of 724 rating scale statements. *Personnel Psychology*, **3**, 285–316.

Vance R J & Colella A (1990) The utility of utility analysis. *Human Performance*, **3**, 123–139.

van Dam K (2003) Trait perception in the employment interview: a five-factor model perspective. *International Journal of Selection and Assessment*, **11**, 43–55.

van Iddekinge C H, Eidson C E, Kudisch J D & Goldblatt A M (2003) A biodata inventory administered via interactive voice response (IVR) technology: predictive validity, utility, and subgroup differences. *Journal of Business and Psychology*, **18**, 145–156.

van Iddekinge C H, Raymark P H, Eidson C E & Attenweiler W J (2004) What do structured selection interviews really measure? The construct validity of behavior description interviews. *Human Performance*, **17**, 71–93.

van Iddekinge C H, Raymark P H & Roth P L (2005) Assessing personality with a structured employment interview: construct-related validity and susceptibility to response inflation. *Journal of Applied Psychology*, **90**, 536–552.

van Iddekinge C H, Sager C E, Burnfield J L & Heffner T S (2006) The variability of criterion-related validity estimates among interviewers and interviewer panels. *International Journal of Selection and Assessment*, **14**, 193–205.

Van Rooy D L & Viswesvaran C (2003) *The Emotionally Intelligent Female: a Meta-Analysis of Gender Differences*. Unpublished paper, University of Florida.

Van Rooy D L & Viswesvaran C (2004) Emotional intelligence: a meta-analytic investigation of predictive validity and nomological net. *Journal of Vocational Behavior*, **65**, 71–95.

Van Rooy D L, Alonso A & Viswesvaran C (2005) Group differences in emotional intelligence scores: theoretical and practical implications. *Personality and Individual Differences*, **38**, 689–700.

Vasilopoulos N L, Cucina J M & Hunter A E (2007) Personality and training proficiency: issues of bandwidth-fidelity and curvilinearity. *Journal of Occupational and Organizational Psychology*, **80**, 109–131.

Vasilopoulos N L, Cucina J M & McElreath J M (2005) Do warnings of response verification moderate the relationship between personality and cognitive ability. *Journal of Applied Psychology*, **90**, 306–322.

Verive J M & McDaniel M A (1996). Short-term memory tests in personnel selection: low adverse impact and high validity. *Intelligence*, **23**, 15–32.

Vernon P E (1950) The validation of Civil Service Selection Board procedures. *Occupational Psychology*, **24**, 75–95.

Vernon P E (1982) *The Abilities and Achievements of Orientals in North America*. Academic Press, New York.

Vernon P E & Parry J B (1949) *Personnel Selection in the British Forces*. University of London Press, London.

Vinchur A J, Schippmann J S, Switzer F S & Roth P L (1998) A meta–analytic review of predictors of job performance for sales people. *Journal of Applied Psychology*, **83**, 586–597.

Vineberg R & Joyner J N (1982) *Prediction of Job Performance: Review of Military Studies*. Human Resources Research Organisation, Alexandria, VA.

Viswesvaran C (1993) *Is there a general factor in job performance?* Unpublished doctoral dissertation, University of Iowa, Iowa City.

Viswesvaran C (2002) Absenteeism and measures of job performance: a meta-analysis. *International Journal of Selection and Assessment*, **10**, 53–58.

Viswesvaran C & Ones D S (1999) Meta-analyses of fakability estimates: implications for personality measurement. *Educational and Psychological Measurement*, **59**, 197–210.

Viswesvaran C & Ones D S (2000) Measurement error in 'big five factors' personality assessment: reliability generalization across studies and measures. *Educational and Psychological Measurement*, **60**, 224–235.

Viswesvaran C & Ones D S (2005) Job performance: assessment issues in personnel selection. In: A Evers, N Anderson & O Voskuijl (eds) *The Blackwell Handbook of Personnel Selection*. Blackwell, Oxford.

Viswesvaran C, Ones D S & Schmidt F L (1996) Comparative analysis of the reliability of job performance ratings. *Journal of Applied Psychology*, **81**, 557–574.

Viswesvaran C, Schmidt F L & Ones D S (2002) The moderating influence of job performance dimension on convergence of supervisory and peer ratings of job performance: unconfounding construct-level convergence and rating difficulty. *Journal of Applied Psychology*, **87**, 345–354.

Viswesvaran C, Schmidt F L & Ones D S (2005) Is there a general factor in ratings of job performance? A meta-analytic framework for disentangling substantive and error influences. *Journal of Applied Psychology*, **90**, 108–131.

Voskuijl O F & van Sliedregt T (2002) Determinants of interrater reliability of job analysis: a meta-analysis. *European Journal of Psychological Assessment*, **18**, 52–62.

Wagner R (1949) The employment interview: a critical summary. *Personnel Psychology*, **2**, 17–46.

Waldman D A & Avolio B J (1986) A meta-analysis of age differences in job performance. *Journal of Applied Psychology*, **71**, 33–38.

Weekley J A & Jones C (1999) Further studies of situational tests. *Personnel Psychology*, **52**, 679–700.

Weiss B & Feldman R S (2006) Looking good and lying to do it: deception as an impression management strategy in job interviews. *Journal of Applied Social Psychology*, **36**, 1070–1086.

White L, Nord R D, Mael F A & Young M C (1993) The assessment of background and life experiences (ABLE), In: T Trent and J H Laurence (eds) *Adaptability Screening for the Armed Forces*. Office of Assistant Secretary of Defense, Washington, DC.

Whitney D J & Schmitt N (1997) Relationship between culture and responses to biodata employment items. *Journal of Applied Psychology*, **82**, 113–129.

Wiens A N, Jackson R H, Manaugh T S & Matarazzo J D (1969) Communication length as an index of communicator attitude: a replication. *Journal of Applied Psychology*, **53**, 264–266.

Wiesner W H & Cronshaw S F (1988) A meta-analytic investigation of the impact of interview format and degree of structure on the validity of the employment interview. *Journal of Occupational Psychology*, **61**, 275–290.

Wilk S L & Cappelli P (2003) Understanding the determinants of employer use of selection methods. *Personnel Psychology*, **56**, 103–124.

Wilk S L & Sackett P R (1996) Longitudinal analysis of ability-job complexity fit and job change. *Personnel Psychology*, **49**, 937–967.

Williamson L G, Malos S B, Roehling M V & Campion M A (1997) Employment interview on trial: linking interview structure with litigation outcomes. *Journal of Applied Psychology*, **82**, 900–912.

Wilson N A B (1948) The work of the Civil Service Selection Board. *Occupational Psychology*, **22**, 204–212.

Witt L A, Burke L A, Barrick M R & Mount M K (2002) The interactive effects of conscientiousness and agreeableness on job performance. *Journal of Applied Psychology*, **87**, 164–169.

Woehr D J & Arthur W (2003) The construct-related validity of assessment center ratings: a review and meta-analysis of the role of methodological factors. *Journal of Management*, **29**, 231–258.

Woodzicka J A & LaFrance M (2005) The effects of subtle sexual harassment on women's performance in a job interview. *Sex Roles*, **53**, 67–77.

Wright P M, Gardner T M, Moynihan L M & Allen M R (2005) The relationship between HR practices and firm performance: examining causal order. *Personnel Psychology*, **58**, 409–446.

Yoo T Y & Muchinsky P M (1998) Utility estimates of job performance as related to the Data, People, and Things parameters of work. *Journal of Organizational Behavior*, **19**, 353–370.

Zazanis M M, Zaccaro S J & Kilcullen R N (2001) Identifying motivation and interpersonal performance using peer evaluations. *Military Psychology*, **13**, 73–88.

Zeidner M (1988) Cultural fairness in aptitude testing revisited: a cross-cultural parallel. *Professional Psychology: Research and Practice*, **19**, 257–262.

Zeidner M, Matthews G & Roberts R D (2004) Emotional intelligence in the workplace: a critical review. *Applied Psychology: an International Review*, **53**, 371–399.

Zhao H & Seibert S E (2006) The big five personality dimensions and entrepreneurial status: a meta-analytical review. *Journal of Applied Psychology*, **91**, 259–271.

Zickar M J (2001) Using personality inventories to identify thugs and agitators: applied psychology's contribution to the war against labor. *Journal of Vocational Behavior*, **59**, 149–164.

Zickar M J & Drasgow F (1996) Detecting faking on a personality instrument using appropriateness measurement. *Applied Psychological Measurement*, **20**, 71–87.

Zickar M J & Gibby R E (2006) A history of faking and socially desirable responding on personality tests. In R L Griffith & M H Peterson (eds.) *A Closer Examination of Applicant Faking* Behavior. Information Age Publishing, Greenwich, CT.

Zickar M J & Robie C (1999) Modeling faking good on personality items: an item-level analysis. *Journal of Applied Psychology*, **84**, 551–563.

Zimmerman R D (2008) Understanding the impact of personality traits on individuals' turnover decisions: a meta-analytic path model. *Personnel Psychology*, **61**, 309–348.

Zimmerman R D, Triana M C & Barrick M R (2008) *The criterion-related validity of a structured letter of reference using multiple raters and multiple performance criteria.* Paper presented at 23rd Annual Conference of SIOP, San Francisco.

Zottoli M A & Wanous J P (2000) Recruitment source research: current status and future directions. *Human Resource Management Review*, **10**, 353–382.

Author Index

Subject Index